ENTREPRENEURSHIP

A Comparative
and Historical Study

MODERN SOCIOLOGY:
A Series of Monographs, Treatises, and Texts

Edited by
GERALD M. PLATT

ENTREPRENEURSHIP

A Comparative and Historical Study

Paul H. Wilken
University of Virginia

ABLEX Publishing Corporation
Norwood, New Jersey 07648

Library of Congress Cataloging in Publication Data

Wilken, Paul H
  Entrepreneurship: a comparative and historical
study.

  (Modern sociology)
  Bibliography: p.
  Includes index.
  1. Entrepreneur—History. I. Title. II. Series.
HB615.W54   338′.04′09   79-4236
ISBN 0-89391-020-1

ABLEX Publishing Corporation
355 Chestnut Street
Norwood, New Jersey 07648

To Jane,
for the happy times
that even sociologists need

Contents

Preface

On the Trail of the Heffalump

Peter Kilby (1971) has recently compared those who study entrepreneurship to the characters in the Winnie-the-Pooh stories who have all heard about the awesome creature known as the "heffalump" but who have failed to capture one. This study continues the search for the evasive entrepreneurial heffalump. During the past several decades scholars from a number of disciplines have baited their conceptual and methodological traps in a valiant attempt to snare the entrepreneurial heffalump and have succeeded in capturing a variety of "animals." This has caused much disagreement as to which of the captured specimens is really the *true* representative of entrepreneurship. Part of the confusion stems from the fact that the entrepreneurial heffalump is a variegated sort of animal, which appears in different habitats and in different forms. It also appears to have undergone some evolutionary changes or mutations since the first reports of its existence were made public by heffalump hunters in the past. So it is not surprising that there is disagreement about the nature of the beast.

There seem to be three more specific reasons for the confusion about the entrepreneurial heffalump. First, in the last century or so an "animal" that looks very much like the entrepreneur has appeared in many of the habitats which entrepreneurs formerly occupied. This animal goes by the name of "manager" in most accounts, and, although its appearance is very similar to that of the entrepreneur, many morphologists are wary of considering it part of the entrepreneurial species. It is not clear whether it is a close relative, or whether entrepreneurs have become extinct and this new breed has replaced them.

Second, other animals resembling entrepreneurs, although not as closely as managers, also have been reported in habitats totally unlike the usual entrepreneurial or managerial haunts. For example, there have been reports of *political* (Apter, 1965; Ilchman & Uphoff, 1971), *moral* (Becker, 1966), and *antilaw* (Bustamante, 1972) entrepreneurs. This has perplexed entrepreneur hunters even more, because it raises the possibility that entrepreneurs are not a species, but a family or a genus instead.

Third, there also has been a significant change in the entrepreneurial heffalump's chief habitat. In earlier times it was widely agreed that entrepreneurs were found only in a habitat known as the *private sector*. Competition for survival was believed to be especially severe in that setting, so that only extremely virile entrepreneurs survived. But in recent times that habitat has increasingly been encroached upon by a habitat known as the *public sector* in which the aforementioned managers, who appear less aggressive than the entrepreneurs of old, predominate.

So there is almost complete disagreement among entrepreneurial heffalump hunters as to what their prey is *really* like, whether or not the size of the entrepreneurial population has increased or decreased in recent decades, and how to go about developing a program of selective breeding in order to prevent the extinction of this "endangered species." For, although there is controversy about the nature of the entrepreneurial heffalump, there is much more agreement concerning the importance of it—or of an animal that behaves similarly—in societies currently struggling to raise their economic productivity and to improve their standards of living. The entrepreneurial heffalump often is credited with having been a major force promoting economic growth and development in the past. And the lack of these animals in contemporary developing societies, as well as the inhospitality of these societies to the few that do exist there, are often singled out as serious retardants to economic growth and development.

A comprehensive study that analyzes the importance of the entrepreneurial heffalump for economic growth and development and the conditions under which these animals flourish has been lacking. This volume provides the beginning for such a study through a detailed analysis of industrial entrepreneurship in six societies—Great Britain, France, Prussia-Germany, Japan, the United States, and Russia—during the eighteenth and nineteenth centuries. We hope it will enlighten other heffalump hunters and motivate all who are interested in, and concerned about, the processes of socioeconomic change to examine the entrepreneurial beast more closely.

PAUL H. WILKEN
Charlottesville, Virginia

Acknowledgments

An earlier version of this study constituted my Ph.D. dissertation, submitted to the University of North Carolina in Chapel Hill. Three individuals particularly—Henry Landsberger, Gerhard Lenski, and Richard Simpson—offered comments and suggestions on that version which enabled me to clarify my thinking regarding the entrepreneurial "heffalump." I especially wish to thank Henry Landsberger, whose enthusiasm and encouragement kept me going at those times when I thought I was hopelessly lost in the jungle and would not return from my safari to report my adventures on the trail of the heffalump. I of course bear full responsibility for whatever inadequacies or excesses may exist in this volume.

Several other individuals have had an impact on me during my relatively short career in the academic world, and I also want to acknowledge my indebtedness to them, both for their influence on my thinking about things sociological and for the examples they have provided of humanism in academia: August Baetke, who first acquainted me with the sociological perspective; Art Johnson and Roy Francis, two of my mentors at the University of Minnesota; and, most recently, Tad and Ann Blalock, whose many kindnesses to me will always be remembered and appreciated.

I also wish to thank Jerry Platt for providing the opportunity for this study to see the light of day, rather than being sentenced to a dusty corner of my bookshelf, and for his patience in waiting for me to deliver the final product. Thanks also are due to the University of Virginia for providing a grant toward publication costs, to Gail Wooten-Votaw and Lorraine Indermill for typing the manuscript, and to Debbie Bogdan for chasing down those bits of bibliographical information that I always seem to forget.

My parents also have been a source of encouragement and assistance over the years and I wish to thank them for that. Lastly, a special "thank you" to my daughters, Kristina Renée and Stephanie Anne, who, in their own individual ways, have helped to brighten my life.

1

The Emergence of Entrepreneurship and Its Significance for Economic Growth and Development

What causes economic growth and development? This simple question has absorbed the attention of scholars of socioeconomic change for decades. The complexity which the simplicity of this question belies is evident from the variety of answers that has been offered to it. In this volume we attempt to shed additional light on an important aspect of that larger question, the phenomenon of entrepreneurship.

That societies differ in their capacity to achieve economic growth and development is obvious, both from the historical record and to the contemporary observer. Only a little over two centuries ago there was relatively little variation in the economic well-being of the vast majority of the world's residents. But soon after that a transformation was to begin, first in the British Isles and then on the European continent, that was radically to change the course of world history. As these societies began to experience the transition which has subsequently earned the title of the Industrial Revolution economic growth rates began to accelerate. Increases in the level of per capita income surpassed increases in population in these societies and thus the standard of living of their members improved.

This basic quantitative change was accompanied by revolutionary qualitative changes as well. Patterns of living based upon agricultural and pastoral modes of production were superseded by the industrial mode of production, in which manufactured goods produced by machines took the place of the products of the craftsman and artisan. Workers who had owned and controlled their physical capabilities saw their skills being treated like commodities and subject to the vagaries of the market. At the same time new goods and new techniques for producing those goods freed mankind from reliance upon the limits of human strength and endurance.

1

The focal point of mankind's existence was changed simultaneously. Small rural communities disappeared, replaced by mammoth concentrations of people, as industrial production came increasingly to be concentrated in urban settings. Social roles that had been unheard of proliferated, and individuals became specialized actors in the intricate machinery of industrial society. People who in an earlier age might have lived their lives unaware of their compatriots in other regions of their societies became tied to them by bonds of economic interdependence, and their societies became complex webs of exchanges of goods and services.

Today the evidence of differences in the level of economic growth and development is even more starkly clear than it was during this earlier period. The early industrializers, those who led the march to industrialization, now struggle with the problems accompanying advanced industrialization—the provision of employment opportunities for growing populations; the eradication of remaining pockets of poverty, the imperfections in the social fabric where economic growth has not kept pace with that of the mainstream of society; the depletion of resources by a voracious industrial machine; and the control of the pollution created by consumers and by the millions of energy-consuming machines which have served as the basis of their rapid economic growth. In these societies, critical questions are raised about the real benefits that these momentous changes have brought, and some yearn for a return to a time when the evils were not present.

Among the majority of the world's population, however, which occupies the sectors labeled the Third and Fourth Worlds, concerns are diametrically different. There the struggle is not to control the excesses of industrialization, but to achieve the economic benefits enjoyed by their industrialized predecessors. Many of them remain mired at levels of well-being possibly lower than those of the early industrializers when they began their industrial transformations. In these societies, as well as in those sectors of the industrialized societies that have not participated fully in the improvements in living standards accompanying industrialization, the question of what causes economic growth and development is a particularly relevant one.

THE SIGNIFICANCE OF ENTREPRENEURSHIP

This study does not provide a definitive answer to the larger question of the causes of economic growth and development. Instead it concentrates on an aspect of that larger question which at times serves as a surrogate for the more general question. Entrepreneurship has been regarded by many as one, perhaps the most, significant causal factor in the process of economic growth and development. Hence differences in entrepreneurship among societies are believed to account for their differential rates of growth and development. According to this belief, those societies that possess individuals willing and eager to perform the entrepreneurial function or role can accelerate the growth and development process; those societies lacking this necessary component lag behind. Furthermore, advocates of this point of view are most likely to attribute the amount of entrepreneurship within a society to a constellation of factors that are generally noneconomic in nature. According to them, entrepreneurship is most likely to emerge either under a specific set of social conditions or when a society has a sufficient supply of individuals possessing particular psychological characteristics. Thus proponents of this viewpoint provide two closely related answers to the basic question of what causes economic growth and development. "Entrepreneurship" is the mediate answer, and implicit within this answer is the supposition that entrepreneurship in turn is caused by particular social and psychological factors.

But some students of the problem offer an opposite argument regarding the significance of entrepreneurship and its causes. From this point of view entrepreneurship is neither a significant causal factor in economic growth and development, nor are social and psychological factors crucial facilitating factors. Rather, entrepreneurship is regarded as fulfilling the function of a conductor or transmitter of more fundamental causes. And these causes are held to be economic in nature. Thus this argument can be simply summarized as follows: Economic growth and development, and entrepreneurship are most likely to occur in situations where particular economic conditions are most favorable. If the economic conditions are favorable, then, given the basic human motivation to maximize one's gains, entrepreneurship will emerge and economic growth and development will result. If the economic conditions are not favorable, entrepreneurship will not emerge and the society's economy will stagnate. From this point of view, entrepreneurship is primarily a dependent variable and social and psychological characteristics receive relatively little attention.

So we have two quite different points of view about the significance of entrepreneurship in the process of economic growth and development. An analogy from the field of electricity shows the contrast even more vividly. On the one hand, we may regard entrepreneurship as a sort of electrical conductor by means of which electrical energy is transmitted from one point to another with almost no change in its strength between sender and receiver. This corresponds with the latter view just described, in which entrepreneurship only transmits the economic impulses present in a situation. On the other hand, we may describe entrepreneurship as analogous to an electrical transformer or generator. Both of these devices significantly alter the amount of electrical energy which reaches the receiver. Whereas the transformer diminishes the energy flow, the generator creates electrical energy from other types of energy, such as water power. As we shall show later, entrepreneurship can be visualized as producing either of these consequences. The latter part of the analogy of course represents the point of view that claims causal significance for entrepreneurship.

Chemistry provides a second set of analogies which clarify the distinction between the two points of view. On the one hand we may regard entrepreneurship as similar to a process of spontaneous combustion. When the appropriate conditions are met, a chemical reaction, such as fire, occurs automatically. On the other hand, combinations of elements may remain inert unless an additional ingredient, a catalyst, is added. Using this analogy we could describe entrepreneurship as the catalyst which "provides the spark" for the economic growth and development process.

Not surprisingly, the differences in opinion regarding the significance of entrepreneurship have generally followed disciplinary lines. Economists have usually played down the significance of entrepreneurship and have emphasized the economic conditions promoting its emergence, and concomitantly, the occurrence of economic growth and development. Thus Hirschman (1965) has claimed that a lack of entrepreneurship is not an obstacle to economic growth and development, and Gerschenkron (1966) suggests that entrepreneurship is not "necessarily necessary" as a precondition for economic growth and development. Therefore economists can be described as generally viewing entrepreneurship as a *dependent* variable.

Noneconomists, particularly sociologists and psychologists, have taken the opposite position. For them, and for those economists who allocate more significance to the impact of noneconomic factors on economic processes, entrepreneurship constitutes a significant *independent* variable. Schumpeter (1961), as we shall note later, visualized the entrepreneur as the key figure in economic development because of his role in introducing innovations. Parsons and Smelser (1956) describe entrepreneurship as one of the two necessary conditions for economic growth and development, the other being the increased input of capital. Harbison (1965) includes entrepreneurs among the prime movers of innovation, and Sayigh (1962) simply describes entrepreneurship as a necessary dynamic force.

Therefore one of the two major questions we address in this study is: What is the significance of entrepreneurship for economic growth and development? Does it add an important independent influence to that of other factors widely agreed to promote economic development, in a manner analogous to the transformer or the generator? Or does it primarily play a role similar to that of a conductor, transmitting the influence of these other factors without appreciably altering their force?

Definitional Versus Causal Significance

In answering these basic questions it is important to make a distinction between what may be called *definitional* and *causal* significance. Entrepreneurship will have *definitional* significance in all situations, because, by definition, it is a term referring to the initiating activity of human actors in economic activities. Obviously money does not invest itself; labor does not hire itself; factories do not build themselves. These developments are the result of actors carrying out the entrepreneurial role. Hence if these behaviors occur one can say that entrepreneurship is present in a situation and if they do not occur that it is absent. As a result, economic growth and development will clearly not occur if entrepreneurship is absent, and *ergo* entrepreneurship is of monumental significance for the growth and development process.

As both Harris (1970) and Kuznets (1968) have pointed out, though, this approach is not particularly helpful. As Kuznets (1968, p. 66) indicates, "If we identify those that make changes as entrepreneurs without at the same time specifying the group apart from their actions, we explain economic change by definition rather than by substantive analysis." An approach which makes entrepreneurship significant by definition does not necessarily preclude an analysis of the conditions which promote or retard this significant activity, but it does not show as clearly the relevance of entrepreneurship for economic growth and development as does an approach which analyzes the causal significance of the phenomenon.

In this study we analyze the relevance of entrepreneurship for growth and development in terms of its *causal* significance. In other words, our concern is with the extent to which entrepreneurship *adds to, or detracts from,* the influence of other factors affecting economic growth and development within a society. Keeping in mind our comparison of entrepreneurship with a transformer or a generator, we investigate the degree to which entrepreneurship has had an independent additive influence on economic growth and development. This influence may be either positive (analogous to the generator) or negative (analogous to the transformer). We shall spell out the procedure we have followed in making this determination of entrepreneurship's *causal* significance in the next chapter.

Therefore, rather than treating entrepreneurship as primarily a dependent variable, as economists are inclined to do, or primarily as an independent variable, as noneconomists have done, we have conceptualized it as an *intervening* variable, between prior conditions, on the one hand, and economic growth and development on the other. The question of causal significance involves determining the influence of this intervening variable on economic growth and development. In a statistical sense the problem of determining causal significance can be seen as the "partialling out" of the influence of entrepreneurship from the influence of other factors on economic growth and development.

CONDITIONS INFLUENCING THE EMERGENCE OF ENTREPRENEURSHIP

The second basic question we answer in this study is closely related to the first. It can be stated simply: What conditions, both economic and noneconomic, influence the emergence of entrepreneurship? Does entrepreneurship appear primarily in response to a particular set of economic conditions? Or does it appear only when specific social, political, and psychological conditions are present within a society? These conditions may have both a *positive* and a *negative* influence on the emergence of entrepreneurship. Positive influences constitute facilitating conditions for entrepreneurship, those which increase the likelihood of individuals behaving entrepreneurially. Negative influences constitute inhibiting conditions, factors which serve as barriers to the emergence of entrepreneurship.

Given the fact that entrepreneurship may have either causal significance or only definitional, but not causal, significance in a particular situation, it is necessary to make a subtle distinction at this point regarding the relevance of those conditions which promote the emergence of entrepreneurship. Since our most important distinction in regard to the significance of entrepreneurship is between situations in which entrepreneurship has causal significance and situations in which it does not have causal significance (but has only definitional significance), we are correspondingly interested in those economic and noneconomic conditions under which entrepreneurship falls within one of these two categories. One must keep in mind two different sorts of distinctions—between causal significance and causal insignificance and between the emergence and the nonemergence of entrepreneurship. As we visualize it, these are independent distinctions (as shown in Table 1). Entrepreneurship may emerge within a society and be either causally significant or insignificant. Conversely, the failure of entrepreneurship to emerge may also be either causally significant or not. As we shall soon point out, we are interested in those situations in which either the emergence or nonemergence of entrepreneurship has causal significance for economic growth and development, contrasted with those

Table 1
Relationship Between Emergence and Significance of Entrepreneurship

| | | Significance of Entrepreneurship | |
		Definitionally Significant but Not Causally Significant	Definitionally Significant and Causally Significant
Emergence of Entrepreneurship	Yes	Entrepreneurship present but not causally significant	Entrepreneurship present and causally significant
	No	Entrepreneurship absent and absence not causally significant	Entrepreneurship absent and absence causally significant

situations in which the presence or absence of entrepreneurship is not causally important. And we are further interested in the conditions promoting or hindering the appearance of entrepreneurship in those two types of situations.

Nearly all discussions of the conditions influencing the emergence of entrepreneurship have assumed that it is a significant causal influence, and so these analyses have focused on conditions which make it more or less likely to appear. These discussions have also divided along disciplinary boundaries, as has been true of the issue of the significance of entrepreneurship. Economists have claimed priority for economic factors; sociologists and anthropologists have emphasized the equal importance of noneconomic factors. According to Harris (1970) and Dales (1949), the former have regarded economic factors as determining the *demand* for entrepreneurship, whereas the latter have presented noneconomic factors as determinants of the *supply* of entrepreneurship. Consequently, as with all supply-demand models, the appearance of entrepreneurship involves an "identification" problem (Harris, 1970). Kilby (1971, p. 22) raises the question, "When a change in entrepreneurial performance is observed, how can it be ascertained whether it has happened because of a shift in the supply of entrepreneurial effort or because of an improvement in the economic environment?" We do not believe that this problem is insoluble. The most satisfactory way of solving it would be to find situations in which the demand for entrepreneurship was strong or favorable and the factors influencing the supply of entrepreneurship were weak or nonexistent *or* vice versa and then to observe the extent to which entrepreneurship emerged in these contrasting environments. In this study we have attempted to provide this type of test by means of a comparative historical approach, involving an analysis of entrepreneurship in six different societies.

Economic Factors Promoting Entrepreneurship

From a strictly economic viewpoint the same factors that promote economic growth and development account for the emergence of entrepreneurship. The important factors are economic in nature and they are construed to constitute both necessary and sufficient conditions for entrepreneurial emergence. These economic conditions can be broadly divided into two classes: those which provide market incentives for entrepreneurs and those which influence the availability of capital. Market incentives show entrepreneurs opportunities to be exploited, and capital is the major resource needed to carry out the entrepreneurial function. Hence as economic growth and development occurs, the conditions promoting entrepreneurship also improve. With increased levels of per capita income, the demand for goods increases and a greater amount of savings is available for investment. The accumulation of capital results in productivity increases that further raise the level of economic well-being. By contrast, societies that are stagnating economically offer limited market incentives, and the level of capital accumulation is too small to enable potential entrepreneurs to take advantage of the limited opportunities that do exist.

These two broad classes of factors can be broken down into a large number of more specific economic characteristics. For example, Kilby (1971, pp. 24–26) mentions the following as being particularly relevant for the emergence of entrepreneurship: the level of demand for industrial products, the availability of required labor and raw material inputs, the degree of inflation, the level of taxation, and the ease of importing essential inputs. He further notes that with favorable product and factor markets the entrepreneurial role can be reduced to decisionmaking under uncertainty. And Nafziger (1971, p. 315) summarizes the presence of entrepreneurship as ''a direct function of the quality and an inverse function of the costs of inputs, labor, and capital.''

Later we discuss these economic factors in more detail; here we simply wish to indicate the major influences on entrepreneurship stressed by economists to show the contrast with the type of conditions noneconomists think promote or retard the entrepreneurial phenomenon.

Noneconomic Factors Influencing Entrepreneurship

Scholars of entrepreneurship from disciplines other than economics (primarily sociology, psychology, anthropology, and history), as well as those economists who are more oriented to the influence of noneconomic factors on economic processes, have described a wide variety of conditions that either increase or decrease the supply of entrepreneurship. From their perspective economic factors may be necessary conditions for the emergence of entrepreneurship, but they are not also sufficient conditions. A variety of social and psychological factors also are regarded as necessary conditions for the appearance of entrepreneurship. We shall not discuss these at length here, as each of them could easily merit a chapter of its own. (Our discussion of them also is organized somewhat differently than many such discussions, as we are interested in describing major classes of factors instead of specific theories of entrepreneurship that may be better-known.) These major noneconomic factors alleged to influence the emergence of entrepreneurship can be categorized as follows:

Legitimacy of entrepreneurship. A major emphasis among this group of scholars is upon the relevance of the system of norms and values within a sociocultural setting for the emergence of entrepreneurship. We refer to this as the legitimacy of entrepreneurship because these scholars argue that the degree of approval or disapproval granted entrepreneurial behavior will influence its emergence and its characteristics if it does emerge. Schumpeter (1961) himself emphasized the importance of an appropriate social climate for entrepreneurship, and, among current theorists, Cochran (1949) has particularly called attention to the importance of cultural themes and sanctions.

Marris and Somerset (1971) have suggested that the value system in a setting has three possible functions—institutional, justificatory, and imperative. Our use of the term *legitimacy* focuses upon the last two of these three. A normative-evaluative system may not only accord approval to entrepreneurial behavior but it may also more actively encourage individuals to behave in that manner.

The actual content of such a normative-evaluative system has been less clearly specified. Positive attitudes toward business and technology have been mentioned, as well as the social status of those playing entrepreneurial roles (Cochran, 1959; Kilby, 1971; Marris and Somerset, 1971). Katzin (1964) has suggested that entrepreneurs should be given high status, Alexander (1967) emphasizes status respect, and Parsons and Smelser (1956) have stressed the granting of high status to those dissatisfied with the operation of the economic system. Parsons and Smelser have also discussed the importance of a tolerant and supportive system, which suggests that values need not be actually positive regarding entrepreneurship, but that they should not be negative.

Parsons' pattern variables have been cited to exemplify the normative-evaluative system most conducive to entrepreneurship. For example, sociocultural settings in which achievement and universalism rather than ascription and particularism are value orientations are emphasized by Lipset (1967) as being conducive to entrepreneurship. Brozen (1954) adds functional specificity to this list. But McClelland (1961), in relating the five sets of pattern variables to measures of economic growth, has concluded that only role specificity is of significance.

In addition, the need for a change of traditional values, which are assumed to be opposed to entrepreneurship, has been proposed, although several writers have pointed out that a complete change may not be necessary (McClelland, 1961). Instead, traditional values may be reinterpreted or synthesized with newer values which give greater legitimacy to entrepreneurship (Lipset, 1967; McClelland and Winter, 1971). Existing elites may play a significant role in this process, as they do in influencing values and norms in general (Hoselitz, 1957; Smith, 1968; Taylor, 1965).

Various effects of norms and values upon entrepreneurship also have been suggested. Their primary effect will be upon the attitudes and role expectations of entrepreneurs (Kilby, 1971). More specifically, norms and values are regarded as influencing the likelihood of innovation, the degree of entrepreneurial security, and the probability of entrepreneurs merging their efforts (Cochran, 1959; Parsons and Smelser, 1956; Riggs, 1964). Hagen (1968) notes the influence on innovations and also suggests that the system of norms and values will influence the field of production into which an entrepreneur goes. And Kriesberg (1963) observes that entrepreneurs from outside the system will have advantages in situations in which the legitimacy of entrepreneurship within the system is low.

The opinion that values supporting the legitimacy of entrepreneurship are crucial for entrepreneurial emergence is not unanimous. Gerschenkron (1962, 1966) has emphasized the part played by governments in influencing values, by arguing that negative values will be significant only if they are supported by specific government actions and that governments can also overcome negative orientations. Hoselitz (1957) and Bendix (1956) have emphasized another aspect, claiming that entrepreneurship can emerge, and has emerged, even when entrepreneurial legitimacy has been low.

Our position is that the legitimacy of entrepreneurship will be significant in determining the likelihood of entrepreneurial emergence because entrepreneurs will be more likely to emerge in settings in which legitimacy is high. But we do not consider norms and values sufficient by themselves either to cause or prevent the appearance of entrepreneurship. Their influence must be seen in the context of other noneconomic factors.

Social mobility. Closely related to the normative-evaluative system of a society are the existent structured patterns of interaction within that society, which we regard as *social* structure in contrast to the *cultural* structure consisting of norms and values. This social characteristic is regarded as being significant for entrepreneurial emergence, too. Although different writers have referred to it by several different terms, the factor involves the degree of mobility, both social and geographical, and the nature of mobility channels within a situation.

One can discern three different points of view about this factor. The first holds that a high degree of mobility is conducive to entrepreneurship (Bruton, 1960; Cameron, 1961; Katzin, 1964). Hoselitz (1960) and Marris (1969) both refer to the need for "openness" of a system, and McClelland (1961) speaks of the need for "flexibility" in role relationships. All these comments imply the need for the possibility of mobility within a system, or for accessible mobility channels.

The opposite point of view, expressed most strongly by Hagen (1968), is that a lack of mobility possibilities promotes entrepreneurial behavior. Hagen refers to this as *relative social blockage* to indicate that only some channels of mobility must be blocked. Specifically, the possibility of mobility in nonentrepreneurial roles must be limited, while the possibility of upward mobility by means of entrepreneurship is available to particular groups or individuals. Marris and Somerset (1971) similarly emphasize the importance of the inability of individuals to find rewards in established, nonentrepreneurial occupations. And Cole (1959) describes entrepreneurship as coming through the crevices in a rigid society.

The third position may be seen as combining the first two. Thus Rostow (1956) mentions the need for both flexibility and the denial of conventional routes to prestige. And Brozen (1954) simply notes that a setting should not be too rigid nor too flexible. If it is too flexible, then individuals will gravitate toward other roles; if it is too rigid, entrepreneurship will be restricted along with other activities.

Existing elites also play a significant role in influencing the degree of mobility and the nature of mobility channels. Typically they will attempt to maintain their position against entrepreneurs attempting to be upwardly mobile, and therefore elites may use their power to manipulate mobility channels to the disadvantage of rising entrepreneurs (Hoselitz, 1963).

We concur with Brozen's prediction of a curvilinear relationship between social mobility and the emergence of entrepreneurship. The patterning of mobility channels in a society will be particularly important, in that they will determine the relative opportunities offered by entrepreneurial roles and other roles. But the degree and nature of social mobility within a society do not stand alone as influences upon entrepreneurship. They will vary most likely in accord with the legitimacy of entrepreneurship, and the combined influence of these factors will relate significantly to the influence of the next noneconomic factor.

Marginality. A prominent argument presented by another group of scholars is that entrepreneurship very often is promoted by social marginality (Brozen, 1954; Kerr, Dunlop, Harbison, and Myers, 1960; Young, 1971). Individuals or groups on the perimeter of a given social system or between two social systems are believed to provide the personnel to fill entrepreneurial roles. They may be drawn from religious, cultural, ethnic, or migrant minority groups, and their marginal social position is generally believed to have psychological effects which make entrepreneurship a particularly attractive alternative for them.

The conditions under which marginality is likely to promote entrepreneurship are largely determined by the two preceding factors—the legitimacy of entrepreneurship and social mobility. Marginal individuals and groups will be excluded, by definition, from access to the established mobility channels in a situation. "Mainstream" individuals and groups, however, will have primary access to these channels. Hence marginals are likely to play entrepreneurial roles under opposite conditions than are actors from the societal mainstream. The legitimacy of entrepreneurship will influence which of these two potential sources of entrepreneurship will be predominant in a society. In situations in which entrepreneurial legitimacy is low, mainstream actors will be attracted to nonentrepreneurial roles, and entrepreneurial roles will be relegated to marginals. But in situations in which entrepreneurial legitimacy is high, mainstream actors will use the entrepreneurial role as a mobility channel, and marginals will have to find other roles as means of mobility. This latter situation is characteristic of some racial and ethnic minorities in the United States, and in some cases individuals from these marginal groups have opted for even more deviant roles, becoming entrepreneurs in crime, for example. The relationship between entrepreneurial legitimacy and the access of actors to mobility channels is shown in Table 2. We use the terms *outsider* and *mainstream* entrepreneurship to represent the two cases.

The importance of legitimacy and social mobility have been stressed in the literature on marginality. First, it has been pointed out that marginal entrepre-

Table 2
Relationship Between Entrepreneurial Legitimacy
and Access to Mobility Channels

| | | Degree of Entrepreneurial Legitimacy | |
		Low	High
Access to Mobility Channels	Low	Outsider Entrepreneurship	Nonentrepreneurial roles
	High	Nonentrepreneurial roles	Mainstream Entrepreneurship

neurship is more likely where entrepreneurship is not valued (Hoselitz, 1957; Kriesberg, 1963; Lipset, 1967). Second, relative social blockage has also been emphasized as a condition promoting entrepreneurship by marginals (Kilby, 1971; Marris and Somerset, 1971; McClelland, 1961). Several other factors also are believed to increase the likelihood of marginals becoming entrepreneurs. One of these is the presence of positive attitudes toward entrepreneurship *within* the group (Hagen, 1962; Lipset, 1967). Entrepreneurship must be accorded legitimacy within the group to compensate for the lack of legitimacy it faces outside the group. The second important factor is a high degree of group solidarity or cohesion (Marris and Somerset, 1971; Young, 1971). This is necessary to counteract whatever opposition may be forthcoming from mainstream groups within the larger social situation. In addition, Marris and Somerset (1971) note the importance of a belief in the superiority of the group on the part of its members.

Both Glade (1967) and Riggs (1964) have described the advantages marginal or minority groups bring to the entrepreneurial role. The former notes the experience they typically have in mercantile roles, their greater contact with the environment, their tendency to recruit and reward within the group, their wider information networks and more informal in-group contacts, their mechanisms of mutual assistance which can be used to raise capital (cf. Young, 1971), and their exemption from "customary leveling and wealth control mechanisms" found in the larger social system. The latter has emphasized marginals' freedom from the network of obligations found in the larger system and the networks which tend to form among marginals and between marginals and the outside world.

Given these supposed advantages, however, marginality, like many other factors, cannot be considered a sufficient condition for entrepreneurship (Glade, 1967). Not all marginal groups are entrepreneurial (Ilchman and Uphoff, 1971; Lipset, 1967), although this may be true primarily in situations in which mainstream sources of entrepreneurial supply exist. Furthermore, marginal actors may be vulnerable to political attacks which may negate their entrepreneurial efforts (Lipset, 1967). So it appears that whether marginality produces entrepreneurship will depend upon a favorable combination of other factors.

Social integration. In contrast to the emphasis on marginality, there is also an emphasis upon the necessity of some degree of social integration existing if entrepreneurship is to emerge. It appears that if marginality is too great, so that individuals or groups are too far removed from the network of relationships within a social system, then entrepreneurship will not be promoted. We have earlier noted the importance of cohesion within a marginal group; this factor emphasizes the need for some integrative bonds between entrepreneurs and the larger social system.

Marris and Somerset (1971) have emphasized this factor most strongly, claiming that an increase in the scale or range of interaction is necessary and that barriers to interaction must be broken down if entrepreneurship is to occur. Solo (1967) has also suggested the need for an integrating culture. The important points are that the social ties are sufficient to provide potential entrepreneurs with access to resources and markets and that they are positively oriented to entrepreneurial behavior. It is obvious that strong group ties may draw actors into nonentrepreneurial roles (Lipset, 1967; Marris and Somerset, 1971). We find it significant that McClelland and Winter (1971) have found a sense of group identity, which is indicative of social integration, to be an important characteristic among entrepreneurs in currently developing societies.

Thus it appears that social integration will facilitate entrepreneurship if the ties are to groups or societal sectors that are supportive of entrepreneurship and if they are not so strong that they place priority claims for nonentrepreneurial modes of behavior upon those striving to be entrepreneurs.

Security. Several writers have described entrepreneurial security as an important facilitator of entrepreneurial behavior. Security may have either economic or noneconomic bases, and in this context we consider the latter. Easterbrook (1949, 1963) has been among the major advocates of this point of view, suggesting that security in all the roles—entrepreneurial, social, ethical, and political—of the entrepreneur is desirable. According to him, these types of security essentially involve protection from uncertainties, want, social disapproval, and political interference. Brozen (1954) also regards security as especially significant, claiming that it may be the most important factor promoting entrepreneurship. His emphasis is upon protection from unnecessary risks. Katzin (1964) stresses freedom from governmental control, whereas Brandenburg (1962) simply cites security for person and property as being significant.

There is, however, no consensus on the amount of security that is needed. Cole (1959) suggests that "minimal" security is necessary; McClelland (1961) emphasizes moderate certainty. There is an opposite point of view, though, represented by Peterson and Berger (1971) and by Kirzner (1973), which maintains that entrepreneurship is more likely to appear under turbulent conditions than under conditions of equilibrium. (We assume that turbulent conditions will be less secure than an equilibrial situation.) This point of view also contrasts sharply with Schumpeter's claim that entrepreneurship occurs as a disequilibriating force in stable situations (Clemence and Doody, 1950). Perhaps Redlich (1958) provides the correct middle position here when he suggests that insecurity does not prevent entrepreneurship, but rather that different kinds of insecurity will result in different kinds of entrepreneurship.

We do consider security to be a significant factor. It seems reasonable that if individuals are fearful of losing their economic assets or of being subjected to various negative sanctions, they will not be inclined to increase their insecurity by behaving entrepreneurially. But if they are in a completely secure situation, we anticipate also that entrepreneurship will not be likely. Thus we believe a curvilinear relationship between the degree of security and the emergence of entrepreneurship is most probable.

Ideology. The importance of some kind of entrepreneurial ideology has been stressed by several prominent sociological theorists. We define an ideology as *a comprehensive organized set of beliefs regarding the nature of the world and the behaviors that should be enacted within it.* An ideology supportive of entrepreneurship may be specifically oriented to entrepreneurial behavior, or its content may indirectly, and perhaps unintentionally, encourage individuals to behave entrepreneurially. Thus we include several different ideologies within this category, and we distinguish this factor from our first noneconomic factor, the legitimacy of entrepreneurship, to emphasize the specificity of an ideology in contrast with the diffuseness of a normative-evaluative system.

The best-known example of an entrepreneurial ideology, in our sense of the term, has been Weber's Protestant Ethic (1958). It constituted an organized set of beliefs about the world and enjoined its adherents to behave in the mode which Weber described as worldly asceticism. The "calling" which it incorporated, when heeded by its followers, resulted in the saving and investment of capital and in entrepreneurial behaviors although that was not its manifest intent. Thus the Protestant Ethic illustrates the fact that the content of the ideology need not be explicitly entrepreneurial.

Both Rostow (1956) and Parsons (1960) have emphasized the promotive function that *nationalistic* ideologies may have for entrepreneurship. Entrepreneurial behavior may be advocated explicitly within such an ideology, or the ideology's stress upon nation-building and upon the superiority of a nation may be interpreted so that entrepreneurship becomes perceived as a means of increasing the strength of a nation.

Bendix (1956) has described a somewhat different kind of entrepreneurial ideology. According to him, the presence of this kind of entrepreneurial ideology promotes entrepreneurship mainly by integrating the work force into the industrial process and thus gaining its cooperation. He describes such an ideology, with Great Britain as his primary example, as initially justifying entrepreneurial activities, and particularly, the exercise of authority within the workplace. Over time the emphasis changes to the desirability of nonentrepreneurs emulating the lifestyle of the entrepreneurial class as well as the possibility of their becoming part of this class.

Therefore there appears to be sufficient agreement on the importance of some kind of ideology to include it as one of the noneconomic factors promoting entrepreneurship.

Other social factors. A number of scholars have suggested a miscellany of social factors promoting entrepreneurship which we group together. Both Bruton (1960) and Brozen (1954) have emphasized the importance of a middle class in providing a supply of entrepreneurs. Brozen, for example, describes the middle class as the source of promotable people in a society. The degree to which the middle class serves as this source appears to depend upon the social mobility and legitimacy of entrepreneurship factors. Similarly, several writers have noted the importance of actors possessing power or control over resources if they are to behave entrepreneurially (Awad, 1971; Marris, 1969; Papanek, 1962; Smith, 1968; Solo, 1967). It may be that this is the characteristic of a strong middle class which promotes entrepreneurial behavior on its part. A specific resource which is likely to be of importance for an entrepreneur is information (Aubrey, 1961; Cochran, 1959), and the middle class in a society may have a relatively large share of this resource.

These factors may be subsumed under the general topic of the social stratification system of a society, and we have considered them in that respect in this study. A society's distribution of the resources required for entrepreneurial behavior, especially wealth and knowledge, has major implications for the pattern of entrepreneurship found within that society. Not only must actors have an interest in entrepreneurship, but they must also possess at least a minimal supply of the resources needed to enact that role. Thus many of the earliest entrepreneurs were drawn from either mercantile or artisanal occupational backgrounds partly because they had the requisite resources for entrepreneurship. Merchants had the advantage of possessing relatively liquid capital, and artisans brought their knowledge of producing goods to the industrial entrepreneurial role.

Riggs' theory of entrepreneurship. Frederick W. Riggs has developed a theory of entrepreneurship which, although not as well known as some of the theories we have discussed, is significant because of its incorporation in a comprehensive framework of a number of the social factors we have discussed. This theory has been developed most fully in his book *Administration in Developing Countries: The Theory of Prismatic Society (1964).*

Riggs makes a distinction among three types of societies in which entrepreneurship will have distinctive features. At one extreme is the *fused* society, characterized by strong restrictions imposed upon entrepreneurial behavior by the existing elite. In this type of society any accumulation of wealth by entrepreneurs constitutes a threat to the elite and the rigidity of the social system, so entrepreneurship is necessarily restricted. In some cases budding entrepreneurs may be assimilated into the elite, or they may develop a symbiotic relationship with them. But neither of these patterns is conductive to innovative and/or expansive entrepreneurship. In the fused society, entrepreneurship will be most dynamic if entrepreneurs are excluded from access to the elite.

The *diffracted* society is the opposite of the fused society and is characterized by universalism and a high degree of social mobility and flexibility. In this type of society entrepreneurship will be encouraged and entrepreneurs will be upwardly socially mobile into the ranks of the elite.

Riggs discusses at greatest length the characteristics of entrepreneurship in the *prismatic* type of society, which is intermediate to the fused and diffracted types. In a prismatic society greater encouragement is given to entrepreneurship than in the fused society, but it is only partial encouragement, and *pariah* entrepreneurship becomes the usual pattern. A prismatic society allows selective mobility, with access to mobility channels based upon communalism. Thus individuals and groups who are not part of elite communal groups are most likely to adopt entrepreneurial roles as a response to the relative social blockage in the system.

The elites in a prismatic society are ambivalent toward entrepreneurs, and consequently they simultaneously protect and persecute them. They need the wealth and industrialization provided by entrepreneurs to maintain their position, but the entrepreneurs, by gaining wealth, become a threat to their position. Hence, the elite maintains power over the entrepreneurial actors by confiscating their wealth. Members of the elite may enter the entrepreneurial role themselves while maintaining their political positions. They are thereby able to siphon off some of the wealth created by entrepreneurship and also to retain their power positions.

The position of entrepreneurs in such a society is very insecure because of their dependence upon the elite. Upward mobility into the elite is somewhat greater than in the fused society, but it is also severely controlled by the elite. Entrepreneurs are characteristically required to buy protection from the elite in the form of tax tribute, and this understandably prevents them from amassing sufficient resources to change their dependent position. As a result the most satisfactory position they can attain is a pariah, or middleman, role, between the elite and primary producers within the society.

Riggs' greater attention to the prismatic society reflects his belief that many contemporary developing societies fall within that category. We find his approach intriguing because of its relationship to several of the factors previously discussed. His three types of societies are differentiated mainly on the basis of their patterns of social mobility and the amount of legitimacy accorded entrepreneurship. In addition, the fused society shows the importance of marginality for entrepreneurship when entrepreneurial legitimacy is low. The prismatic society shows the negative effects of a particular kind of integrative tie between an elite and entrepreneurs, namely, a dependent relationship. And each of the societies differs in the degree of entrepreneurial security which is present. So, although Riggs has developed his theory on the basis of currently developing societies, we have found his perspective informative for our historical study as well.

Psychological Factors

So far our discussion of noneconomic factors promoting entrepreneurship has concentrated upon sociocultural factors. Although each of the foregoing factors can be regarded as significant ultimately because of its psychological impact upon potential entrepreneurs, several other entrepreneurial theorists have provided theories of entrepreneurship that concentrate specifically upon psychological factors. We consider these theories separately for that reason, but we also note that these theories make substantial use of sociocultural variables. Hence a sharp division between psychological and sociocultural theories is not possible.

Need-achievement. No doubt the best-known of these primarily psychological theories is David McClelland's theory of need-achievement, as presented in *The Achieving Society* (1961) and in *Motivating Economic Achievement* (1971) in collaboration with David Winter (cf. McClelland, 1963, 1965). According to McClelland, a constellation of personality characteristics which are indicative of high need-achievement can be identified. Individuals who have these characteristics are especially likely to behave entrepreneurially. Therefore if the average level of need-achievement in a society is relatively high, one would expect a relatively great amount of entrepreneurship in that society. Or one would expect to find entrepreneurship in those segments of a society in which need-achievement is high. In either case entrepreneurship becomes the link, or the intervening variable, between need-achievement and economic growth (McClelland, 1963). Consequently McClelland advocates increasing the level of need-achievement in a society in order to stimulate entrepreneurship and economic growth.

McClelland (1961) regards the following as the distinctive characteristics of high need-achievement: (a) a preference for moderate risks and a propensity to work harder in such situations; (b) a belief that one's personal efforts will be influential in the attainment of some goal and pleasure derived from this belief; (c) a tendency to perceive the probability of success in attaining a goal as being relatively high; (d) a need for feedback regarding success or failure of one's efforts; (e) the capacity to plan ahead and to be particularly aware of the passage of time; (f) an interest in excellence for its own sake. In addition, he suggests that individuals with high need-achievement will not be motivated by monetary incentives, but that monetary rewards will constitute a symbol of achievement for them. Achievement itself will be their primary reward. He further suggests that Protestants and Jews generally possess higher levels of need-achievement than

Catholics, and that the Protestant Ethic should be seen as a special case of the need-achievement thesis.

McClelland has been more equivocal in his account of the factors which promote high levels of need-achievement than in his description of the characteristics of a person with high need-achievement. In *The Achieving Society* (1961) he emphasized the significance of parental influence in developing need-achievement, with the most crucial factor being the mother-son relationship. If mothers expected self-reliant mastery of their sons neither too early nor too late, if they had high expectations for them, and if they had strong emotional ties with them, then high need-achievement would be most likely to develop. Need-achievement would be least likely to develop in situations in which the father was domineering or authoritarian, if the child were not confronted by high standards of excellence, and if achievement demands were made of him too early.

Subsequently, in *Motivating Economic Achievement*, McClelland and Winter (1971) have radically reduced the significance of the dynamics of the relationship between parents and children in the genesis of need-achievement. In this work a greater emphasis is placed upon sociocultural factors, such as norms and values which stress achievement and support from groups. Thus the authors speak in terms of an achievement "mystique" in a culture arousing latent need-achievement and making it manifest. They do retain the emphasis upon standards of excellence, however, emphasizing particularly the need for an individual to compete with such standards. Also emphasized is the importance of an individual's seeing himself as the source of changes in his environment. And, relatively greater emphasis is also placed upon the part played by education in making latent need-achievement manifest; McClelland (1966) and McClelland and Winter (1971) claim that a significant interaction effect exists between these two factors.

The theory of need-achievement has been subject to substantial criticism, which we will not discuss fully here. We will simply note that this criticism can be divided into three general categories. First, it has been claimed that the correlations between need-achievement and economic growth which McClelland found for the countries he studied are spurious. Second, there have been a variety of methodological criticisms, particularly of his indicators of economic growth and need-achievement. And third, he has been criticized for failure to consider negative evidence. We do not think that these criticisms have completely demolished the need-achievement hypothesis, however, so we retain it as a potentially significant psychological factor promoting the emergence of entrepreneurship.

Withdrawal of status respect. Everett Hagen's theory (1962, chaps. 9–12) of the genesis of entrepreneurship makes substantial use of social variables. But we include it in this context because the crux of his argument concerns the psychological changes which result from certain social changes. As the phrase which has been applied to his theory implies, Hagen believes that the initial condition leading to eventual entrepreneurial behavior is the loss of status by a group or collectivity. This can occur in one of four ways: (a) the group may be displaced by force; (b) it may have its valued symbols denigrated; (c) it may drift into a situation of status inconsistency; (d) it may not be accepted in a new society. Hagen suggests that there are several possible reactions to this loss of group status: retreatism, ritualism, innovation, reformism, and rebellion. The most significant of these for entrepreneurship is retreatism, which is characterized by psychological repression of the trauma associated with the status loss. The suppressed rage resulting from the loss of status ultimately results in a later generation in standards of achievement being held up by mothers within the group to their sons. If the sons' fathers are simultaneously weak or erratic, then the likelihood of the sons' becoming innovators is increased and entrepreneurship becomes a feasible outlet for such tendencies.

Hagen supplements this basic model with a number of other variables. As we noted earlier, he regards relative social blockage as being crucial in determining the channel into which creative energies flow. Hence the personality changes resulting from the withdrawal of status respect in prior generations are not sufficient to produce entrepreneurship. He further notes that the state of knowledge available, the size of markets and the amount of savings available for investment, and attitudes toward manual labor will be significant (Kilby, 1971). Or in other words, the opportunities present in the individual's situation will be an important factor in determining whether the psychological process yields entrepreneurship (Hagen, 1963).

Hagen's description of the innovative entrepreneurial personality has many similarities to McClelland's. He notes that high levels of need-achievement and of need autonomy, the latter being similar to McClelland's emphasis upon personal effort and personal responsibiliy, will be characteristic of this type of personality. But to these he adds high degrees of need succorance, need order, and need nurturance, and a system of moral values with broad scope, characteristics which do not correspond precisely with those described by McClelland.

Hagen, like McClelland, has been the object of much scholarly criticism. Probably the most damaging of these critiques is the allegation that his theory is *post hoc*, that he has discovered instances of the withdrawal of status respect by looking first at situations in which economic growth occurred and then by looking for status losses that might have preceded that growth (Kilby, 1971). A second major criticism has centered on the long period of time—as much as five or more generations—required for the withdrawal of status respect to result in the emergence of entrepreneurship (Young, 1971). Despite these criticisms we retain this factor as a potential influence on entrepreneurial emergence.

Motives. A prominent feature of discussions of the psychological factors promoting entrepreneurial behavior is the analysis of motives. Whereas need-achievement constitutes a combination of psychological predispositions which theoretically may lead to attempts to attain a variety of goals, the emphasis on motives stresses specific goals that entrepreneurs are likely to pursue. This discussion of motives is probably one of the major supports for the argument that noneconomic factors are significant for entrepreneurship, because it has been claimed that pecuniary motives are not the only ones operative among entrepreneurs (Cochran, 1950; Parsons and Smelser, 1956). If pecuniary motives were the sole motives of entrepreneurs, then one could argue that economic factors would be sufficient to stimulate the emergence of entrepreneurship.

Cole (1959) suggests security, prestige, power, and social service as potential motives in addition to profit maximization; he further suggests that providing security for one's family has been an especially important motive historically. Stepanek (1960) provides a list of nonmonetary motives which includes the desire for independence, community esteem, power, and the chance to prove oneself superior. And Evans (1949) makes an interesting distinction among different types of entrepreneurs. According to him, the managing entrepreneur is primarily motivated by a desire for security, the innovating entrepreneur seeks adventure, and the controlling entrepreneur is after power. Collins and Moore (1970) make the unique suggestion that entrepreneurship is a means of demonstrating maleness. Rostow has suggested that motives will change between generations of a family and has labeled this alleged phenomenon the *Buddenbrooks* dynamic after the novel by Thomas Mann. In Rostow's model the desire for financial gain characteristic of the first generation of entrepreneurs is replaced in the succeeding generation by a desire for social and civic prestige, and subsequently, in the following generation by the pursuit of artistic values (Feller, 1967).

Other psychological factors. Several of the other psychological characteristics described as being important for the emergence of entrepreneurship are in general accord with McClelland's description of need-achievement. These include the setting of definite and realistic goals and the ability to defer gratification, the willingness to take risks (Harris, 1970; Thiagarajan and Whittaker, 1969; Anderson, 1969; Stepanek, 1960), and a tendency to see self-induced changes as possible (Brandenburg, 1962; Hagen, 1967). The emphasis placed by some upon a high energy level or the possession of "drive" can also be considered as a probable characteristic of a person high in need-achievement (Harris, 1970; Schaw, 1968; Stepanek, 1960). By contrast, perception (Marris, 1969; Negandhi and Prasad, 1971) and cognition (Solo, 1967), two psychological factors which some have emphasized, have not been particularly important components in the need-achievement model.

Another emphasis in the literature on the psychological factors promoting entrepreneurship which merits comment is that of the psychological implications of unrewarding or negative experiences for entrepreneurship. Hagen's theory of the withdrawal of status respect is the best-known example of this emphasis. In addition, Parsons and Smelser (1956) have stressed the importance of dissatisfaction with existing modes of production, Marris and Somerset (1971) have cited frustration as a factor generating entrepreneurship, and Evans (1959) has described several different kinds of fear that may encourage entrepreneurial actions. Although this emphasis upon negative experiences is not particularly pronounced in the literature, it does suggest that entrepreneurship is not always generated by favorable circumstances.

Given the nature of the data we have used in this study, it is difficult for us to say anything very precise about either the psychological factors which have induced individuals to behave entrepreneurially or the psychological characteristics they have manifested within the entrepreneurial role. We have attempted to determine the extent to which nonmonetary motivations have been operative for entrepreneurs because the relative importance of monetary and nonmonetary motives is of significance for determining the relative importance of economic and noneconomic factors as promoters of entrepreneurship.

Summary of Noneconomic Factors Influencing the Emergence of Entrepreneurship

We can distill two distinct models of the noneconomic factors influencing entrepreneurial emergence from the foregoing discussion. These two models suggest that entrepreneurship, or perhaps different types of entrepreneurship, will emerge under quite different social conditions. We have retained the terms *mainstream* and *outsider* entrepreneurship to characterize these two models, which are presented in Table 3. Generally the models suggest that entrepreneurship may arise either under favorable or unfavorable sociocultural condi-

Table 3
Relationship Between Noneconomic Factors Influencing
the Emergence of Entrepreneurship and Two Basic
Types of Entrepreneurship

Mainstream Entrepreneurship	Outsider Entrepreneurship
1. High entrepreneurial legitimacy	1. Low entrepreneurial legitimacy
2. High access to mobility channels	2. Low access to mobility channels
3. Nonmarginality	3. Marginality
4. High integration within system	4. High integration within subsystem, low integration within larger system
5. High security within system	5. High security within subsystem, low security within larger system
6. Entrepreneurial ideology	6. Entrepreneurial ideology within subsystem
7. High need-achievement	7. Withdrawal of status respect

tions, and the table indicates the characteristics of each of the noneconomic factors for the two cases. Mainstream entrepreneurship is most likely to emerge under favorable conditions, whereas entrepreneurship will more likely emerge from outside sources when sociocultural conditions are unfavorable. We have assigned the two major psychological theories, need-achievement and withdrawal of status respect, to these two types respectively. This cannot be made a hard and fast distinction because the withdrawal of status respect may be psychologically significant through the high levels of need-achievement which it engenders. But the theory of need-achievement, especially with McClelland's more recent emphasis upon its mobilization through stimulation by the larger sociocultural setting, instead of merely the family, clearly relates more closely to the other characteristics of mainstream entrepreneurship than to the other characteristics of outsider entrepreneurship.

Another significant point illustrated by this pair of ideal types is that, for outsider entrepreneurship, many of the social factors promoting the emergence of entrepreneurship are located in the subsystem, or a group within society, rather than in the larger system. From this perspective, the characteristics included under mainstream entrepreneurship in Table 3 may be considered the factors promoting entrepreneurship, and outsider entrepreneurship may be seen as a special case of the more general model which appears when conditions in the larger social system, or a whole society, are not conducive to mainstream entrepreneurship.

SUMMARY

The phenomenon of entrepreneurship is elusive. In this book we are attempting to make it less elusive by focusing upon two issues. First, how important is entrepreneurship for economic growth and development? Second, what economic, social, and psychological conditions lead to its emergence?

We have shown that quite different points of view prevail regarding these two issues. Economists generally have given entrepreneurship little credit for significantly affecting the course of economic growth relative to other more fundamental causes of economic change. We have suggested a reformulation of this issue involving a distinction between the definitional and the causal significance of entrepreneurship. We have argued that entrepreneurship will always be definitionally significant for economic growth and development because it refers to the human element in economic activities. We have, however, argued further that the fundamental issue concerns its *causal* significance—whether it has an independent effect upon economic change. This may be deduced by determining the extent to which it has an influence separate from the influence of other factors known to affect economic growth and development.

Very different points of view are also apparent regarding the closely related issue of the factors which promote, or hinder, the emergence of entrepreneurship. Whereas economists tend to regard its appearance as a consequence of economic factors, sociologists and psychologists have suggested a variety of noneconomic factors which influence its emergence. We have described a variety of sociocultural factors—legitimacy, social mobility, marginality, social integration, security, ideology—and psychological factors—need-achievement, withdrawal of status respect, and other motives—which have been proposed as influential for the appearance of entrepreneurship.

We turn next to a more detailed consideration of the way in which we have inferred the causal significance of entrepreneurship in the six societies that we have used as case studies.

2

Assessing the Significance of Entrepreneurship for Economic Growth and Development

In our initial discussion of the significance of entrepreneurship for economic growth and development we said that it will be *causally* significant to the extent that it adds to, or detracts from, the influence of other factors which affect growth and development. In Table 1 we noted that either the emergence or the nonemergence of entrepreneurship may or may not have causal significance. We also noted the different points of view regarding the significance of entrepreneurship—one emphasizing it as a dependent variable and the other focusing upon it as an independent variable. We now describe how we have sought an answer to the question of the significance of entrepreneurship in this study.

The two points of view regarding the significance of entrepreneurship can be represented heuristically by means of the two models in Figure 1. In these models O represents the economic *opportunity* conditions characterizing a particular situation.[1] E stands for entrepreneurship, X represents the noneconomic factors alleged to influence the emergence of entrepreneurship, and Y represents the rate of economic growth and development. Model (a) exemplifies the point of view which regards entrepreneurship as primarily a dependent variable and a response to the opportunity conditions present in a given situation. From this point of view, E and Y will be correlated with each other because of their

[1]Our designation of the economic factors influencing entrepreneurship as *opportunity conditions* is consonant with the emphasis placed upon opportunites by several students of entrepreneurship. Kunkel (1970), McClelland and Winter (1971), and Glade (1967) have all emphasized the opportunity structure to which entrepreneurs respond. Cole (1959) and Parsons and Smelser (1956) have similarly emphasized opportunities.

dependence on O, but E will not have a significant independent influence upon Y. In other words, the opportunity conditions will be the only significant factor, causing both the emergence of entrepreneurship and the occurrence of economic growth and development. If these conditions are unfavorable, then entrepreneurship will not emerge and economic growth and development will not take place.

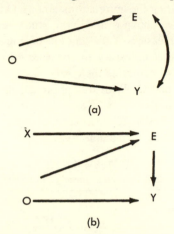

Figure 1   Alternative Models of Entrepreneurship

Model (b), which represents the argument that entrepreneurship is an important independent variable, differs from Model (a) in two main ways. First, an independent influence of entrepreneurship upon economic growth and development is shown by means of the arrow drawn from E to Y. Second, entrepreneurship is made partially dependent upon the noneconomic factors, X, rather than being totally influenced by the economic opportunity conditions. Thus this model shows entrepreneurship as being significant for economic growth and development and noneconomic factors as being significant for entrepreneurship.

These two models can also be represented by means of equations. For Model (a) the equations are:

$$Y = O \tag{1}$$
$$E = O \tag{2}$$

For Model (b) they are:

$$Y = O + E \tag{3}$$
$$E = O + X \tag{4}$$

We have presented equations (3) and (4) in an additive form. It is conceivable that the relationships are actually multiplicative so that the equations should be $Y = O \times E$ and $E = O \times X$, implying that both O and E are necessary for Y and both O and X are necessary for E. But we started from the premise that the relationships were additive rather than multiplicative.

CHOOSING BETWEEN THE MODELS

How does one choose between these models? Ideally one would derive measures of O, E, and Y from a variety of situations and determine the correlations among them. One could then ascertain whether entrepreneurship had a significant causal influence on Y by comparing the correlations among O and E, E and Y, and O and Y. But this approach was not possible in this study because of the impossibility of obtaining a direct measure of the amount of entrepreneurship in a situation.[2] Consequently, it was necessary to measure E by means of a residual approach. This was done by assuming the correctness of Equation (3) and deriving measures of both Y and O. With this approach therefore, the value of E depends upon the difference between Y and O. If Y and O are approximately equal, then the value of E will be near zero; if there is a large discrepancy between Y and O then this is attributable to E.

Table 4
Possible Relationships among O, E, and Y

		Value of Y	
		Low	High
Value of O	Low	E = 0	E > 0
	High	E < 0	E = 0

This approach corresponds precisely with our earlier discussion of the causal significance of entrepreneurship, as can be seen from Table 4. This table shows the four patterns of relationships among O, E, and Y that are possible when O and Y are simply dichotomized. In two of these cases entrepreneurship will have causal significance and in the other two it will have only definitional significance. If the values of O and Y are both low or both high, then the value of E will be near zero, indicating that O accounts for most of the value of Y. The two crucial cases in which entrepreneurship *will* have causal significance are those in which the correlation between O and Y is lower than the correlation between E and Y. First, if the value of Y is high and the value of O is low, then the value of Y is attributable to E's being significantly greater than zero, or to a *positive* influence of entrepreneurship on economic growth and development. Second, if the value of Y is low and the value of O is high, then we attribute the value of Y to an E that is significantly less than zero, or to a *negative* influence of entrepreneurship on Y. In the former case E makes a significant *addition* to the influence of O on Y; in the latter case E makes a significant *detraction* from the influence of O on Y. In the two cases in which E lacks causal significance it neither adds to, nor detracts from, the influence of O on Y.

[2]McCloskey and Sandberg (1971) have noted the impossibility of measuring entrepreneurship directly.

This can be made clearer by considering what O, E, and Y represent. For the two cases in which E lacks causal significance we find either favorable opportunity conditions accompanied by a high rate of economic growth and development, or unfavorable opportunity conditions resulting in a low rate of economic growth and development. But in the case in which entrepreneurship has a positive causal influence, entrepreneurs have significantly improved upon the unfavorable opportunity conditions to create a high rate of economic growth and development. And in the case in which entrepreneurship has a negative causal influence, entrepreneurs have failed to take advantage of the favorable opportunity conditions that are present; hence the rate of economic growth and development has been relatively low. Therefore these two kinds of situations are crucial for making the inference that entrepreneurship is a significant cause of economic growth and development.

Another way to visualize the causal significance of entrepreneurship is to think in terms of two situations, for example two societies, in which the level of O is the same but in which the levels of Y are different. One could say either that the entrepreneurs in the society in which Y was higher have made more effective use of the opportunity conditions available to them, or that the entrepreneurs in the society in which Y was lower have failed fully to exploit the opportunity conditions available to them. Or, one might think in terms of two societies with unequal opportunity conditions and equal rates of economic growth and development. The potential of this approach is limited by the difficulty of finding cases in which the levels of O or the levels of Y are exactly equal, but it does exemplify the argument that entrepreneurship is causally significant when it adds to, or detracts from, the influence of opportunity conditions on economic growth and development.[3]

It is important to keep separate the *causal significance* and the *amount* of entrepreneurship in a situation. As we noted in Table 1, either the emergence or nonemergence of entrepreneurship may be causally significant. A large amount of entrepreneurship, or a significant degree of entrepreneurial emergence, will be

[3]It should be pointed out that our discussion of the significance of entrepreneurship is not incompatible with the possibility that Y is a multiplicative function of O and E, i.e., $Y = O \times E$. The value of E in the cases we have described as involving causal insignificance may actually be one rather than zero, since $Z + O = Z \times 1$. And a value of one may be more appropriate than a value of zero for E in cases in which entrepreneurship has definitional, but not causal significance. If we were to represent definitional significance in this manner, then a positive influence of entrepreneurship would be represented by a value for E that was greater than one and a negative influence by a value that was less than one. As it turns out, the critical test for determining whether an additive or multiplicative model is the correct one is provided by situations in which the value of O is zero. If such a case were found to exist, and if the value of Y in that situation were not zero, then it would be clear that an additive model was the appropriate one to use. But it is doubtful whether there are any situations in which one may assume that the opportunity conditions are zero. Furthermore, for our purposes it really does not make much difference whether the basic model is additive or multiplicaive. In either case the causal significance of entrepreneurship is inferred from the magnitude of the discrepancy between O and Y.

causally significant if the opportunity conditions in a situation are not very favorable and if the situation is characterized by a relatively high Y. It will not be causally significant if the opportunity conditions are quite favorable, so that Y and O are approximately equal. Conversely, the nonemergence of entrepreneurship, or a small amount of entrepreneurship, will be causally significant if opportunity conditions are quite favorable—and yet Y remains significantly lower than O. It will not be causally significant if opportunity conditions are unfavorable, since in that case Y, O, and E will all be near zero. Normally one would expect that the causal significance of entrepreneurship would be directly related to the amount of entrepreneurship but in our formulation that is not so.

Therefore, in this study we have inferred the causal significance of entrepreneurship from the magnitude of the discrepancy between the opportunity conditions for entrepreneurship present in a situation (O) and the rate of economic growth and development (Y) achieved in that situation. In cases where Y was significantly greater than O, entrepreneurship was judged to have positive causal significance; in cases where Y was significantly less than O, it was concluded that it had negative causal significance. And where Y and O were approximately equal, entrepreneurship was deemed causally insignificant.

THE RELATIVE SIGNIFICANCE OF ECONOMIC AND NON-ECONOMIC FACTORS FOR ENTREPRENEURSHIP

Once it has been determined whether entrepreneurship was causally significant or insignificant in a particular situation, the crucial question becomes: Why was it causally significant or insignificant? What accounts for its disproportionate emergence in a particular situation, or for its acute failure to emerge in other situations? It is at this point that the issue of the relative importance of economic and noneconomic factors becomes significant.

Given the two models of entrepreneurship presented in Figure 1, we can show that the conclusion we make regarding the causal significance of entrepreneurship will also determine the conclusion that will be made regarding whether economic factors, the variables included within O, are sufficient to account for the emergence of entrepreneurship, or whether noneconomic factors, the variables included within X, are also necessary to explain its emergence.

This can be shown quite easily if we assume that the same factors in O influence both Y and E. If it should be discovered that there is little or no discrepancy between Y and O, and hence that entrepreneuship is not causally significant, then the inference is that Model (a) in Figure 1 is correct and that both entrepreneurship and Y are determined by the nature of economic opportunity conditions. Where these conditions have been favorable, entrepreneurs have come forth and economic growth and development have occurred; where they have been unfavorable, entrepreneurs have not come forth and economic growth and development have not taken place.

But, if it is discovered that there is a significant discrepancy between O and Y so that entrepreneurship is causally significant, then the E term will be significantly greater or less than zero (or one if we use a multiplicative model). Furthermore, the greater the discrepancy there is between O and Y, and the greater therefore the value of the E term, the greater also will be the discrepancy between O and E. And if a discrepancy exists between O and E, then E *cannot* be a function only of O. Hence it will be necessary to bring in other factors to account for E's being either less than, or greater than, O, and it is at this point that the noneconomic factors, X, become relevant.

Table 5
Relationships among O, E, and X

		Value of E		
		< 0	= 0	> 0
Value of O	Low	X < 0	X = 0	X > 0
	High	X < 0	X = 0	X > 0

The major possibilities are shown in Table 5, which is based on a multiplicative influence of X and O on E, i.e., $E = C \times O$.[4] E may be assumed to have one of three values on the basis of the relationship between O and Y. It may be less than zero, approximately equal to zero, or greater than zero. Given these values of E and dichotomous values for O, X will take on the values included in the table. The most interesting cases are the extremes. If the value of O is low, and E is greater than zero, indicating that Y is significantly greater than O, then X will also be significantly greater than zero. This may be interpreted in terms of noneconomic factors being present in the situation which caused a significantly higher level of entrepreneurship to occur than was justified by the low level of opportunity conditions. Consequently the rate of economic growth and development was also significantly higher than the level of O. Or to phrase it somewhat differently, a low value of O and a high value for Y imply a relatively high positive value for E. A relatively high positive value for E and a low value for O in turn imply a relatively high positive value for X.

At the opposite extreme we have a high O and low Y implying a negative value for E, or a failure of entrepreneurs to take advantage of the opportunity conditions available in a situation. A negative E and a high O imply a negative value for X, which we interpret as the presence of noneconomic factors which constitute barriers to entrepreneurship.

---

[4]A multiplicative relationship is more in accord with the argument of those who claim that noneconomic factors are necessary conditions for entrepreneurial emergence.

Between these extreme cases we have the other two cases shown in Table 5, in which E is inferred to be approximately zero because of the near or actual equality of O and Y. In these cases X will also be approximately zero, connoting the absence of noneconomic factors which would have led to the emergence of entrepreneurship and its causal significance.

These noneconomic factors include the sociocultural characteristics of the environment in a particular situation and the psychological characteristics of the entrepreneurs themselves which we have discussed in the previous chapter. In addition there may be certain significant characteristics of the entrepreneurship in a situation, which we discuss later, that may be found to be related to causal significance and which will provide clues as to the reason for its causal significance. The important point is that where entrepreneurship is causally significant, that significance cannot be attributable to the influence of economic factors.

Therefore we may conclude that entrepreneurship will have the greatest causal influence on economic growth and development and that noneconomic factors will be most significant for the emergence of entrepreneurship in two cases. First, if a relatively high rate of economic growth and development is attained in a situation with only limited economic opportunity conditions, then this rate will be attributable to the influence of noneconomic factors which promoted the disproportionate emergence of entrepreneurship in that situation. Second, if only a relatively low rate of economic growth and development is achieved in a situation with very favorable economic opportunity conditions, then entrepreneurship will have a significant negative influence and this influence will be attributable to the effects of noneconomic factors which hindered the emergence of entrepreneurship.

And, if entrepreneurship does not appear to be causally significant because of the similarity of the favorableness of the opportunity conditions and the achieved rates of economic growth and development in situations characterized by either favorable or unfavorable opportunity conditions, then we may assume that both entrepreneurship and the rate of economic growth and development were primarily the result of the nature of the economic opportunity conditions.

This procedure makes logical sense and it is also buttressed by the usual social scientific canons of causal inference. Furthermore it follows the approach suggested by several writers for determining the relative influence of economic and noneconomic factors on entrepreneurship. Feller (1967), for example, suggests that one must show that favorable opportunity conditions were not responded to by entrepreneurs if one wishes to show an influence of noneconomic factors. The procedure we have used, of allowing the economic opportunity conditions to explain as much of the variance in economic growth and development as they can before introducing either entrepreneurship or noneconomic factors, is the logical one to follow, rather than its opposite, because entrepreneurship is basically *economic* behavior. Ilchman and Uphoff (1971) and Glade (1967) have argued for the priority of economic variables in the study of entrepreneurship. It is conceivable, however, that noneconomic variables may be important determinants of the opportunity conditions present in a situation. This is the position taken by Gould (1972) who suggests that economic and noneconomic, especially sociocultural, variables exist at different levels in a model of entrepreneurship. According to him, opportunity conditions impinge directly upon entrepreneurial decisionmaking, but sociocultural factors may affect the nature of those opportunity conditions through their influence on characteristics such as the propensity to save. These potential influences, of X on O, have been outside the purview of this study.

In the following section we describe the specific research strategy and the sources of data we have used in this study to answer the two basic issues we have considered: the significance of entrepreneurship for economic growth and development and the relative significance of economic and noneconomic factors for entrepreneurial emergence.

STRATEGY OF THE STUDY

The need for a comparative study to answer these questions should be obvious. Basically we have been interested in the correlations between O, Y, and E. Therefore it has been necessary to analyze situations in which there was some reasonable expectation that the values of these variables would vary. By comparing societies in which O has varied, and determining the value of Y in those societies, we have been able to ascertain the significance of E for Y. In addition, we have analyzed the characteristics of the noneconomic factors in those societies, with an eye to cases in which entrepreneurship was causally significant and cases in which it was causally insignificant. In cases in which entrepreneurship has had causal significance, our major interest has been in the noneconomic factors related to its positive or negative influence on economic growth and development.

Countries Studied and Periods of Analysis

The approach we have described to study the significance and the emergence of entrepreneurship could be used in a variety of situations. One might compare situations at the level of specific entrepreneurs within a single community. Or one might compare situations within a country, for example, different regions. We have selected a larger unit of analysis for this study, that of the entire society. Thus our comparisons are between societies, and we have asked such questions as: What were the opportunity conditions for entrepreneurship like in society A as compared to society B? How did the rates of economic growth and development differ in these societies? On this basis we have inferred the significance of entrepreneurship in the various societies and also ascertained the relative influence of noneconomic factors on the emergence of entrepreneurship.

Five of the six societies we selected—Great Britain, France, Germany, Japan, and the United States—achieved industrialization between 1750 and 1925. In addition our comparative study has been strengthened by the inclusion of a negative case, a society that did not achieve industrialization—Russia before the Bolshevik Revolution. These six societies were selected for several reasons. First, the five which achieved industrialization, and are often referred to as the *early* developers, are widely regarded as the most significant societies on the world economic scene during this period. Second, our choice was partly influenced by the potential availability of data regarding the key variables in our study. Given their economic preeminence during this period, we assumed that more data would be available for them than for other societies for that time period. Third, we also believed that they would offer substantial variance on all four variables—O, Y, E, and X—of interest to us. Four of the six societies are in Europe, one in the New World, and one in Asia; hence this geographic diversity presented the opportunity to analyze entrepreneurship in widely varying situations.

We have limited our analysis of entrepreneurship in these six societies to the *manufacturing* sector of their economies. This limitation was imposed partly to keep the scope of the study within manageable proportions. More importantly, manufacturing was clearly the leading sector, as Rostow calls it, in the industrial transition in these societies. As he puts it, ". . . takeoff requires that a society find a way to apply effectively to its own peculiar resources. . . the tricks of manufacture" (1956, p. 48). In addition, more historical data are generally available regarding the manufacturing sector than regarding other economic sectors. So we have excluded agricultural entrepreneurship and entrepreneurship in tertiary areas, such as finance and transportation, from this study. Within the manufacturing sector, we have followed Hagen's (1968) suggestion and concentrated on the transition from cottage or domestic modes of production to factory production, rather than upon the prior transition from production by independent artisans or craftsmen to domestic production. It is in the transition from domestic to factory production that the most variance in our major variables is to be found, and furthermore it is far the more significant transition in the process of industrialization.

It was also necessary to place chronological constraints on our study. The beginning of the process of industrialization in the early developers could be traced back to the point at which inhabitants of those societies first produced goods. But this would not be a particularly helpful starting point because of the centuries of extremely slow change between that time and the ultimate achievement of industrialization. Thus entrepreneurial behavior would reveal only limited variance, if in fact it existed at all, during this period. It is fairly widely agreed, however, that the Industrial Revolution in these societies was characterized by a quickening of the rate of economic growth, an upturn in indicators of production. So we have attempted to locate this historical benchmark and begin our analysis of each society at that point. Ideally we would have used some quantitative indicator of this point, comparable to the one we will note presently that we are using for the end point of our analytical periods. But historical data have proved inadequate for this. Consequently we have been strongly influenced by the opinions of economic historians, as well as by monumental historical events which constitute logical starting points.

In the case of England there is substantial evidence of an increase in industrial and general economic growth around 1750, and this can be regarded as the approximate beginning of the Industrial Revolution. In the case of France, there was relatively rapid growth from about the same period, but we have chosen to start our analysis with the French Revolution since we feel that event marked a significant point in French history. We start our analysis of Prussia-Germany at 1815, the date of the Congress of Vienna, and the beginning of a period of slightly more rapid growth. Japan provides us with a natural starting point, the Meiji Revolution in 1868. For Russia, we have selected 1800 as our point of departure. And for the United States we have started our analysis at 1810, the beginning of a period of increased interest in manufacturing.

Similarly, it was difficult to determine the appropriate end point for our analysis of each society. We wanted to conclude our analysis at the point at which industrialization was achieved because we were interested in the significance of entrepreneurship in the industrialization process. But unfortunately there is no consensus on when a society reaches that point. Therefore we have selected as our indicator of the degree of industrialization the proportion of a society's national product derived from industry. We consider a society to be industrialized when the proportion of its national product derived from industry *surpasses* the proportion of its national product attributable to agriculture.[5]

Table 6 shows the resultant end points of our periods of analysis for each of the six societies. The percentages for Russia in 1913, four years before the Bolshevik Revolution, clearly show a failure to achieve industrialization, thereby affirming its status as a negative case.

There are several problems, even with the fairly definite indicator that we chose. First, the proportion of national product from agriculture includes forestry and fishing in two cases (France and Great Britain for 1821). Therefore the strictly agricultural percentages are less than those given in the table, so that one

---

[5]Gould (1972) suggests that sector shares will be more highly correlated with economic growth and development than will another potential indicator, the proportion of the labor force in either sector. Kuznets (1968), however, claims that labor force proportions are a better indicator of structural changes. Since we were interested simply in determining a historical point that might be considered to mark the achievement of industrialization, we believe our proportion-of-national-product indicator is more satisfactory than a proportion-of-labor-force indicator. It is also more satisfactory than selecting an arbitrary percentage as our indicator.

Table 6

Date of Achievement of Industrialization in Five
Societies and Degree of Industrialization in
Russia as of 1913

Country	Date or Period	Percentage of National Product from Agriculture	Percentage of National Product from Industry	
Great Britain	1812	27.0		30.0a
	1821	26.0b		32.0a
France	1908–10	35.0b		37.0a
Prussia-Germany	1865–74	30.0		31.0c
Japan	1923–27	23.0d		28.0e
	1928–32	22.0d		28.0e
United States	1869–79	20.5		21.0a
Russia	1913	44.0	c.	20.0f

aMining, manufacturing, and construction
bAgriculture, forestry, and fishing
cIndustry excluding handicrafts
dPrimary sector
eSecondary sector
fMining, manufacturing, and handicrafts
Source: Deane (1957, p. 165, table 3); Deane & Cole (1967, p. 166, table 37); Goldsmith (1961, pp. 442, 444); Kuznets (1957, pp. 68–73, table 2).

could conclude that industrialization was achieved earlier in France than the 1908–1910 period shown. And including forestry and fishing places the British achievement of industrialization in 1821 rather than 1812. Moreover, the bases for the proportion of national product derived from industry also differ among countries. The data for Great Britain, France and the United States include mining and construction with manufacturing. We regard this as acceptable since the industrial transition involves more than the development of manufacturing. The Prussian-German percentage is based upon industry excluding handicrafts, whereas we assume that the three indices just mentioned include handicrafts. Consequently, it probably understates the degree of industrialization relative to that of the countries which include handicrafts. The Russian data exclude construction, so they may understate the degree of industrialization, too. They undoubtedly do not understate it to the extent that we could conclude that industrialization had been achieved in Russia by 1913.

The Japanese percentages involve comparisons between the primary and secondary sectors of the economy which are not synonymous with agriculture and industry. Mining, which is included under industry for several of the other countries, is often considered as part of the primary rather than the secondary sector, so the Japanese agricultural percentage may be inflated in comparison with that of the other countries. Hence industrialization, by our definition, may have been achieved earlier in Japan than the dates we indicate.

Therefore we have analyzed entrepreneurship essentially during the period of the transition from an economic system based on agriculture to one based upon industrial production, with manufacturing as the chief component. We consider this period to represent the "takeoff" to industrialization in these societies. This conception differs from Rostow's (1956) in that it covers a more general change than his. His view of the "takeoff" refers to the period when industrial growth "takes hold" or becomes self-reinforcing. The periods we analyze in this study and Rostow's estimates of the takeoff periods are compared in Table 7. This table reveals that in all cases our period of analysis includes Rostow's takeoff period within it. In most cases his takeoff periods lie closer to the end than to the beginning of our periods. So in terms of his conceptualization, our periods of analysis cover a portion of the pre-takeoff period, in which the preconditions for takeoff occur; the takeoff period itself; and the beginning of the period of self-sustained growth.

Table 7
Historical Periods of Analysis of This Study
Compared to Rostow's "Takeoff" Periods

Country	Period of Analysis	"Takeoff" Period*
Great Britain	1750–1815	1783–1802
France	1789–1910	1830–1860
Prussia-Germany	1815–1875	1850–1873
Japan	1868–1927	1878–1900
United States	1810–1880	1843–1860
Russia	1800–1917	1890–1914

*Rostow (1956, p. 31).

The lengths of the periods we have selected also give an indication of the rapidity of economic growth in these societies; the contrast between England and France, which we emphasize later, is particularly noteworthy, even more so if we consider that we could have begun the French period at the same time as the English period. Lastly, it should also be noted that our analysis of German entrepreneurship is mainly of the various states, particularly Prussia, which united to form Germany in 1871. Our period of analysis ends only four years after that political development.

It is also interesting to note the differences in the specific percentages of national product derived from agriculture and industry at the time when industrialization was achieved according to our operationalization. The percentages for industry range from a high of 37 percent for France to a low of 21 percent for the United States. Likewise the percentages for agriculture range from a high of 35 percent for France to a low of 20.5 percent for the United States. These differences indicate a substantially different socioeconomic structure in these two societies. Another way of looking at this difference is to say that the United States would not have been industrialized until the period 1947–54, if it had had to reach the 37 percent level, whereas France could have been considered industrialized in 1815 if the 21 percent level had been the criterion. Despite this variance in our indicator of industrialization, we believe it to be preferable to an arbitrary selection of a specific percentage of national product derived from industry.

The major difference between France and the United States is, of course, that the agricultural sector remained far more significant in France. But other interesting differences also show up when we look at the contributions of other sectors of the two economies to their national product, as shown by Kuznets' (1957) data. A major difference shows up in the sector which Kuznets has classified as *trade*. At the time when France achieved industrialization by our standard this sector accounted for only 7 percent of French national product, whereas in the United States it accounted for 16 percent of national product at the time of its achievement of industrialization. In contrast, the sector Kuznets labels as *government* accounted for only 4.4 percent of national income in the United States, but 11 percent of French national product, when the two societies achieved industrialization. This presents a picture of an agricultural-administrative French society in comparison with a business-industrial American society.

DATA SOURCES

This study is based on data from a wide variety of sources. We have used the analyses of numerous economic and social historians, both regarding specific cases of entrepreneurship and the more general industrialization process in each society. Where feasible we have also used quantitative data to support major points or as illustrative material. Our goal has been to consider the broadest possible range of points of view.

We should mention some problems with the use of data of this type, if only to assure readers of our awareness of them. First, a problem endemic to all historical studies is that of missing data. We do not know whether the available historical accounts of entrepreneurship constitute a random sample, or whether only those entrepreneurs who were most visible or who left the most extensive records are included. The latter is more likely and it is also probable that many cases of entrepreneurial failure left no record. But it is also possible that the entrepreneurs who have been most influential have also been most visible and left evidence of their efforts for succeeding generations.

A second, possibly more serious, problem is the tendency of writers to concentrate on specific cases of entrepreneurship, often the more novel or dramtic ones, and to fail to generalize from these cases. This inferential exercise is left to others who cannot be certain that the cases constitute a random sample. The study of entrepreneurship is especially likely to yield such specific studies because in the past individual actors have been the most visible manifestations of the phenomenon.

Third, it is questionable whether all types of variables—economic, sociocultural, and psychological—have been given equal consideration in the historical accounts of entrepreneurship. Conceivably, given the individualistic nature of much past entrepreneurship and the tendency to emphasize specific cases, psychological variables have been overemphasized and economic and sociocultural ones neglected.

Fourth, since entrepreneurship has been studied by investigators from a number of disciplines—including economics, sociology, psychology, and history—there has been an understandable tendency toward disciplinary insularity, or perhaps myopia. As Kilby (1971, p. 4) has put it, "Practitioners in each of the social sciences tend to define the problem so that the principal determinants of entrepreneurial performance fall within their disciplines." Earlier we noted the distinction between scholars emphasizing the importance of the *demand* for entrepreneurship and those emphasizing its *supply*. We have attempted to compensate for this disciplinary narrowness by including both economic variables (the O factors) and noneconomic ones (the X factors) and by considering the arguments presented by scholars from different disciplines. Therefore, although our background is sociological, we have attempted to give greater credence to nonsociological variables than has been the case in most studies of entrepreneurship carried out by sociologists. Although this inclusion of both economic and noneconomic variables has complicated our task enormously, the study has persuaded us more strongly than ever that both kinds of variables must be considered in a study of entrepreneurship.

We know of no way to overcome these problems except to procure data from as wide a variety of sources as possible, and this is the strategy we have used.

MEASUREMENT OF THE VARIABLES

Given our approach, it has been necessary to estimate values for three major categories of variables: O, economic opportunity conditions; Y, the rate of economic growth and development; and X, noneconomic factors believed to influence entrepreneurship, or what we might call *noneconomic opportunity conditions*. Also it has been necessary to consider the major characteristics of, and sources of variance in, entrepreneurship itself, for reasons we shall discuss presently.

The Rate of Economic Growth and Development (Y)

Since we have analyzed the significance of *industrial* entrepreneurship, our dependent variable has been the rate of *industrial* growth of a society rather than the rate of overall economic growth, which would also include the primary and tertiary sectors. Data on industrial growth are available for at least part of the historical period we have analyzed for each society.

We regard industrial growth as involving *quantitative* changes in goods production and industrial development as involving *qualitative* changes in the manner in which goods are produced. Quantitative change has constituted our major dependent variable because it is much more quantifiable than qualitative change. Wherever it has been meaningful to refer to significant qualitative changes accompanying industrial growth, such as in the composition of the labor force or in modes of production, we have done so. We have also, however, provided quantitative evidence of these qualitative changes to the extent that such data have been available.

Economic Opportunity Conditions for Entrepreneurship (O)

Determining the favorableness of opportunity conditions in each of the six societies clearly has been our most critical task. Because of the very large number of potentially significant economic variables it has been necessary to select only the most general and most essential. Our choice of these determinants of the opportunity conditions has required us to consider the elements of a micro-level theory of entrepreneurship, or the factors which affect the decisions made by existent or potential entrepreneurs.

Although we can think of "opportunity conditions" as describing an economic situation, when we observe that situation from the perspective of the entrepreneur as decisionmaker it is more helpful to think in terms of the *profit potential* of a situation. Favorable opportunity conditions will offer high profit potential, and hence we assume that they would be conducive to profit seeking entrepreneurial behavior. The profit potential of situations with unfavorable or limited opportunity conditions will be limited; thus one would assume that less entrepreneurship will occur. If this is in fact what occurs, then entrepreneurship will not be causally significant. *But* if entrepreneurs provide either more or less entrepreneurship than is warranted by the opportunity conditions, i.e., extensive entrepreneurship in a situation with low profit potential or limited entrepreneurship in a situation with high profit potential, then their efforts will be causally significant, i.e., $Y \neq O$.

Assuming that the favorableness of opportunity conditions is synonymous with the profit potential of a situation, then the favorableness of opportunity conditions for entrepreneurship, *relative* to other roles, is synonymous with the *relative* profit potential of entrepreneurship compared to nonentrepreneurial roles. Therefore, in the economists' model of entrepreneurship, the probability of its emerging in a situation will be *proportional* to the relative opportunity conditions of that situation. The more favorable the relative opportunity conditions, the greater the probability of entrepreneurship, rather than other roles, emerging, and the greater the likelihood of the occurrence of economic growth and development.

In the noneconomic model, though, the probability of entrepreneurship's emerging will *not* be necessarily proportional to relative opportunity conditions. Entrepreneurs may emerge to a greater or lesser extent than warranted by the opportunity conditions. So, in terms of our framework, entrepreneurship will be causally significant to the degree that it beats the odds, so to speak. It will have a positive causal influence if its emergence, relative to the emergence of other roles, is greater than the ratio of the relative opportunity conditions for nonentrepreneurial roles. It will have a negative causal influence if its emergence is less than this ratio. And it will not be causally significant if its degree of emergence is equal to this ratio; in this case it will have emerged in proportion to the relative opportunity conditions as specified in the economists' model.

Hoselitz (1955b) argues that, in general, industrial entrepreneurship is riskier than entrepreneurship in finance and trade because the capital that is invested is less liquid and turns over more slowly. If this is so, then in the economists' model financial entrepreneurship may be proportional to relative opportunity conditions, whereas industrial entrepreneurship may be somewhat less than proportional. This will not affect our strategy, however, as we are not comparing industrial and financial entrepreneurship.

General Determinants of Rewards and Costs

What then determines the profit potential of a situation? We assume that it will be a direct function of the potential economic *rewards* and economic *costs* of that situation. Rewards and costs will in turn be functions of several determinants. These determinants can be divided into three categories: (a) the quantity of factor inputs available; (b) the quality of available factor inputs; (c) the level and composition of the market. The first two will mainly affect the entrepreneur's potential costs, and the last one will mainly affect his potential rewards. We shall discuss each of these in turn.

Quantity of factor inputs. Economists have traditionally discussed three factors of production—land, labor, and capital—which constitute inputs for the entrepreneurial role. Technology, or the actual techniques used to produce a good, is assumed to be embodied in capital; hence it does not constitute a separate factor. Some economists have suggested that it be regarded as a separate factor of production (a suggestion some have also made regarding entrepreneurship), and we have done so in this study. Although the amount of technology used in production and the amount of capital are highly correlated, the correlation is not perfect. It is possible for capital to increase up to a point without any change in technology (capital widening), and it is also possible for technology to increase without a net increase in capital (Hagen, 1968). Therefore we have found it advantageous to regard it as a separate factor of production.

Generally one assumes a negative relationship between the supply of factor inputs and their cost. The more of a given raw material (land) that is available to an entrepreneur, the less will be the cost per unit. Likewise the larger the supply of labor available, the lower will be its cost. The cost of capital will be evidenced by the interest rate, and this too will be negatively related to capital supply. And, for a given level of technology, or a specific technique, the more of it that is available the less costly it will be.[6]

The negative relationship between factor supply and factor cost is not a perfect one, however. For one thing, factor cost will also be partly determined by the demand for the factors. At a given level of factor supply, the cost will be greater the larger the number of competing users there are for the factor. We consider this aspect in our analysis of specific factors in specific situations. Second, the possibility of *substitutability*, up to a point, of factors for each other can ameliorate the negative effects of a high-cost factor. Entrepreneurs can substitute low-cost factors for higher-cost ones. For example capital may be substituted for labor via technology, i.e., the adoption of capital-intensive rather than labor-intensive techniques. Or a lower-cost raw material may be used to replace a high-cost one.

Therefore we would expect opportunity conditions to be least favorable when all factors were in short supply, demand was high for these factors, and there were limited substitution possibilities. Confronted by this unfavorable situation, an entrepreneur or potential entrepreneur has several choices. First, it should be made clear that a possible option for an entrepreneur in any situation is to *do nothing*, or to simply continue his existing mode of operation. If this is the response, and if the opportunity conditions (O) are unfavorable, then it is a certainty that Y will also be low and entrepreneurship will have little or no causal significance.

But there are also possible responses which will make entrepreneurship causally significant. On the one hand, entrepreneurs may respond to high-cost factors by means of *cost-cutting* innovations, perhaps by adopting a technological innovation that requires less of a high-cost factor. On the other hand, they may search out and discover new sources of the high-cost factor which will increase its supply and thereby lower its cost. Either of these two responses will likely have a greater impact on Y than merely substituting factors for each other, and thus they will increase the causal significance of entrepreneurship.

Conversely, entrepreneurs may have a negative causal influence on economic growth and development by failing to take advantage of the favorable opportunity conditions provided by low-cost factors of production. They may fail to expand the scale of their operations, for example, even though they could do

---

[6]If a particular technique has not been invented, so that its supply is zero, then it is clear that making it available would be more costly than if the technique were already in existence.

so relatively inexpensively by simply duplicating their existing facilities. Substantial amounts of low-cost labor also may be available, but they may continue to operate on a small scale, content with a relatively lower level of profits. In these cases we would expect Y to be lower than O.

Quality of factor inputs. The major effect of the quality of factor inputs will be upon *productivity*, which will influence the cost per unit produced by the entrepreneur. The greater the quality of factor inputs, the greater their productivity, and the greater the productivity, the lower the cost per unit. The productivity of technology, labor, and raw materials will be of greatest significance to the entrepreneur. Capital-intensive technologies generally will be more productive than labor-intensive technologies. Holding technology constant, skilled labor will generally be more productive than unskilled labor. One raw material may yield more of a finished good than another, or in the case of a raw material used as a source of energy, such as coal, it may provide more energy per unit than another.

Entrepreneurial responses similar to those discussed in conjunction with the quantity of inputs are possible. More productive factors may be substituted for less productive ones. Thus an entrepreneur may adopt a technology that is more productive than the one currently in use, or he may substitute more productive technology for less productive labor. He may try to improve the productivity of labor by means of training programs. If the productivity of factors is low, and opportunity conditions therefore unfavorable, any steps taken by the entrepreneur which involve more extensive use of more productive factors will increase the level of Y relative to O and make entrepreneurship causally significant.

Of course, the entrepreneur may again do nothing, in which case Y and O will both be low and E of little causal significance. And, in cases in which O is high because of the existence of highly productive factors, entrepreneurs may fail to utilize these factors and instead continue using less productive technologies, forms of labor, and raw materials. If they make this response, then entrepreneurship will show a negative causal influence.

Size and composition of the market. We have said that market size and composition will be the major determinants of the amount of reward an entrepreneur can anticipate in a situation. Normally the greater the size of the market, the greater the potential reward. But market composition must also be taken into consideration. The effective demand of the market for manufactured goods must be appropriate for the goods that the entrepreneur is able to produce. And, as was the case with the supply of factor inputs, the number of competitors vying for that market will be a significant factor. For a given market size, the larger the number of other entrepreneurs competing for that market, the less favorable will be the opportunity conditions.

Therefore market opportunity conditions will be least favorable if the market is small, i.e., a limited number of people with limited wealth with which to purchase manufactured goods; if it is demanding goods other than an entrepreneur is producing; and if market competition is great. The possible responses to this situation are many, including the ever-present possibility of acceptance of the situation. First, entrepreneurs may attempt to increase the size of the existent market for their goods by cutting the cost of their goods, by improving their quality, by diversifying into the production of goods more in accord with the tastes of the market, or they may attempt to manipulate the tastes of the market.[7] Second, they may attempt to find new markets, either among an untapped segment within their society or in other societies. If they make any of these responses, then it is probable that entrepreneurship will have a positive causal influence on economic growth and development.

Again, entrepreneurs may fail to take advantage of market opportunities. They may be content to provide goods for only a limited market rather than expand to obtain a larger share of the available market. They may price their goods too high, or they may insist upon producing goods desired by only a limited segment of the market. In all these cases entrepreneurship will likely also be causally significant, but the influence will be a negative one.

The relationships among these three general determinants of opportunity conditions and the opportunity conditions in a given society are summarized in Figure 2. Although our discussion has presented the nature of the relationship between these determinants and opportunity conditions, it has not indicated how one might determine the actual characteristics of these determinants in our six societies. In order to make this determination we found it necessary to ascertain characteristics which might be considered specific determinants of these general determinants.[8] We next discuss these specific determinants for each of the factors, as well as for the market.

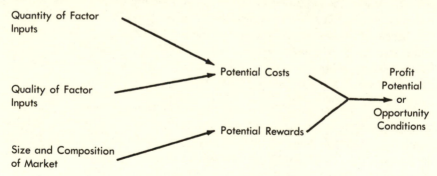

Figure 2 Relationship Between Determinants of Opportunity Conditions and Opportunity Conditions

[7]Modern industrial corporations are often accused of producing goods and then manipulating the market to demand these goods rather than simply responding to the actual wants of the consuming public.

[8]We consider these to be determinants of the determinants rather than indicators of the determinants because they are farther removed from our three major determinants than indicators would be.

Specific Determinants of Opportunity Conditions

Capital. We have been concerned primarily with the amount of investment or venture capital available in a society for entrepreneurial activities rather than with the size of the existent stock of physical or real capital. Physical or real capital, i.e., buildings, equipment, and inventories, will be a *consequence* of entrepreneurship. Investment capital will be a particularly crucial factor for entrepreneurs since it can be used to purchase other inputs, i.e., raw materials, labor, and technology. The more investment capital available, the less will be its cost, and the more favorable the opportunity conditions for enterpreneurship.

We have assumed the quantity of investment capital within a society to be a function primarily of the amount of wealth within that society, or of its per capita income (Alexander, 1967). Theoretically, the greater the per capita income of a society, the more investment capital should be potentially available for entrepreneurship. But whether this is actually true will depend upon at least four other factors. We have already alluded to one of these, namely, the number of competitors for the existent supply of capital. These competitors may include other industrial entrepreneurs, nonindustrial entrepreneurs, or the government. A second important factor will be the existence of mobilizing facilities within the society, such as the existence of a capital market, or, more generally, a financial infrastructure. Third, the propensity of the society's people to make surplus resources available for industrial entrepreneurship, as opposed to investment in agricultural pursuits, for example, will also modify the relationship between per capita income and the supply of investment capital. Lastly, the impact of the supply of capital on the favorableness of opportunity conditions will be *relative* to the capital requirements for entrepreneurship in a given situation. It is well known that capital requirements have increased over time; hence a given capital supply will have a less favorable effect on opportunity conditions when capital requirements are high than when they were lower.

Therefore, for each of our six societies we have considered not only per capita income but also the characteristics of these four modifying factors in estimating the supply of capital available for entrepreneurship. And again we wish to note that in the face of a shortage of capital, entrepreneurs may accept the situation, or they may make innovative responses. They may cut costs to make the available supply of capital go farther, devise other devices whereby more capital may be procured from existing sources, or they may search out new sources of capital.

Raw materials. Most economists have played down the significance of the supply of raw materials for entrepreneurship because of the potential for purchasing those that are scarce or of substituting technology for them. Thus, Kuznets (1968) suggests that lack of a raw material may affect the direction of economic growth, but that it should not affect economic growth itself.

Even though raw material supplies may not be as significant as the supply

of other factors, we have included them in this study. Clearly, if two entrepreneurs are confronted by identical opportunity conditions except that one has
access to an important raw material and the other does not, the overall opportunity conditions for the two entrepreneurs will not be equal. Or if entrepreneur A
can procure a raw material within his society whereas entrepreneur B can get the
raw material only from another society, then A's opportunity conditions will
likely be more favorable than B's. More entrepreneurship probably will be required of B than of A to achieve the same return.

In this study we have concentrated on the availability of those raw materials that were significant for the major industries of the historical periods we
studied: textiles, metallurgy, the machine industry, and the chemical industry.
As in all other cases, the entrepreneurial response to a lack of ready access to raw
materials will be crucial in determining whether entrepreneurship has causal
significance or not. This significance will be greater to the extent that entrepreneurs discover new sources of the raw material or discover new raw materials
that may be substituted for them, especially if the new raw materials are more
productive than the old.

Labor. The supply and the productivity of the labor available to an entrepreneur will be a particularly important determinant of his opportunity conditions. In fact, Gould (1972) has suggested that labor costs were the most important determinant of entrepreneurial decisions during the general historical period
we have studied because labor constituted the major factor of production and its
costs were the only ones that could be estimated with any reasonable accuracy at
that time.

We have assumed the quantity of labor to be determined mainly by the size
of the adult population of a society. In addition, population growth is significant
in determining whether the supply of labor is increasing or not. If it is not
increasing, then employing additional labor probably will be more costly to an
entrepreneur. The degree to which population size can be directly translated into
labor supply is also affected by the degree of labor *mobility* within a society
(Gould, 1972). If restrictions which hinder labor from entering industrial
employment or prevent geographic movement within a society exist, then labor
will be more costly than if these restrictions are absent.

Labor productivity can be assumed to be a direct function of the proportion
of skilled workers within a society. An increase in this proportion will be one of
the major consequences of economic growth and development in all likelihood,
as workers learn to use technologies that require more skill. It will also partly be
a function of the level of *social* development of a society. The level of education
and its availability, for example, will significantly affect the skill level of labor.
This exemplifies our earlier assertion that the nature of the opportunity conditions
in a society may well be a function of noneconomic factors.

Technology. We have considered this factor, which economists generally regard as a residual, as a separate distinct factor of production. Therefore its supply and its productivity also affect the opportunity conditions for entrepreneurs. We have attempted to assess the availability and the productivity of the major technologies in the most important industries of the time. As we noted earlier, creating a new technology from nothing is more costly than borrowing it from someone who has already shown its feasibility. And the more productive an available technology is, the more favorable will be its influence upon opportunity conditions.

Availability and productivity of technology may be partially diminished by a characteristic we refer to as *suitability*. If the technologies in existence are suitable for an entrepreneur's needs, so that adoption of the technology is relatively simple, then opportunity conditions will be even more favorable. But if these technologies are not suitable, perhaps being useful only in industries other than the one in which an entrepreneur is involved, then the effect on the favorableness of opportunity conditions will be far less positive.

Market size and composition. We have assumed the *size* of the domestic market available to entrepreneurs to be primarily a function of a society's per capita income and of the degree of development of market mechanisms. The former provides the potential demand for manufactured goods, the latter influences the ease of meeting that demand. In addition, we have given special attention to the rate of increase in population growth, assuming that per capita income does not decline, since increasing demand is especially likely to encourage entrepreneurs to expand (McClelland, 1961; Hagen, 1968). We have also taken into account any reductions of imperfections in market mechanisms that may have been present (Gould, 1972). The degree of competition for a given market has constituted another modifier of the relationship between per capita income and market size; the larger the number of entrepreneurs competing for a market, the smaller will be the potential share for any one of them.

We have also attempted to take into account the potential foreign market which existed for entrepreneurs in each of the six societies. The size of this market is mainly a function of the availability of transportation—so that goods may be carried internationally at some reasonable cost—the existence of a demand for goods; and the degree of competition from other entrepreneurs, both from one's own and other societies.

The *composition* of markets has been especially difficult to judge because of the potentially great variety and impreciseness of tastes. Domestically, market composition may be considered partly a function of the pattern of wealth distribution of a society. If this distribution is very inequitable, then it is probable that there will be a large demand for luxury goods and limited demand for more common goods. This is the major aspect of market composition that we have considered in this study, for both domestic and foreign markets.

Summary of Specific Determinants of Opportunity Conditions

In Table 8 we present a summary of the specific determinants of our three general determinants—quantity and quality of factor inputs and market size and composition. A serious complication encountered in using these determinants in order to estimate the opportunity conditions in each society is that many of them underwent significant changes over the period of time which we studied. These changes occurred both within and between the societies we analyzed, with significant consequences for the opportunity conditions in both the same and different societies at different points in time. Some specific examples will make this clearer.

Table 8
Specific Determinants of Opportunity Conditions

Factor	Determinants
Capital Supply	Per capita income
	Degree of competition
	Existence of mobilizing facilities
	Investment propensities
	Capital requirements
Raw Material Supply	Available domestically or not
Raw Material Productivity	As known at particular time point
Labor Supply	Size of adult population
	Rate of population growth
	Labor mobility
Labor Productivity	Proportion of skilled laborers
Technology Supply	Existing at particular time point
	Suitability of technology
Technology Productivity	Existing at particular time point
Market Size (Domestic and	Per capita income
International)	Existence of market mechanisms
	Rate of population growth
	Degree of competition
	Availability of transportation
Market Composition	Pattern of distribution of wealth
	Luxury vs. nonluxury goods demand

In the case of the availability of investment capital, we note first that within each society the supply of such capital increased as economic growth and development occurred. Economic growth implies an increase in per capita income by definition. In addition, growth and development were accompanied by the development of capital mobilizing facilities. Furthermore, over time an international capital market developed, so that capital from some societies became available to entrepreneurs in other societies. These secular trends all suggest that opportunity conditions, in regard to capital supplies, were more favorable in later periods than at earlier times. But how much more favorable? The increase in capital requirements which occurred simultaneously must be balanced against this increase in capital supplies, but it is not clear just how much of an effect this had. At the same time once certain scales of operations had been attained economies of scale appeared that negated some of the influence of increased capital requirements. So making comparisons among different societies at different points in time has been especially problematic.

Similarly, as new sources of raw materials were found and technologies were discovered which could make use of new raw materials the supply of raw materials increased significantly over time. Competition for these raw materials also increased but probably not to the degree that their supply did.

An even bigger change occurred with respect to technology. The period we have studied was characterized by a proliferation of new technologies, so that in later periods it was possible for entrepreneurs simply to borrow what earlier entrepreneurs had had to create themselves. Many of these later technologies were capital-intensive and much more expensive than the earlier technologies had been. And there is some evidence that there was also a decline in their suitability, as they became more and more complex. But it is doubtful that these two trends were sufficiently great to lead one to conclude that opportunity conditions with respect to technology did not improve over time because of the increases in availability and productivity.

Finally, significant market changes also took place over time. International trade increased greatly as transportation became much more rapid and less costly. Consequently market competition was greater in later periods than it had been formerly. But at the same time the increases in per capita income and in population sizes and the development of market mechanisms very likely improved the market situation for entrepreneurs. Insofar as market composition is concerned, it is also probable that the greater familiarity with manufactured goods that developed over time improved opportunity conditions for entrepreneurs.

Labor is possibly the one factor for which these changes over time are least obvious, at least if we consider it in isolation from technology. Its lesser degree of change can be attributed to the fact that it is the factor least affected by extra-societal factors. In other words, each society had to recruit and train its own labor force. In a few cases there were significant international migrations of labor, but for the most part entrepreneurs in each society were limited to the workers available within that society. As industrialization became more widespread and as the level of education increased, labor productivity also clearly increased. But this change was probably more obvious within a society than in a comparison of different societies. The education gained by the labor force within one country was not as easily transferable from one society to another as was capital, for example.

These historical changes in opportunity conditions have been termed ''the advantages of backwardness'' by Gerschenkron (1962) and Landes (1969). The major advantage of backwardness, i.e., beginning the industrialization process later than other countries, was that a society did not have to recapitulate the experiences of its precursors. This was particularly true in regard to technology; it was less true for labor. Our question has been to what extent we can regard the changes in opportunity conditions as improvements in opportunity conditions for entrepreneurs who were located later in our period of study. We shall return to this perplexing issue in our final chapter.

Noneconomic Factors Influencing Entrepreneurial Emergence (X)

In Chapter 1 we described the major noneconomic factors that have been suggested as influencing the emergence of entrepreneurship. We shall not discuss these in more detail at this point, but will simply repeat them to indicate their status as the components of X in our analysis. They include the legitimacy of entrepreneurship, access to mobility channels, marginality, social integration, security, ideology, the nature of the social stratification system, need-achievement, withdrawal of status respect, and motives. We have attempted no specific measures of these noneconomic factors but have attempted to judge their presence or absence on the basis of our various sources of data.

We anticipated that in situations in which entrepreneurship had positive causal significance, these psychological and sociocultural factors could be shown to have had one, or both, of two major effects. First, they may have influenced entrepreneurs to be more willing to take risks, so that they reacted to the existent opportunity conditions assertively rather than cautiously, Second, these factors may have decreased the risk present in a situation, most likely by offering additional rewards that negated some of the costs associated with entrepreneurship in a situation in which the opportunity conditions for entrepreneurship were unfavorable.

In cases in which entrepreneurship was found to have negative causal significance, we expected these X factors to have opposite effects. Either they caused entrepreneurs to be less willing to take risks, or they increased the risk of entrepreneurial behavior by introducing additional costs into the situation which made entrepreneurship more costly than it would have been simply on the basis of the favorable opportunity conditions in the situation.

ENTREPRENEURSHIP (E)

Up to this point we have been discussing entrepreneurship as an undifferentiated phenomenon, the causal significance of which can be determined indirectly from the size of the discrepancy between economic opportunity conditions and rates of economic growth and development. But there is much variance in certain characteristics of entrepreneurship that may be relevant for answering the question *why* entrepreneurship was causally significant in some situations and not in others.

We shall discuss these characteristics more extensively in the next chapter. Here we wish to point out two particularly important characteristics. One is the *identity* of entrepreneurial actors, or simply *who* plays the role. The second concerns *what* the entrepreneur does, that is, the specific activities he undertakes in the role. We term this the *type* of entrepreneurship.

We can indicate how analysis of the characteristics of entrepreneurship enables us to specify the reasons for its causal significance more precisely by extending the logic of the approach we have used to determine the causal significance of entrepreneurship. Thus if entrepreneurial identity varies consistently with the causal significance of entrepreneurship, then this obviously indicates that who entrepreneurs are is relevant for causal significance. If, for example, we should find that entrepreneurs from mercantile occupational origins are predominant in situations in which entrepreneurship is causally significant and not well represented when entrepreneurship is causally insignificant, then this implies there is something about mercantile occupational origins which accounts for entrepreneurship's being causally significant. Or it may imply that when certain other noneconomic factors are present in a situation, entrepreneurs from those origins are more likely to emerge and entrepreneurship is more likely to be causally significant. Which of these two inferences is more correct may be determined by analyzing the conditions under which entrepreneurs from mercantile backgrounds are present compared to the conditions under which they are not present. If we should find that they are present under a variety of noneconomic conditions, then it would seem probable that they possess some characteristic, perhaps a psychological predisposition, which explains why their entrepreneurship is causally significant.

Similarly, it may be discovered that some types of entrepreneurship are more likely to be associated with the causal significance of entrepreneurship than are other types. If so, then this suggests that there is something about those types of entrepreneurship that promotes causal significance. If, for example, entrepreneurship tends to be causally significant when technological innovations are present, and insignificant when they are absent, then technological innovation can be assumed to promote causal significance.

Furthermore, it is also plausible that the identity of entrepreneurs and the type of entrepreneurship will be linked with both the causal significance of entrepreneurship and the noneconomic factors influencing its emergence and with each other. That is, under certain conditions entrepreneurs of a certain identity may be particularly likely to come forth and undertake types of entrepreneurship which make entrepreneurship positively causally significant. Or under other conditions, entrepreneurs of a particular identity may be particularly *unlikely* to come forth and certain types of entrepreneurship will be especially *unlikely* to be displayed so that entrepreneurship will have negative causal significance.

So we have included these two general characteristics of entrepreneurship in our analysis to answer the question *why* entrepreneurship was causally significant or insignificant more precisely. They enable us to *specify* the relationships between causal significance and the factors believed to account for the emergence of entrepreneurship. Our use of these characteristics for this end was guided by the two major influences we expected the noneconomic factors to have on entrepreneurship. We felt that the characeristics would provide clues regarding the effects of the noneconomic factors on the willingness of entrepreneurs to take risks and/or regarding the presence of other rewards and costs which either increased or decreased the risks of entrepreneurial behavior.

THE ROLE OF THE STATE

We have left the description of one other important influence on entrepreneurship until this point. That is the role of the state, or the government, of a society, which constitutes an *exogenous* variable in our model. It will have an impact upon all the other variables in our model, so it has seemed fitting to conclude this chapter with a discussion of its significance,

Easterbrook (1949) has described the governmental role as being one of three possible types: protective, promotional, or corrective. A government may protect the entrepreneurs within a society from competition from other entrepreneurs; it may directly or indirectly promote entrepreneurial behavior; or it may correct deficiencies in the combination of opportunity conditions confronting entrepreneurs. It should also be noted that the governmental role will not necessarily be conducive to entrepreneurship. Instead of protecting entrepreneurs, a government may attack them. Instead of promoting entrepreneurship it may create barriers to it. And instead of correcting deficiencies in the economic system, it may reinforce them. Both the positive and negative possibilities need to be considered for each of the major variables in our model.

Influence on Opportunity Conditions

The manifold ways in which a government can affect the opportunity conditions for entrepreneurship are almost too numerous to list, so we mention only the most significant.

Capital. The state can increase the supply of investment capital in several ways, including direct subsidies to entrepreneurs, taxation of the nonindustrial sector of the economy and transfer of revenues to industrial entrepreneurs, the maintenance of "easy money" monetary policies, and promotion of the development of capital-mobilizing facilities. Conversely, the state can make opportunity conditions less favorable by draining the supply of investment capital through practices such as extensive public expenditure for nonindustrial purposes, heavy taxation of industrial entrepreneurs, the maintenance of high interest rates, and restrictions on the development of mobilizing facilities.

Labor. Similarly, the state may either increase the availability and productivity of labor or decrease it. The former may be accomplished by means of policies encouraging labor mobility out of nonindustrial activities and into industrial ones and immigration in cases where the labor supply is limited, by assistance to entrepreneurs in regulating workers, and by encouragement to entrepreneurs to provide programs training workers in necessary skills. Conversely, a government may use available labor supplies for its own purposes (perhaps military exploits), restrict the mobility of labor, and possibly even require entrepreneurs to employ excess labor thereby increasing labor costs and lowering labor productivity.

Raw materials. The main positive effect of the state on opportunity conditions in this area probably occurs through the encouragement it may give to the discovery of new sources of old materials or of new substitute materials. In addition, it may facilitate importation of materials not available within the society, and it may provide a guaranteed source of supply by maintenance of a colonial system. By contrast, it may fail to do all of these things; an especially likely negative practice in this respect is the maintenance of a tariff system which makes importation of necessary raw materials too costly for indigenous entrepreneurs.

Market. Finally, the state may play a key role in both the regulation of and the determination of the size and composition of the market (Swerdlow, 1963). Particularly important in this regard will be the tariff policies adopted by the state. These may increase the market for domestic entrepreneurs by promoting import substitution. The state may also increase the foreign market through export-expansion policies. Domestically, it may influence both the size and the composition of the market through its taxation policies. By supporting the development of a distributive infrastructure, including transportation facilities and market mechanisms, it can also enlarge the market. And it may itself constitute an important segment of the market through its own demand for goods.

The maintenance of a system of foreign colonies will in most cases also increase the market for domestic entrepreneurs, especially if restrictions are placed upon the purchasing practices of those colonies. In addition, the state may encourage the growth of international trade through its policies regarding foreign exchange, transportation development, and so forth. And, for both the domestic and foreign markets, the state's selection of different policies may constitute a negative influence on opportunity conditions.

The actions of the government in each of the six societies we have studied have been directly incorporated in our estimates of the favorableness of opportunity conditions. One other effect of the state on opportunity conditions, which cuts across the foregoing categories, is manifested through the extent to which the state is a *competitor* with entrepreneurs from the private sector, whether for factors of production or for markets. The greater the extent of this competitive role, the less favorable the opportunity conditions for private entrepreneurship will be.

Influence on Noneconomic Factors

Not only may the state influence the economic opportunity conditions available to entrepreneurs, but it may also influence the noneconomic factors which are supposedly significant for the emergence of entrepreneurship. Thus it may increase the legitimacy of entrepreneurship through its pronouncements and policies or it may decrease it. It may manipulate the access of certain individuals and groups to mobility channels through legal restrictions on role behavior. It may be responsible for the withdrawal of status respect from certain groups and their relegation to a situation of marginality. It may itself constitute a centralizing focus of integrative ties. It may provide a high degree of security to entrepreneurs through laws protecting their property and investment, or it may allow chaos and confiscation. And it may play a significant role in the provision of an ideology which is supportive of entrepreneurship. We noted earlier that nationalism may constitute such an ideology, and the state is likely to play a major role in the development of a nationalistic ideology.

Influence on Entrepreneurship

The most significant way in which the state affects entrepreneurship itself is through its direct assumption of the entrepreneurial role. One of the distinctions that must be made in regard to entrepreneurial identity is between private and public entrepreneurship. This *direct* entrepreneurship of the state contrasts with its *indirect* influence on entrepreneurship through its effects on either Y or O.

The causal significance of public entrepreneurship is a more important issue than the factors accounting for its emergence. The emergence of entrepreneurs from the public sector can be explained by *fiat*, although it may be interesting to know the combination of economic and noneconomic factors under which this *command* form of entrepreneurship, as compared to *demand*-induced private entrepreneurship, appears. Since there was relatively little public entrepreneurship in any of the six societies we studied, we have not been able to shed much light on the causal significance of private as opposed to public entrepreneurship. A study of currently developing societies would provide far more evidence on this issue.

The state may also affect *how* the entrepreneurial role is played. For example, it may influence the manner in which entrepreneurs obtain factor inputs, such as capital. Its policies will also be likely to affect the types of goods that entrepreneurs produce and the changes they institute in their production of goods. So a significant influence of the state can be ascertained here also.

A Complication

We have described how the government of a society may affect entrepreneurship through a number of effects on the X, O, and E variables in our model. Overall it may constitute either a positive or a negative influence on both entrepreneurship and economic growth and development, or, as we shall find in some societies, it may constitute a mixed influence, with some of its policies promoting entrepreneurship and others simultaneously hindering it.

The complication we refer to is that it is not possible to consider the state as a solely exogenous factor. For the actions of entrepreneurs themselves are very likely to influence the policies of the state, and, in fact, in some cases the entrepreneurs themselves may be regarded as major actors in the political system. Hence, entrepreneurs themselves help create the characteristics of our key variables, O and X, within a society through their influence on the state. They may press for governmental policies which improve the opportunity conditions, or they may transform the nature of the noneconomic factors within a society. To the extent that they are socially upward mobile, for example, they may not only influence the degree of social mobility in the society but they may also affect governmental policies regulating social mobility.

This effect of entrepreneurial actions on both X and O may be expressed in terms of our original model as a feedback from E to both X and O. If such feedbacks were found to be significant determinants of X and O, then this fact might be regarded as evidence of an *indirect* causal significance of entrepreneurship. We shall return to this issue also in our concluding chapter, after we have had the opportunity to present the evidence from our six societal case studies. In these case studies we shall show that there was variance in the degree to which entrepreneurs became politically mobilized and to which they were able to affect both economic and noneconomic factors.

Several scholars have emphasized the importance of an interaction between entrepreneurial political mobilization and the role of the state in influencing entrepreneurship. Bendix (1956), for example, has drawn a contrast between Great Britain and Russia in this regard that we shall discuss more fully when we consider entrepreneurship in those two settings. Here we just note that he emphasizes the implications of differences in entrepreneurial political mobilization and in the relationship between entrepreneurs and the state. Smith (1968) has provided a more comprehensive theory regarding this interaction which has received relatively little notice. According to him, the duration and intensity of the political initiative for national development, which will be influenced by a sense of political urgency motivated by an awareness of national backwardness, will be an important determinant of the effects of the state on entrepreneurship. The nature of the initiative will interact with existing attitudes toward entrepreneurship and the degree of power concentration of entrepreneurs, as well as their status, to determine the characteristics of entrepreneurship within a society.

SUMMARY

In this chapter we have laid out our strategy for determining whether entrepreneurship is causally significant for economic growth and development and whether economic or noneconomic factors are relatively more important for the emergence of entrepreneurship. We have argued that the two issues are inseparable. If the extent of economic growth and development in a situation is proportional to the favorableness of the economic opportunity conditions in that situation, then entrepreneurship does not have an independent causal influence on economic growth and development and its emergence is explainable solely on the basis of the existent opportunity conditions, If, however, the extent of economic growth and development in a situation differs from the favorableness of the economic opportunity conditions, being disproportionately greater or less than one would expect given the favorableness of these conditions, then not only does entrepreneurship have an independent causal influence on economic growth and development, but its emergence cannot be explained wholly by economic factors.

Thus a high degree of economic growth and development in a situation characterized by relatively unfavorable economic opportunity conditions is evidence of both a positive causal influence of entrepreneurship and the presence of noneconomic factors promoting its emergence. By contrast, a low degree of economic growth and development in a situation in which the economic opportunity conditions are relatively favorable exemplifies entrepreneurship's negative causal influence and the existence of noneconomic factors hindering entrepreneurial emergence.

We have applied this strategy to the analysis of entrepreneurship in manufacturing in six societies—Great Britain, France, Prussia-Germany, Japan, Russia, and the United States—that participated in the first Industrial Revolution. We have used secondary data from several disciplines to focus upon the historical period during which five of these societies achieved industrialization (Russia being the exception), with the end point of the period for each society determined by the relative proportions of national product derived from industry and agriculture. We have assumed that industrialization was achieved by a society when the former exceeded the latter.

In order to utilize our strategy, it has been necessary to assess the rates of industrial growth and evidence of industrial development, the favorableness of economic opportunity conditions, and the noneconomic factors characterizing each of the six societies. Determination of the favorableness of economic opportunity conditions has required the formulation of a micro-level theory of entrepreneurship in which the *profit potential* of a situation corresponds to the degee of favorableness. A situation's profit potential is determined by the probable rewards and costs confronting the entrepreneur, and these in turn are a function of three general determinants: the quantity and quality of factor inputs and the size and composition of the market. We have suggested a number of specific determinants of these three general determinants as well.

Two characteristics of entrepreneurship itself are also important for more precisely specifying the impact of entrepreneurship on economic growth and development, on the one hand, and the effects of economic and noneconomic factors on entrepreneurship, on the other hand. These are entrepreneurial identity—who is behaving entrepreneurially—and type of entrepreneurship—the specific activities engaged in. Lastly, we have discussed the significance of the state as a partially exogenous factor influencing entrepreneurship and the economic and noneconomic factors which promote or hinder entrepreneurship. We have noted that it is not a completely exogenous factor because it may be influenced by the actions of entrepreneurs.

Our final step before considering our six case studies is to focus more closely on exactly what entrepreneurship is, and we devote the next chapter to this topic.

3

The Nature
of Entrepreneurship

One of the major problems in the study of entrepreneurship has been the lack of conceptual consensus regarding the phenomenon. Elsewhere we have summarized the history of the concept at length (Wilken, 1976). Here we simply provide a brief discussion of the major conceptual developments that have occurred up to now, to serve as an introduction to the analysis of the conceptualization of entrepreneurship that we have used.

EXISTING CONCEPTUALIZATIONS

The most comprehensive theory of entrepreneurship has been that of Joseph Schumpeter, presented in *The Theory of Economic Development* in 1934. Prior to Schumpeter two different approaches to the phenomenon are discernible. One concentrated on defining the specific entrepreneurial function or role in order to distinguish it from other economic behavior. Major figures representative of this approach were Alfred E. Marshall (1936), who argued that "organization" should be considered a factor of production, and Frank Knight (1965), who described entrepreneurship primarily as risk-taking.

The other approach was more general, involving a number of writers well known to sociologists, such as Saint-Simon, Comte, Marx, Sombart, Veblen, and Weber. The analysis of entrepreneurship was secondary to the description of the rise of capitalism for these scholars, but they all provided significant insights into the impact of entrepreneurship upon economic growth and development and the factors which promoted its emergence. Weber's (1958) classic analysis of the significance of the Protestant Ethic for entrepreneurial emergence, Marx and

Engels' (1954) description of the revolutionary implications of the rise of an entrepreneurial class, and Veblen's (1963, 1965) critical analysis of the negative characteristics of entrepreneurship are the most noteworthy contributions of this more general approach.

Schumpeter's theory of entrepreneurship may be considered as a synthesis of these two approaches because he not only regarded entrepreneurship as the primary cause of economic development but also delineated its distinguishing features and suggested conditions that promoted its appearance. Innovation, the carrying out of new combinations of the factors of production, constituted the entrepreneurial function for him, and these new combinations comprised the qualitative economic changes which he regarded as the essence of economic development. Hence, entrepreneurship, which he believed emergent in response to noneconomic motivations, was a crucial factor in economic change.

Although Schumpeter claimed that the entrepreneurial function had declined in significance, his conceptualization does allow for the inclusion of the public and collective forms of entrepreneurship that superseded the individual forms of the eighteenth and nineteenth centuries on which he based his theory. In this study we have endeavored to develop a conceptualization of entrepreneurship applicable to the various forms in which it may be manifested.

Schumpeter's theory of entrepreneurship stimulated extensive writing on the subject. Subsequent writings can be categorized on the basis of what they emphasize as the distinctive entrepreneurial role. These include a continuation of Schumpeter's emphasis on innovation as well as emphases on the deviant nature of entrepreneurship, organization-founding, leadership, risk-taking, decision-making, authority, and coordination. There also has been a substantial development of multi-functional conceptualizations, of what may be called *multi phase* conceptualizations, and of entrepreneurial typologies (Wilken, 1976).

Several more general issues have crosscut these conceptualizations. These have included the question of the appropriate conceptual relationship between entrepreneurship and management, the issue of individual versus group-level conceptualizations, and the question of whether the concept should apply only to economic activities or also to noneconomic activities (which we refer to as the issue of the *scope* of entrepreneurship).

Therefore there is currently no consensus in the literature on the most satisfactory conceptualization of entrepreneurship. In the remainder of this chapter we describe the conceptualization used in this study, one that we believe helps to resolve the disorganization which presently prevails.

CONCEPTUALIZATION ISSUES

Before discussing the conceptualization of entrepreneurship that we have used we comment briefly on several conceptual issues we faced and goals we sought to achieve with our conceptualization. The first of these involves the *level* of conceptualization. Entrepreneurship may be conceptualized at several different levels. For example, it may be considered a psychological characteristic of individuals, which can be described in terms such as *creativity, daring, aggressiveness,* and the like. Second, it may be regarded as a type of social position, in which case one would identify that position and then analyze the behaviors of all individuals occupying that position. Third, it can be conceptualized as a social role, or a set of similar behaviors, that may be enacted by individuals in different social positions. McClelland (1961) distinguishes between the study of the behavior of entrepreneurs and the study of entrepreneurial behavior to represent the difference between the social position and the social role approaches respectively. Fourth, one also may conceptualize entrepreneurship as a social process, consisting of a variety of behaviors combining to produce an observable sequence of activities within a system.

We have chosen to conceptualize entrepreneurship as a social role, but as a very general and multifaceted role. Most significantly, our conceptualization enables us to study entrepreneurial behavior rather than the behavior of entrepreneurs in McClelland's sense of these terms. A conceptualization at this level offers the most satisfactory compromise between specificity and generality in our opinion.

Second, we wished to retain a distinction between entrepreneurship and management, on the grounds that combining them under one heading does not allow for differentiation of features which we regard as distinctive.

Third, we desired our conceptualization to be applicable to types of economic entrepreneurship in addition to that of individual actors from the private sector.

Fourth, we wanted to utilize the contributions of Schumpeter and his successors as extensively as possible.

Fifth, we felt that entrepreneurship relates to both economic growth and economic development and hence must be conceptualized accordingly.

And sixth, although it was not a major goal, we did attempt to develop a conceptualization also applicable to noneconomic types of entrepreneurship.

Entrepreneurship as a Role

Therefore, we have been concerned in this study with the significance of the entrepreneurial *role* for economic growth and development and the factors that cause this role to emerge. What are the similar behaviors that define the parameters of this role, and how are these behaviors of significance for economic growth and development? These are difficult questions to answer because the entrepreneurial role is complex, consisting of a great variety of behaviors. The role may be divided into *phases*, as we shall show presently. It may also be divided among *persons*, with different individuals enacting different phases. It may be enacted by a collective actor, or an organization, in which different persons are given responsibility for different phases. In the previous chapter we noted that two kinds of variance in the enactment of the role will be particularly important—the identity of the actors and the specific activities enacted. So the role is a difficult one to analyze, as Schumpeter clearly indicated. In some cases it may not be possible to ascertain which individuals are enacting the different phases of the role and it may be necessary simply to attribute the role to an organization. But, despite this complexity and the variety of ways in which the role is exemplified in the world, it is possible to distill from this variety of behaviors the commonality which constitutes the entrepreneurial role.

ENTERPRENEURSHIP AS "COMBINING FACTORS OF PRODUCTION"

Entrepreneurship fundamentally involves combining factors of production to achieve a specific consequence. By defining it generally in these terms, one allows for the possibility of delineating types of entrepreneurship other than economic entrepreneurship. These other types, such as political entrepreneurship, will be distinguished from economic entrepreneurship both by the factors that are combined and the consequences that are achieved. Political entrepreneurship will involve the combination of *political* factors of production, whatever they may be, and the achievement of political consequences. Economic entrepreneurship involves the combination of *economic* factors of production—land, labor, capital, and technology—and economic consequences, usually the production of goods and services.[1]

Therefore the question of the significance of entrepreneurship for economic growth and development may be rephrased in terms of the significance of the *combining* role relative to the significance of the economic opportunity conditions for entrepreneurship. Entrepreneurship will have positive causal significance if more *combining* of the factors of production occurs than would be expected on the basis simply of the opportunity conditions. Or it will have negative causal significance if less *combining* of the factors of production occurs than is implied by the existent opportunity conditions. In terms of our prior discussion, if the opportunity conditions are different in two situations, then more combining, i.e., more entrepreneurship, will be required in one situation than in the other to yield equal amounts of economic growth and development in the two situations. Or, if the opportunity conditions are equal in two situations, but in one situation the rate of economic growth and development is greater than in the other, then this indicates that less combining of the factors of production, i.e., less entrepreneurship, has been present in the situation in which economic growth and development is less.

One more qualification is necessary to arrive at a final definition of entre-

[1]One also can conceive of entrepreneurship in the *distributive* sphere of economic activities, in which case the consequence is the *distribution* of goods and services, e.g., wholesaling and retailing.

preneurship, however. Since economic growth and development consitute economic *change*, we are not interested in the production of goods and services in general, but in *changes* in their production. By definition, economic change consists of changes in the production of goods and services. Hence we are necessarily interested in the combining of factors of production *to initiate changes* in the production of goods and services, rather than in the combining of factors of production simply *to produce* goods and services.

It is at this point that entrepreneurship can be differentiated from management. Both may be regarded as involving combining, but the former involves combining *to initiate changes* in production whereas the latter involves combining *to produce*. Management therefore refers to the *ongoing coordination* of the production process, which can be visualized as a continual combining of the factors of production. But entrepreneurship is a discontinuous phenomenon, appearing to initiate changes in the production process, by changing the manner in which factors are combined or by combining more of the factors of production, and then disappearing until it reappears to initiate another change. This infrequency in the appearance of entrepreneurship is in keeping with the emphasis in the entrepreneurial literature on the relative rareness of the phenomenon. Conceptualizing management as *coordination* is also in line with the main trend of thought in that literature. Since combining implies *organization*, both entrepreneurship and management can be considered as organizing activities. But entrepreneurship involves organizing to initiate changes, whereas management involves organizing within a given structure.

An example will help to clarify this distinction. When someone begins producing a good, such as cars, this constitutes a change in the production of goods and hence involves entrepreneurship. But once the production of cars has begun, then management takes over and coordinates the continuing production of cars. Entrepreneurship reappears to initiate changes in that production, either in the number of cars produced or in the manner in which they are produced. Once that change has been initiated, then management again takes charge of the production process, within the new structure of the production process and/or at the new level of production.

Therefore our definition of entrepreneurship for this study has been *the combining of factors of production to initiate changes in the production of goods*. We must now consider the types of changes that are initiated by entrepreneurs.

Types of Changes Initiated

Two basic types of changes may be initiated by entrepreneurs in the production of goods (from here on we refer only to goods and omit services since we are interested only in entrepreneurship in *manufacturing* in this study). Basically, changes may be either *quantitative* or *qualitative*. We shall use the term *expansion* to refer to quantitative changes, or changes in the amount of goods produced. The extent to which entrepreneurs initiate such changes in a society will show up in indicators of economic growth for that society. We use the term *innovation* to refer to qualitative changes, the production of new goods, or changes in the manner in which existing goods are produced. This represents a somewhat different use of the term than is usual, since it generally refers to the degree of *newness* of a given change. The effects of innovations will also show up in indicators of economic growth because of their quantitative consequences. For example, if an innovation initiated by an entrepreneur increases the productivity of a factor, such as labor, then this will have quantitative effects. These changes will also have important qualitative effects, which we regard as economic development, involving the mode of production within a society, the relations between employers and employees, and so forth. In this study we have concentrated mainly on the effects of innovations on economic growth.

Because entrepreneurship involves the initiation of these two types of change, we can characterize entrepreneurship in a given society on the basis of which of these types of change are represented, as shown in Table 9. We refer to cases in which expansion and innovation are both present as *dynamic* entrepreneurship. This distinction between broad types of entrepreneurship improves upon previous present-absent characterizations of entrepreneurship.

Table 9
Summary Characterizations of Entrepreneurship

| | | Expansion | |
		Present	Absent
Innovation	Present	Dynamic Entrepreneurship	Innovative Entrepreneurship
	Absent	Expansive Entrepreneurship	No Entrepreneurship

Thus, in cases where entrepreneurship is found to be causally significant, this is attributable as a first approximation to the fact that entrepreneurs in those cases initiated more (or fewer) expansions and/or more (or fewer) innovations than one would expect on the basis of the favorableness of the opportunity conditions for entrepreneurship in those situations. But it is necessary to become more specific than that in order to determine why they acted in that way. We will return to this point later.

Expansion

Expansion may occur in one of two main ways. Either an individual who has not produced goods before may assume the entrepreneurial role and initiate production, or someone who has already done so may increase (or decrease, in which case it would constitute *negative* expansion) the amount of goods he is producing. These can be referred to as *initial* and *subsequent*, or *new* and *old*, expansions respectively. Subsequent expansions may involve enlarging one's output in the location where he has been producing goods, or it may involve initiating production in a new location.

It is impossible to disaggregate the relative proportions of initial and subsequent expansions from indicators of economic growth, such as the economic growth rate for a society, and it is not especially important whether economic growth occurs as a result of initial or subsequent expansions or both. What is important to recognize, however, is that *expansion*, as we are using it, refers to the enlargement of the production of the same goods in the same manner in which they have been produced before. It is synonymous therefore with *capital widening* as defined by economists. Entrepreneurship in a given situation may be causally significant simply because entrepreneurs have been extremely expansive or extremely reluctant to expand along traditional lines.

Innovation

A large variety of qualitative changes may be initiated by entrepreneurs, and we have considered only the most significant of these. They can be divided into three categories: those involving the factors of production, those involving the production process itself, and those involving the market. We call them *factor, production,* and *market* innovations respectively.

Factor innovations. The most significant qualitative changes that may be initiated in regard to the factors of production are those that either increase the supply of these factors or increase their productivity. *Financial* innovations involve changes which increase the supply of investment capital. They include the discovery of a new source from which to procure this capital, or the creation of a new form in which it may be procured. *Labor* innovations involve changes which increase either the supply of labor or its productivity. The former includes procuring labor from a new source—from categories of people who have not been used before as labor—or the use of a different type, such as skilled, than has been used before. The latter may also involve the use of a different, more productive type of labor, or it may involve methods whereby the productivity of existing labor is improved. *Material* innovations will include the procurement from a new source of a material that is being used, or the adoption of a material that has not been used before in the production of goods, with the new material likely to be more productive or less costly than the old.

Production innovations. Some of the most significant innovations that can be initiated by entrepreneurs fall into this category. *Technological* innovations are changes in the physical techniques whereby raw materials are transformed into a final product. Since we are concerned with the *initiation* of changes, such innovations will not be the same as technological inventions, or the creation of new techniques; innovations involve the *application* of an invention. *Organizational* innovations involve changes in the structure of relationships among the persons involved in the production of the good. Since entrepreneurship comes very close to management at this point we distinguish between changes *of* the form of organization and changes *in* its form. The former, which will generally involve the entire productive organization, are entrepreneurial; the latter, which involve only parts of the organization, are managerial.

Market innovations. This category of innovations refers to changes in the way in which the entrepreneur relates to the market for his goods. *Product* innovations include the production of a good that has not been produced before, or an improvement in quality or a lessening in cost of a good that is being produced. The first of these may also be termed *diversification*. A strictly *market* innovation will involve the discovery of a market that has not been exploited before by the entrepreneur. It may include a new geographical area or a new category of consumers.

The innovations initiated by entrepreneurs will have varying effects which it also will be impossible to disaggregate from indicators of economic growth. Factor innovations will have a feedback effect upon opportunity conditions by increasing factor supplies, thereby lowering their cost, or by increasing their productivity. Production innovations will mainly affect productivity, or the amount of output obtainable from a given amount of input; thus their effects will show up more directly in indicators of economic growth. Market innovations will also affect opportunity conditions, by changing the size of the market, whereas product innovations, unlike expansion, will involve new goods and may change the mix of goods available in the market.

The causal significance of entrepreneurship in a given situation therefore may be due to the fact that entrepreneurs either innovated extensively, and thereby were able to achieve a relatively high rate of economic growth in spite of unfavorable opportunity conditions, or to the fact that they failed to initiate innovations that would have improved productivity, for example, but continued to produce goods in a traditional manner which yielded only relatively limited economic growth.

In Table 10 we have listed the types of changes initiated by entrepreneurs with which we have been concerned in this study. In some cases entrepreneurial actions will include more than one of the types of change that we have listed. For example, a new product will often involve a new technology as well. Likewise a material innovation will often involve a simultaneous technological innovation. And an instance of expansion very likely may be accompanied by one or more types of innovation. Cases involving several types of change at the same time undoubtedly will have a greater effect than cases in which only one type of change is involved.

The aggregate expansions and innovations initiated by entrepreneurs in a

Table 10
Types of Changes Initiated by Entrepreneurs

1. Initial expansion—original production of goods
2. Subsequent expansion—subsequent change in the amount of goods produced
3. Factor innovation—increase in supply or productivity of factors
   a. Financial—procurement of capital from new source or in new form
   b. Labor—procurement of labor from new source or of new type; upgrading of existing labor
   c. Material—procurement of old material from new source or use of a new material
4. Production innovations—changes in the production process
   a. Technological—use of new production technique
   b. Organizational—change of form of structure of relationships among people
5. Market innovations—changes in the size or composition of the market
   a. Product—production of new good or change in quality or cost of existing good
   b. Market—discovery of a new market

society will constitute economic growth and development. But there will also be an important feedback from economic growth and development to opportunity conditions. Since economic growth involves increases in per capita income in a society, it should lead both to an increase in the potential supply of investment capital and to expansion of the market, provided that the income is not diverted to other purposes. Hence opportunity conditions should improve as growth takes place. Innovations, to the extent that they are diffused throughout a society, will also improve opportunity conditions for the most part. Factor innovations will increase the supply and productivity of land, labor, and capital. Technological innovations will increase the supply of technology and very likely increase its productivity as well. And market innovations will increase the size of the market and alter its composition.

So the actions taken by entrepreneurs will have ultimate effects on the opportunity conditions to which they respond. As the entrepreneurial pool grows within a society the competition for factors and markets will increase, however, which can be seen as decreasing the favorableness of opportunity conditions to some degree. Although this feedback from entrepreneurship to opportunity conditions via economic growth and development does complicate the estimation of the opportunity conditions in a society, it does show that entrepreneurs are not merely passive respondents to opportunity conditions but may affect them through their actions.

Phases of Entrepreneurship

We have defined *entrepreneurship* as the combining of factors of production to initiate changes in the production of goods. This role can be further subdivided into three phases. First is the *perception* phase. An individual or individuals must perceive the possibility of behaving entrepreneurially. Basically, this will involve an analysis of the opportunity conditions existent in a particular situation. The characteristics of the situation must be seen as *opportunity* conditions for entrepreneurship. And this further will involve seeing the resources present in the situation, whether the perceiver owns them or not, as *factors of production* which are combinable. It will also involve seeing people as a *market*, and not merely as persons.

Perception will be followed by *planning*, with the amount of planning dependent upon the nature of the contemplated change and the situation. The larger the change that is being considered and the less structured the situation, the greater the amount of planning that will be required. The actual initiation of the change will constitute the *implementation* phase. During this phase the actual combining takes place. Factors of production are procured and combined by the entrepreneur during this phase.

Any individuals who play a major role in any of these three phases should be considered as part of the "entrepreneur" for a given case of entrepreneurship. If the change being initiated is quite extensive, then it is probable that it will not be possible to identify all who are so involved, and one will have to consider it simply a case of collective or organizational entrepreneurship. But if a relatively small number of individuals can be identified who have primary *responsibility* for some of the phases, especially planning and implementation, then this will simplify matters. The perception phase will be the least likely of the three to have someone in charge of it. The primary actor in that phase will be the one who conceived the idea for the change that is ultimately initiated.

CHARACTERISTICS OF ENTREPRENEURSHIP

We come again to the two characteristics of entrepreneurship mentioned previously—identity, or who carries out the phases of the entrepreneurial role, and type, the actual activities that are carried out. As we indicated earlier, we have analyzed these in this study in order to trace more precisely the linkages between factors promoting the emergence of entrepreneurship and its causal significance to answer the question why entrepreneurship is causally significant or insignificant in different situations. We add to these two a third characteristic, the degree of change involved in entrepreneurial actions.

Entrepreneurial Identity

We anticipated at the outset of this study that the identity of the entrepreneurs in a given situation would be relevant both for the causal significance of entrepreneurship and for the factors promoting its emergence. More specifically, we expected that entrepreneurs with certain identities might have certain psychological characteristics conducive to expansive and innovative entrepreneurship, such as a willingness to take risks, that entrepreneurs with different identities would not have, or that entrepreneurs with certain identities would be more likely to emerge under some conditions than under others. So in cases where entrepreneurship was causally significant, we believed that it might be attributable to a preponderance of entrepreneurs with these characteristics or to the presence (or absence) of factors which promoted or hindered the emergence of entrepreneurs of particular identities. Or a combination of these two factors might be involved—under certain conditions entrepreneurs with strong entrepreneurial propensities would be most likely to emerge.

The identity of entrepreneurs may be categorized in many different ways. We categorized it as follows:

Individual-collective. All phases of the entrepreneurial role may be carried out by one individual, they may be divided among individuals, or they may be carried out by a corporate actor—an organization. The transition from individual to collective entrepreneurship has been a major historical trend, representing a response to the capital limitations of individual actors and to increases in capital requirements for many entrepreneurial actions. The typically greater resources of combinations of individuals should enable them to behave entrepreneurially more easily than individuals, or should at least influence their perception of opportunity conditions. So the causal significance of entrepreurship in a particular situation may be due to a greater or lesser willingness of individuals to join with others in entrepreneurial endeavors. It has been suggested, for example, that entrepreneurs in France were particularly hesitant to cooperate with others and hence failed to expand or innovate. And it also has been claimed that with the transition to collective forms of entrepreneurship expansion and innovation are likely to decrease, either because of the greater caution of collective actors or the unwieldiness of attempting to act in concert. So we expected that whether entrepreneurship is individual or collective might well be related to its causal significance for economic growth and development.

Mainstream-outsider. In Chapter 1 we proposed a distinction between two major types of entrepreneurship, which we labeled *mainstream* and *outsider*. We can use these terms to describe entrepreneurial identity as well. As our discussion there indicated, this distinction relates primarily to the factors causing entrepreneurship to emerge; but it has also been suggested that outsider entrepreneurs will be more willing to take risks because of their marginal situation. This category can be subdivided into two others based on differences in the basis of marginality.

1. Indigenous-migrant-foreign.   Marginality may be mainly geographical. On this basis an indigenous entrepreneur, born in the society in which he is an entrepreneur, is a mainstream entrepreneur. A foreign entrepreneur, born in, and a citizen of, a society other than the one in which he plays the entrepreneurial role, constitutes an outsider. In between these two is the migrant, who is born in

a different society but moves to, and becomes a citizen of, the society in which he is an entrepreneur.

2. Dominant-minority. Marginality may also be predominantly social. Thus individuals or groups within a society vary in social distance from the societal mainstream. We regard entrepreneurs from the dominant group in a society as belonging to the mainstream, and entrepreneurs from distinct subordinate groups within a society as outside the mainstream.

Therefore, entrepreneurship may be causally significant in a situation because conditions were such that large proportions of entrepreneurs from either mainstream or outsider origins emerged, or entrepreneurs from either of these origins may have been especially expansive and innovative.

Family-nonfamily. Entrepreneurship carried out by members of the same family has not been regarded as more likely to emerge under certain conditions than under others. Rather it is regarded as a virtually universal feature of the early stages of industrialization. An extensive literature suggests that entrepreneurs belonging to the same family are likely to be nonexpansive and noninnovative. Much of this literature refers to the *family firm*, which Hagen (1968) describes as operated for the benefit of the family, managed by the senior family member, dependent on relatives for capital, and recruiting managerial personnel only from within the family membership. The family firm is often regarded as being inimical to economic growth and development, because of its unwillingness to take advantage of opportunity conditions, but it is not clear why this should be an inherent characteristic of family entrepreneurship. Some have tied the failings of family-run firms to their system of management, and especially to their failure or unwillingness to bring in nonfamily members (Cochran, 1959; Hagen, 1968; Harbison and Myers, 1959). Another prominent argument describes the inadequacies as an intergenerational phenomenon. The failure of talent to be inherited or the lack of interest in entrepreneurship on the part of succeeding generations are cited by representatives of this approach (Cole, 1959; Davis, 1968). Yet another point of view attributes whatever inadequacies there may be to an overwhelming concern with security of the family which results in an unwillingness to take risks (Strassman, 1964). There also have been suggestions that a strong family bond may actually facilitate entrepreneurship (Hagen, 1962), but this point of view has been less prominent than the more critical point of view.

Hence we anticipated that family entrepreneurship would very likely predominate in cases in which entrepreneurship was found to have negative causal significance and that entrepreneurship involving individuals from different families would more likely be found in cases in which entrepreneurship had positive causal significance.

Socioeconomic origins. The socioeconomic, particularly occupational, origins of entrepreneurs have been considered in relation to the factors causing entrepreneurial emergence. Thus entrepreneurship may be causally significant in a situation because conditions are such that large proportions of entrepreneurs from certain origins are encouraged to emerge. Merchants often have been regarded as especially likely to become industrial entrepreneurs because of certain advantages they bring to the role—capital, knowledge, networks of business contacts, and the ability to perceive and exploit opportunities (Glade, 1967; McClelland and Winter, 1971). Merchants involved in international trade are also believed to bring advantages to the entrepreneurial role; their major assets are contact with the outside world and the possession of capital (Stepanek, 1960). Some, however, have suggested that entrepreneurs of merchant origin are likely to be nonexpansive and noninnovative because they are shortsighted, possess a "trader" mentality, and are unable and unwilling to plan for the future (Hoselitz, 1955a; Stepanek, 1960). But this appears to be a minority opinion, and we did not expect mercantile origins to be related to the negative causal significance of entrepreneurship as the opinion implies.

Artisans or craftsmen are a second occupational category likely to turn to industrial entrepreneurship. Their assets—knowledge of the product and a long-term view of profits—are complementary to those of merchants (Stepanek, 1960), and we shall show later that actors from those two occupational backgrounds have often merged their efforts in entrepreneurial endeavors.

The relationships between these occupational origins and entrepreneurship suggest that the emergence of entrepreneurship requires that an individual have certain resources which transform the situation in which he finds himself into a favorable opportunity condition. These resources include not only capital but also less tangible commodities, such as knowledge or contact with others.

Religious orientations. In light of Weber's emphasis on the Protestant Ethic as a promoter of entrepreneurship, it is conceivable that the positive causal significance of entrepreneurship in certain situations may be attributable to a preponderance of entrepreneurs with a Protestant religious orientation and to sociocultural conditions encouraging them to emerge. Or, if entrepreneurship has negative causal significance, it may be due to the absence of entrepreneurs with this orientation. Thus we have included religious orientation as another category of entrepreneurial identity,

Old-new. Entrepreneurial expansions and innovations may be carried out by *new* entrepreneurs, those who have not behaved entrepreneurially before, or by *old* entrepreneurs, those who have acted in that fashion before. Which of these categories of entrepreneurs is more significant in a given situation is not particularly important from the standpoint of the economic growth of a society. There have been suggestions that old entrepreneurs may be somewhat less expansive and innovative than new ones, but it is difficult to separate this factor from the influence of the transition from individual to collective forms of entrepreneurship. It is also plausible that entrepreneurship will be more likely to have positive causal significance in situations in which the rapid influx of new entrepreneurs is promoted, than in situations in which they do not enter the role so that it remains the province of established entrepreneurs. So we included this category of entrepreneurial identity on an exploratory basis in this study.

Private-public. The entrepreneurial role may be played by representatives of the government of a society or by nongovernmental members of the population. In some cases, individuals from these two sectors may combine their efforts in an entrepreneurial action; these we refer to as cases of *mixed* entrepreneurship.

Private and public entrepreneurship both involve a response to opportunity conditions, and both may be related to the causal significance of entrepreneurship. But the conditions promoting the entrepreneurial response are markedly different in the two cases, as is suggested by the distinction between *command* and *demand* economic systems to denote the public and private cases respectively. Because the response of public entrepreneurs to opportunity conditions is the result of "commands," and because the state usually possesses greater resources than does any private individual or organization, one might expect that public entrepreneurship would be more likely to have positive causal significance. Entrepreneurship may be commanded, even though opportunity conditions are unfavorable. It also has been suggested that public entrepreneurship tends to be less expansive and innovative than entrepreneurship by private individuals, which might mean that public entrepreneurship would either have negative causal significance or be causally insignificant. Private entrepreneurs are generally not commanded to respond by any higher authority but rather react to the advantages of the economic situation as they perceive them.[2] Hence the explanation of the response of private entrepreneurs is much more problematic, and much more important for determining the factors that cause entrepreneurship to emerge.

Type of Entrepreneurship

The second significant way in which entrepreneurship varies involves the *type of change* that is initiated. We have simply used the types of expansion and innovation listed in Table 10 as categories for this characteristic of entrepreneurship. With the aid of this list we were able to answer questions such as: Did the entrepreneurs in society Z primarily expand or did they introduce significant innovations and thereby expand? What types of expansion were predominant in society Z? What types of innovation were most often introduced by the entrepreneurs in society Z?

We anticipated that the causal significance of entrepreneurship in a situa-

---

[2]If they should be commanded to respond, then it would constitute a case of mixed entrepreneurship since public officials were carrying out the perception and planning phases of the role and ordering private individuals to implement an expansion or innovation.

tion might be directly related to the types of changes that were initiated in that situation. Since innovations have often been regarded as the primary entrepreneurial contribution, we further anticipated that entrepreneurship would be more likely to have positive causal significance in situations where innovations were prominent than in cases where entrepreneurship primarily involved expansion along traditional lines.

Degree of Change

One must also consider a third important aspect of entrepreneurship, involving the *size* of changes that are initiated. Generally one would expect large changes to result in greater economic growth than small changes and hence to be related to entrepreneurship's having positive causal significance. Therefore we also attempted to assess the *size* of the changes initiated by entrepreneurs in different situations, and we discuss this facet of the study in terms of the *degrees* of expansion and innovation of various entrepreneurial actions.

Degree of expansion. The size of a quantitative change can be handled quite easily, in terms of the percentage increase in the production of goods represented by a specific case. But because the base amount of goods produced, on which such percentages would be calculated, is zero for cases of initial expansion, we have used the *cost* of an expansion as the indicator of its size. Thus we have utilized data on the capital investments involved in particular cases of expansion where possible.

Degree of innovation. It has been much more difficult to determine the "size" of innovations, since they involve qualitative change. What aspect of a qualitative change is most likely to be related to economic growth and development, so that one can translate larger changes directly into larger amounts of economic growth and development and thereby relate it to the causal significance of entrepreneurship? As with expansions, we intuitively expected that entrepreneurship would be more likely to have positive causal significance in cases where entrepreneurs initiated "large" innovations than in cases where they made only "small" changes.

The usual meaning of innovation, involving newness, can be transformed into a "size" indicator by referring to the degree of newness of an innovation. We can distinguish between innovations that are absolutely new, i.e., a change that is the first of its kind in the world, and those that are relatively new, i.e., the first of its kind in a given situation, such as a society, but not the first of its kind in the world. Absolute innovations might be considered to be larger, and hence more likely to make entrepreneurship causally significant than relative innovations.

This aspect of an innovation, however, seems unlikely to account for the causal significance of entrepreneurship. It involves the temporal sequencing of qualitative changes, so its major effect will be upon the priority of a society in achieving economic growth and development, assuming that innovations have positive effects of growth and development. Societies in which a significant proportion of the innovations introduced by entrepreneurs are absolutely new very likely attain a higher rate of economic growth earlier than those societies in which the innovations have been borrowed, or developed independently at a later date. But temporal priority will not necessarily result in the causal significance of entrepreneurship, as we have defined it. Hence the degree of newness of an innovation is not relevant for the causal significance of entrepreneurship. It does, however, have relevance for another matter which we shall point out.

What we needed was an indicator of the size of innovations that was comparable to our indicator of the size of expansions, namely, indicating the *magnitude* of the changes, or the difference between the characteristics of a situation before the change is made and after its introduction. Since the types of innovation that we have outlined vary in terms of the nature of the change that is made, it is not possible to utilize a common indicator for all of them. We have noted that factor innovations primarily increase factor supplies or improve factor productivity, that production innovations usually improve factor productivity, and that market innovations increase the size of the market. Therefore the most appropriate measure of the degree of innovation of these changes would be in terms of the degree to which they increase factor supplies, improve factor productivity, and increase the size of the market. The more factor supplies are increased, factor productivity is improved, and the size of the market is increased by entrepreneurs, the more likely it will be that the rate of economic growth and development will be relatively high, and entrepreneurship will reveal an independent positive causal influence. Conversely, the smaller these changes, the less likely entrepreneurship will have this influence; it may be either insignificant or negatively significant.

This has been a difficult indicator to use in this study. Technological innovations are most susceptible to measurements of increases in productivity, and we have used such data where they have been available. But the extent to which innovations improve factor supplies or increase the size of the market, for example, may be impossible to measure. Thus our analysis of the size of these types of innovation has been necessarily impressionistic. But our approach is no doubt the closest one can come to determining the size of qualitative changes.

Another complication is that the effects of both expansions and innovations on economic growth and development are not only a function of their sizes and types. The *number* of such changes that are initiated and the *rate* at which they are initiated are also significant. In the case of innovations, the speed at which they *diffuse* among entrepreneurs will constitute the rate of innovation. Thus it is not clear exactly what combination of number, type, size, and rate of expansions and innovations is represented by a given aggregate rate of economic growth. This complication does not cast doubt on our conclusions regarding the causal significance of entrepreneurship in a society, because those are based on differences between growth rates and the favorableness of opportunity conditions, but it has made it more difficult to specify relationships between types of entrepreneurship and its causal significance.

Therefore we analyzed the types of entrepreneurship present in different societies, and the sizes of expansions and innovations initiated by entrepreneurs, to see whether they might account for the causal significance or insignificance of entrepreneurship. We expected, for example, that entrepreneurship would be more likely to have positive causal significance if it involved large expansions and innovations than if it involved small ones. We also hoped to show linkages between entrepreneurial identity and the type of entrepreneurship—for example, that entrepreneurs from one social category were more likely to initiate large innovations whereas entrepreneurs from another social category were more likely to initiate small expansions. And we were interested also in the conditions which promoted different types of entrepreneurship—the conditions promoting innovations as opposed to expansions, for example.

The discovery of a relationship between the type of entrepreneurship and the causal significance of entrepreneurship does not tell one much about *why* entrepreneurship was causally significant. If we say that entrepreneurship had positive causal significance in society Z because the entrepreneurs there initiated large innovations this still does not tell us *why* they initiated large innovations. So an analysis of types of entrepreneurship is most useful in providing information concerning links between factors promoting the emergence of entrepreneurship and the consequences of entrepreneurship, i.e., economic growth and development. This analysis may provide evidence, for instance, regarding the importance of some of the noneconomic factors we have discussed. It is in this context that the degree of newness of an innovation becomes most significant.

Let us assume that the entrepreneurs in a given society are especially likely to initiate large innovations. Not only will their entrepreneurship be more likely to have positive causal significance than if they had initiated small innovations or no innovations at all, but their pattern of innovation *also* reveals something about other characteristics of theirs, such as their willingness to take risks. Other things being equal, one would expect that large innovations would involve greater risk than small ones. Thus, if in two societies opportunity conditions are equally unfavorable, and in one of those societies entrepreneurs initiate large-scale innovations whereas in the other society entrepreneurs fail to do so, it is probable that entrepreneurship in the former society will have positive causal significance. And the entrepreneurs in that society possibly may be considered to have a greater propensity for risk-taking than entrepreneurs in the other society. Furthermore, the degree of newness of an innovation should be positively related to the amount of risk involved in introducing it, because being the first in the world to do something entails greater risk than following the example of someone else. Hence if entrepreneurs in a given society—Great Britain being the primary example in this study—initiate many absolute innovations, this may well imply their great willingness to take risk. In fact, the degree of risk associated with an innovation can be considered an additive function of *both* the degree of newness of that innovation and its degree of innovation. Initiating a large absolute innovation will be far riskier than initiating a small relative innovation.

Likewise, we would expect large expansions to involve greater risk than small expansions, and initial expansions to be riskier than subsequent expansions. Whether expansions are generally riskier than innovations, or vice versa, is impossible to say and depends on the opportunity conditions present in a particular situation. Although innovations have the connotation of being riskier, because of the usual emphasis on their newness, it is conceivable that in some situations an expansion may present greater risk for an entrepreneur than an innovation.

Thus one can use the types and sizes of entrepreneurial actions to infer the willingness of entrepreneurs to take risks. But one must also consider the possibility that they imply the presence of other noneconomic factors as well. A prevalence of large-size expansions and innovations in a society may indicate not so much that entrepreneurs in that society were especially willing to take risks, but rather that other noneconomic factors were present which minimized the risks of these actions or provided significant rewards for risk-taking. For example, if an entrepreneur anticipates significant noneconomic rewards as a result of his initiating an innovation, then his initiation of that innovation cannot be explained exclusively in terms of his risk-taking tendencies.

In sum, therefore, our analysis of the types of entrepreneurship present in different societies, and our linking of this characteristic of entrepreneurship to the causal significance or insignificance of entrepreneurship in those societies, have been major components of our attempt to determine why entrepreneurship was either causally significant or merely definitionally significant for economic growth and development.

In Table 11 we summarize the several categories of the characteristics of entrepreneurship that we have analyzed in this study.

RELATIONSHIP OF OUR CONCEPTUALIZATION
TO OTHER CONCEPTUALIZATIONS

Our conceptualization of entrepreneurship relates closely to the conceptualizations of others mentioned earlier in this chapter. *Innovation* is one of the two main types of change initiated by entrepreneurs in our conceptualization. *Organization-founding* is synonymous with our term *initial expansion*. *Leadership* is not an explicit part of our conceptualization, but we show the entrepreneurial actions that may constitute economic leadership. *Decisionmaking* is involved in all three phases of the entrepreneurial role and may be used to

Table 11
Characteristics of Entrepreneurship

I. Identity of Entrepreneurs
   a. Individual-Collective
   b. Mainstream–Outsider
      1. Indigenous-Migrant-Foreign
      2. Dominant-Minority
   c. Family-Nonfamily
   d. Socioeconomic Origins
   e. Religious Orientations
   f. Old-New
   g. Private-Public
II. Type of Entrepreneurship
   a. Expansion
      1. Initial
      2. Subsequent
   b. Innovation
      1. Factor
      2. Production
      3. Market
III. Degree of Change
   a. Degree of Expansion
   b. Degree of Innovation

identify entrepreneurial actors. Similarly, *authority* may serve as a criterion for identifying entrepreneurial actors in the planning and implementation phases of the role. And, at one point, we described entrepreneurship as the *coordination* of change in order to distinguish it from management. In addition, our conceptualization is applicable to forms of entrepreneurship other than individual private entrepreneurship and to economic growth *and* development. We have also briefly suggested how it might be applied to noneconomic types of entrepreneurship.

We have not emphasized *deviance* in our conceptualization, although it is implicit in innovation. The extent to which entrepreneurship is deviant behavior will be determined primarily by the legitimacy of entrepreneurship in a given situation. Nor have we defined entrepreneurship in terms of *risk-taking*, as some have done. Instead we have defined it in terms of the specific behaviors involved, namely, the initiation of expansions and innovations. But implicit in that definition is the risk-taking nature of entrepreneurial behavior. The initiation of any change may be assumed to involve a certain degree of risk. Hence entrepreneurs are inherently risk-takers, just as they may be described as necessarily coordinators or decisionmakers by virtue of their role. The degree of risk-taking their actions involve will depend on two factors. First, the favorableness of opportunity conditions in a situation may be defined in terms of potential risk. The more favorable these opportunity conditions are, the less potential risk an entrepreneur faces as he contemplates initiating an expansion or an innovation. So one who acts entrepreneurially despite unfavorable opportunity conditions may be described as an extreme risk-taker. Second, we have also noted that the actions an entrepreneur takes will vary in riskiness, with larger changes being typically more risky than smaller changes.

Therefore, since the degree of potential risk confronting an entrepreneur decreases with an increase in the favorableness of opportunity conditions and increases with an increase in the size of expansions and innovations, an entrepreneur who initiates a large change in the face of unfavorable conditions—an action most likely to make his entrepreneurship positively causally significant—becomes virtually by definition an extreme risk-taker. By contrast, an individual who hesitates to make even small changes in the face of favorable opportunity conditions can be defined as one who does not take risks. We have found it preferable to conceptualize entrepreneurship in terms of specific behaviors, rather than in terms of risk-taking in general, and then to relate these behaviors to different degrees of risk.

SUMMARY

We have conceptualized entrepreneurship as a role which involves *combining factors of production to initiate changes in the production of goods*. Two major types of changes, expansions and innovations, are initiated by entrepreneurs. *Expansions* are defined as quantitative changes, and *innovations* as qualitative changes, in the production of goods.

The entrepreneurial role can be divided into three phases: perception, planning, and implementation. Empirically there are three major sources of variation in the role—who plays the role, the type of changes initiated, and the size of the changes initiated—which we refer to as *entrepreneurial identity, type* of entrepreneurship, and *degree of change*, respectively. We have suggested seven categories into which entrepreneurial identity can be subdivided, two major types of expansions, and three major kinds of innovations. The degree of change simply refers to the magnitude of the expansions and innovations initiated.

These three characteristics constitute important linkages between the factors influencing the emergence of entrepreneurship and economic growth and development. They were included in the study in anticipation that they would help to explain the differential causal significance of entrepreneurship across situations. Our general hypothesis has been that entrepreneurship is causally significant in some cases because of the characteristics of entrepreneurship in those cases and that these characteristics are consequences of the existing combinations of economic and noneconomic factors in those situations.

We now turn to our six historical case studies for evidence on the causal significance of entrepreneurship and the factors which promote its emergence.

__4__

Great Britain

It is indisputable that the surge to industrialization which constituted the Industrial Revolution began in the British Isles. Hartwell (1971, p. 160) summarizes the pioneering quality of the British experience quite well:

> Of all the historical examples of growth, none is more important or more interesting than the industrial revolution in England; it was the first industrial revolution; it led to the first example of modern economic growth; . . . it was "the engine of growth" for other economies, stimulating them by example, by the export of men and capital, and by trade.

This leadership naturally raises the question: Why did the Industrial Revolution begin there? For us the important questions are: What was the significance of British entrepreneurship in this process? Was the emergence of British entrepreneurship primarily the result of favorable economic opportunity conditions, or were there unique sociocultural and psychological factors present that encouraged entrepreneurs to come forth and substantially improve upon the existing opportunity conditions?

We will analyze mainly the British textile and metallurgical industries during the period from 1750 to 1820 in order to answer these questions. Our analysis will follow the strategy previously described to determine both the causal significance of entrepreneurship and the factors promoting its emergence. We shall look first at the economic opportunity conditions; second, at the characteristics of the entrepreneurial response to these opportunity conditions; and third, at the rate of industrial growth that was achieved. As outlined previously, we shall compare the favorableness of the opportunity conditions and the rate of industrial growth to determine whether entrepreneurship had an independent causal influence on industrial growth. We then look at the noneconomic factors presumed to influence entrepreneurship to see their relevance in the British situation. The role of the state will be included as an exogenous factor, affecting both opportunity conditions and these noneconomic factors.

OPPORTUNITY CONDITIONS FOR BRITISH ENTREPRENEURSHIP

What were the economic conditions like for British entrepreneurs? Can they be regarded as quite favorable, so that entrepreneurship had limited causal significance? Or did entrepreneurship emerge despite unfavorable opportunity conditions, and thereby propel Great Britain to its position of economic leadership?

The first thing to note is that as of 1750 Britain was economically ahead of the other European societies, with the possible exception of Holland, in terms of standard of living and per capita income (Gould, 1972; Hartwell, 1971; Landes, 1965b). Gould traces this economic leadership to the Tudor and Stuart periods, and Wallerstein (1974) dates it from about 1600. The argument that British per capita income was only about 10 percent higher than that of France (Gerschenkron, 1955) appears to be a minority opinion. Thus, compared to potential entrepreneurs in most other European societies at this time, the British had the advantage of a higher economic level from which to start.

This economic level offered the potential of relatively abundant domestic capital supplies, which could be supplemented by capital from Holland and the Caribbean colonies. But whether it meant that substantial capital was available for *industrial* entrepreneurship depends upon several other factors, as we noted earlier. Of these factors we have a mixed picture.

First, industrial investment propensities appear to have been strong. More important, capital requirements for expansions were very low, particularly in textiles, although they did increase over time.[1] Fixed capital requirements were within the reach of domestic manufacturers and workers in most industries (Ashton, 1948) and could be met generally by a single person or family (Landes, 1969). Furthermore, capital requirements in manufacturing were less than they were in other areas, such as agriculture, mining, and transportation.

One of the major reasons for the modest cost of expansions in the cotton industry in the early years was the great potential for the conversion of existing facilities. According to one writer, in the years after 1788, "The old looms being insufficient, every lumber room, even old barns, outhouses and outbuildings of any description were repaired, windows broke through the old blank walls, and all fitted up for loom shops" (Chapman, 1971, p. 59). Entrepreneurs who did not do this were able to start with only a minimal outlay of funds because they could rent a plant, borrow funds for equipment and raw materials and gain funds for

[1]Gould (1972) argues that they did not become really large until the last third of the nineteenth century.

wages by making contracts for the finished products (Landes, 1969).[2] In addition, profits were quite high, so that capital was available for reinvestment. Hoselitz (1955a, p. 324) says, in regard to the iron industry in Wales, "The supply of capital funds became so great after the first important successes . . . that the result was the development of the joint-stock companies and the lavish extension of plants."

But the situation was not perfect. For one thing, industrial entrepreneurs faced competition from other economic sectors. Credit was more easily procured by commercial entrepreneurs. Consequently the capital needs of industrial entrepreneurs were not as well met as those of entrepreneurs in other sectors. "Many important enterprises were in repeated financial difficulties despite their high profit rates" (Gould, 1972, p. 163). This situation was exacerbated by the relatively limited development of capital-mobilizing facilities, such as banking. Capital was usually only available on a short-term basis from banks, although it has been argued that the demands of industry and agriculture for capital were seasonal and reciprocal and that the banking system, particularly the country banks, transferred capital back and forth between the two sectors (Shapiro, 1967). It has also been claimed that industry was able to finance its own activities (Gould, 1972). Self-financing, however, was somewhat limited by restrictions on the use of corporate forms of organization. The Bubble Act of 1720, which remained in effect until 1825, limited the size of partnerships and prohibited limited liability. The reluctance of the government to issue corporate charters appears to have hindered the flow of capital to industry, although the ease with which partnerships were formed made them an attractive alternative. Nevertheless a majority of the most rapidly growing enterprises had to make extensive use of credit (Cameron, 1967a).

The major capital problem facing entrepreneurs was the procurement of working capital to pay for raw materials, to extend credit to buyers, and particularly to pay wages. This pattern also had existed under the domestic system of manufacturing, and it distinguished manufacturing from other sectors, such as agriculture, transportation, and public works in which fixed capital requirements were proportionately much greater. The highest fixed/working capital ratios in manufacturing were found in cotton spinning after the introduction of steam power, although even there the proportion of investment devoted to plant and equipment constituted only one-seventh or one-eighth of total assets (Crouzet, 1972, p. 36).[3]

Our conclusion is that capital supplies were sufficient for British entrepreneurs, but that they could have been greater.[4] The major problem appears to

[2]The amount of capital involved can be put into perspective by noting that it, including stocks, amounted to about four months' wages per member of the industrial labor force in the years before 1800 (Gould, 1972, p. 385).

[3]Gould (1972, p. 151) estimates that in the early years of the British industrial revolution plants and equipment accounted for only about 0.5 percent of national income.

[4]Hartwell (1971) asserts that there is little evidence of any industrial entrepreneurs being starved for capital.

have been the lack of suitable mobilizing facilities. It has been claimed that the Industrial Revolution could have taken place a *century* before it did, simply on the basis of the total supply of wealth (Gould, 1972). Also, it has been shown that there was a decline in the interest rate in the period after 1760 (Ashton, 1948), which we would attribute partly to an increased supply of investment capital. Furthermore, Britain became a net exporter of capital by 1815 at the latest (Gould, 1972); this suggests that by the end of our period capital supplies had become sufficient. Only Landes (1969) argues that capital supplies were insufficient and inferior to those on the Continent where entrepreneurs could rely upon government subsidies.

Potential British entrepreneurs confronted a mixed situation in procuring raw materials after 1770. Supplies of coal and iron ore were plentiful, but water for power and cotton were lacking. But the increases in the supply of cotton from the United States resulting from the invention of the cotton gin in 1793 reduced the cost of cotton appreciably. Hoselitz (1955a) claims that British and French opportunity conditions were equal on this factor; Murphy (1967) grants the British an advantage on the basis of their coal and ore supplies. We concur with Murphy on this issue.

A variety of opinions exist regarding the supply of labor available to British entrepreneurs, with the majority opinion being that it was inadequate, although it has also been described as abundant (Saul, 1970) and adequate (Henderson, 1965). It has been suggested that the enclosure movement in agriculture actually increased the demand for labor, thus squeezing the supply for industry (Landes, 1965b), but the same writer acknowledges that the supply of labor for industry increased after 1750. And Murphy (1967) claims that the greater mobility of British workers gave the British an "overwhelming advantage" over Continental entrepreneurs. There is much more agreement regarding the relatively high skill level of British workers, however, compared to workers on the Continent. So it appears that the supply of labor was limited but that what was available was rather highly skilled and quite mobile.

The level of British technological development, like the level of economic development, exceeded that of other societies in 1750 (Landes, 1965b). By that date there was an existing stock of rudimentary machines in the textile industry. In metallurgy, the crucible technique for making steel had been developed around 1740. Coke had been introduced for smelting in 1709 though it was rather slow to replace charcoal because of the impurity of available ores. The Newcomen steam engine had been in use since 1705. Societies on the Continent lacked technologies such as these.

According to Habakkuk (1968), the British market constituted a more significant influence on entrepreneurship than either capital or labor supplies. Several others have emphasized the favorableness of the market, both domestic and foreign. The domestic market was favorable because of the high level of per capita income. Both the relatively large middle class and the working class demanded substantial goods, rather than luxuries, so it was also favorable for the mass production of inexpensive goods. Moreover, Britain was more urbanized than other societies and hence more dependent on manufactured goods. And the growing British population promoted increases in demand after 1750.[5]

The foreign market, in which Britain already had a competitive advantage in 1750, has been stressed as especially important, particularly in textiles. This market included the British colonies, which were more extensive than those of other countries, and the Continent. Its exploitation was facilitated by an excellent external transportation system. Involvement in wars after 1780 removed the French and American as competitors, and at the conclusion of these wars in 1815 the British advantage was even greater than it had been before.

So the potential rewards offered by the market were quite large for British entrepreneurs. The only major inadequacy was the lack of substantial demand from railroad construction that characterized several of the societies which industrialized later. Possibly also the British market was not large enough to accommodate the introduction of interchangeable parts in manufacturing (Landes, 1969). But these appear to have been the only drawbacks.

We conclude that the opportunity conditions for British industrial entrepreneurship were quite favorable between 1750 and 1820. Capital and labor supplies were adequate, raw material and technology supplies were above average, and the market potential was excellent. Even though science was more advanced in France in the eighteenth century, the Industrial Revolution occurred in Britain.

> . . . where there were richer resources of coal and iron, where foreign trade was greatly expanding, where capital could more easily be mobilized, . . . and where there were therefore greater opportunities of *applying* scientific knowledge. (Musson & Robinson, 1969, p. 81; italics in the original)

It is conceivable, however, that these opportunity conditions were even more favorable for forms of entrepreneurship other than industrial. This does not seem to have been true. In the nineteenth century at least, returns were greater in industry than in farming (Hoffman, 1955). So we further conclude that *relative* opportunity conditions were also favorable for industrial entrepreneurship in Great Britain.

CHARACTERISTICS OF BRITISH ENTREPRENEURSHIP

Innovations

How did British entrepreneurs respond to these favorable opportunity conditions? Their primary response can be summed up in one word: innovation. First and foremost were a number of technological innovations which were absolute,

---

[5]Landes (1969, p. 46) calls the British domestic market "the largest coherent market in Europe" because of its lack of customs and toll barriers and improvements in transportation after 1750.

i.e., the first of their kind. These innovations necessitated organizational innovations in the production process as well, and they also stimulated factor and market innovations (Crouzet, 1972).

These innovations can be grouped into three classes: the replacement of manual methods of production with machine methods, the discovery of new processes, and the application of new forms of power to the production process. Great Britain's chronological leadership in industrialization derived directly from these technological changes.

The cotton industry exemplified the introduction of mechanical production methods. After 1750 there appeared in rapid succession Hargreaves' spinning jenny (1767); Arkwright's spinning frame or water frame, patented in 1769; carding machines developed under Arkwright's leadership in the 1770s; and Cartwright's power loom, patented in 1785. The introduction of these interrelated innovations in spinning and weaving has been described as a marriage of the right kinds of machines with the right kind of industry (Landes, 1965b).[6]

The discovery of new production processes occurred primarily in the metallurgical industry, with Darby's improvement of the process of using coke for smelting in 1750 and Cort's development of the puddling and rolling processes for refining in 1784 the major accomplishments. After 1750 this industry was mainly involved in the "adaptation of the processes of smelting and refining to ores and fuels of different characteristics" (Landes, 1965b, p. 322), which shows the close relationship of technological and material innovations. Innovations of this sort were also occurring in the nascent chemical industry at this time. Its production of sulphuric acid for bleaching and dyeing contributed to the progress of the textile industry.

Improvements in the use of steam for power were the major development in the third category of technological innovations. The Newcomen steam engine was superseded in 1769 by the Watt engine. Subsequent improvements by Bell and Trevithick and by Woolf further increased the power of the engines and their fuel economy. Steam power was first applied to cotton spinning in 1785, and after 1800 it was applied to transportation. At the same time larger and more efficient water wheels were being developed. They too contributed to the growth of the cotton industry, although innovations in the use of water for power were far less significant than those connected with the use of steam.

An especially important development accompanying these innovations was the rise of a machine industry about 1775.[7] It began largely in response to the mechanical innovations occurring in the cotton industry, and by the 1790s firms specializing in the manufacture of textile machines were in existence. The machine industry was dependent upon metallurgy for materials so it was aided by

---

[6]Chapman (1972) also credits the cotton industry with several technological innovations not directly related to production, including the erection of iron-frame buildings and using gas for lighting, which had ramifications for other industries.

[7]Recently British entrepreneurs have also been credited with leadership in the development of this industry, an honor formerly given to American entrepreneurs (Musson & Robinson, 1969).

technological improvements in refining and fabricating. And it produced the steam engines for the developing power industry.

The machine industry was also responsible for major innovations of its own. The first of these was the use of specialized machinery to produce the components of textile machines. The second was the development of "self-acting" machine tools. In 1800, for example, Maudslay developed a self-acting lathe which was able to machine parts much more accurately than existing machines. This and other self-acting tools led to the standardization of machine production in the 1830s (Chapman, 1972).

The rate at which these innovations diffused among entrepreneurs varied considerably. Entrepreneurs often copied from nearby entrepreneurs (Pollard, 1965). The rather high degree of geographic concentration of much of British industry, particularly cotton spinning, due to the location of power and material supplies therefore facilitated diffusion. The spinning jenny and the spinning mule diffused very rapidly because they could be assimilated into either the domestic system of production or the factory system. Arkwright's water frame also spread quite rapidly (Chapman, 1971, 1972). Diffusion of the power loom was much slower, however, because of its greater cost, its imperfections, and the large supply of handloom weavers.[8] By 1820 there were only 14,150 power looms in operation in England and Scotland, but by 1833 there were 100,000 (Smelser, 1959, p. 147).

We lack specific data on the diffusion of the puddling and rolling techniques, but it must have been fairly rapid as well. But the diffusion of steam technology, at least in the cotton industry, was relatively slow until about 1800. After that time the growth in mule spinning was accompanied by an increase in the use of steam, but water power still predominated over steam in 1820.[9]

The initiation of innovations and their diffusion were not without complications. A first obstacle was the opposition of skilled workers to innovations which replaced them, the most famous opponents, of course, being the Luddites. This opposition was significantly greater in Britain than it was in the United States (Strassman, 1959). Second, technological innovation in one industry, or a segment of an industry, often created inadequacies, or bottlenecks, in another industry or segment. But rather than stifling innovation, these bottlenecks promoted it (Landes, 1969). This occurred in many areas. In the cotton industry a lack of yarn led to innovations in spinning which increased its output and that of thread. This increased output in turn stimulated innovations in weaving. The increased output of cotton cloth encouraged the development of new techniques for bleaching and dyeing by the chemical industry. Within that industry a surplus of waste products of chemical processes stimulated innovational uses for them. And the

[8]Domestic workers outnumbered factory workers in weaving until about 1835 (Chapman, 1972).

[9]By 1835 steam was to account for three-fourths of the power supply of the cotton industry (Chapman, 1972, p. 19).

steam engine prompted innovations both in metallurgy and in the precision construction of machines (Strassman, 1959).

Third, the secretiveness of many of the entrepreneurs slowed the diffusion of innovations (Musson & Robinson, 1969). British entrepreneurs were able to overcome this and other obstacles partly as a result of their technological adeptness and their interest in "gymcracks" (Landes, 1969). Although many of them lacked technological knowledge, particularly in metallurgy, they obtained it through experimentation or from whatever scientific training they could find (Carr & Taplin, 1962; Gould, 1972; Musson & Robinson, 1969). They also had great faith in technology, which has been described as the ideology of a social movement (Bendix, 1956).

These technological innovations facilitated and necessitated innovations in the organization of production which were perhaps equally important (Hartwell, 1971). These organizational changes were important in the pottery and chemical industries, as well as in textiles and metallurgy. The replacement of the putting-out system by the factory system was the first major organizational change. Although factory systems can be traced back to the fifteenth century, the mechanization of production made possible their development on a much larger scale. This innovation involved several components—the use of mechanical power, the concentration of production processes under one roof, the use of specialized machines, and the organization and direction of the labor force by specialized management (Chapman, 1972). It did not merely involve an increase in scale, as entrepreneurs sometimes employed hundreds, and even thousands, of workers under the putting-out system (Pollard, 1965).

The factory system was adopted most extensively in the textile industry. Although the spinning jenny and spinning mule could be incorporated in the putting-out system, the water frame and the subsequent development of carding engines radically increased the productive potential of the factory system. Arkwright established the first cotton factory run entirely by water power in 1771, and by 1780 there were between fifteen and twenty factories using the spinning frame and water power. By 1787 this number had swelled to one hundred and forty-three (Smelser, 1959, p.97), and by 1797 there were nine hundred factories of all types in the cotton industry (Chapman, 1972, p.33). The increased use of steam power for mule spinning after 1800 led to the decline of the rural factory colonies and to an increase in urban factories, so that by 1815 the latter were predominant. Thus in the textile industry a system of large single production units developed, whereas in the iron industry smaller units linked together remained more important (Pollard, 1965).

The second major organizational innovation, the development of a corps of managers, was much slower in coming. This step was taken by entrepreneurs in most cases only with the utmost hesitation. The major reason for this hesitance was the perceived untrustworthiness of potential managers. They were hired to oversee operations only as a last resort, and in many cases subcontracting survived as a bridge between the putting-out and factory systems. Mining and metallurgy were the first industries to be forced down this path, primarily because of their greater complexity, their larger scale, and their greater geographical dispersion. Some putting-out masters in the textile industry were using managers even before 1750. The use of managers in this industry increased after about 1760, and the increase in factory production necessitated even greater reliance on them. Yet, the textile industry remained the one most likely to use subcontracting (Pollard, 1965).

When management techniques were adopted, they were borrowed from three existing models of large-scale enterprises—agricultural estates, merchants who combined large-scale trade with control of a network of domestic manufacturers in the putting-out system, and mining. Gradually innovations were also introduced in such areas as the training of managers and their hiring on the basis of merit rather than family affiliation (Pollard, 1965). The slowness of innovation in this area was not too serious, however, because the scale of production was generally not large enough to require significant management innovations until the late nineteenth century (Gould, 1972).

The use of "new and far more abundant raw materials" was another of the major British innovations (Landes, 1965b, p. 274). This was most true in the metallurgical industry where the puddling process made it possible to use coal in refining.[10] It was also a major innovation in the chemical industry, in which vegetable materials replaced animal, inorganic materials replaced organic, and the byproducts of chemical reactions were used to produce new products. We lack information on diffusion of the use of new materials in the chemical industry. The use of coke in metallurgy was relatively slow after 1750, and it did not replace charcoal until about 1800.

New producer goods, such as steam engines, machine tools, textile machinery, and the new products of the chemical industry, also were a significant component of the British industrial transition. The major product innovation in consumer goods was the production of *better-quality* and *lower-cost* textiles, although there is some dispute regarding the extent to which improvements in quality occurred. Chapman (1972) claims that machine-spun yarn was far superior to handmade and that British printed calicoes and lace outclassed similar French products, but he also notes that a decline in the quality of cloth occurred in the first half of the nineteenth century. Hagen (1968) argues that the high quality and low cost of British goods enabled Britain to capture the foreign textile market. Landes (1965b, p. 286) asserts, "The sacrifice of quality to quantity was an old story in English manufacture." So we believe that there was definitely a reduction in the cost of textile goods and probably some improvements in their quality.

Improvements in the quality of cast and wrought iron goods accompanied the decline in costs associated with new production techniques in metallurgy.

---

[10]The use of coal for smelting had been introduced before 1750.

The engines and machines being produced by the fledgling machine industry were continually upgraded through numerous modifications. The chemical industry exemplified the same pattern—introduction of a new, imperfect product and its subsequent improvement.

Two major market innovations were important during this period. The first was the *mass* production of *consumer* goods, particularly cotton cloth and yarn, made possible by the transition to mechanical methods of production.[11] The second was the exploitation of the foreign market with these inexpensive goods. Although the majority of goods was marketed domestically, British expansion into the foreign market was substantially greater than that of any of her European competitors. According to Landes, (1969, p. 53), "This was Britain's forte: the ability to manufacture cheaply precisely those articles for which foreign demand was most elastic."

If any of the types of innovations initiated by British entrepreneurs can be considered relatively less important, it is those involving capital and labor. Several devices were developed to provide liquid capital for the payment of wages. Shop notes, bills of exchange, and checks were used, tokens were issued, or sometimes workers were paid only when coins were available, a practice known as *long-pay* (Shapiro, 1967). In some cases—in metallurgy more than in textiles—entrepreneurs diversified into banking to provide themselves with working capital.

Mechanisms to provide fixed capital were also instituted, such as borrowing on bond. But the financial-organizational innovation which was substantially to increase the supply of capital in other societies, the corporate form of organization, was uncommon. Before 1750 joint-stock companies had been almost uniformly unsuccessful and had fallen into disfavor. They did become somewhat more popular after 1750 and many entrepreneurs were organized virtually as corporations even though they did not have that legal form (Dunham, 1955). The joint-stock companies which did exist were more prevalent in metallurgy than in textiles.[12]

Solving the problem of labor supply was most crucial for the entrepreneurs in the textile industry and for those who introduced technological innovations. This problem was solved primarily by the use of unfree pauper labor and of women and children, the latter having been an important source of labor in the putting-out system. It is estimated that, at maximum, unfree labor comprised one-third of the labor force, and that 40 to 45 percent of the cotton industry work

[11]Ashton (1948) credits cheap calicoes made from cotton with building the first stage of the industrial revolution in textiles. As late as 1871 consumer goods still constituted 52 percent of British industrial output (Patel, 1961, p. 322).

[12]Accounting, which can be considered as partly a financial and partly an organizational innovation, was also slow to develop. Existing methods of accounting were particularly inadequate for dealing with fixed capital. But Pollard (1965, p. 245) notes that "accuracy in accounting was less essential at a time when selling prices were so far above total costs that almost any pricing policy was bound to show a net surplus."

force consisted of workers under eighteen (Pollard, 1965, pp. 172, 185). In addition, entrepreneurs sometimes poached workers from each other, which led to the development of formalized work rules and systems of fines as means of retaining them.

Improving labor productivity by upgrading the skills of workers was most problematic in the metallurgical industry. Here relatively little progress was made. Some on-the-job training was instituted and entrepreneurs also relied partly upon formal education outside the factory. Ultimately incentive payments were adopted and workers' hours were reduced, with consequent improvements in productivity.[13] Innovations in labor management did not diffuse as rapidly as technological innovations, mainly because entrepreneurs believed that specific changes would not be beneficial. Rather they felt that workers would have to internalize entrepreneurial character and morals before their work would improve (Pollard, 1965). This entrepreneurial ideology (Bendix, 1956) may also be considered an innovation, although entrepreneurs were not solely responsible for its development.

Because most of the early factories were built in rural areas where the putting-out system had flourished, many entrepreneurs also provided services to their workers to entice them to remain. These included houses and schools, and in some cases transportation facilities were also constructed, farms were established to provide food, and systems of civil power were established. These factory colonies were most prominent in the years before 1800 and can be considered indirectly as a labor innovation (Pollard, 1965).

Degree of innovation. We have shown that technological innovations were the most significant contribution of the British entrepreneurs, and that they also precipitated other innovations—organizational, material, product, and market. But financial and labor innovations were relatively less important. Now we must ask: How innovative were these innovations? How much change from the existent situation did they involve?

These questions clearly are answered most easily for technological innovations, as one can compile at least rough data on improvements in productivity. Many of the earliest machines were not far different from manual methods of production (Landes, 1969). The earliest spinning jennies could be run manually, for example. Despite their simplicity, they yielded significant gains in productivity. When first used the spinning jenny multiplied the spinner's output eight times (Smelser, 1959, p. 87); by 1812 one jenny equaled the output of two hundred spinners of the pre-jenny period (Deane & Cole, 1967, p. 183).

The adoption of steam power also brought significant improvements in productivity. It tripled the spinning mule's output, for example (Chapman, 1971,

---

[13]Gould (1972) points out that most achievements in this regard were accidental rather than planned.

p. 77). Furthermore, it was an *inanimate* form of power, not dependent on the energy of man or beast. And it relied on a specific form of inanimate energy— mineral fuel. Manufacturers were no longer dependent upon the vagaries of the wind or water for adequate power (Landes, 1965b).[14] In addition, significant improvements were made in fuel economy. Consumption of fuel relative to output for Watt's steam engine was only one-fourth that of the Newcomen engine (Landes, 1965b, p. 331). And, given Britain's relative supplies of coal and wood, the use of coal for the steam engine and coke in metallurgy resulted in significant cost reductions (Landes, 1969).

The development of a machine industry, with the innovations it incorporated, supported developments in textiles, power, and metallurgy. The effects of these changes were heightened by the rapidity at which they were adopted. As Pollard (1965, p. 90) puts it, "Technical changes followed so quickly on the heels of each other that the man who failed to innovate was unable to compete." This was no doubt most true for the cotton spinning industry.

Determining the degree of change involved in the nontechnological innovations is much more difficult. Smelser (1959, p. 66) does estimate that factory production had a sixfold advantage over hand production in spinning and allied activities. But we have not been able to determine how much the use of managers affected productivity. We have not been able to estimate accurately the size of the effects of the product, market, and financial innovations of the period. Nor can we say how much the supply and productivity of labor was increased.

But we can note the impact of the transition to factory production upon workers of the time, which "in many respects . . . , required the fiercest wrench from the past" (Pollard, 1965, p. 160).[15] Higgins (1951) describes the loss of ownership of raw materials and products by cottage workers who became factory workers as more significant than the rise of factory production *per se*. And Marx (1929, p. 451) penned an impassioned protest against this consequence of the industrial transition:

> In manufacture and in handicrafts, the worker uses a tool; in the factory he serves a machine. In the former cases the movements of the instruments of labor proceed from the worker; but in the latter, the movements of the worker are subordinate to those of the machine. In manufacture the workers are parts of a living mechanism. In the factory, there exists a lifeless mechanism independent of them, and they are incorporated into that mechanism as its living appendages.

Thus the former vassalage to feudal masters was transformed into servitude to the machine.

[14]The development of bleaches and of synthetic dyes by the chemical industry was similar to the use of mineral fuel in that it reduced the dependence of the entrepreneur upon his natural environment.

[15]By 1830 65 percent of all British cotton workers were in factory settings (Hayes, 1939, p. 21).

Expansions

These innovations were accompanied by numerous expansions by industrial entrepreneurs between 1750 and 1820. The expansion of production is shown by several indicators. Annual pig iron production increased from 30,000 to 452,000 tons between 1770 and 1823 (Carr and Taplin, 1962, p. 6). In 1760 there were fewer than twenty operating blast furnaces in existence; by 1805 there were 177, and by 1830, 372. The number of cotton spindles increased from less than two million in 1780 to ten million in 1830. Average annual imports of raw cotton increased from 7.65 million pounds in the period 1776–80 to approximately 250 million pounds in 1830 (Hartwell, 1971, pp. 121–22).

Undoubtedly both initial and subsequent expansions were occurring during this period. New entrepreneurs continued to enter the cotton industry, for example, at least until the 1830s. Subsequent expansions took place in several ways (Crouzet, 1972). The number of factories surpassed the number of firms in the cotton industry, which indicates that some entrepreneurs expanded by adding factories. Second, there was also an increase in output per factory, since between 1797 and 1834 the number of factories increased only from 900 to 1,200 whereas the amount of raw cotton consumed increased ten times (Chapman, 1972, p. 33). And third, there was also an increase in the size of factories. Landes (1965b, p. 297) says, regarding the earliest of them, "Most so-called factories were no more than glorified workshops: a dozen workers or less; one or two jennies, perhaps, or mules; and a carding machine to prepare the rovings." By 1822 the average Manchester firm employed one to two hundred workers, but factories in other areas were probably smaller (Chapman, 1972, p. 26). But the transition to factory production was also accompanied by the establishment of small-scale units engaged in subcontracting for operations such as carding and spinning. So there was probably substantial heterogeneity in plant size in the textile industry (Chapman, 1972).

The situation was similar in metallurgy, although the increase in scale in it, and in the chemical and machine industries, preceded that in cotton (Landes, 1965b; Pollard, 1965). Two increases in scale occurred after 1750, the first after Darby's refinement of the use of coke for smelting; the second, after the appearance of Cort's puddling technique. But there was heterogeneity in size in this industry, too. Three of the largest ironworks—Carron, Dowlais, and Cyfarthfa—each employed over two thousand workers by 1800. But the average wrought ironworks of the 1850s still employed only about 250 men (Carr and Taplin, 1962, p. 2). Both initial and subsequent expansions took place in this industry also (Landes, 1965b).

Capital for initial expansions generally came from entrepreneurs' own resources or from their families and friends. Some initiated the production of goods with only the capital they had accuumlated through petty local trading

(Landes, 1969). As the cost of expansions became greater, entrepreneurs typically were forced to go farther afield in order to procure capital. We have already noted their innovations in this area, including diversification into banking.[16]

Subsequent expansions were financed almost completely by the reinvestment of profits. British entrepreneurs typically lived on 5 percent of their invested capital and returned all income above that to their enterprises (Cameron, 1967a). Because profits were very high, particularly for the earliest and most innovative entrepreneurs, subsequent expansions could take place very rapidly. Furthermore, there was no taxation to hinder reinvestment. So, although these entrepreneurs sometimes sustained serious losses, they generally had sufficient profits to reinvest, and they did reinvest them.

Degree of expansion. There is substantial agreement that most cotton entrepreneurs began on a small scale, at least in the early years of the period. Chapman (1971, pp. 61–63) has provided the most detailed information regarding costs in this industry on the basis of a study of insurance records for 1770–1803. He reports that there were three different types of cotton factories. The first type, which used horse capstans for driving carding machines, were maximally valued at 2,000 pounds if they used steam power and at 1,000 pounds if they did not. The second type utilized water power and had average valuations of from 3,000 to 5,000 pounds. The third type, which used steam power and began to appear in the 1790s, cost a minimum of 10,000 pounds. So these data indicate a substantial increase in the cost of expansions over time.

The cost of technological innovations also increased over time; hence expansions involving the simultaneous adoption of an innovation became even more costly. Around 1795 jennies cost 6 pounds and mules 30 pounds. By 1811 hand looms cost 5 pounds, stocking frames 15 pounds, a small steam engine 150 to 200 pounds, and large steam engines 500 to 800 pounds (Crouzet, 1972, p. 37). Thus the steam engine constituted a more costly innovation than did the early textile machines. It is not surprising that wealthier entrepreneurs were the ones most likely to purchase them (Smelser, 1959). This increase in costs also undoubtedly had a restrictive effect on the entry of new entrepreneurs into industry.

There is a difference of opinion regarding the cost of initiating production in metallurgy, which is probably attributable to the heterogeneity of the industry. Bendix (1956) and Hoselitz (1955a) emphasize the high costs of expansion; Cameron (1967a) says that a number of firms started on a small scale. Crouzet (1972, pp. 37–38) estimates that most iron enterprises around 1800 represented an investment of between 12,000 and 30,000 pounds, which would make them

---

[16]Cameron (1967a) notes that this practice often led to business failures because of an overextension of credit and the absence of limited liability.

more costly than the most expensive cotton mills described earlier. There is more agreement on the greater cost of later metallurgical innovations, such as the puddling technique.

Thus from relatively small beginnings the size and cost of entrepreneurial expansions increased in the years after 1750.

Entrepreneurial Identity

The third characteristic of entrepreneurship to be considered simply involves *who* the British entrepreneurs were. There is consensus regarding their identity in several areas, as well as a couple of points on which there is dissension.

First, British entrepreneurship was more individual than collective. Very often one person carried out all three phases of the entrepreneurial role. As Hartwell (1971, p. 301) describes it, "During the English industrial revolution, more than in any subsequent industrialization, . . . one man often combined two or more of the roles of capitalist, inventor, innovator, and manager, so that high success demanded wide ability."

Although a large number of entrepreneurs acted individually, the partnership was the predominant entrepreneurial form. Partnerships were usually small, being legally limited to six members until about the mid-nineteenth century, and generally consisted of family members or close friends.[17] In some cases partners contributed no capital to the partnership. Joint-stock companies were insignificant except in metallurgy where larger amounts of capital were needed.

Second, British entrepreneurship was overwhelmingly private. The only direct entrepreneurial role of the government appears to have been in the armaments industry (Trebilock, 1969). Third, it was also predominantly indigenous. Immigrant entrepreneurs had been significant before 1750 but were unimportant after that date.

Fourth, family entrepreneurship was significant, both in cotton and metallurgy, particularly in the early years of the period. Individuals often sought capital from, and formed partnerships with, family members. There were, however, noteworthy cases of partnerships being formed with nonfamily members, such as Arkwright's partnership with Need and Strutt to promote his water frame and the Watt-Boulton partnership in developing the steam engine. British entrepreneurs are credited with a great willingness to enter into partnerships with unrelated individuals (Landes, 1969; Kindleberger, 1964). Quite often though, partners became family members through marriage, and managers were often selected from the families of entrepreneurs and their partners. There was also much inheritance of industrial enterprises, more than occurred in France (Landes, 1949). Chapman (1970) has shown the extent to which this happened in

---

[17]Partnerships were slightly larger in Scotland because of different legal provisions there.

the cotton industry. British family entrepreneurship does not appear to have had the negative effects on expansion and innovation that family entrepreneurship often is alleged to have (Cole, 1959). The possibility of family members' inheriting enterprises perhaps motivated entrepreneurs to be expansive and innovative (Gould, 1972).

Finally, both old and new entrepreneurs were important in Britain, according to Bendix's (1956, p. 24) description of the period after 1760 as one in which "the families of new entrepreneurs consolidated their economic positions or . . . already established families succeeded in maintaining and enlarging their enterprises."

The areas of disagreement concern the occupational origins and the religious affiliations of British entrepreneurs. It is agreed that many of them came from one of two occupational backgrounds. First, entrepreneurs in the putting-out system simply made the transformation to the factory mode of production, either on their own or in partnerships. This was particularly likely in the cotton industry, in which the putting-out system had been predominant, but putters-out who had been involved in smelting also made the same transition in metallurgy.

Second, a large number of artisans and craftsmen became industrial entrepreneurs, especially in metallurgy, but also in the textile industry in the early years.[18] Weavers and spinners often went into business for themselves after the introduction of the spinning jenny and the spinning mule. Somewhat surprisingly, however, two of the individuals who played prominent roles in the cotton industry by inventing *and* innovating—Arkwright and Cartwright—came from neither of these occupational origins. Arkwright was an uneducated barber and horsedealer and Cartwright was an Anglican clergyman (Hayes, 1939).

The disagreement regarding occupational backgrounds involves a third group, consisting of merchants who had been involved in the putting-out system. A number of scholars have attested to their significance in both the cotton industry and in metallurgy. They became important suppliers of capital as the scale of production and capital requirements increased, often forming partnerships with artisans. Quite often it was the larger merchants with more capital at their disposal who were so involved. Over time they gradually became dominant in their partnerships and relegated the artisans to technical positions.

Hoselitz (1955a) has described their importance in the spread of iron manufacturing to South Wales and Scotland. In South Wales their capital, often invested in partnerships with local artisans, precipitated a period of very rapid growth and by 1788 they comprised about one-half of the entrepreneurs in this area.[19] In Scotland, several major ironworks were founded at this time. Chapman (1970, 1971) attributes the introduction of the cotton industry to Scotland to these

---

[18]Chapman (1970) observes that Stockport had a large number of entrepreneurs from this occupational background.

[19]South Wales is a possible exception though because it appears to have had a larger scale of production than other areas where artisans and craftsmen remained more important.

merchants and says that they were generally predominant after 1795. And Crouzet (1972) claims that merchant capital was more important than self-financing as a source of working capital until 1815.

Hagen (1962, pp. 301–03), though, has shown that only a few individuals in a sample of entrepreneurs whose median date of death was 1810 made the transition from trade to manufacturing. The largest proportion—almost 40 percent—were sons of industrial proprietors and hence from within manufacturing. Bendix (1956, p. 24) notes that two-thirds of a sample of prominent industrialists in the period 1750–1850 were from families established in business, which seems to support Hagen's point of view, although "business" could refer to either trade or manufacturing.

The apparent confusion probably indicates a chronological sequence. Craftsmen and putting-out entrepreneurs who made the transition to factory production very likely were most prominent in the years immediately after 1750. With the advent of steam power in textiles and the spread of textiles and metallurgy to Scotland and Wales, merchant capital became more significant. By 1820 these merchants had consolidated their entrepreneurial positions and their descendants were beginning to assume entrepreneurial roles.

There were instances of industrial entrepreneurs coming from other occupations. Landowners occasionally participated in metallurgy, but they were more involved in mining. Some small farmers were active in the cotton industry (Shapiro, 1967). Large landowners were more likely to be creditors than entrepreneurial partners (Landes, 1965b). And individuals employed as managers also became entrepreneurial partners.

The disagreement over religious affiliations concerns the extent to which Dissenters occupied entrepreneurial roles. Smelser (1959) and Landes (1969) both claim that a number of leading entrepreneurs were Nonconformists, and the latter also suggests that they were numerous in the areas of most rapid industrial development. There is also evidence of the importance of Quakers in the iron industry. Hagen (1962, 1968) shows that Nonconformists were overrepresented in England, contributing ten times as many innovating entrepreneurs and fourteen times as many manufacturing entrepreneurs as did the Anglicans. Furthermore, a number of Nonconformist sons joined the Anglican church, presumably as a means of insuring their respectability, so the representation of Nonconformists may actually be understated.

Hagen has also shown, however, that Nonconformists were *not* overrepresented among Scottish entrepreneurs and that Scots *were* overrepresented, in comparison with English and Welsh, among British entrepreneurs. There are also notable individual exceptions, such as Cartwright, the Anglican clergyman. So it appears that entrepreneurs in England were disproportionately from non-Anglican religious backgrounds; hence entrepreneurship there had somewhat of an outsider quality, but this was not so in Scotland.

Thus British entrepreneurship was primarily individual or family, private, and indigenous. It included old and new entrepreneurs who came primarily from mercantile or artisan backgrounds, but from other occupations as well, and a disproportionate number of Nonconformists in England.

THE RATE OF BRITISH INDUSTRIAL GROWTH

We now turn to the third link in the chain of our argument, the rate of industrial growth in Britain resulting from the entrepreneurial responses to the economic opportunity conditions we have described. Although there was rapid growth in particular industries, notably cotton in which rates of growth almost always exceeded rates of growth of all other consumer goods industries (Shapiro, 1967), and in particular time periods, especially after about 1780 (Ashton, 1948), the overall rate of British industrial growth between 1750 and 1820 was surprisingly low compared to most of the other countries that we are considering. But it was higher than the growth rates of these countries in the period 1750–1820. Thus Great Britain, already ahead of these countries in 1750, was able to pull farther ahead of them by increasing her growth rate only slightly.

The British annual rate of growth of industrial output has been estimated at less than 2 percent before 1780, between 3 and 4 percent from 1780 to 1792, and between 2 and 3 percent from 1792 to 1818 (Hartwell, 1971, p. 120). Some have remarked upon the relative slowness of the industrial transition in Britain (Deane, 1957; Gould, 1972). Hartwell (1971) suggests that this slowness makes it inappropriate to refer to this transition as the Industrial *Revolution*. Although the innovations initiated by British entrepreneurs were ultimately to have revolutionary consequences, the quantitative evidence shows that overall change came relatively slowly.

THE CAUSAL SIGNIFICANCE OF BRITISH ENTREPRENEURSHIP

We find it difficult to accord a great deal of causal significance to entrepreneurship for British industrial growth during the period 1750–1820 on the basis of our preceding analysis. Setting off in 1750 with the advantage of an economic and technological head start over other European countries, Britain increased its industrial growth rate only moderately and thereby increased its economic advantage. Compared to the other countries we are considering, its industrial growth rate was below average, except for the twelve years between 1780 and 1792.

Economic opportunity conditions for entrepreneurship were generally rather favorable in the years after 1750. First, capital supplies were adequate. British entrepreneurs often were able to initiate expansions on a small scale and to increase their scale of operations gradually by reinvesting profits, which appear to have been available in substantial amounts. As capital requirements increased, entrepreneurs made greater use of some devices to provide the necessary capital, but they made only limited use of joint-stock forms of organization. They made no major innovations which might have increased capital supplies.

Second, the labor supply was also adequate. Its relatively high cost was balanced by its relatively high productivity. No major innovations were instituted to improve labor productivity.

Third, supplies of necessary raw materials, such as coal and iron ore, were very good and innovations were introduced which took advantage of these supplies and which simultaneously increased productivity. Cotton was lacking originally, but it was later converted into a low-cost factor through no effort of the entrepreneurs.

Fourth, in 1750 Britain was technologically ahead of other societies. The early innovations introduced by entrepreneurs were developed upon this base of technological leadership and were often quite simple devices; this suggests that the entrepreneurial contribution in this regard was not as revolutionary as it might seem, although innovations did provide large increases in productivity.

British entrepreneurs introduced organizational innovations, such as the factory mode of production, in conjunction with these technological innovations. But they were able to model these innovations after existent examples of large-scale organization, which makes their actions appear less revolutionary. In addition, we have seen how very slowly they adopted the practice of using managers to run these organizations.

Lastly, we have described the potential market, both domestic and foreign, available to British entrepreneurs as excellent. They did make the appropriate responses to this situation—concentration on mass-produced consumer goods for both markets and a rapid expansion of foreign trade. But here they were aided by the extensiveness of the British colonial system, an excellent merchant marine, and their position of chronological priority.

Therefore, it appears that the British entrepreneurs were least innovative in the areas in which the economic opportunity conditions for entrepreneurship were least favorable, namely capital and labor supplies. In areas where these conditions were more favorable—markets and materials—they were more innovative. They were most innovative technologically, and they relied on technological innovations to compensate for the limitations in other areas. Their technologies were laborsaving and the costs of these technologies were financed out of the profits resulting from the increased productivity which they provided. Had they been more innovative in respect to the factors of capital and labor, they might conceivably have achieved a higher rate of industrial growth and increased the economic gap between their society and other societies even more rapidly.

We also feel that the degree of risk British entrepreneurs faced was relatively low because of the favorableness of these opportunity conditions. The greatest risks they confronted were associated with their introduction of a number of absolute innovations. However, we believe the risks these innovations involved were modified by the favorableness of other opportunity conditions, such as the size of the potential market. And we have seen that those who adopted these innovations were often rewarded handsomely.

The costs of initiating either expansions or innovations did increase during the course of the British industrial transition, thereby increasing the risks associated with making these changes. But we believe that improvement of opportunity conditions resulting from the economic growth that had occurred probably cancelled out the effects of these increased costs on the degree of risk.

Thus we regard British entrepreneurship as having limited independent causal significance for British industrial growth and as emerging primarily in response to favorable and improving economic opportunity conditions. This responsiveness to these conditions can be shown more concretely by the differential rates of diffusion of various technological innovations. More costly and less improved innovations, such as the power loom and the steam engine, diffused less rapidly than did less expensive and less problematic innovations like the spinning jenny and the water frame.

NONECONOMIC FACTORS PROMOTING THE EMERGENCE OF ENTREPRENEURSHIP

What then can we say about the significance of the noneconomic factors which supposedly cause entrepreneurship to emerge? If British entrepreneurship was not causally significant for British industrial growth, and if they were both responses to generally favorable economic opportunity conditions, were these noneconomic factors of no significance? Before attempting to answer this question, we must analyze these noneconomic factors, as well as the role of the state.

First, the degree of sociocultural legitimacy accorded the entrepreneurial role in Britain is debatable. On the one hand, some have stressed the favorable attitudes toward the role. It has been argued that neither the middle class nor the aristocracy, the latter particularly in comparison with the French aristocracy, despised manual labor (Kindleberger, 1964; Landes, 1969). It has also been suggested that the entrepreneurial activities of some members of the nobility and the gentry gave such activities legitimacy (Landes, 1969).

On the other hand, Bendix (1956) has vigorously emphasized the aristocracy's opposition to entrepreneurship. According to him, they regarded the entrepreneur's faith in technological progress with "undisguised contempt" and looked down upon traders concerned with material things. Their opposition was largely due to the threat they sensed this potentially socially mobile group of actors represented. But in Bendix's opinion, their opposition had unexpected consequences, motivating entrepreneurs to strive more diligently to overcome it. Eventually the entrepreneurs' efforts paid off in gains in political power, including the right to vote in 1832. So it appears that the aristocracy granted entrepreneurship less legitimacy than did other groups in British society, but that it was not able to deter it.

The existence of a relatively high degree of social mobility in Britain is somewhat clearer. The barriers to mobility were less and the definitions of status looser than elsewhere in Europe, as shown by the indistinctness of the nobility. The influence of tradition was also weaker and individuals engaged in agriculture and manufacturing simultaneously, implying a high degree of social flexibility. The relatively high degree of social mobility was especially significant for the market because it promoted emulation and thereby standardization which was conducive to mass production (Landes, 1965b, 1969).

Guilds and corporations were relatively weak in Britain, the upper middle class more accessible, and many of the entrepreneurs were actually upwardly mobile, thus creating a strong belief in the *possibility* of upward mobility which was a force encouraging others to enter the entrepreneurial role (Hoselitz, 1955a; Kindleberger, 1964). Even though the aristocracy was opposed to entrepreneurship, some of them were entrepreneurs themselves. Nonaristocratic entrepreneurs, with the exception of those who were Dissenters, were increasingly able to merge with the aristocracy. As the scale of production increased, and as more entrepreneurs inherited enterprises, the mobility provided by entrepreneurship no doubt declined. It appears, however, that early in the period 1750–1820 mobility via entrepreneurship was increasing.

Although there was aristocratic opposition to entrepreneurship, entrepreneurs cannot be considered as coming predominantly from marginal positions. The merchants, either from the putting-out system or from regular trade, and the artisans who comprised the majority of entrepreneurs were not far removed from the mainstream of British society. The Dissenters, significant in England but not in Scotland, can certainly be considered a marginal group. But the important question is whether their entrepreneurship was due mainly to their marginality or to their religious ideology. Were they more marginal or more religious in England than they were in Scotland? If Hagen's (1962) claim that the Scots were more Calvinist than the English is correct, then "marginality" appears to be the answer to that question.

A type of marginality not previously discussed is geographical. It has been pointed out that the earliest British innovations occurred primarily in areas other than those where industry was already established. This fact has been attributed to the lack of tradition, guilds, and craft groups in those areas (Hoselitz, 1955a). This then may be the aspect of marginality most conducive to entrepreneurship. Freedom is necessary for innovation, and marginal locations, whether social or geographic, are more likely to offer that condition.[20] Thus the distinctive characteristic of the Dissenters may have been their freedom from restrictions, exemplified in both their religious and economic behavior.

---

[20]Landes (1965b) has emphasized the importance of freedom for light industries, such as textiles. We have seen that many of the first innovations in Britain occurred in textiles.

Is there any evidence regarding the Dissenters' religious beliefs which would suggest that their ideology, rather than their marginality, promoted their entrepreneurship? The only evidence we have, other than Hagen's assertion, is not conclusive, but it does not support an argument that religion had an important influence. Both the Nonconformist and Scottish entrepreneurs have been singled out for having been relatively well educated.[21] And both Scots and Nonconformists in England have been shown to be overrepresented among British entrepreneurs. Therefore, if the Scottish education system was better than the English, and if Nonconformists were generally better educated than Anglicans, then the overrepresentation of Nonconformists in England might be linked to their greater *relative* education, compared to that of Anglicans, and their not being overrepresented in Scotland to the approximate parity between their education and that of Scots who were not Nonconformists! By this logic education, and not religion, was the significant factor promoting entrepreneurship. Support for this interpretation is provided by those who emphasize the significance of the education provided by the Dissenting academies for the entrepreneurs of this period (Hartwell, 1971; Musson and Robinson, 1969).

Another characteristic promoting the entrepreneurship of the Dissenters may have been their high degree of social integration as a group (Landes, 1969). As for the degree of integration in British society as a whole, we suspect that it was relatively great because of the fairly high population density and the quite good systems of transportation and communication existing at the time. But, the inability of the government to be a strong directing force at this time (Moore, 1966) suggests that the mixture of flexibility and stability most conducive to entrepreneurship may have been present in British society.

Even though we have noted the presence of factions opposed to entrepreneurship in Great Britain, it appears that entrepreneurial security was quite high. For example, British entrepreneurs have been described as less fearful than those on the Continent (Landes, 1969). A major reason for their security was the legal support given to private property, which was greater in Britain than on the Continent (Hartwell, 1971). A second reason was the correlative lack of government interference. And a third reason was the relative immunity of British society to extensive internal or external conflict during this period.

Thus British society appears to have been relatively supportive of entrepreneurship during the period 1950–1820, more supportive than was the French social environment (Hoselitz, 1955a; Musson & Robinson, 1969). The major obstacle, the opposition of the aristocracy, was not sufficiently strong to stop it and may actually have stimulated it.

Some characteristics of British entrepreneurship support this assertion of sociocultural support for entrepreneurship. That entrepreneurs were not significantly drawn from marginal sources verifies our prediction for situations in

---

[21]It has also been suggested that the Scottish educational system was more accessible than the English (Gould, 1972).

which the legitimacy of entrepreneurship is relatively high and social mobility extensive. Entrepreneurs from the Dissenting religious groups are the major exception to this generalization, but we have indicated the complexity involved in explaining their emergence and raised the possibility that their entrepreneurship was due to their high level of education. In addition, the broad representation of social classes and occupations among British entrepreneurs is indicative of entrepreneurship of the mainstream rather than the outsider type.

We indicated earlier that it would be difficult to reach definite conclusions about the impact of psychological factors on entrepreneurship in the historical periods we have studied. The British case is important, however, because it has been used as evidence for two major arguments regarding the influence of these factors. So our analysis of these factors is more extensive for Britain than for the other societies we analyze.

McClelland (1961) has argued that a general rise in need-achievement imagery in British literature between 1700 and 1800 preceded an increase in the economic growth rate by thirty to fifty years and that this rise in need-achievement therefore accounted for the increased growth rate. He also argues that the increase in need-achievement was most pronounced among Nonconformists. Flinn (1967) has provided partial support for McClelland's claim by noting that the Congregationalists of the period, who were the most ardent Nonconformists, had child-rearing patterns which, according to McClelland's theory, are especially likely to produce high levels of need-achievement. But he also asserts that the increase in need-achievement occurred *simultaneously* with the increased rate of economic growth.

A major criticism of McClelland has been that he has failed to use the growth of output as a measure of economic growth but has relied instead upon indicators such as increases in coal imports or electric consumption. When we relate his description of increases in need-achievement imagery to our data regarding increases in the industrial growth rate the results are inconclusive. He (1961, p. 135) shows a steady increase in need-achievement imagery from the period 1676–1725 to the period 1776–1830. We noted earlier that the industrial growth rate increased after 1780, declined somewhat after 1792, and then increased again after 1818. So it did not follow the steady upward trend characterizing need-achievement imagery, which suggests that his case is overstated.

Hagen's (1962) argument concerning psychological factors is more encompassing than McClelland's. He holds that a withdrawal of status respect from the lesser gentry and the common folk in the period 1087–1422 ultimately culminated in the entrepreneurship of the Dissenters in the eighteenth century, after the Peasants' Revolt of the fourteenth century and the Civil War failed to right this wrong. Calvinism provided a refuge for alienated groups after 1422 and thus it and the withdrawal of status respect combined to yield Nonconformist entrepreneurship. But Hagen confuses the issue by arguing that the higher elites also experienced the withdrawal of status respect, even earlier than the lower elites, and hence became innovators earlier. We find Bendix's (1956) argument regarding the desire of the rising entrepreneurs to achieve *status recognition* to be more persuasive than Hagen's emphasis on a process which took seven centuries to produce entrepreneurship. Although the opposition of the aristocracy might be dated all the way back to 1100, as Hagen does, it is probable that the immediate opposition of the aristocracy after 1750 meant more and was more oppressive to contemporary entrepreneurs, and hence was a more important motivating force.

There has also been substantial disagreement concerning the extent to which the British common people, and entrepreneurs drawn from them, were motivated by monetary incentives. The people have been described as being particularly sensitive and responsive to such incentives (Landes, 1969), and the utilitarian orientation of British entrepreneurs has been contrasted with the status orientation of entrepreneurs in France (Rothman, 1956). But the importance of noneconomic motives—conspicuous consumption, the maintenance of "position," and hospitality—to British entrepreneurs has also been proposed (Gough, 1969). And several have described the frugal, ascetic life of many early entrepreneurs and their lack of interest in adopting the aristocratic lifestyle (Ashton, 1948; Gould, 1972; Moore, 1966). In all likelihood economic and noneconomic motives were both operative for entrepreneurs, but their responsiveness to economic opportunity conditions suggests the primacy of economic motives for them.

We do not perceive the British entrepreneurs as extreme risk-takers because we do not believe the degree of risk associated with entrepreneurial behavior was particularly high. In fact the British situation may have provided the situations of *moderate* risk proposed as most desirable for individuals with high need-achievement. The entrepreneurs' apparent ability to perceive economic conditions as *opportunities* very well may have been a more important psychological factor than their willingness to take risks. They have been credited with ability to foresee potential profitability (Hartwell, 1971), with having a sense of market opportunities (Wilson, 1955), and with an acute consciousness of the competitive environment in which they operated (Pollard, 1965).[22] They probably would have been less likely to take advantage of the favorable opportunity conditions if they had not had these characteristics.

THE INFLUENCE OF THE STATE

The overt activity of the state, either in promoting or restricting industrial entrepreneurship, was less in Britain that in any of the other countries we are considering with the possible exception of the United States. This is attributable to one or more of several factors—the historical priority of the British experi-

---

[22]Landes (1969) claims that they were more oriented to marketing than to production, a characteristic which may have facilitated the market innovations discussed.

ence, the government's lack of power to influence entrepreneurs' actions, the opposition of the aristocracy, and the fact that industrial growth was proceeding without government intervention (Henderson, 1958; Moore, 1966).

When the state did act to influence opportunity conditions for entrepreneurship its influence was mixed. It possibly limited the mobilization of capital by restricting the formation of corporations under the Bubble Act, and it also restricted development of the banking system (Cameron, 1967a). But it also occasionally loaned money to entrepreneurs, and it did not tax them, except during the Napoleonic Wars. In addition, it promoted technological innovation through financial incentives to inventors; it perhaps increased the labor supply through its support of the enclosure movement (but also limited labor mobility by settlement laws and the system of parish relief), and it helped entrepreneurs in the market through its regulation of trade. Little tariff protection was provided, but little foreign competition threatened British entrepreneurs at the time. Possibly its greatest contribution was the maintenance of an extensive colonial system which provided entrepreneurs with markets and sources of raw materials and capital.

A characteristic of British entrepreneurs which we have not mentioned, their political mobilization through the formation of trade associations, is also indirectly indicative of the state's support of entrepreneurship. Although entrepreneurs were not as politically active before 1820 as they were to become after that date, their activities suggest that they were relatively integrated into British society and that they enjoyed a relatively high degree of security. It is doubtful that they would have felt free to form such organizations if they had been fearful of hostile actions by the government.

Another important factor was the government's provision of relative freedom for the pursuit of the entrepreneurial role and of simultaneous security from the loss of property through the legal protection of property and patent rights. Eventually also it yielded political power to the rising entrepreneurial class, thereby avoiding political conflict which would have created insecurity.[23] Therefore its overall role, or lack of a definite role, appears to have been generally supportive of entrepreneurship.

RELATIVE SIGNIFICANCE OF ECONOMIC AND NONECONOMIC FACTORS

We have suggested that the emergence of British entrepreneurship can be explained largely as a consequence of the favorable economic opportunity conditions existing after 1750. According to our earlier argument, this implies that the sociocultural and psychological characteristics present in British society were

---

[23]It has been criticized for its failure to provide free elementary education until late in the nineteenth century, but it is questionable whether that substantially impaired British entrepreneurship.

inconsequential for the emergence of entrepreneurship. But we have also described a variety of ways in which these factors, as well as the state, were supportive of entrepreneurship.

This combination of favorable economic *and* noneconomic conditions leads us to revise our earlier argument. It appears more accurate to say that, if these noneconomic conditions and the state had been less favorable to entrepreneurship, it is probable that British entrepreneurship would not have emerged to the degree that it did. In that case, it would have had *negative* causal significance, given the favorableness of the economic opportunity conditions. But neither did the noneconomic factors and the state promote a *disproportionate* emergence of entrepreneurship which would have led us to infer *positive* causal significance for British entrepreneurship. Instead the noneconomic factors and the state seemingly promoted, or allowed, the emergence of entrepreneurship *in proportion to* the favorableness of the economic opportunity conditions.

Therefore we believe that a variety of noneconomic factors encouraged the emergence of entrepreneurship in Great Britain. If the economic opportunity conditions for entrepreneurship had been less favorable, then the favorableness of these factors might have been sufficient to promote entrepreneurship to the degree that it would have had positive causal significance. Or if these factors had been unfavorable, then entrepreneurs might have failed to come forth, as we have speculated. But in the British case neither the economic nor the noneconomic conditions for entrepreneurship were unfavorable and entrepreneurship emerged proportionately.

5

France

British entrepreneurs often are hailed as examples par excellence of the Schumpeterian entrepreneur. Entrepreneurs in France, Britain's chief national rival of the eighteenth and nineteenth centuries, are often presented as examples of entrepreneurial failure. We shall assess the accuracy of that accusation during the period from 1790 to 1910. It is clear that France fell behind Great Britain industrially after 1750, and by World War I it had also been surpassed by Germany and the United States. But the responsibility of French entrepreneurship for this failure to keep pace is less obvious. It has been suggested recently that the issue of the quality of French entrepreneurship is far from resolved and that its record is not as bad as often depicted, looking worse than it actually was because of its comparison with British entrepreneurship (Holmes, 1972).[1]

OPPORTUNITY CONDITIONS FOR FRENCH ENTREPRENEURSHIP

Just how favorable were the opportunity conditions for entrepreneurship in France from the French Revolution to 1910? Were they comparable to those in Great Britain, or were they markedly less favorable? We turn to this issue first, making comparisons with our discussion of Britain where appropriate.

We have noted that British entrepreneurs had the advantage of economic

[1]Holmes (1972) has also suggested that the French experience bears strong resemblance to the situations of many currently industrializing societies. We shall not consider that possibility, but the reader may wish to do so.

and technological leadership in 1750. This represented a reversal of Britain's earlier position of economic disadvantage relative to France.[2] But the relative levels of economic development in France and Britain in 1790 are unclear. The disadvantageous French position at that time has been emphasized by some (Gould, 1972; Moore, 1966; Wallerstein, 1974). Hoselitz (1955b, p. 386), for example, estimates that average income in France in 1800 was 200 francs compared to Britain's average of 375 francs in 1798–99. Gerschenkron (1955), however, claims that Britain had only about a 10 percent lead in per capita income, and it also has been claimed that France was the leading industrial country in the world at the beginning of the nineteenth century (Holmes, 1972). The latter claim must be balanced by noting that the French population was more than twice as large as the British, so that Britain no doubt led in industrial production on a per capita basis.

In addition, the economic effects of the Revolution of 1789 probably increased the French disadvantage. Kemp (1971, p. 95) has described these as follows:

> After an initial stimulus, the Revolution had a baneful effect on some important sectors of industry owing to lack of raw materials, loss of markets and labor difficulties . . . outside a few fields, the conditions prevailing in the decade after 1789 were hardly propitious for healthy industrial growth.

Thus we find the claim of French economic inferiority to Britain more persuasive. But France was undoubtedly the most economically advanced country on the Continent, except perhaps for Holland.

Given France's relatively lower level of economic development, it is not surprising that there was a lack of capital for industrial entrepreneurship until about 1850, or possibly until after the Revolution of 1830 (Dunham, 1955).[3] Gerschenkron (1955) claims that the lack of capital was more serious than the lack of entrepreneurial talent. This lack, which primarily involved working capital at the outset as it did in Britain, was due to several factors, each of which was probably more important than the level of per capita income.

First, the propensity of French investors to provide capital for industrial activities was limited. Or to say it another way, the competition for capital from nonindustrial areas was high. Investors poured money into land, government securities, and trade in commodities and currency (Kemp, 1971). The Revolution did not substantially diminish this characteristically aristocratic *rentier* orientation. There was also competition for capital from construction of infrastructure, such as transportation, which was occurring at the same time as the growth of manufacturing. "While in Britain the initial stages in the development of the iron

---

[2] Recently the change in economic positions of the two countries has been dated from about 1575, during England's "first" Industrial Revolution (Wallerstein, 1974).

[3] Landes (1969) says the lack of capital was a more serious problem in France than it was in Britain, but in the last chapter we noted that in another context he claimed the problem was more serious in Britain than it was on the Continent.

and cotton industries had preceded the railroad boom, in France the building up of the entire complex of basic industries . . . and the provision of more modern transportation facilities had to be accomplished simultaneously.'' (Hoselitz, 1955a, p. 306).

A second factor limiting capital supplies was the sizeable flow of investment capital to foreign countries, particularly after 1850.[4] Much of this foreign investment was in banking, railroad construction, and government bonds. Germany and Russia were the major recipients before the 1880s; after that date investments were made in Latin America, eastern Europe, Asia, and colonies such as Algeria. Some critics have argued that French industry was starved of capital in the process. But it also can be argued that the foreign investment benefitted domestic entrepreneurs by increasing foreign demand for French goods (Cameron, 1961). The outflow of capital was balanced somewhat by an inflow of foreign capital, thus creating the paradox of French capital being used to develop Russia at the same time that Belgian capital was promoting French economic development (Palmade, 1972). This pattern represents the beginning of a trend that we shall see being more pronounced in later cases of industrialization. A different kind of foreign capital outflow, which apparently did not affect French industry seriously, was the reparation of five billion francs France was forced to pay Germany in 1871 after the disastrous (for the French) Franco-Prussian War.

Third, France lacked facilities for mobilizing capital. Until about 1830 restrictions on corporate organization were more severe than they were in Britain. The principle of limited liability was not legalized until 1867, when the *société à responsabilité limité* was granted government approval (Landes, 1965b, p. 426). The French banking system was particularly poor, mainly because of the policies of the Bank of France founded in 1800. The banking system maintained a five times greater reserve of gold and silver than did the English system, and it has been estimated that the French annual growth rate could have been increased by 50 to 100 percent if it had operated with the same fractional reserves as did the British banking system (Cameron, 1967b).[5] French people's hesitance to use the banks has been blamed for the bank's failure (Dunham, 1955), but the public very likely had good reason to be hesitant.

French bankers became more involved in industrial promotion, primarily in

---

[4]The French foreign portfolio increased from 2 billion to 15 billion francs between 1850 and 1880 (Palmade, 1972, p. 175), and it is estimated that one-third to one-half of French savings was invested in foreign countries between 1880 and 1914 (Kemp, 1971, p. 269).

[5]Cameron (1967b, pp. 110, 121) has provided the most stinging indictment of that institution. According to him:

> France had fewer bank assets per inhabitant in the mid-nineteenth century than England or Scotland had had in 1770 and in 1870 had not reached the position that they had held before the beginning of the nineteenth century. . . . until 1848 the average value of bills discounted [by the Bank of France] never fell below 1,000 francs, and that at a time when per capita annual income was between 200 and 300 francs.

textiles and railroads, after 1830, and especially after 1850. The legalization of joint-stock banks in 1848 also increased the supply of capital from this source. The establishment of the *Crédit Mobilier* by the Saint-Simonian Pereires in 1852 further enlarged the supply of investment capital.[6] Although it was essentially an industrial development bank, the *Crédit Mobilier* also took on the entrepreneurial role, primarily in public works rather than in manufacturing. It did not last long, meeting its demise in 1867 because of the hostility it had aroused among more traditional bankers, but during the period 1850–70 it did increase capital supplies.[7]

Fourth, the problem of a limited capital supply became severe because capital requirements had increased and continued to increase, especially in metallury. These requirements were greater than they had been in Britain at the start of its industrial transition (Cameron, 1967b).[8] Consequently, "the size of the initial lump of investment now required was itself an obstacle to change" (Landes, 1969, p. 147). By the 1870s and 1880s the initial capital requirements for a modern iron and steel works amounted to 250,000 pounds, and the most costly new cotton mills required an investment of between 75,000 and 100,000 pounds (Landes, 1965b, p. 452n). This contrasts with Chapman's (1972, p. 26) estimate of an initial cost of 80,000 pounds for cotton mills in England in the 1830s and Crouzet's (1972, p. 38) estimate of the value of English ironworks at between 12,000 and 30,000 pounds around 1800, and indicates a substantially greater increase in capital requirements in metallurgy than in textiles.

Yet, new opportunities for entrepreneurship which did not require substantial capital became available in the 1880s with the introduction of the automobile. It was possible to begin on a small scale both in automobile production and the manufacture of automobile components. Overall, though, the supply of capital appears to have been less adequate in France than it was in Great Britain some years earlier.

Habakkuk (1968) claims that the inadequacies of the French labor force were a more serious problem than the lack of capital. This was partly due to the lower rate of natural increase in France than in other European countries, but the resultant limited labor supply was further restricted by the very low labor mobility. Workers remained close to the land, moving into industry in prosperous times and back into agriculture in depressed periods. France, unlike Britain, did not experience an enclosure movement of any significance (except a small one in the Normandy region); hence the peasantry remained strong. The close ties of the labor force to agriculture did result in a willingness to accept low wages so that

[6]This organization, which Kemp (1971, p. 166) describes as "an investment bank, floated as a joint stock company, which was to raise additional capital both by accepting deposits and by selling stock" was based on the Belgian *Société Générale* which had been established in 1822.

[7]Kemp (1971) warns against bestowing too much credit upon it, at least in manufacturing.

[8]Capital investment amounted to six to eight months' wages per member of the industrial force in France after 1800 compared to the British average of four months' wages after 1750 (Gould, 1972).

labor was a relatively low-cost factor. But this characteristic, which should have constituted a favorable opportunity condition, actually strengthened the putting-out system. Dunham (1955, p. 425) says that it gave the putting-out system a strength "that made it almost irresistible" and singles it out as probably the most important reason for the slowness of French industrial growth.[9]

Furthermore, labor productivity was low, so that French entrepreneurs were forced to use relatively more labor than were the English, thereby probably negating any cost advantages they may have had. The low productivity was partly attributable to the workers' peasant origins and lack of training, but the small scale of many industrial enterprises discouraged expenditures on labor training and also kept productivity low. The French system of technical education has been credited with providing high-quality skilled manpower (Holmes, 1972), however, so there probably was diversity in labor productivity. This diversity was likely promoted by, or at least correlated with, a dualistic industrial development which we describe later.

One school of thought blames the sluggishness of French industrial growth on a lack of raw materials, particularly coal suitable for coking. The high cost of coal which resulted slowed the diffusion of steam power and metallurgical innovation. French iron ore endowments were more satisfactory, although the ore was scattered and quite phosphoric so that it could not be used effectively. Wool and cotton also were lacking, but only the lack of the former distinguished France from Britain.[10] Apparently the only material advantage France had over Britain was in the supply of water for power.[11]

The potential of the French market also has been subject to criticism. The domestic market for consumer goods was quite limited because of the relatively low level of per capita income and the predominately rural character of the population.[12] The domestic demand for producer goods also was limited, which hampered the machine industry. The beginning of railroad construction in the 1830s, and its increase in the 1840s, partially alleviated this problem, but it is questionable whether it had any significant impact until after 1850 because of its slow growth (Marczewski, 1963).

The domestic market expanded very slowly because of the low rate of

---

[9]Similarly Marczewski (1963) claims that the French agricultural structure was the major cause of the inferiority of the French performance relative to England's.

[10]Moore (1966) makes an interesting observation on the inability of viniculture, which was prominent in France, to support a textile industry in the way that sheep-raising, characteristic of Britain, could.

[11]Hoselitz (1955a) argues that French raw material supplies were comparable to those of the British, but he seems to have overlooked the differential in coal resources which we think was sufficiently great to put France in a less favorable raw material position.

[12]As of 1850 only one-fourth of the French population was urban compared to one-half of the English population (Schapiro, 1946, p. 83).

population growth—only 4 percent between 1869 and 1939 (Kemp, 1971).[13] In this respect therefore France differed markedly from Britain. In addition the period from about 1815 to 1851 was characterized by an economic depression which further stifled the French market (Palmade, 1972). The heterogeneous composition of the domestic market, resulting from the great variance in standards of living, has been considered a disadvantage, too. The gap between rich and poor appears to have been greater in France than it was in Britain. Coupled with the antipathy of French consumers to standardized, mass-produced goods, it made the option of producing inexpensive goods in large volume, the English response, less viable for the French (Youngson, 1961).

It might appear that the foreign market had greater potential than the domestic market because France was the most industrially advanced country on the Continent. Only Belgium provided a modicum of competition. But demand in this market was greatest for the inexpensive goods which Britain was able to offer and not for the high-priced luxury goods which the French were accustomed to producing.[14] The potential of this market was further limited around 1800 by the Napoleonic Wars and government policies which backfired. The Continental System, imposed by Napoleon in 1806 to prevent British goods from entering European ports, resulted instead in the British blockading of French ports and the restriction of French trade. The far superior British merchant marine, plus the lack of good French ports, placed French entrepreneurs at an additional disadvantage in this endeavor, and in foreign trade in general. Furthermore, the French colonial system was much less extensive than the British and consequently a less important component of the French market. The Continental System disrupted the colonial trade; hence this segment was even less significant after 1815. Thus, the French market was far less favorable for entrepreneurship than was the British market. But, as we shall soon see, the French entrepreneurs compounded this disadvantage by their response to it.

To all outward appearances, a supply of highly productive technologies was the one factor on which the French had an advantage over the British. By 1790 a number of technologies were available from Britain which the British entrepreneurs had had to produce for themselves. This stock of productive techniques swelled after that date, but its flow to France was restricted severely around 1800 by the Napoleonic Wars and the British blockade.[15] The British prohibition of the emigration of artisans, which was in effect until 1825, and of

[13]Kemp says (1971, p. 281), in regard to this low rate of growth, "France . . . conserved a demographic pattern unlike that of practically every other country in the course of industrialization, a pattern which grew out of the practices and preferences of a peasant and petty bourgeois society."

[14]Wallerstein (1974) suggests the British textile industry had a competitive advantage over the French as early as 1600.

[15]Dunham (1955) calls this isolation from England the greatest obstacle that France had to overcome.

the export of textile machinery, which lasted until 1842, were less restrictive. These prohibitions were circumvented widely and many machines were smuggled to France to be copied by machine-makers there with the apparent willing participation of numerous British entrepreneurs.

Two major innovations in metallurgy—the Bessemer and Siemens-Martin processes for making steel—became available after 1850, followed in the 1870s by the Gilchrist-Thomas process which utilized phosphoric ores. These innovations, particularly the last, improved opportunity conditions in metallurgy. In addition, a number of chemical inventions became available for industrial application—the fuchsine process in dyeing, the Sainte-Clare Deville process for making aluminum by electrolysis, and the discovery of uses for coal byproducts. So the availability of technological innovations increased during the nineteenth century.

The suitability of the available British innovations has been questioned, however. From the beginning the British textile innovations were not immediately applicable for a number of reasons, according to Henderson (1965). The Bessemer and Siemens-Martin processes also were less applicable in France than they had been in Britain because of the greater phosphoric content of French ores, so opportunity conditions in metallurgy did not improve greatly until the appearance of the Gilchrist-Thomas process. The disruption of the flow of innovations around 1800 also is believed to have created a technological gap between Britain and France, so that French entrepreneurs were unable to utilize the latest British innovations after 1815. This resulted from the large capital requirements of these innovations and the fact that their marginal advantage over less advanced technologies was smaller in France (Landes, 1969). The smaller marginal advantage in metallurgy was partly due to the relatively high cost of coal in France. Thus lower-cost traditional methods of production, such as the use of charcoal to manufacture iron, continued to expand.[16]

The likelihood of these technological innovations being developed in France, rather than borrowed from abroad, depended partly upon French scientific knowledge, and its relevance for French industry has been questioned repeatedly. It has been argued that French scientists often did not transform abstract scientific principles into practical technological innovations although they surpassed scientists in other countries in the discovery of these principles (Kindleberger, 1964; Palmade, 1972).[17] The contrast with other countries is exemplified by the development of the steam engine, which resulted from theoretical speculation rather than practical experimentation in France (Landes, 1969). Cameron (1961, p. 44), though, argues that "the French had talent for synthesizing science and

[16]The geographical dispersion of French industry, especially textiles, may also have hindered the diffusion of many innovations.

[17]The French development of scientific knowledge was epitomized by the *École Polytechnique* which Klemm (1964, p. 317) has called "the first great seeding ground of a technology based strictly on science."

applying it to practical ends.'' Further, many French discoveries in chemistry were applied to industry in foreign countries, which indicates that French science was more suitable for industry than has been claimed.

Therefore, opportunity conditions for French entrepreneurship appear to have been less favorable after 1790 than British opportunity conditions were after 1750, but conditions did improve in France from about 1850 on. Technology, of which an ample supply was available from Britain, was the one area in which the French possessed a relative advantage, even though there were impediments to diffusion between the countries. On all other factors—capital, labor, raw materials, and the market—the French were at a relative disadvantage.[18] The unfavorableness of opportunity conditions also may be inferred from the outflow of capital described earlier, if we assume that capital gravitated toward places where opportunity conditions were more favorable. The *Crédit Mobilier,* for example, actually financed many foreign projects even though it was intended to develop *domestic* industry. This is only indirect evidence, of course; it may simply indicate a failure to perceive favorable opportunity conditions in France.

We have no direct evidence that *relative* opportunity conditions were less favorable for industrial entrepreneurship than for other roles. Landes (1949, p. 56) says that ''the best talents . . . almost invariably turned to the traditional honorific careers such as law, medicine, or government. This was true even of the children of businessmen.'' From this it might be inferred that opportunities were greater in these areas than in industry. Wealthy landowners sought to enter the nobility or purchased bureaucratic offices, rather than attempt industrial entrepreneurship. This, too, may be regarded as indirect evidence of unfavorable relative opportunity conditions. However, this group was not a significant source of industrial entrepreneurship in Britain either.

THE ROLE OF THE FRENCH GOVERNMENT

The roles of the British and French governments represent a major point of contrast between the two cases. Whereas the British government was one of the least involved in the societies we are considering, in the manipulation of opportunity conditions the French state was one of the most active. Hence we consider its role at this point in our discussion. Its actions improved unfavorable opportunity conditions in some cases, but in other cases it created barriers and made a bad situation worse. The pendular character of its involvement is especially important. It swung between actions improving opportunity conditions and policies which made them less favorable, and at times both kinds of influences can be discerned simultaneously. We shall follow the government's actions chronologically to show this general pattern.

[18]It has been suggested that the potential economic rewards from entrepreneurship were also substantially lower in France than in the United States (Holmes, 1972).

France inherited a long tradition of public entrepreneurship and state intervention in the economy in 1790. The *ancien régime* had been responsible for much of the industrialization, especially in metallurgy, that had taken place in the last half of the eighteenth century.[19] This pattern of government direction continued under Napoleon and perhaps increased as a result of his policy of political and economic centralization. He did create an orderly financial system and also provided subsidies to industrial entrepreneurs, particularly in silk (Henderson, 1968). But we also have observed the generally negative economic impact of his Continental System.

The government of the Restoration (1815–30) continued the subsidization of entrepreneurs, and the July Monarchy of Louis Philippe (1830–48) was distinguished by its concentration on social overhead—roads, canals, and railroads. But government stimulation of railroad construction was really rather lackadaisical, compared to the strong effort being made in Germany at the time, so it did not constitute the spur to industry or the support to trade that it could have. Government influence over entrepreneurs declined after 1830, but it never disappeared completely (Hoselitz, 1955a).

The tariff policies of these last two periods have received especially strong criticism, although their effects may have been exaggerated because of the relative availability of information concerning them (Dunham, 1955). Cameron (1961, p. 18) describes the French tariffs as "the most stringent system of . . . any major trading nation." As such, they had manifold negative effects. First, they promoted inefficiency by shielding entrepreneurs, especially in the iron industry, from foreign competition. Second, they *increased* the costs of both raw materials and finished products. The effect on raw material costs was greatest in textiles, particularly in cotton, where the entire supply of raw cotton had to be imported and was subject to duties. The costs of finished products were affected most in metallurgy where consumers had to buy inferior steel at artificially high prices. Third, they damaged an already poor foreign trade position by increasing costs and inviting reprisals from other countries.

The lowering of tariffs under the Second Republic significantly improved opportunity conditions (Gerschenkron, 1955; Kemp, 1971). The most important consequences were the elimination of less efficient enterprises and an increase in foreign trade. In 1892 the government returned to a policy of high tariffs, but its action was part of a general trend among nations at that time and hence was less damaging.

Under the Second Republic the state also legalized corporate organization and adopted a national development plan. It supported the establishment of the *Crédit Mobilier,* but it equivocated in its continued support of that organization

---

[19]Prior governmental actions, such as the revocation of the Edict of Nantes in 1685 which resulted in the migration of French Huguenots to other European countries, especially England, thereby depriving France of a significant entrepreneurial group, also had been directly inimical to entrepreneurship.

and let it succumb to the opposition of the Bank of France and private bankers. The involvement in the Franco-Prussian War was another action that had negative consequences. It resulted in the loss of Alsace-Lorraine, which had the most advanced segment of the textile industry and important iron-ore deposits, to Germany, plus the financial indemnity noted previously.

The contradictory nature of the French government's actions becomes clearer when we look at the specific determinants of economic opportunity conditions. On the one hand, it gave subsidies directly to entrepreneurs, but on the other hand, it raised costs for them with the tariff system, it severely restricted corporate forms of organization until the 1860s, and it rendered the banking system ineffective. Its policies encouraging agriculture at the expense of industry likely restricted labor supplies and productivity. The continued strength of the agricultural sector restricted labor mobility, and the unwillingness of labor to leave rural occupations reciprocally reinforced the continued strength of that sector.

The tariff system, by raising the costs of raw materials and products, also restricted the potential of the market. Other policies which reduced market potential included the inducements given to the production of luxury goods rather than to mass production and the failure to develop and utilize a colonial system comparable to the British one. The stimulation of the armaments industry and of railroad construction did not compensate for these errors, and the former constituted a drain on scarce supplies of capital and raw materials.

The state's actions were most supportive in regard to technology, the one factor we have regarded as more favorable in France than in Britain. There was some government interest in it even under the *ancien régime* and the state actively promoted the importation of both technology and entrepreneurs from Britain. This interest increased as British technological superiority became more evident. French entrepreneurs were encouraged to travel to England to obtain technological secrets. National expositions were held and prizes awarded to inventors. The state's role in this area continued until at least 1850, so it appears to be the brightest spot in an otherwise gloomy picture.

Many reasons have been offered for the equivocal character of the government's actions, which we will not discuss in depth. No doubt it was partly due to the continued strength of the aristocracy before 1850, although some of the poorer policies, such as high tariffs, were advocated by entrepreneurs as well. It also resulted partly from the weakening of the July Monarchy before 1848 (Gerschenkron, 1955). And the competition of the British surely must have been a major reason. The French, seeing their place in the sun eclipsed by the British, clearly were interested in reestablishing their preeminence in the world balance of power. But their eagerness to regain it, coupled with the unstable social situation after 1790, seems to have forced them into serious miscalculations. Thus they failed to improve the opportunity conditions for French industrial entrepreneurship.

CHARACTERISTICS OF FRENCH ENTREPRENEURSHIP

We have described some aspects of the French entrepreneurial response to opportunity conditions in our analysis of these conditions. In this section we look at this response in more detail.

Innovations

Whereas the chief claim to fame of British entrepreneurs was their development of a multitude of new technologies, the most noteworthy characteristic of the French was their *borrowing* of innovations. France can be considered the first of the *latecomers,* the societies that made industrial progress on the basis of innovations developed elsewhere (Palmade, 1972).[20] This pattern of borrowing developed soon after 1750. In the cotton industry for example, France "received the machines . . . from England, in the order in which they were invented and perfected . . ." (Dunham, 1955, p. 256). This was most common in Normandy, which was closest to England, but it also occurred in the eastern Alsatian region. Steam engines also had been introduced prior to 1790, and in metallurgy, the Le Creusot ironworks, which was to become one of the major French firms, had been established in 1782. The machine industry relied upon technologies and machines from both Britain and Belgium.

We have noted the disruption of the flow of innovations from Britain before 1815 and have seen that the French entrepreneurs often did not adopt the latest British techniques after that date. But a series of additional innovations, including the steam hammer and the compound steam engine, carried French industry forward in the 1840s. The 1870s and 1880s marked the adoption of the three metallurgical processes—Bessemer, Siemens-Martin, and Gilchrist-Thomas—mentioned earlier. The latter decade, a period which has been referred to as the *Second* Industrial Revolution (Landes, 1965b), saw the introduction of a number of innovations in power—the harnessing of electricity, the refinement of the internal combustion engine, and the development of the diesel engine. So, the pattern of borrowing, from Britain and later from other countries, such as Germany and the United States in the case of metallurgy (Kemp, 1971), continued throughout the nineteenth century.

This did not mean that the French failed to produce any innovations of their own. Entrepreneurs in the machine industry responded to the cut-off of British innovations under the Continental System by making technological improvements (Henderson, 1968). The Jacquard loom for weaving patterns on silk was a French production. The textile entrepreneurs are credited with leadership in

---

[20]Cameron (1961, pp. 106–07) summarizes the comparative significance of the British and French contributions thus: "Britain pioneered the introduction of new technology, but in acclimatizing that technology and in adjusting legal and financial institutions to its pace France pioneered no less."

112

dyeing, calico-printing, and bleaching, and with developing a mechanical wool comber before one was developed in England. The high cost of coal prompted improvements in the use of water wheels and in the fuel efficiency of steam engines, and Frenchmen played a part in developing the internal combustion engine. French metallurgists went to Britain to help the British with their steel industry. The chemical industry also made major contributions, and late in the 1800s the French were responsible for innovations in the development of the pneumatic tire and of synthetic fibers; in the production of automobiles, taxis, and trucks; and in some areas of the electrical products industry (Kemp, 1971; Palmade, 1972). Thus independent innovations were significant after 1850.

Diffusion of many of the technological innovations was relatively slow until after about 1850. The diffusion of steam power was much slower than it had been in Britain, primarily because of the high cost of coal.[21] In contrast to Britain also, the adoption of steam power was connected more closely with metallurgy and mining than with textiles, in which it did not really begin until after 1840. France did have more fixed steam engines than all the other Continental countries combined by 1840 (Landes, 1969, p. 448), and power machinery was competing with manual production in most industries. But water power was still dominant over steam at mid-century because of its relative cost advantage.

Textile innovations also diffused rather slowly, but there was much regional variation. Alsatian and northern entrepreneurs adopted the innovations more readily than did entrepreneurs in Normandy (Landes, 1969). Diffusion was more rapid in the woolen industry while the Continental System was in effect, but after that it was more rapid in cotton, and most rapid in cotton spinning as had been the case in Britain.[22]

The chemical industry's performance was particularly lackluster. In spite of its major scientific breakthroughs, such as the electrolysis of aluminum and the production of synthetic dyes, its entrepreneurs failed to adopt innovations rapidly, and the German chemical industry surpassed it very quickly (Kemp, 1971; Landes, 1965b; Palmade, 1972).

The diffusion of metallurgical innovations was very slow before 1850. Adoption of the Bessemer and Siemens-Martin processes in the 1870s was more rapid, and the Gilchrist-Thomas process was adopted very rapidly in the 1880s by entrepreneurs who leased the patent rights to it. So the rate of diffusion of technological innovations picked up speed after 1850 except in the chemical industry.

French entrepreneurship had several distinctive characteristics in regard to innovations. First, it was generally slow to adopt mass production methods.[23] This was especially true in the machine industry, which was very hesitant to

[21]By 1825 only 65 French firms were using steam power (Palmade, 1972, p. 42).

[22]The silk industry remained unmechanized well beyond 1850.

[23]Kemp (1971, pp. 286–87) cites this as "the principal defect of French industry," and says that these techniques were not utilized to any great extent before World War I.

move to standardization and the use of interchangeable parts compared to the British. Second, at least in textiles, the *better*-quality segments of an industry were first to mechanize (Landes, 1969). This, too, contrasts with the British pattern of earlier mechanization of the production of cheaper, lower-quality goods, and implies the greater significance of, and possibly the greater profitability of, the luxury sectors of industries in France. Third, innovations, particularly in chemicals, that were developed in France were put into widespread use in *other* countries. In the chemical industry this most likely indicates a failure on the part of French entrepreneurs, whereas it probably indicates the relatively less favorable opportunity conditions existing in France in the case of other industries.

So even though French entrepreneurs made substantial use of foreign technological innovations, they did so only relatively slowly until after 1850. And they adopted technological innovations slowly in some industries, such as the machine industry, until the end of our period of study.

The innovations of French entrepreneurs which were next in significance to the technological innovations they borrowed were financial, in response to the limited capital supplies we have described. The French appear to have outclassed the British in this area (Dunham, 1955). The major device they adopted was the *commenda* or *société en commandite,* a medieval form of organization that required only registration with a notary and allowed sleeping partners limited liability (Cameron, 1967b; Dunham, 1955).[24] The *commenda* avoided the severe legal restrictions against corporations and the difficulty of getting government approval for corporate organization. It was used first in transportation, insurance, and savings banks. In manufacturing it was used more widely in textiles than in metallurgy, and it became increasingly significant after about 1840.

Joint-stock investment banks provided additional capital also, but they were not as significant as they were to be in Germany, and they cannot be credited solely to *industrial* entrepreneurs. They were, however, used more extensively in France than in Belgium where they had originated. And there were cases of industrialists going into banking as had happened in Britain, too.

The transition to the factory system of production, the most significant organizational innovation in Britain, was relatively lacking in France. By contrast, the putting-out system appears to have remained much more prominent in France.[25] It remained particularly strong in the silk industry, although there also were cases of it in metallurgy in the early part of our period. French entrepreneurs also combined factory and domestic production under their aegis in a manner similar to the British practice of subcontracting in some instances.

The prevalence of other organizational innovations is unclear. The Saint-

---

[24]There were cases of sleeping partners in Britain but they did not have the protection of limited liability.

[25]At least it has received greater emphasis; we noted in the last chapter that in Britain domestic cotton workers still exceeded factory workers in 1835—eighty-five years after 1750.

Simonians who promoted the *Crédit Mobilier* also have been credited with developing techniques for managing large-scale organizations (Cameron, 1961). And it has been suggested that organizational innovations diffused more rapidly than technological ones before 1850 (Kemp, 1971). But the claim has also been made that the French lagged far behind the British in their use of the division of labor and specialization in manufacturing (Dunham, 1955; Henderson, 1968). It is probable that organizational innovations such as these, which are associated with mass-production techniques, were less necessary in France because of the limited development of mass production there.

The high cost of coal discouraged the use of coke and processes involving it before 1850.[26] But the French did use it in refining before they used it in smelting, which is the more logical technological sequence and which should have given them an advantage, whereas the British followed the less natural reverse ordering (Landes, 1969). Iron production using charcoal actually increased relative to production using coke for a short time after 1850, but charcoal use declined rapidly after 1857 when a period of economic depression set in. Another change that the French made, which, like the use of coke, we consider a material innovation, was the replacement of wooden machine parts with iron ones, a step ''which Englishmen often forgot they had to take'' (Dunham, 1955, p. 245).

The French entrepreneurs did manufacture new products, particularly producer goods. France and Belgium were the first countries on the Continent to make their own machines, and France was the first Continental country to produce its own steam engines (Landes, 1969).[27] Unlike the British, French machine manufacture was tied more closely to heavy industry than to textiles. The chemical industry also developed new products, including synthetic dyes and rayon, in the nineteenth century. The introduction of the automobile late in that century led to the establishment of an industry that was especially important in France. The full impact of these product innovations probably was not felt until after World War I, but they played a part in France's achievement of industrialization by that time.

But French entrepreneurs have gained greater notoriety for their continued concentration on the production of luxury goods than for their product innovations.[28] This concentration was especially pronounced in the silk industry, an industry which was nonexistent in Britain. The French silk industry was ''geared to changes in high fashion'' (Kemp, 1971, p. 116) and led the world in production until it was badly damaged by silkworm disease in the 1860s and lost its position to Japan.[29] The woolen industry was also a quality leader, particularly in

[26]It was first used at the Le Creusot ironworks in 1785, about three-quarters of a century after its first use in Britain (Palmade, 1972, p. 61).

[27]The first French locomotive was built in 1838, for example.

[28]Wallerstein (1974) dates this characteristic of French industry from about 1550.

[29]More than half of French exports in 1846 consisted of silk and wine (Schapiro, 1946, p. 84).

its production of worsteds. And the French automobile industry excelled in the production of quality goods.

France has been roundly criticized for not following Britain's example and switching to the mass production of inexpensive textiles. But the French strategy appears reasonable given British leadership in that type of production. According to Kemp (1971, p. 118),

> The emphasis on quality was not . . . irrational in the circumstances in which many French entrepreneurs found themselves. . . . They were . . . able to take advantage of rising incomes produced by industrialization elsewhere in Western Europe and North America at a time when they were ill-equipped to challenge the hold on the markets for cheaper and semi-finished goods possessed by their English rivals.

Yet the French might be faulted for not switching to the production of heavy producer goods earlier, the pattern we shall describe in the next chapter. Even though the British dominated the market for inexpensive textiles, there was potential for surpassing them in the production of iron, steel, and machinery, as the Germans were to show. Here, though, the French came up against their relative lack of coal and iron ore, so that alternative also was limited for them.

French entrepreneurs possibly could have done more than they did to overcome their poor market situation. Their failure to make innovations constituted one of their major errors. They have been accused of an inability, or unwillingness, to adapt to changing tastes and needs (Kemp, 1971) and criticized for despising the English large-scale production of cheap goods (Dunham, 1955). Their attitude toward foreign trade was also not very helpful.[30]

We found no evidence of any significant French labor innovations.[31] The continuation of the putting-out system and of the tendency of workers to alternate between agriculture and industry suggests that innovations breaking these patterns were not forthcoming.

In sum, French entrepreneurs made significant financial innovations and borrowed numerous technological innovations. But their record for other types of innovation is less respectable. Their failure to initiate market innovations and their slowness to move to a factory system of production were their most serious shortcomings.

Degree of innovation. The failure to attain productivity gains equal to those of the British constitutes another significant characteristic of French en-

---

[30]They also were inclined to assume that a foreigner would, if really intelligent, prefer French goods because of their excellence and would seek them out. They seldom . . . tried to find out what foreigners wanted, and in nearly all cases they scorned to produce unusually cheap goods for foreign markets. . . .

As long as most French manufacturers regarded export simply as a means of disposing of a surplus that could not be sold at home, there was no hope of building a sound foundation for the development of French foreign trade. (Dunham, 1955, pp. 377, 383).

[31]Henderson (1968) does mention the introduction of welfare services by Alsatian textile entrepreneurs.

trepreneurship. This was partly due to their not adopting the latest techniques after 1815, but no doubt it was also partly due to the quality of the French labor force. French entrepreneurs achieved far less output per worker than did the British (Dunham, 1955). According to Landes (1965b, p. 443), "Other things equal . . . it would appear that English power looms ran faster and wasted less; while the English weaver minded more machines—generally twice as many as his French . . . counterpart." Furthermore there was a very large difference in efficiency between entrepreneurs. This resulted from the dual-sector nature of French industry which we shall describe shortly.

Expansions

Yet another criticism of French entrepreneurship is that it was nonexpansive. Entrepreneurs are believed to have been content to continue with small-scale operations once they had initiated production. This pattern was not uniform, however. For example, there was expansion in both metallurgy and textiles during the Revolution and some entrepreneurs expanded under the Continental System while others were eliminated (Henderson, 1968). The silk industry is regarded as particularly unexpansive. Small workshops with only four or five hand looms were the norm even after 1850 (Kemp, 1971). The cotton industry revealed the same regional diversity it showed in innovations, with the north and Alsace being most expansive and Normandy the least. In metallurgy the period before 1850 was characterized by some expansion along traditional lines, involving the use of charcoal. (Traditional methods of production tended to expand during good times in that industry particularly.) Expansion was more rapid after 1850, though.

The French machine industry expanded much more slowly than the German machine industry, and we have already noted the poor performance of the chemical industry, which went through an expansive phase after 1850 but quickly succumbed to the superior German chemical industry. The automobile industry expanded quite rapidly in the late nineteenth century, though, when opportunity conditions were more favorable, and it stimulated the initiation and expansion of supportive industries.

The failure of French entrepreneurs to expand has been blamed on their unwillingness to reinvest their profits in their enterprises and their preference for investments in land (Henderson, 1968; Landes, 1949, 1969; Palmade, 1972). But it has been claimed that there was substantial reinvestment in France, as there had been in Britain (Cameron, 1967b; Kemp, 1971). The greater capital requirements French entrepreneurs faced compared to the British, plus their reluctance to seek capital from banks, would have made a reliance on reinvested profits more necessary for them. Undoubtedly there was great variance on this characteristic.

Degree of expansion. So expansion did occur at certain times and in particular industries and regions.[32] But the unevenness of the expansion resulted in a two-sector industrial structure with some large expansive enterprises and a large number of very small nonexpansive firms (Cameron, 1967b). This heterogeneity was present in Britain also, but it appears to have been more extreme in France. For example, in 1851 there were 124,000 large industrialists employing about ten workers each on the average and 1.5 million small employers employing three million, or an average of two workers apiece (Palmade, 1972, p. 96). As of 1911 there were still only about 2.5 workers on the average for every French employer (Palmade, 1972, p. 206).

This variance in size apparently was present before 1790. Le Creusot, for example, involved an initial investment of 10 million francs (Palmade, 1972, p. 63), but in 1815 the majority of iron enterprises had ten workers or less (Dunham, 1955, p. 199). The cotton industry appears to have operated on a large scale from the beginning. For instance, a cotton firm in Lyon employed almost a thousand workers around 1790.[33] The majority of enterprises in other industries, however, were "traditional town workshops," small-scale and old-fashioned (Palmade, 1972, pp. 49, 50, 61).

The first major increase in the scale of initial expansions took place after either 1815 or 1830, except in metallurgy where it did not happen until after 1850. Before 1850 the average French metallurgical enterprise was smaller than contemporary English ones but larger than those in Germany (Landes, 1965b, p. 408). By the end of our period of study French metallurgical enterprises were smaller than the German ones (Kemp, 1971, p. 258).[34] The automobile industry also followed the pattern of small-scale initial expansion in its early phase, as did the industries that supplied it with components, but in that industry some firms grew rapidly.[35] So there was an increase in the scale of operations in all industries comparable to the one in Britain and continuing the trend begun there, though in some industries a large number of small firms continued to exist.

Entrepreneurial Identity

There were some noteworthy differences in the identity of French and British entrepreneurship. First, French entrepreneurship was slightly more collective because of the later historical period we are studying, although there were still

---

[32]According to Landes (1965b), Alsatian textile entrepreneurs began operations on a large scale around 1800, northern entrepreneurs began on a somewhat smaller scale, and Normandy entrepreneurs began on the smallest scale and remained that way.

[33]Around 1815 the Richard-Lenoir firm in cotton had 39 establishments and 15,000 workers (Palmade, 1972, p. 68).

[34]We noted earlier the capital requirements in metallurgy and textiles in the 1870s and 1880s—250,000 pounds for the former and 75;000–100,000 pounds for the latter.

[35]The firm of Peugeot, for example, produced its first car in 1889 and in 1913 it produced over 9,300 cars, 80,000 bicycles, and other products (Palmade, 1972, p. 205).

significant cases of individual French entrepreneurs in both textiles and metallurgy in the last half of the nineteenth century. Individuals often remained influential in the position of director-general in organizations formed on a corporate basis at that time. Furthermore, some innovations of this period, such as the automobile, opened up new opportunities for individuals like Renault and Citroën (Palmade, 1972). So individual entrepreneurship was never completely superseded.

French entrepreneurs have been accused of being overly individualistic and unwilling to cooperate with others (Dunham, 1955; Kindleberger, 1964), but they have also been criticized for disliking economic competition (Palmade, 1972), and hence for being overly cooperative with each other. The development of the *commenda* implies at least some degree of willingness to cooperate on their part. It and partnerships predominated by about 1850. After 1850 joint-stock forms of organization increased in importance except in textiles where partnerships remained most important. Heavy industry moved completely to joint-stock forms of organization after 1870. Some family firms also made this conversion although for them it was largely a "legal convenience" (Kemp, 1971, p. 250).

French entrepreneurship also had more of an outsider quality than did British entrepreneurship. A large number of Englishmen had migrated to France in the eighteenth century and established enterprises in the textile, iron, and machine industries. These included entrepreneurs and artisans who became entrepreneurs upon coming to France. Swiss entrepreneurs were significant in the first half of the nineteenth century, and Germans were important later in the century. So, although French entrepreneurs were primarily indigenous, migrants and foreigners were more important in France than they had been in Britain.[36]

Public entrepreneurship had been very significant in France before 1790, as we noted previously. Under the *ancien régime* the state had operated the *manufactures d'etat* and initiated the *manufactures royales* by granting monopoly rights, interest-free loans, and occasionally titles of nobility to private individuals. The direct entrepreneurial role of the state declined significantly after 1790, and particularly after 1815, and subsidization of private entrepreneurs became more important. But the ties between the public and private sectors remained closer than they were in Britain, even though the private sector was predominant in both societies.[37]

The tradition of state entrepreneurship and intervention in the economy is believed by some to have made French entrepreneurs too dependent upon state initiatives (Henderson, 1968; Hoselitz, 1955a). They did clamor for tariff protection from English competition, and they expected the government to bail them out of difficulties. But it also has been claimed that they were not dependent and that their initiative was not destroyed (Gerschenkron, 1955). Examples of

[36]One scholar claims, however, that many domestic French entrepreneurs were drawn from marginal groups (Holmes, 1972, p. 12).

[37]Graduates of the government's technical schools alternated between private business and government positions, for example (Hagen, 1968).

both dependent and independent behavior can be adduced to support either point of view on this issue.

The importance of family entrepreneurship in France has been much disputed. Proportionally it was perhaps no more significant than in other societies at a comparable stage of industrial development. It was especially important in the textile industry in which a number of family dynasties had been formed by 1850. Mulhousian and Alsatian entrepreneurs were prime examples of family entrepreneurship in this industry (Kemp, 1971; Palmade, 1972), and the Gillets and the Carnots, two of the major families in the industry, were responsible for the production of the first synthetic fibers (Palmade, 1972).

A similar pattern was evident in metallurgy. The typical ironworks between 1800 and 1850 was either family-run or a small partnership. Several important family dynasties—the Schneiders, de Wendels, and Talabots—were in existence after 1850, and "Many other steelmaking enterprises, even when they appeared to be new, were . . . linked with old family businesses" (Palmade, 1972, p. 156). In general there was much intermarriage among entrepreneurial families and "repeated interplay of inherited capital between families from dynasty to dynasty" (Palmade, 1972, pp. 165–66).

The family firm has been described as the "typical unit of production" in the early twentieth century (Henderson, 1968), which extends its tenure in France somewhat longer than in societies where corporate forms of organization had become dominant by that time. But Landes (1949, p. 56) has claimed that the inheritance of industrial ownership was really quite rare among smaller entrepreneurs in France as compared to England. This was partly due to the practice of partible inheritance which hindered bequeathing an enterprise intact to one's descendants.

A host of accusations have been made about the poor business practices of French family firms. These include the limitation of expansion, the avoidance of mergers and of the public sale of stock, the recruitment of managers from within the family, the reversion of profits to savings rather than investment, the maintenance of too high a level of liquidity, and "secrecy, suspicion, fear of banks, the government, and the consuming public" (Kindleberger, 1964, pp. 115–16). Other negative characteristics that have been mentioned include the avoidance of credit because of the fear of debt, pursuit of the highest possible profit, an excessive concern with security and a tendency to overestimate risk, unwillingness to cooperate with nonfamily members, and a concern for the status and consumptions needs of the family (Hoselitz, 1955a; Landes, 1965a, 1969).

The charges are harsh, and clearly there were examples of families that they do not fit—the Alsatian families and the families in metallurgy just mentioned. Perhaps the appropriate distinction to be made is between those families that became involved in the more progressive large-scale industrial sector and those who were in the less progressive small-scale sector, and the charges applied to the latter group. But it has also been suggested that the restricted nature of the

French market promoted some of the negative characteristics of these family firms (Landes, 1965a). So we believe it is necessary to consider them in light of the unfavorable opportunity conditions we described earlier.

The occupational origins of the French entrepreneurs were very similar to those of the British. In textiles they were predominantly from merchant backgrounds, either from the putting-out system or from general trade. Landowners, who often doubled as merchants, were most numerous in the metallurgical industry in its early stages, but they were gradually displaced by merchants and traders during the nineteenth century. Entrepreneurs from artisan backgrounds were more prominent in other industries. For example, the founders of the automobile industry were primarily from technical backgrounds. Bankers were somewhat more important than they had been in Britain, although they were not well represented before 1848 (Kemp, 1971).

The nobility was apparently more active in industrial entrepreneurship in France than in Britain.[38] Noble participation in metallurgy and glassmaking continued well into the nineteenth century, and in eastern France nobles remained prominent ironmasters for much of the century. In addition, members of the nobility were often included for prestige value on the boards of directors of industrial firms in the latter part of the century (Palmade, 1972, p. 214).

Religious differences overlapped regional differences. Alsatian entrepreneurs were predominantly Protestant and entrepreneurs from northern France primarily Catholic, for instance. We lack evidence on the proportions of Catholic and Protestant entrepreneurs in the country as a whole.

Therefore collective, marginal, and public forms of entrepreneurship were somewhat more prominent in France than in Britain, but the differences are not great. The greater participation of the French nobility leads us to conclude that French entrepreneurs came from slightly higher social class backgrounds and, perhaps, a more restricted range than did British entrepreneurs. Family entrepreneurship was very common in both cases and very likely less dynamic in France than in Britain.

THE RATE OF FRENCH INDUSTRIAL GROWTH

We have maintained that economic opportunity conditions for industrial entrepreneurship were less favorable in France than they had been in Britain. We also have analyzed the characteristics of French entrepreneurship, agreeing with some criticisms of it and questioning others. Now we consider the rate of French industrial growth to see just how inferior it was to the British rate.

Marczewski (1961) has provided the most complete data on French rates of industrial growth. These are shown in Table 12 and reveal that the French rate

[38]They included Count de Chardonnet, founder of the artificial silk industry, and Marquis de Dion, "one of the pioneers of the motor vehicle industry" (Palmade, 1972, p. 214).

varied from slightly less than 2 percent to a high of about 3.5 percent in the 1830s. The average of these averages is approximately 2.7 percent. These data are compared with estimates of the British rate of industrial growth in Table 13. The periods included in this table do not match precisely, but they indicate a remarkable similarity between British and French rates. The only period when the French rate was decidedly inferior was from 1785 to 1807, during the Revolution and a portion of the Napoleonic period; this was the period when the British rate of growth was at its apex. From about 1850 to 1880 the French rate was less than the British, but after 1880 the French rate *exceeded* the British, although it was lower than that of the United States and Germany (Patel, 1961, p. 319).

Table 12
Annual Rates of French Industrial Growth

Period	Rate (%)
1785–1807	1.98
1807–1829	2.86
1829–1839	3.52
1839–1849	2.45
1849–1859	2.76
1859–1869	2.72
1869–1879	2.75
1879–1889	2.20
1889–1899	2.47
1899–1909	2.85

Source: Marczewski (1961, pp. 380–381, table 7).

Table 13
Comparison of British and French Annual Industrial Growth Rates, Selected Periods

Great Britain		France	
Period	Rate (%)	Period	Rate (%)
–1780	< 2	1705–1785	1.91
1780–1792	3–4	1785–1807	1.98
1792–1818	2–3	1807–1829	2.86
1820–1860	3+	1829–1859	2.90
1880–1913	2	1879–1909	2.50

Source: Hartwell (1971, p. 120); Marczewski (1961, pp. 380–381, table 7); Patel (1961, pp. 317, 319, table 2).

Furthermore, a similarity in the *pattern* of industrial growth is apparent when we compare these two tables. The British annual rates jumped from less than 2 percent before 1780 to a high of 3 to 4 percent between 1780 and 1792, then dropped to less than 3 percent before stabilizing at a little over 3 percent in the period 1820–60. The French annual rates also jumped from slightly less than 2 percent before 1807 to a high of 3.5 percent in the 1830s, dropped in the 1840s, and then stabilized at about 2.75 percent after 1850. It appears that France recapitulated the British pattern almost perfectly, but with a lag of about thirty years.

Thus this comparison shows that the difference in the rate of industrial growth between the two countries was much smaller than it is often portrayed. The British had the advantage of a head start chronologically and economically. The French still would have lagged behind the British if they had started their period of more rapid growth about 1750, when the British did, but the gap very likely would not have been as great.

THE CAUSAL SIGNIFICANCE OF FRENCH ENTREPRENEURSHIP

French entrepreneurship differed substantially from British entrepreneurship, just as French society differed from British society. But, like the British case, we find it difficult to attribute any significant degree of independent causal significance to French entrepreneurship on the basis of the evidence we have considered. This conclusion is identical to our conclusion regarding British entrepreneurship. It is based on our judgment that economic opportunity conditions for entrepreneurship were somewhat less favorable in France than they were in Britain and on the fact that the French rate of industrial growth also was somewhat lower than the British rate, although not as much lower as one would expect simply on the basis of many descriptions of French entrepreneurship. The key to the French ability to attain a growth rate approaching the British rate appears to be their adoption of many British innovations. Their surpassing of the British growth rate after 1880 was partly due to the decline in the British rate and partly to the appearance of new industries connected with the Second Industrial Revolution.

Technology constituted the one area in which the French possessed an advantage in opportunity conditions over the British because they did not have to develop many of the new techniques on their own. But it is significant that these technologies did not provide the cost advantages in France that they did in Britain. The adoption of steam power was hindered by the relative lack of coal and the abundance of water, for example. The French did make progress in developing the latter for power, but unfortunately for them it did not provide the productivity increases offered by steam. Their adoption of new techniques in metallurgy was also hindered by their limited supplies of coal and iron ore. They were slow to adopt mass production techniques, but we attribute this largely to their relatively poor market situation and the difficulty of overcoming British competition. We find it especially noteworthy that mechanization tended to occur first in the *better*-quality segments of industry, the opposite of the British case. This implies that French entrepreneurs were willing to mechanize where it offered substantial benefits. They were slow to turn to factory production, but this was a result of the relatively slow diffusion of technological innovations.

We have singled out their reaction to the market as the area in which they were least able to overcome the disadvantages they faced. But upon closer examination few viable options appear to have been available. It would have taken a monumental effort to overcome the British advantage in the production of inexpensive consumer goods. The option of extensive development of heavy industry was less feasible for them than it was to be for German entrepreneurs. Consequently, continuing the production of luxury goods, which had been a suitable strategy before, appears to have been a sensible choice. The silk industry had enjoyed great success and it would have been difficult to abandon a sure thing for industrial pursuits that were riskier. French entrepreneurs were forced to develop the heavy industrial sector following the loss of this sure thing after 1860, but the availability of the necessary technologies by that time had increased its potential.

We also have observed that capital supplies were less favorable for French entrepreneurs than they had been for the British. This was partly the result of their later start, because capital requirements had increased in the interim, but it was primarily due to the lack of mobilizing devices and to competition from non-industrial, including foreign, sectors. Their adoption of forms of organizations such as the *commenda* and the joint-stock company constituted an entrepreneurial response to this situation.

A major portion of the blame for the relative unfavorableness of French opportunity conditions must be laid upon the government. We have described the "robbing-Peter-to-pay-Paul" nature of its policies. If it had decisively taken steps to improve opportunity conditions, then we believe the performance of French entrepreneurs would have been more like that of the British. But its actions both reflected and influenced the halfway nature of the opportunity conditions.

The degree of risk associated with entrepreneurship was undoubtedly higher in France than it had been in Britain. French entrepreneurs' awareness of these risks is indicated by their fear of British competition and their advocacy of government protection. Given the relative favorableness of the opportunity conditions in the two societies, it would have taken a *greater* willingness to take risks on the part of French entrepreneurs than was required of British entrepreneurs to attain the same ends.

It is significant that French entrepreneurs did come forth at times when opportunity conditions improved. We have noted their positive response to the ending of the tariff system. The availability of increased amounts of capital in the 1830s and 1850s is correlated with improvements in the industrial growth rates for those periods. Entrepreneurs also were relatively quick to adopt British metallurgical innovations after 1850, and they adopted innovations and products, such as the automobile, late in the nineteenth century which resulted in a higher industrial growth rate after 1900. Their willingness to undertake industrial activities in other societies also indicates a general responsiveness to opportunity conditions. Finally the dualistic development of French industry indicates a responsiveness of at least some entrepreneurs. We believe the dualism would not have been as extreme if opportunity conditions had been more favorable.

NONECONOMIC FACTORS INFLUENCING FRENCH ENTREPRENEURSHIP

Therefore, if French entrepreneurs were significantly to improve upon their economic opportunity conditions and French entrepreneurship were to have positive causal significance, it would have been necessary for some noneconomic factors to be present that would have produced a disproportionate emergence of entrepreneurship. We conclude this chapter by analyzing the nature of these noneconomic factors in France.

In doing so, it is necessary to start with the impact of the event which began our period of study—the French Revolution—because that upheaval cast a shadow over French society at least until the Revolution of 1848 and very likely beyond that. Did it unleash forces which were conducive to the emergence of entrepreneurship, or was it an incomplete revolution, merely rearranging relationships without fundamentally altering them?

Palmade (1972, p. 70) has described the impact of the Revolution thus:

> . . . the right of property which was at the centre of the capitalist machine triumphed over the restrictions and complications which had impaired its effectiveness under the feudal and manorial system. . . . In addition, the abolition of the old corporations and regulations resulted in the emergence of unregulated commercial and industrial enterprises.

Kemp (1971, p. 58) has provided a similar description:

> . . . the Revolution and the Empire brought into existence and consolidated a social and legal order thoroughly attuned to bourgeois property owners, clearing the ground of all preexisting barriers to industrial enterprise.

Yet, he (1971, p. 102) also describes "the essential paradox of nineteenth-century France," that "the very events which brought the bourgeoisie to power at the same time retarded the development of industrial capitalism . . . the base of the revolutionary bourgeoisie was not in industry, but rather in trade, the professions and the land." Therefore, it seems that the Revolution broke the power of the aristocracy, thereby increasing the legitimacy of entrepreneurship and the access of entrepreneurs to mobility channels, and increased entrepreneurial security through its support of private property. But it also seems that it was incomplete insofar as *industrial* entrepreneurship was concerned.

The actual degree to which the legitimacy of entrepreneurship increased as a result of the Revolution is in doubt. There is much agreement regarding the strength of aristocratic values opposed to entrepreneurship prior to the Revolution. Under the *ancien régime* the practice of *derogation* threatened nobles who engaged in commercial activities with loss of their status. A constellation of values emphasizing prowess; belittling manual labor, trade, and mass-produced goods; and extolling luxury goods and the ownership of land reigned supreme. So the question is the degree to which these values remained salient after 1790.

It has been suggested that they did, at least until 1850 (Palmade, 1972). It has also been suggested that aristocratic opposition to entrepreneurial activities became *more* severe after the Revolutions of 1789 and 1830 (Landes, 1949). The spread of Marxist doctrines in the nineteenth century has been described as reinforcing the traditional negative attitudes toward entrepreneurship (Sawyer, 1952). Consequently, the entrepreneurs themselves had anticapitalist attitudes because of these influences (Rothman, 1956).

A slightly different interpretation, however, suggests that the values of achievement, egalitarianism, specificity, and universalism, which should have spurred entrepreneurship, were present in French society, but that they were not shared widely enough to support either economic growth or democracy (Kindleberger, 1964, pp. 105–08). This may be a more perceptive view because the leaders of the Revolution of 1789, with their ideological emphasis on liberty, equality, and fraternity, certainly attempted to disseminate these values, but the incompleteness of the Revolution and the rise of the Restoration government prevented their widespread acceptance.

Thus it is highly probable that entrepreneurship was accorded less legitimacy in France, at least until about 1850, than in Britain. The aristocracies in both societies were opposed to it, and if nothing else, the greater strength of the French aristocracy made its opposition more powerful.[39] But it is also possible that the legitimacy of entrepreneurship was greater than is sometimes supposed. Another criticism of French entrepreneurs has been that they viewed the role as a source of status rather than as a means to an end, unlike the British (Rothman, 1956). It hardly seems likely that they would have exemplified this characteristic if the entrepreneurial role offered them little or no status.

The comments of Palmade and Kemp indicate that an increase in the possibility of upward social mobility for entrepreneurs was a major consequence of the Revolution. The medieval guilds, which limited mobility, had actually increased in strength under the *ancien régime* (Landes, 1969). Thus the ending of guild and occupational restrictions would have made entry into the role easier. That French entrepreneurs did attain higher social status under the Second Em-

---

[39]Wallerstein (1974) contrasts the aristocracies in the two societies by suggesting that English aristocrats lost in the short run and gained in the long run by transforming themselves into bourgeois capitalists, whereas the French aristocracy won in the short run and lost in the long run by forcing the bourgeoisie to abandon its function.

pire may be taken as *de facto* proof of the increased potential for social mobility, but it may also be interpreted as the result of entrepreneurs' own greater efforts to rise in the stratification system.

It is probable that entrepreneurship was less a means of social mobility in France than in Britain, primarily because of the continued strength of the French nobility until after the mid-nineteenth century. The gap between the aristocracy and the rest of the population remained greater in France and the upper middle class less accessible (Landes, 1969). The restrictiveness of the French educational system also limited the possibility of upward mobility (Kindleberger, 1964). All in all, less change from the past took place socially in France than in Britain (Hoselitz, 1955b), there was less overall social mobility in France, and French entrepreneurs had less access to mobility channels.

The degree to which French entrepreneurs, as compared to British entrepreneurs, were integrated into society is difficult to determine. They were more likely to have outsider origins than were British entrepreneurs, which is indicative of less integration. France was probably a less integrated society than Britain (Kindleberger, 1964), partly because of its greater size and diversity and partly because of the social instability of the period we are studying.

But the centralization policies of the French government were a counterforce. For example, French entrepreneurs were more closely regulated by the state than were British entrepreneurs, although the effectiveness of the state's manifold rules and regulations has been questioned. These ties to the "center" may have yielded substantial social integration. We suggested earlier that a moderate degree of integration may be the most conducive to entrepreneurship, and it is possible that French entrepreneurs were too highly integrated into the system as a result of the state's policies.

The degree of security provided entrepreneurship in France is also unclear. The several revolutions which punctuated the period of our study very likely created much insecurity, although it may have been only temporary and the long-run effect may have been greater security. Protestant Frenchmen supposedly were commercial rather than industrial entrepreneurs because of the former's greater security (Hoselitz, 1955a; Palmade, 1972), but they were a special case, a religious minority, and their situation cannot be generalized to all French entrepreneurs.

It is also conceivable that French entrepreneurs were *too* secure. The consistent inability of the French economic system to eliminate inefficient producers has attracted comment. This distinctive characteristic has been attributed to the negative attitude toward competition in French society (Landes, 1965a). Less efficient producers were not forced out of the market but given a share of it. There was thus little need for cartels to regulate competition, in contrast to Germany. In addition, the very high tariffs before 1850 provided security against foreign competition, although competition for the protected French market was quite high (Dunham, 1955). Therefore entrepreneurial security may have been greater in France than in Britain, where those who failed to innovate fell by the wayside.

Because France was predominantly Catholic and Great Britain predominantly Protestant, the two countries would appear to offer a critical test of the Protestant Ethic hypothesis regarding religion as an ideological force promoting entrepreneurship. Although Protestant Alsatian entrepreneurs were more dynamic than Catholic entrepreneurs from northern France, differences in economic performance allegedly were greater among the Catholic regions than between Catholic and Protestant regions (Kindleberger, 1964). Obviously, this does not support an argument for the importance of Protestantism. The greater importance of regionalism than religion is shown by the fact that some regions, such as southern France, converted from Protestantism to Catholicism without a change in their economic characteristics (Wallerstein, 1974).

So religious ideology does not seem to have been very significant, and nationalism does not appear to have provided an ideological lever either. This may be owing to the failure of entrepreneurs to identify with national goals and ideals (Sawyer, 1952), however, and not to the absence of nationalistic appeals.

There is little definite evidence of either a high or low degree of need-achievement in France after 1790. Various descriptions of French "national character" have included characteristics exemplary of low need-achievement, such as noncompetitiveness, interest in personalized relationships, and discouragement (Landes, 1965a; 1965b; Palmade, 1972). Two very different characterizations, one emphasizing nonadventurousness and the other "prowess—the cult of the exceptional feat" (Kindleberger, 1964) both contrast with the desire for *moderate* risks supposedly characteristic of high need-achievers. But the French have also been described as realistic, practical, rational, calculating, and prudent (Dunham, 1955; Hoselitz, 1955a)—descriptions consonant with relatively high need-achievement.

Nor is there evidence of any significant *withdrawal* of status respect. Rather, as in Britain, the long-term opposition of the aristocracy makes *a desire for* status respect a more cogent explanation of entrepreneurial motivations.

Pecuniary motives often have been described as less salient in France than in Britain. French entrepreneurs have been described as motivated by class and status goals rather than by monetary ones (Sawyer, 1952),[40] and as more interested in becoming part of the nobility and in preserving family status than in economic achievement (Barber, 1965; Landes, 1949, 1965a). This may have changed as the legitimacy of entrepreneurship increased and as entrepreneurs became more successful, because they also have been described as being primarily concerned with profits after 1848 (Palmade, 1972). It seems logical that economic success would have been necessary for achievement of noneconomic

---

[40]The *ultimate* value placed on private property also is regarded as having limited risk-taking (van der Haas, 1967).

goals, such as the attainment of a landed estate, however, so there appears to be danger of overstressing the significance of noneconomic motives in the French situation.[41]

In general, we conclude that the noneconomic factors believed to promote entrepreneurship were less favorable in France than they were in Britain. They clearly were not favorable enough to overcome the unfavorable economic opportunity conditions and promote a disproportionate emergence of entrepreneurship that would have led to a high rate of industrial growth and to our regarding French entrepreneurship as having positive causal significance. These noneconomic factors did become more favorable during the nineteenth century, but not sufficiently favorable to promote extensive entrepreneurship. For instance, if the legitimacy of entrepreneurship, or the possibility of social mobility by means of entrepreneurship, had increased radically it is probable that more entrepreneurship would have emerged.[42]

The effects of entrepreneurial security and integration are more complex. We have suggested that French entrepreneurs may have been too secure. If they had been less secure, it is probable that more of them would have been eliminated, but possibly too many would have because of British competition. Perhaps the problem was that they were economically secure, but not socially secure, so that a decline in the former and an increase in the latter would have promoted more entrepreneurship. Similarly, it is conceivable that they might have been more entrepreneurial if they had been less integrated into the system. More entrepreneurs might have arisen from marginal origins. These arguments suggest that the French sociocultural environment provided intermediate support for entrepreneurship—sufficient to promote some but insufficient to promote enough to overcome the unfavorable economic opportunity conditions.

Finally, an ideological force to promote entrepreneurship was lacking in France, as were motives sufficiently strong to influence French entrepreneurs to overcome the odds against them. We feel that the desire for status recognition was a motive force in France, as it was in Britain, but it is probable that its force was dissipated in nonentrepreneurial activities, such as attempts to join the nobility, because less status was accorded entrepreneurship in France than in Britain. The responsiveness of French entrepreneurs to opportunity conditions at various times implies that economic motives were operative, but the nature of the opportunity conditions often deflected action on these motives into noneconomic areas.

The characteristics of French entrepreneurship reflect the sociocultural characteristics we have described. That relatively few entrepreneurs came from

[41]Interestingly enough, they also have been accused of being *too* concerned with profits: "The majority of entrepreneurs were rather careless about the volume of production and the level of cost and selling prices; in their management they were directly concerned with the amount of overall profit they could obtain" (Palmade, 1972, p. 165).

[42]It appears, from an inspection of industrial growth rates, that the improvement in industrial growth *preceded* a significant improvement in legitimacy, which casts doubt on the importance of legitimacy as a factor promoting entrepreneurship.

marginal sources indicates that French society did not fully fit the requirements of our model of outsider entrepreneurship. That there was *no blockage* of access to nonentrepreneurial roles that served as mobility channels has the same implication. And, that French entrepreneurs generally came from the same occupations as did the British also indicates the mainstream nature of the French case. In France, however, the mainstream was not very supportive of entrepreneurship, whereas in Britain it was much more so.

The heterogeneity characterizing French entrepreneurship also is indicative of a system neither completely supportive nor completely opposed to entreprenurship. Some French families were expansive and innovative, many were not. Some industrial sectors expanded, others did not. A transition to collective forms of entrepreneurship occurred, but a significant number of individual entrepreneurs remained. French society became more industrial, but an unusually large agricultural sector continued to exist.

Throughout the period we have studied, therefore, the noneconomic factors influencing entrepreneurship were favorable enough to stimulate some entrepreneurship, but not so favorable as to stimulate extreme amounts, nor so unfavorable as to block it completely. This situation is attributable to the *incompleteness* of the French *Revolution* referring now not to the Revolution of 1789, nor to succeeding specific revolutions, but to France's break with its medieval past. There were significant changes in France during the nineteenth century, but there were also many survivals. The succession of governments reflected this situation, neither moving decisively in favor of industrialization nor against it. Their fluctuations can be traced directly to the political struggle going on between an aristocracy attempting to retain its position and a rising entrepreneurial class attempting to improve its status. In Britain the same struggle had occurred in the context of a *weaker* aristocracy, a *weaker* state, and a *stronger* entrepreneurial class. Hence British entrepreneurs were able to attain a position of political influence more quickly and to promote policies which they favored.

Consequently, although the French case differs greatly from the British, we come to identical conclusions regarding the relative importance of economic and noneconomic factors in the two cases. French entrepreneurs also emerged *in proportion to* the favorableness of economic opportunity conditions. Noneconomic factors were favorable enough to promote or permit a proportional emergence, but not favorable or unfavorable enough to lead to either a disproportionate emergence or lack of emergence. In Britain both economic and noneconomic factors were relatively favorable for entrepreneurship; in France both were relatively unfavorable.

6

Prussia-Germany

Entrepreneurship in the states and principalities that formed the German Reich in 1871 represents a contrast with both French and British entrepreneurship. Great Britain was France's predecessor and industrial mentor. France in turn was the exemplar of industrialization for the Germanic states and aided them in their industrial quest. In fact a comparison between French and German entrepreneurship is more revealing than a comparison of British and French. France and Germany shared a similar geographic setting, they were both latecomers relative to Britain, and it is probable that numerous remnants of the medieval period existed in both when they began to industrialize. Hence these similarities should make any differences in entrepreneurial performance between them important for our determination of the causal significance of entrepreneurship. Of course there were also major differences between them. France had been politically unified for centuries, whereas the unification of the Germanic states did not take place until 1871. This momentous event accounted for some of the differences we shall describe.

We will analyze entrepreneurship in the Germanic states, primarily in Prussia, during the period from 1815, the date of the Congress of Vienna, to 1875, the point at which we believe Germany achieved industrialization. Thus only the last four years of the period of study concern Germany as such. Our emphasis on Prussia is justified by its predominance among the German states in industrial output before 1871. Table 14 indicates the proportions contributed by Prussia to the industrial output of these states during the 1860s.

We can see that Prussia was especially predominant in heavy industry—coal and metallurgy—but that she also possessed a majority of the equipment of

131

Table 14
Proportion of German Industrial Output and
Equipment Attributable to Prussia (1860s)

Product or Equipment	Prussian Percentage
Coal	90
Pig iron	90
Lead	77
Iron ore	66
Steam engines	67
Flax spindles	79
Worsted spindles	53
Woolen looms	60

Source: Henderson (1958, pp. xvi–xvii).

the woolen and flax industries. The cotton industry, predominant in Britain and slightly less important in France, was relatively less significant in Prussia and in the Germanic states as a whole. The annexation of Alsace-Lorraine after the Franco-Prussian War dramatically increased the size of the German textile industry. The number of textile spindles increased by 50 percent and the relative sizes of the French and German textile industries were reversed (Dawson, 1911, p. 57).

We follow the format of the previous chapter, examining the opportunity conditions for Prussian-German entrepreneurship, the role of the government, the characteristics of German entrepreneurship, the rate of German industrial growth, and the nature of the sociocultural environment in that order. (We now drop the *Prussian-German* designation and simply refer to *German* entrepreneurship.)

OPPORTUNITY CONDITIONS FOR GERMAN ENTREPRENEURSHIP

As of 1815 the Germanic states were less prosperous, on both a total and a per capita basis, than Great Britain, the United States, and probably also France (Gould, 1972; Landes, 1969). Consequently the supply of investment capital was limited. As in Britain and France, the lack of working capital was the major inadequacy.[1] Entrepreneurs faced an absolute shortage of this type of capital, as well as more specific problems, such as a lack of coins with which to pay wages.

The amounts of fixed capital needed did increase radically from their low initial level. This change started in the 1840s with the construction of railroads

---

[1]Even as late as 1880 investment in plant and equipment represented only 13 percent of total German industrial investment; transportation facilities, for example, required far larger amounts of fixed capital (Gould, 1972, p. 151).

and the more rapid development of the producer goods sector, and increased rapidly after about 1850. Thus there was a relative scarcity of savings available for industry from about 1840 on (Tilly, 1967). There was also a strong tendency after 1840 for investment capital to flow into nonindustrial pursuits.

The German response to this situation was distinctive and significant: the extensive and vigorous development of capital-mobilizing facilities. Two components of this response were the assumption of the investment function by private bankers and the rise of joint-stock investment banks (Tilly, 1966a). The extensiveness of their roles and their innovative and liberal policies distinguish the German case from both the British and French cases.

German private bankers made increasing amounts of capital available to industrial entrepreneurs starting in the 1830s, if not earlier. Most of this was relatively short-term working capital, although they also provided fixed capital, and much was provided only locally. They moved to a dual, or "mixed" role, not only providing capital to industrial entrepreneurs but also engaging in the entrepreneurial role themselves with the beginning of railroad construction in the 1830s and 1840s. In this respect they differed radically from British and American bankers. From railroad construction they moved into manufacturing, especially in Rhineland-Westphalia and Silesia. Their policies were often very liberal and very different from the conservative practices of French bankers. They would loan amounts up to one-half the assets of an entrepreneur's firm, for example. But there also were weaknesses in their performance, such as their hesitance to loan capital beyond their own localities and their tendency to favor established entrepreneurs over new ones.

These inadequacies prompted the second component of the financial response in the 1850s—the joint-stock investment banks patterned after the French *Crédit Mobilier*. The German investment banks became increasingly important, whereas the *Crédit Mobilier* collapsed after only fifteen years. Planned from the beginning to be initiators of industry and not merely passive sources of credit, the investment banks continued the private bankers' dual role of founding and funding industrial enterprises. They too, followed quite radical policies, advancing loans of up to as much as two-thirds of the purchase price of an enterprise. They also demanded voting rights in the enterprises they funded and thus they assisted in managing them as well. By 1867 nineteen such banks were involved in a variety of industries (Cameron, 1961, p. 199). The tie between these banks and manufacturing enterprises became even more intimate after 1871 as capital requirements became larger, especially in heavy industry. Other devices for mobilizing capital, such as the stock exchange, were relatively less well developed in Germany than in countries such as the United States because of the significance of these banks (Tilly, 1967). Foreign capital also was of limited significance.

German bankers and the joint-stock investment banks surely improved capital supplies for industrial entrepreneurs. Germany became a capital-exporting country at a very early stage of development (Stolper, Hauser, & Borchardt, 1967), which implies that capital supplies increased sharply. The closeness of the relationship between banks and manufacturing enterprises undoubtedly facilitated the flow of capital also. Thus Visser (1969) has singled out the development of the German financial system as the major reason for Germany's impressive industrial performance after 1850. But Tilly (1966a) describes the banks as important although hardly strategic, on the grounds that they complemented, but did not take the place of, German entrepreneurs. Our conclusion is that, compared to the British and French banking systems, the German banking system created much more favorable opportunity conditions. The histories of the *Crédit Mobilier* and the German investment banks exemplify quite different responses to limited capital supplies.

The quality and quantity of the raw materials available to German entrepreneurs gave them a further advantage over the French. Most significant was the ample supply of coal in areas such as the Ruhr and Upper Silesia. Discovery of the massive coal deposits in the Ruhr and their development after 1850 gave a tremendous boost to industries using coal and coke, such as metallurgy and the fledgling chemical industry which at the time was developing dyes from coal tars. The German edge in iron ore was not as great because its ore was phosphoric like the French. But after 1871, annexation of Alsace-Lorraine, where the largest iron ore deposits in western Europe were located, reversed that situation. The more rapid development, compared to the French, of the German railroad system before 1850 provided Germany with another advantage through its facilitating utilization of these raw materials. Railroad development was very important because the major known coal and iron ore deposits lay in distant areas, such as Upper Silesia and the Saar, at the time. The lack of wool, which handicapped the worsted industry, appears to have been the only serious raw material problem confronting the Germans.

We think that Germany's advantage over France in raw material supplies was sufficient to account for at least some of the variance in their industrial performances, even though Pounds (1959) does not consider it a major factor. That French capital and entrepreneurship played a significant role in the development of mining in areas such as Silesia and the Ruhr also suggests that opportunities were greater there than in France.

The German labor force in the nineteenth century has received much acclaim. Veblen (1939, p. 196), who described it as having "ready pliability under authority" and being "well trained to an impecuniously frugal standard of living," believed it to be of higher quality than the British labor force, and we have previously noted the superiority of the British labor force to the French. The German labor force has been commended on several counts. First, there appears to have been an ample supply of labor, larger than that available to early British entrepreneurs (Landes, 1969). Hence labor was relatively low cost, definitely lower cost than in Britain and probably lower than in France. This abundant supply of cheap labor did encourage the continuation of small-scale operations in textiles and of the putting-out system, but these effects were not as serious as they had been in France.

Second, it was quite highly skilled. Pounds (1959, p. 189) describes its "tradition of careful craftsmanship," for example. The German educational system played a significant role in developing this high-quality labor force.[2] Compulsory elementary education had existed in some areas as early as the sixteenth century. The educational system was expanded in the 1820s, with the founding of technical schools, such as the Polytechnic, founded in 1825 in Karlsruhe on the pattern of the French Polytechnique. Thus the relationship between the educational system and industry differed from what it had been in Great Britain. The development of an educational system *prior* to industrialization in Germany produced a highly skilled labor force, with the system of technical schools providing highly educated technicians. The level of education required by the more complex technologies of the post-1850 period therefore was matched by the personnel being supplied by the educational system. By comparison, Britain's relative neglect of its educational system placed it at a disadvantage in maintaining an industrial lead over Germany (Landes, 1969).

German entrepreneurs possessed an advantage over British and French entrepreneurs by virtue of following in their wake and thus having access to a greater stock of available technological innovations. This was true for several industries—metallurgy, textiles, and machinery. But, as we shall see, German entrepreneurs made significant additions to the supply of existing techniques. And they provided leadership in technological innovation in the chemical and electrical industries, two of the leading sectors of the *Second* Industrial Revolution, in a manner analogous to the leadership provided by the British in the first Industrial Revolution.

The market constituted the area in which the Germans seemingly had relatively disadvantageous opportunity conditions, compared to the British and the French, also by virtue of following them on the path to industrialization. Britain dominated the foreign market both in inexpensive textile goods and heavy industry. France was the leader in the production of luxury goods. In addition, the Germans had no colonial possessions that might have served as a captive market. Therefore there was limited potential for them in the foreign market, although their low-cost labor might have enabled them to undersell Britain and France.

The domestic market also was not very favorable, partly because of the low level of economic development. The fragmentation of this market resulting from the lack of political unity of the Germanic states was perhaps more important. Trade among the states was hindered by the multiplicity and variety of monetary

[2]As Murphy (1967, p. 19) says, "By accident or design, Germany developed an educational framework that meshed with the process requirements of the current industrial frontier."

systems, commercial codes, and tariffs. Transportation was hindered by the lack of access to good ocean ports and a poorly developed system of river transport. A system of roads had not been developed in Prussia because the potential leaders feared they would be used by invading armies. The only aspect of the domestic market that was favorable was the growing population.

But the market situation improved dramatically after 1815. First, economic integration was achieved by means of the *Zollverein,* started in 1834 under Prussian leadership. This customs union facilitated trade by reducing tariffs. Second, the development of the railroad system, beginning in the 1830s, was particularly significant as a stimulus for heavy industry and as a means of moving products and materials (Hoffman, 1963).[3] The rapid development of the German rail system contrasted sharply with the sluggish development of the French system about ten years later. The fact that the German system was not intended primarily as a spur to industrialization, but as a military tool, exemplifies a distinctive characteristic of the German case which we shall discuss more fully later.

German entrepreneurs in the nineteenth century enjoyed more favorable opportunity conditions than did their French compatriots, with the sole exception of the market. These favorable conditions have been termed the *advantages of backwardness,* as we noted in Chapter 2. A major advantage of Germany's backwardness was of course the ability to borrow technology. Although there were macro-economic costs associated with being a follower rather than a leader, these costs were not as great for Germany as were the micro-economic costs which confronted Britain. Moreover, the technological gap between Germany and Britain was small enough to make backwardness advantageous. And, the relatively small size of the gap meant that changes which had been spread out over a long period of time in both Britain and France could be compressed into a short time span in Germany (Landes, 1969).[4] One of the major consequences of Germany's chronological position therefore was the feasibility of initiating enterprises on a large scale, particularly in metallurgy. This required large amounts of capital of course, but these were provided by the German banking system.

Thus we find the arguments concerning the advantages of backwardness persuasive when applied to nineteenth-century Germany.[5] But Germany's backwardness was not advantageous solely because of the availability of usable technologies. It was feasible for German entrepreneurs to use these technologies largely because of the favorableness of other opportunity conditions.

---

[3]In the British case the industrial transition had been achieved without the need for, or the benefit of, an extensive system of rail transport (Tilly, 1966a).

[4]As Ferguson and Bruun (1958, p. 765) put it, "The first and second waves of the Industrial Revolution both struck Germany in the same years."

[5]According to Tilly (1966b) there was an "abundance" of these advantages in Prussia after 1815, although he also says that all but the smallest industrial ventures could be carried out more safely and more cheaply in England than in Germany until 1850 and that investment in manufacturing was riskier than investment in railroad securities yet in the 1850s.

The opportunity conditions for industrial entrepreneurship *relative* to other occupational roles also appear to have been favorable in the Germanic states. Other potential occupations, especially in the civil service, the clergy, and higher education, were already filled (Veblen, 1939). According to Bowen (1950), the German milieu was not conducive to speculative types of entrepreneurship because of its rigidity and the limited supply of wealth. If he is correct, then possibly there were pressures on German entrepreneurs to exhibit the sober rationality of Weber's ideal-type entrepreneur.[6]

THE ROLE OF THE GOVERNMENT

The performance of the Prussian government also provides a significant contrast with the role of the governments in Britain and France. The British government intervened very little, either for or against British entrepreneurs. The French government intervened much more, but many of its actions were contradictory. The Prussian government was very similar to the French in the extent of its intervention, but it appears to have been far more intelligent in its choice of policies, at least as measured by its effects on the achievement of industrialization.[7]

Nineteenth-century Prussia inherited a tradition of extensive direct and indirect government involvement. The government had played a major role in the development of mining and metallurgy in the eighteenth century, being responsible for the introduction of steam engines and a fairly modern iron industry. But by the latter part of the century there were conflicting views among Prussian officials regarding the merits of public entrepreneurship. These differing views were duplicated by the Rhenish businessmen and the Junkers after 1815.

There was substantial opposition to industrialization in the government, largely fomented by the Junkers, in the years between 1815 and 1850. Many restrictions were placed on the banking system and on the borrowing of capital by industrial entrepreneurs. There was some tariff protection, although some have considered it inadequate for the iron industry (Landes, 1969).[8] But in spite of the Junker opposition there were also proindustrial elements in the Prussian government, such as Finance Minister Motz, appointed in 1825. And during much of the period the state continued to be the major force promoting industrialization.

First, it gave continued support to technological innovations. Innovations

[6]Redlich (1944) claims that all German entrepreneurs had to have technical knowledge, which implies that relative opportunity conditions were greatest for those with such knowledge.

[7]If we were to measure the state's actions in terms of the achievement of liberal democracy, the German ledger would be less favorable. According to Dahrendorf (1967), the citizen role did not develop under the German state, a failure that had devastating consequences in the twentieth century. Tilly (1966a, p. 138) cites Germany as an "historical lesson in the compatibility of capitalism with political conservatism."

[8]Henderson (1968, p. 16) claims, though, that it encouraged the Prussian manufacturer to "stand on his own feet."

and skilled craftsmen were imported from Britain and France to transform the metallurgical industry; the adoption of coke for smelting was pushed particularly. State factories and ironworks using the latest technological innovations served as models for the private sector. Societies were established to dispense information on innovations and to add to technological knowledge, and exhibitions of innovations were sponsored. The government also appointed technical directors to sit on the boards of private enterprises to supervise their efficiency and to promote the adoption of innovations, a practice which lasted in metallurgy until 1864 (Pounds, 1959).

Second, the Prussian government improved opportunity conditions through measures increasing economic and political integration. The most significant was the *Zollverein* which eliminated tariff barriers and united seventeen of the German states. Third, its promotion of transportation—both roads and railroads— also promoted integration, but the effect of improved transportation upon the market was perhaps more important.[9] Financial assistance to entrepreneurs was the fourth major contribution of government in the pre-1850 period.

After 1848 the government gave industrial entrepreneurship more unified support, primarily because Junker opposition diminished.[10] Tax reforms in 1851 and 1861 provided additional capital for the private sector. Bismarck's accession to power in 1862 further increased support for heavy industry especially. Bismarck continued the liberalization of economic policies which culminated in 1873 with a large reduction in tariffs on iron and steel. And the combination of political unification under Prussian leadership in 1871 and success in the Franco-Prussian War directly stimulated industrial growth.[11]

The liberalization of corporate formation was the major area in which the state was slow to act after 1850. The establishment of joint-stock companies was restricted until 1869. But in the following year automatic registration of such companies was instituted, thereby facilitating their formation. And later in the century the German government gave legal support to the system of cartels, which we shall discuss soon. The governments of Britain, France, and the United States did not take this step, at least not formally (van der Haas, 1967).

It is widely agreed that the Prussian government supported rapid industrialization after 1850 because it offered the potential of increased military power (Pounds, 1959; Spengler, 1959; Veblen, 1939).[12] This militarism also had negative consequences, such as the large defense budget it required (Henderson, 1958), but it did help to stimulate Germany's strong suit—the heavy industrial

[9]The controversy over public versus private development became focalized on the issue of railroad construction.

[10]Ironically nationalization of the railroad system increased in the 1860s at the same time as sentiment in favor of the private sector in manufacturing was increasing.

[11]This provides an interesting contrast with the period immediately after 1815, when the slow pace of industrialization was partly the result of the damage wrought by the Napoleonic Wars.

[12]Landes (1969) has described the government's role in Prussia as a case of taking the right path on the basis of wrong or irrelevant reasons.

sector. It helped account for the Prussian government's share of the market (5.9 percent of gross national product in 1870) being greater than that of the governments of Great Britain and the United States—4.9 and 3.7 percent of gross national product, respectively, in 1870—(Maddison, 1969, p. 14). French (and Japanese) political leaders also appreciated the significance of industrialization for increasing military power, but the French were much less skillful in translating that goal into effective policies. Overall therefore, the Prussian government was more supportive of industrialization than was the French government, and much more supportive than the British government.[13] Although it had given some support before 1850, its support increased greatly after that date.

CHARACTERISTICS OF GERMAN ENTREPRENEURSHIP

We have asserted that opportunity conditions were more favorable for German entrepreneurs than for French entrepreneurs, and we have shown that they increased in favorableness after about 1850, with the Prussian government having a large hand in their improvement. We shall now see how German entrepreneurs responded to these increasingly favorable economic opportunity conditions.

Innovations

German entrepreneurs were relatively slow to take advantage of the technological innovations available from Britain and France in the years between 1815 and 1850.[14] Like French entrepreneurs, they did not adopt the most recently developed innovations after 1815. Textile entrepreneurs adopted the largest share of these innovations, making use primarily of power-driven machinery. As late as 1846, however, less than 4 percent of the cotton looms in Prussia were power driven, and by 1850 there were only 1,200 power looms in the entire German wool industry (Clapham, 1951, pp. 93, 293). Entrepreneurs were slow to adopt power looms because of their cost disadvantage relative to hand looms which resulted from the relatively low cost of labor and the relatively high cost of fuel. The silk industry also remained unmechanized until after 1870. The diffusion of steam power took place more slowly than it did in France or Britain, although German entrepreneurs tended to make use of larger steam engines than did French entrepreneurs. Iron puddling was imported in the 1820s, and the German machine tool industry began to develop about this time also.

[13]The Germans were also aided in this endeavor by their high-quality civil service, of which Schumpeter wrote, "The social stratum that supplied the personnel of public administration was— . . .—much superior in intelligence, horizon, training and energy to the personnel of such private industry as there was" (Fischer, 1963, p. 94).

[14]The first cotton spinning mill in Germanic territory had been founded in 1794, and the use of steam engines for power had been introduced in 1800. British technicians had also helped to develop the iron industry in Upper Silesia before 1800.

The diffusion of innovations became more rapid, especially in heavy industry, in the more supportive environment after 1850. Power looms were adopted more swiftly and the acquisition of Alsace-Lorraine with its large stock of textile machinery radically increased the size of the mechanized sector of the textile industry. By 1875, however, there were still only 57,000 power looms in use in the cotton industry compared to 125,000 hand looms (Landes, 1969, p. 443), and the industry remained far behind its British competitor.

The adoption of steam power was more rapid after 1850, largely because of the development of the Ruhr coal fields, and German steam capacity soon outpaced that of French industry. In metallurgy, entrepreneurs like Krupp were quick to adopt the Bessemer and Siemens-Martin techniques of steel production, as the stimulus of foreign competition made continued technological innovations essential. Other entrepreneurs were somewhat slower because of the problems encountered in using these techniques with phosphoric ores, the same problem the French ran into. The Gilchrist-Thomas process was adopted more rapidly when it became available. The use of interchangeable parts to standardize production was adopted at this time also (Murphy, 1967). German entrepreneurs, like French entrepreneurs, had been slow to adopt this innovation in production techniques. After 1871, the rate of diffusion of innovations was still more rapid.

Thus German entrepreneurs followed the example of French entrepreneurs and made extensive use of a number of British innovations. But compared to the French, German entrepreneurs initiated more major technological innovations of their own, especially in the heavy industrial sector. For example, the puddling process was adapted to steel making before that feat was accomplished in either Britain or France (Landes, 1965b). Alfred Krupp made major innovations, the most significant being his independent discovery and application of the method of making cast steel and of making it in more than one crucible at a time. His most immediate application of this innovation was to the manufacture of seamless railroad wheels which were substantially safer than wheels with seams.[15] This technique was then applied to the manufacture of armaments and the Krupp firm became a world leader in this area. By 1851 Krupp was able to produce a two-ton block of cast steel which he showed at the British Crystal Palace exhibition, and which collapsed the floor at the Paris World Exhibition four years later (Manchester, 1968).

Major advances also were made by German entrepreneurs in the development of new sources of power, including the Holtzhauser double-acting steam engine and the Otto-Langen atmospheric gas engine (Clapham, 1951).[16] Innovations in the use of electricity, such as Siemens' electric dynamo, the first generator based on the electro-dynamic principle, which was developed in 1866,

---

[15]Three interlocking wheels, symbolizing this accomplishment, were made the Krupp trademark in 1875 (Manchester, 1968).

[16]This was to be followed in the 1890s by Diesel's development of the engine that bears his name.

were of greater significance ultimately. After 1875 a number of other technological breakthroughs were achieved in this industry; Clapham (1951, p. 308) calls these "the greatest single industrial achievement of modern Germany."

The German chemical industry also was beginning a series of major innovations in the years just before 1875. Alizarin, the first artificial dye to replace a natural dye, was produced simultaneously in England and Germany in 1869. This was followed by other major advances in the synthesis of coal-tar dyes, the improvement of the fuchsine process (which had been developed in France), and the development of a variety of products from cellulose. Most importantly, these innovations were adopted far more rapidly by the German chemical industry than by British or French chemical manufacturers. As a result, "In the late 1860s the industry was still small, dispersed, and essentially imitative. Scarcely a decade later, . . . [it] held about half of the world market" (Landes, 1965b, p. 503).[17] Landes (1969, p. 289) has described the similarities in the development of the electrical and chemical industries: "The parallels are numerous: the belated start, the rapid rise based on technological excellence and rational organization, the concentration of production, the strong position on the world market." Development of these two industries, which were spearheads of the Second Industrial Revolution, helped to catapult Germany to a position of world industrial preeminence.

Two related features of the development and adoption of technological innovations by German entrepreneurs stand out. The first was their adoption of highly capital-intensive technologies despite the relatively low cost of German labor (Landes, 1965b). This was partly a consequence of timing—these technologies were increasingly available in the years after 1850 when Germany was making her industrial advance—and partly attributable to organizational innovations which were occurring at the same time (Landes, 1969). But credit also must be given to entrepreneurs and to the influence of the government. The more obvious strategy would have been to utilize labor-intensive modes of production, but if this had been followed it is doubtful that German industrial growth would have been as rapid as it was. The large amounts of capital available from the investment banks and the discovery of large coal supplies also encouraged the selection of this strategy.

The second distinctive characteristic was the close relationship between science and industry which German entrepreneurs achieved. They have been credited with using advances in scientific knowledge for industrial purposes to a greater degree than entrepreneurs in any other country during the nineteenth century (Ferguson & Bruun, 1958). The amalgamation of science and industry was exemplified in the electrical and chemical industries particularly. By contrast, French entrepreneurs failed to make use of comparable contributions from French scientists.

---

[17]Landes (1965b) describes the development of the chemical industry as Germany's greatest industrial achievement.

The adoption of coke followed a pattern similar to that of technological innovations. German entrepreneurs used it in refining before smelting, as did the French, but they were slower to adopt it before 1850 than either the French or the Belgians. It was not used in the Rhineland until the 1840s although it had been used in Silesia in the latter part of the eighteenth century. This was partly due to the large quantities of wood available in the Rhineland. Following the discovery and development of the Ruhr coal deposits, however, coke adoption increased rapidly and helped promote the growth of the metallurgical industry.

Organizational innovations accompanying technological innovations were also significant, and German entrepreneurs made distinctive contributions in this area, too, after 1850. The transition to factory production was quite slow in both metallurgy and textiles before 1850, and both industries remained organized primarily on an artisan or domestic outworker basis (Clapham, 1951). As in France, the output of products produced on a craft basis increased more rapidly than that produced in factories. This continued predominance of traditional forms of production was partly due to the relative insignificance of the cotton industry, in which the major foreign innovations were applicable, in comparison to the woolen and linen industries.[18] It was also partly the result of the cheapness of German labor which encouraged continuation of the putting-out system as it had in France.

Although the cotton industry and factory production become more important after 1850, an important sector of small-scale rural production was retained, which was also similar to the French case.[19] In fact, this, in conjunction with developments that were occurring in heavy industry at the time, may have created a dualistic industrial structure in Germany that was even more pronounced than the one in France. The French agricultural sector, however, remained relatively more important than did German agriculture. The former was still proportionately larger in 1910 than the latter had been in 1875 (Kuznets, 1957, pp. 91-92). The transition to factory production in textiles proceeded much more rapidly after 1870. Clapham (1951, p. 301) observes, "Some trades even passed in a single generation through the three stages—independent handicraft, outwork, and the factory system—an evolution which . . . has taken several centuries in earlier ages."

The most distinctive organizational changes took place in heavy industry after 1850. The first of these was the *integration* of enterprises of different types, a development which proceeded reciprocally with the adoption of capital-intensive techniques (Landes, 1969). Capital-intensive techniques required new forms of integration, and the development of these new forms made the adoption

---

[18]Very few residents of the Germanic territories were wearing cotton clothing by 1850, and the cotton industry was only a third to a fourth the size of the French cotton industry (Clapham, 1951; Landes, 1965b).

[19]As late as 1875, for example, two-thirds of German weavers were domestic outworkers (Clapham, 1951, p. 297).

of such techniques more feasible. The major kind of integration evident before 1857 was *vertical,* involving a combination of mining and metallurgy under the same entrepreneurial leadership.[20] Vertically integrated enterprises generally combined coal and iron-ore mining, iron and steel manufacturing, and engineering (Henderson, 1968). These enterprises, known as *Gemischt-Werke,* became even more prevalent after introduction of the Gilchrist-Thomas process, and thus German heavy industry became far more integrated than its British counterpart (Tilly, 1966a). Landes (1965b, p. 491) makes a simple comparison: "Germany put big and big together and Britain left small and small apart." The payoff of the German strategy was obvious; by 1900 its iron and steel production exceeded, and its total industrial output almost equaled, British production (Landes, 1965b; Patel, 1961).

The rise of the cartels, the second major German organizational innovation, accompanied the trend toward vertical organization. The cartels, which consisted of the major entrepreneurs in an industry, were promoted by the investment banks that financed industrial enterprises. The major function of the cartels was to control pricing policies, and by guaranteeing sales to their members they enabled them to concentrate on improving productivity (Dawson, 1911). Thus the benefits of the division of labor were attained on a very large scale (Kindleberger, 1964), a point to which we shall return later.[21]

German entrepreneurs also made important innovations within the producer goods sector. Krupp produced several of the most significant, which were not only the first of their kinds but also of high quality. Regarding Krupp's railroad wheels, Manchester (1968, p. 79) says simply, "The tire was a masterstroke. There was almost no competition." Krupp also diversified his production. His successful production of spoons by means of rollers financed his experiments in making railroad wheels, and the profits from the wheels in turn financed his production of armaments.

The German machine industry was especially distinctive for the quality of its goods. Entrepreneurs in this industry had turned to producing their own machines, rather than copying British machines, in the 1850s. By the latter part of the century the only areas in which the industry did not excel was that of fine cotton-spinning machinery and reaping machinery, in which the British and Americans predominated respectively (Clapham, 1951). A modern shipbuilding industry also had been developed by this time, and we have mentioned the product innovations—dyes and synthetics—of the German chemical industry previously.[22] So new high-quality products were part of the reason for the success of the German producer goods sector. The major innovation in consumer

---

[20]Redlich (1940) considers August Thyssen the leader in the development and promotion of this innovation. Alfred Krupp was also an enthusiastic advocate of such arrangements.

[21]The spread of the cartels was greatest after 1875. There were only 14 in 1877, but by the turn of the century there were 275 (Clapham, 1951, p. 311).

[22]Landes (1965b) observes that the chemical industry was distinctive because of the diversity of its products even before 1850.

goods was the replacement of linen products by cotton, which also took place after 1850.

The accomplishments of German entrepreneurs in the metallurgical and machine industries enabled them increasingly to invade the foreign market dominated by the British. The lack of competition Krupp faced with his railroad wheels exemplifies this situation. Furthermore, his wheels appeared simultaneously with the beginning of the railroad boom in Germany, and after 1850 they and his steel rails were used extensively in the construction of railroads in the United States.[23]

The price-fixing activities of the German cartels also undoubtedly facilitated exploitation of the foreign market. In general, however, German entrepreneurs sold proportionally more goods in the domestic market than did British entrepreneurs (Hoffman, 1955). This difference was in part a result of the great difference in the colonial systems of the two countries, and probably also partly due to the relatively greater demand for goods of the public sector in Germany as compared to Britain. In contrast to French entrepreneurs, the Germans appear to have been more perceptive about the potential of producing goods for a mass market (Bowen, 1950).

German entrepreneurs' use of technical experts constitutes their most significant labor innovation and distinguishes them from the other European entrepreneurs (Dawson, 1911; Landes, 1969). Their use of technicians enabled them to achieve the marriage of science and industry we have discussed above. Krupp's provision of welfare services to his *Kruppianer* was far ahead of the practices of other entrepreneurs and therefore also constituted a labor innovation.[24] Bismarck was to institute a system of welfare legislation in the 1880s very similar to the system that Krupp had developed.

The use of bills of exchange, a device that had been used earlier in Britain, by German entrepreneurs early in the nineteenth century can be considered a financial innovation. With the rise of the investment banks and the acceleration of capital requirements after 1850, German entrepreneurs increasingly turned to the banks for financial support or made the transition to corporate forms of organization. Even the Krupp firm, whose guiding spirit Alfred "could imagine no more ghastly fate than falling 'into the hands of a joint-stock company,' " (Manchester, 1968, p. 81) became dependent upon the banks for capital. The banks also served as intermediaries for many joint-stock companies, raising capital for them through the sale of shares. Thus the major financial innovations in the German case were made by the banking system rather than by industrial

---

[23] And Krupp knew how to exploit this market, particularly for the later sale of armaments. For example, in 1878 he sponsored a "Bombardment of the Nations," a display of weapons which was attended by military officers from twelve foreign countries (Manchester, 1968).

[24] Manchester (1968, p. 146) has described the situation starkly: "Of course, a man dismissed from his job lost everything, including his pension. Elsewhere, however, pensions did not even exist."

entrepreneurs; the major change made by entrepreneurs was their increased reliance upon the banking system.

Degree of innovation. German entrepreneurs contributed major technological, material, organizational, and product innovations to the stock of techniques they inherited from the British and the French, and these contributions enabled them to surpass their predecessors in industrial output. The Bessemer process, for example, had reduced the twenty-four hours required to produce three tons of pig iron by the puddling technique to twenty minutes (Redlich, 1940, p. 54). The Germans improved upon this, and as a result their metallurgical industry had a higher degree of productivity than did the British. The situation was reversed in their respective textile industries, however (Landes, 1965b). Developments in the electrical industry, although primarily realized after 1875, were also of momentous significance. Coupling the dynamo with the ability to transmit electricity across distances revolutionized the industrial world by providing a mode of power far superior to that of steam. The German role in the forefront of this development further stimulated her industrialization. Many of the German technological innovations therefore can be regarded as manifesting a high degree of change.

Expansions

The pattern of German industrial expansions duplicated the pattern of innovations, being quite slow before 1850 and much more rapid after that date. If opportunity conditions were abundant after 1815, as Tilly (1966b) has suggested, German entrepreneurs were apparently somewhat oblivious to them. Or their lethargy may have been due to a lack of capital.[25]

For whatever reason, expansion was slow on all fronts after 1815, occurring in the form of "step-by-step improvements and enlargements of capacity" (Tilly, 1967, p. 174). There was already a strong tendency toward concentration in the textile industry in this period, with larger manufacturers absorbing marginal ones (Hamerow, 1958). This tendency was heightened after 1850 as part of the general trend toward integration and combination, but it did not become universal, as the textile industry retained a significant small-scale sector even in 1870.

Private entrepreneurs increasingly emerged as opportunity conditions improved after 1850, and expansion was more rapid. New enterprises were initiated and existing ones were expanded. The pace of expansion became extremely rapid

[25]Rother, a Prussian official, wrote in 1839:

The capitalists here are not inclined to pay industrial enterprises their proper due. Even the soundest of incorporation projects fail to attract interest. Rather than making funds available to industry, capitalists prefer to invest their fortunes in government securities or mortgages, and to enjoy the fruits of their investment with the greatest possible amount of peace and calm. The currently low interest rates seem associated only with the purchase of landed estates. (Tilly, 1967, pp. 154–55).

after 1871, coincident with the political unification of Germany. Clapham (1951, p. 284) reports, although he does not support his statement with data, that more businesses for ironsmelting, ironworking, and engineering were started in Prussia between 1871 and 1874 than in all the previous years of the nineteenth century. This suggests that a great deal of initial expansion was still occurring at this time, as does Visser's (1969) observation of a large number of self-made men in a sample of entrepreneurs from heavy industry and the chemical industry who were born after 1830. But Landes (1965b) claims that much of the growth of heavy industry involved established, rather than new, enterprises by this time.

The primary sources of capital for expansions before about 1840 were entrepreneurs' own resources, or those of their family and friends, and reinvested profits. German entrepreneurs supposedly were accustomed to relatively low profits (Veblen, 1939), so the rate of reinvestment would have had to be quite high. According to Tilly (1967), there was a need for substantial reliance upon outside credit even at this early stage. Our impression is that this need was greater than it had been in either Britain or France. The need for outside capital increased greatly after 1850, but it was met by the investment banks; thus the difference between German and British and French entrepreneurs on this characteristic became even greater.

Degree of expansion.[26] The degree of change characterizing expansions in Germany followed a pattern similar to the one we have seen in Britain and France. It was possible to start on a small scale after 1815, but after 1850 this was no longer possible. This change in scale was more pronounced in heavy industry than in a light industry such as textiles, in which the pace of technological innovation had slowed, thereby braking the rate of increase in optimum plant size (Landes, 1969).

Small-scale operations were the norm in all industries—textiles, metallurgy, machinery, and chemicals—prior to 1850. For instance, the average spindleage in Prussia in 1837 was 828, by 1846 it had increased to 1,126. But it was 629 in the *Zollverein* as a whole, which represented about six machines and about fifteen workers per firm. German iron enterprises remained smaller than those of Britain and France in 1845 (Landes, 1965b, pp. 395, 401, 408). Krupp's steel-pouring shed was the only facility in the Germanic states comparable to the British scale of operations in metallurgy.

Most industries moved to a larger scale of production after 1850, with the trend being carried to an extreme in heavy industry as compared to British and French heavy industry. By about 1900, for example, the median firm in the German steel cartel was *four* times as large as its British counterpart (Landes, 1965b, p. 490). The Krupp enterprise in Essen exemplifies the rapid increase in scale after 1850. By 1857, forty-six years after its founding, it had attained a

---

[26]We use data on the scale of operations as our indicator of the size of expansions because we have little data on capital requirements.

work force of only a thousand, but by 1870 this had reached 11,000 and by 1873 it had swelled to 16,000. Equally striking was the fifteen-fold increase in the annual production of pig iron in the Ruhr between 1850 and 1860 (Manchester, 1968, p. 81; Stolper, et.al., 1967, p. 15).

Entrepreneurial Identity

Before the 1840s German entrepreneurs acted individually or in partnership with others just as British and French entrepreneurs did in the early stages of their industrial transitions. Some of the most significant firms were the work of individuals like Krupp. But beginning in the 1840s the private bankers became significant entrepreneurial actors, followed in the 1850s by the investment banks. Compared to the indirect involvement of British and American commercial banks, German investment banks were directly involved in the perception, planning, and implementation phases of the entrepreneurial role. In some cases they acted on their own, but in probably the majority of cases they shared the role with manufacturers (Stolper, et.al., 1967). Later in the 1880s the banks joined together in consortia or syndicates to promote especially costly enterprises.

Joint-stock companies were relatively less important in Germany than in Great Britain before 1870, mainly because of the greater importance of private bankers and the investment banks and the continued prominence of individual entrepreneurs, such as Krupp, Mevissen, and Thyssen, who were prominent in metallurgy throughout the 1850s and 1860s (Redlich, 1940). Liberalization of the legal restrictions on corporate formation in 1869 prompted a rapid increase in the formation of such organizations, however. Only 123 had been formed before 1850, but 295 were formed between 1851 and 1870, and 833 were established in the short period 1871-74 (Landes, 1965b, p. 426). According to Cameron (1961, p. 106), many of the joint-stock companies initiated after 1850, and especially after 1870, were "organized on the initiative or under the aegis of the great corporate banks." Thus German entrepreneurship was predominantly collective after about 1850, and significantly more so than it had been in Britain or France.

According to Bowen (1950, p. 77), "Almost from the beginning and considerably earlier than his opposite numbers in other industrializing countries, the German . . . learned the advantage of team play." This presents a sharp contradistinction to the criticism of French entrepreneurs' inability to cooperate. Cooperation certainly was required to carry out the entrepreneurial role when individuals from different organizations were involved. The increased reliance on bank financing, the trend toward integration, and the rise of the cartels necessitated extensive cooperation and also significantly affected the manner in which entrepreneurial endeavors were perceived, planned, and implemented. Kindleberger (1964, p. 86) describes decision-making in heavy industry near the end of our period of study as divided among the cartel, which was concerned with pricing; the banks, whose concern was finance; the managers, who controlled production; and the executives, who were in charge of investment and plant location decisions. Hence in Germany the entrepreneurial role had become split up, a far cry from the individualistic efforts of British entrepreneurs a century earlier. Furthermore, the *planning* phase of the entrepreneurial role was enlarged by the close ties between banking and manufacturing (Landes, 1969).

Family entrepreneurship characterized the period before 1850, but declined in importance after that date, a pattern also similar to that of Britain and France. The family firm was the typical firm around 1850, particularly in the cotton and machine industries (Wutzmer, 1960). There was also much inheritance of family firms. Redlich (1940, p. 60) notes, for example, that August Thyssen was the only major entrepreneur in metallurgy who did not start from a position of inherited wealth or an inherited enterprise.

The proportion of family firms declined as the investment banks and corporate forms of entrepreneurship became more prominent after 1850. Visser (1969) has shown the decline in the proportion of entrepreneurs inheriting industrial enterprises between a group born before 1830 and a group born between 1830 and 1860. Nevertheless there were noteworthy exceptions. The Krupp family, for example, maintained control of its firm from 1811 until the late 1960s.

German family entrepreneurship has not received nearly the criticism that has been heaped upon French family entrepreneurship, although Tilly (1966a, pp. 57–58) does note that "the preservation and increase of the family firm's capital was the principal goal of all entrepreneurial activity" in the Rhineland before 1850. The system of partible inheritance, which likely had negative effects on expansiveness, was in effect in both France and Germany. And it is probable that many German family firms remained nonexpansive and noninnovative like French family firms, so the relative lack of criticism in the German case is somewhat surprising. Undoubtedly it is due to the notably better overall performance of German heavy industry after 1850, in which families, such as the Krupps, played a major role. The Siemens family was another prominent German entrepreneurial family of the period. Frederick and William Siemens played a leading role in the development of the Siemens-Martin process in Britain, and their relative, Werner, developed the dynamo generator. Other members of the family subsequently were involved in innovations in the electrical industry (Landes, 1965b).[27] We noted in the last chapter, however, that there also were innovative families in France, involved, for example, in the development of synthetic textiles. Thus we feel that the difference between French and German family entrepreneurship has been overemphasized.

German entrepreneurship had more of an outsider quality before 1850 than after that date. Whereas Britain was the primary source of the technological innovations borrowed by German entrepreneurs, France was the main source of outside entrepreneurs. British entrepreneurs did make earlier contributions to the cotton, woolen, and engineering industries, but after 1815 the French were more

---

[27]Landes (1965b. p. 484) calls the Siemens family "the most inventive in history."

active. They were concentrated in mining and the processing of nonferrous metals in Silesia, the Ruhr, and the Rhineland (Cameron, 1961; Henderson, 1968). Cameron (1961) attributes French participation to the superior profit opportunities, as compared to France, resulting from the greater supply of coal and metals in Germany. French firms produced one-fourth of the pig iron in western Germany in the 1860s; about a fourth of the capital invested in the coal and heavy industries of the Ruhr and Rhineland before 1870 was French (Henderson, 1968, p. 148). French capital amounted to 4 to 5 percent of the total capital in German industrial and financial enterprises (Cameron, 1961, p. 402).[28] There also were instances of German workmen trained in France who returned to the Germanic states to become entrepreneurs. Foreign entrepreneurship began to decline after 1850. Germans moved into the technical direction of foreign enterprises in the 1850s and into financial control in the 1860s so that after 1870 foreign entrepreneurship was much less significant (Cameron, 1961).

There is little evidence of indigenous entrepreneurs being disproportionately drawn from marginal or outsider sources, however. Occupationally, merchants and craftsmen were most important, a duplication of the British and French cases. Merchants predominated in the textile industry, particularly in cotton and linen. They also were heavily represented among iron entrepreneurs, and provided the capital for many iron works, as well as entering the chemical industry (Wutzmer, 1960).

Artisans were most significant in the early stages of the metallurgical and machine industries, but there were some in the textile industry as well.[29] After about 1850 they were replaced by "engineer" entrepreneurs, individuals with a background in technical education rather than simply the knowledge gained from personal experience in production (Wutzmer, 1960). We have described earlier the German system of technical education which produced individuals with this training. Engineer entrepreneurs were important in metallurgy and in machine production, particularly in the steam-engine industry (Redlich, 1944).

Few German entrepreneurs came from agricultural backgrounds, and the participation of the nobility in entrepreneurial roles appears to have been less significant in Germany than it was in France. Junkers from Schleswig, who were both agriculturalists and aristocrats, did become linen entrepreneurs (Wutzmer, 1960), but they appear to have been an exception.[30] The major way in which German entrepreneurs differed occupationally from British and French entrepreneurs was in the greater proportion of bankers who were *industrial* entrepreneurs.[31]

[28]In mining and metallurgy the proportion was much higher—10 to 15 percent.

[29]Clapham (1951) claims that many cotton entrepreneurs were originally domestic outworkers.

[30]Redlich (1940, pp. 62–63) reports that the nobleman von Donnersmarck developed the Tidewater metallurgical works but provides no additional information.

[31]Generally the firms initiated by bankers were equipped with the most modern equipment (Tilly, 1967), a characteristic probably resulting from their greater supply of capital.

On the basis of these occupational backgrounds therefore we agree with Visser (1969) that German entrepreneurs were predominantly middle class after 1850. It is possible that individuals from lower classes were represented more extensively in the entrepreneurial role before 1850, but after 1850 German entrepreneurship appears to have been predominantly mainstream.

The greater representation of public entrepreneurship in Germany is another characteristic that distinguishes German entrepreneurship from British entrepreneurship especially, and also from French entrepreneurship. Entrepreneurship by the state was extremely significant before 1815, dating from at least the seventeenth century (Fischer, 1963).[32] But we have noted that there were conflicting views among German officials regarding the relative merits of public and private entrepreneurship by the late eighteenth century. The policies followed in the various states reflected the views of the officials in charge. In Silesia, for example, Reden was a vigorous advocate of public entrepreneurship, and mining and metallurgy were developed on that basis. Stein and Vincke promoted private entrepreneurship in the Ruhr and Westphalia respectively (Henderson, 1958).

The *Seehandlung,* which had been established in 1772 as a trading corporation, was one of the most prominent examples of public entrepreneurship after 1815. In the early 1800s it had diversified into the operation of manufacturing enterprises, particularly in the textile industry. After 1815 it acquired existing enterprises and initiated new ones, often in rural areas where there was little factory production. It also procured technological innovations and artisans from Britain, and served as a model for the private sector by erecting the first worsted power mill in the Germanic states in 1842, for example. But shortly thereafter opposition to it mounted in the private sector, and in 1845 it was ordered to undertake no further expansions. Its enterprises were sold to private entrepreneurs between 1851 and 1854. It is noteworthy that the majority of its operations in the 1840s were joint enterprises in conjunction with local entrepreneurs or bankers (Fischer, 1963; Henderson, 1958; Landes, 1965b, 1969).

After 1850 the government maintained its most active hand in metallurgy and mining.[33] Other manufacturing enterprises operated on a public basis in the post-1850 period included tobacco and porcelain factories, amber works, and breweries (Stolper, et. al., 1967).[34] Overall, however, private entrepreneurship predominated in manufacturing during the period we are investigating; the public role was greater in mining and railroad construction than in manufacturing. But the state did play a larger direct role in manufacturing in Germany than it did in

---

[32]Frederick the Great (1740–86) had been the most active proponent of state involvement in the development of mining and metallurgy.

[33]The state of Prussia still operated twelve smelting works and a larger number of mines in 1906 (Dawson, 1911, p. 208).

[34]Prussia and Saxony both retained their porcelain factories until World War II (Stolper, et al., 1967, p. 39).

Britain and France. Opinions vary regarding the effects of German public entrepreneurship upon private entrepreneurship. Pounds (1959) suggests that it hampered the private sector in Upper Silesia, but Henderson (1958) has commended the *Seehandlung* for being innovative—by establishing industries in rural areas and operating joint enterprises—and suggests that there was "healthy competition" between the public and private sectors in the period before 1870.

We have seen that German industrial entrepreneurship differed from British and French entrepreneurship in several important ways. It was more collective (after 1850); it involved more outsiders (before 1850), individuals with technical training, and bankers; and the public sector was more prominent (before 1850). Entrepreneurship, however, was generally similar in the three societies in the relative significance of the family and the predominance of entrepreneurs from mercantile and craft backgrounds. Like British entrepreneurs, German entrepreneurs appear to have been predominantly Protestant. Redlich (1940, p. 60) takes special note of Thyssen's being Catholic, implying that he was an exception. Moreover, Prussia was overwhelmingly Protestant and it was dominant industrially among the Germanic states, which suggests that the majority of German entrepreneurs were Protestant.

THE RATE OF GERMAN INDUSTRIAL GROWTH

German industrial entrepreneurs have received plaudits for their impressive performance in the nineteenth century, whereas French entrepreneurs have usually received opprobrium. Therefore, one would expect that the German industrial growth rate far exceeded the French rate in the 1800s. But the available evidence reveals that the difference is not nearly as dramatic as is the difference in the descriptions of entrepreneurship in the two cases. Industrial growth was quite slow in Germany before 1850.[35] But even after 1850 the industrial growth rate was not astounding. Patel (1961, pp. 319, 324) provides two different estimates of the annual rate of growth of industrial output between 1860 and 1880—2.7 percent and 2.9 percent—neither of which is radically higher than rates for Britain and France during their industrial transitions.

Where, then, does the traditional view of the rapid growth of German industry originate? True, the *overall* rate of industrial growth was not particularly high before 1875, largely because of the slow rate of growth in the textile industry. The key to Germany's industrial success was the performance of the *producer goods* sector, which had an annual growth rate of 3.9 percent per year between 1860 and 1880, compared to 1.8 percent for the consumer goods sector (Patel, 1961, p. 324). The annual growth rate of the German iron industry was

---

[35]Landes (1965b, pp. 587–88) says, "German industrial growth looks extremely rapid if one dates it from 1850. It is much slower, slower at first than the British for example, if 1815 is the starting point."

remarkably high: 10.2 percent between 1850 and 1869 compared to 6.7 percent for the French iron industry during the same period and 5.2 percent for the British iron industry for the period 1848-70 (Landes, 1965b, p. 447). The output of German heavy industry doubled just in the years between 1871 and 1874 (Manchester, 1968, p. 135).

Therefore the credit for the rapid rate of industrial growth in Germany between 1850 and 1875 must go to the producer goods sector. It cannot be given to German industry as a whole. And in this respect Germany is similar to France. French annual rates of growth in the consumer and producer goods sectors between 1861–65 and 1896 were 1.2 percent and 3.3 percent respectively (Patel, 1961, p. 324). Each of these percentages is only slightly more than 0.5 percent below the comparable German rate.[36]

THE CAUSAL SIGNIFICANCE OF GERMAN INDUSTRIAL ENTREPRENEURSHIP

Does the similarity of the German, French and British industrial growth rates suggest that German entrepreneurs possibly failed to take advantage of their more favorable opportunity conditions and hence that German entrepreneurship should be regarded as having *negative* causal significance? That would be an extremely controversial conclusion in light of the accolades that have been bestowed upon German entrepreneurs.

The question of the causal significance of German entrepreneurship is best answered by dividing the period 1815–75 into three parts: 1815–50, 1850–71, and 1871–75. We have suggested that industrial growth was much more rapid after 1850 than before, and that it was especially rapid after 1871, the year when Germany was finally unified. These differences among the three periods make it impossible to assign either causal significance or causal insignificance to the entire 1815–75 period.

Previously we have stressed the favorableness of economic opportunity conditions in Germany in comparison to France. Although that difference is more pronounced for the post-1850 period because of the increased amounts of capital made available by the investment banks and the development of the Ruhr coal deposits at that time, we also believe that German opportunity conditions were somewhat more favorable than opportunity conditions in France before 1850. After 1850 German opportunity conditions became *much* more favorable.

We judge that even though the level of economic development was lower in Germany than in France in 1815, bankers made capital available to alleviate this problem shortly thereafter. Much of this went into railroad construction

[36]The German industrial growth rate did increase to 5 percent in the period 1880 to 1900 and exceeded the United States rate for that period (Patel, 1961, p. 324). That was the period of most rapid change of the German textile industry, which was reflected in the 3.7 percent annual rate of growth for the consumer goods sector during those years.

which also helped to improve opportunity conditions before 1850. Technologically the two societies can be considered approximate equals before 1850, with British innovations available to both, but we feel the Germans had an advantage in regard to labor because of the earlier development of their educational system. Coal was relatively available, even though the Ruhr region had not yet been developed, so they also had an advantage in raw materials. The German market was restricted by the absence of political unification, but the development of the *Zollverein* and railroad construction helped to lessen this handicap. We have also described the slowness of expansion and innovation in all German industries before 1850. Hence we conclude that German entreprenuership had *negative* causal significance before 1850. Opportunity conditions were not exploited as fully as they could have been.

The picture is very different in the two decades after 1850. We have described the increase in expansions and innovations, particularly in metallurgy, but also in textiles. Major innovations began to appear in the infant chemical and electrical industries at this time. The industrial growth rate moved ahead of the French and British rates, and would very likely have been higher if changes had occurred more rapidly in the textile industry. During this period, therefore, we regard German entrepreneurship as being causally *insignificant*, as it responded in virtual parity with the favorableness of the existent opportunity conditions.

The first signs of a much higher industrial growth rate began to appear between 1871 and 1875, at the very end of our period of study, with the producer goods sector the dominant contributor. Its performance is partly attributable to the continuing improvement in opportunity conditions resulting from the Franco-Prussian War and the availability of new metallurgical techniques. But the improvement in opportunity conditions is not the whole story. We believe the rate of industrial growth surpassed what one would expect on the basis of the improved opportunity conditions, and thus we accord German entrepreneurship *positive* causal significance during the period 1871–75. Hence the causal significance of German entrepreneurship reversed between 1815 and 1875. The tentative entrepreneurial response to the relatively favorable opportunity conditions existing after 1815 was transformed into the vigorous response of the 1870s.[37]

NONECONOMIC FACTORS INFLUENCING
GERMAN ENTREPRENEURSHIP

These conclusions regarding the causal significance of German entrepreneurship suggest that noneconomic factors were of great importance in the German case, acting as barriers to entrepreneurship before 1850, becoming neutral between

[37]We differ from Gerschenkron (1955) who has attributed the difference in French and German industrial growth to differences in the two economies rather than to differences in entrepreneurship. We agree with him in regard to the period 1850–71 but not in regard to the 1815–50 or the 1871–75 periods.

1850 and 1871, and becoming strongly supportive after 1871, thereby promoting a disproportionate emergence of entrepreneurship. We shall see if that was in fact the case.

It is probable that the sociocultural environment was less conducive to entrepreneurship in the Germanic states than in France in the years immediately after 1815. Feudalistic structures, supported by the Junker aristocracy, very likely had changed less than they had in France by this time, except for the Rhineland where there was a greater degree of industrialization and a group of businessmen who were gaining in power (Tilly, 1966a; Wutzmer, 1960). The Junkers remained firmly entrenched, especially in eastern Prussia.[38]

Consequently the legitimacy of entrepreneurship was quite low in the Germanic states, probably lower than in France, after 1815. Landes (1969, p. 129) says, ''The farther east one goes in Europe, the more the bourgeoisie takes on the appearance of a foreign excrescence on manorial society, a group apart scorned by the nobility and feared or hated by (or unknown to) a peasantry still personally bound to the local seigneur.'' This opposition to entrepreneurship was widespread, including artisans, the town and craft guilds, the landed Junkers, the churches, and a substantial portion of the government bureaucracy (Hamerow, 1958; Henderson, 1958; Tilly, 1967). Social mobility was also very limited. Landes (1969, p. 129) claims that the gap between the masses and the aristocracy was even greater than in France—''class prejudice was reinforced by law, and lines were carefully drawn between noble, burgher, and peasant.'' Furthermore the German system of guilds was the most rigid in Europe (Clapham, 1951).

But significant changes came after 1848 and the revolution of that year, which was the culmination of the struggle for power between Junker landowners and the rising businessmen and industrialists (Hamerow, 1958). Cameron (1961) believes that Prussia had been affected greatly by the ideals of the French Revolution. Whether it was that influence, or whether it was a realistic political strategy on their part, the Junkers' change in attitude toward industrialization was the most important consequence of the Revolution for German entrepreneurship.[39] Both the legitimacy of entrepreneurship and the potential for social mobility increased in the aftermath. The German revolution was probably no more complete than was the French Revolution, in terms of eliminating the aristocracy and strengthening capitalist entrepreneurs,[40] but it did increase the sociocultural support for industrial entrepreneurship.

After 1850 therefore entrepreneurs, especially those in export and heavy

[38]Veblen (1939, pp. 159, 172) caustically described Prussia as ''medieval militarism resting on a feudally servile agrarian system'' with a dynastic state ''resting on an authentic tradition of personal fealty.''

[39]Tilly (1966b) credits the Junkers with the initiative in forming the coalition with the Rhenish entrepreneurs in opposition to both the Frankfurt Parliament and the working class. Moore (1966, p. 34) seems to give more emphasis to the bourgeoisie, who ''leaned on the landed aristocracy to protect them against popular discontent.''

[40]Dahrendorf (1967) describes Germany as a ''faulted'' nation which remained quasi-feudal.

industries, such as armaments, received higher prestige. Laws restricting the power of the guilds, which were passed as early as 1845, promoted movement into the entrepreneurial role; by the end of 1859, workshops and factories could be established without licensing. The resultant social mobility has been described as "sufficient," (Kindleberger, 1958, p. 86), and we have noted earlier the blockage of traditionally more prestigious roles. The combination of these two factors—increased social mobility by means of entrepreneurship and blockage of nonentrepreneurial roles—no doubt encouraged entry into the entrepreneurial role. Veblen (1939, p. 195) has described the positive forces supporting industrialization at this time, noting the high degree of interest in industry and the willingness of educated men "glad to find employment in some conventionally blameless occupation" to participate. So it is clear that both the legitimacy of entrepreneurship and the potential for social mobility that it offered increased after 1848.

This implies that entrepreneurship was a marginal role before 1848, but that it became more of a mainstream role after 1848. We have seen that outsider entrepreneurship on the part of foreigners was significant before 1850 and declined thereafter, a fact which supports this interpretation. Entrepreneurs also were much less integrated into society before 1850 than they were after 1850. Their early lack of integration stemmed from both Junker opposition and their location in a number of different sovereignties. Foreign entrepreneurs, however, no doubt formed a highly integrated group, partly because they were *foreigners*. The indigenous entrepreneurs' formation of a coalition with the Junkers after 1848 most certainly increased their integration in the social system. In fact they may have become captives of the system. Moore (1966) suggests, for example, that the ties between the bourgeoisie and the landed aristocracy was greater in Prussia than in England, and that the two formed a "marriage of iron and rye," characteristic of late nineteenth-century Germany.[41] Although these close ties may not have been conducive to the establishment of democracy, they certainly did not hinder industrialization, especially after 1871. Hence the German case indicates that a high degree of entrepreneurial integration into the social system promotes industrial growth, provided that the system is supportive, as Germany was after 1850 and even more so after 1871.

It also has been suggested that a high degree of integration was a distinctive characteristic of Prussian society before 1871 and of German society after 1871. Such suggestions typically emphasize the "discipline" of the people under the authoritarian direction of the state (Bowen, 1950; Veblen, 1939). We noted a similar description of the French citizenry, but we suspect that the control from the center was stronger in Prussia and Germany than in France. If so, then this, combined with the state policies supporting industrialization that we have noted previously, would have provided additional support for entrepreneurship. A high

[41] In Dahrendorf's (1967) view, this absorption into the system explains why Germany became an industrial, but not a capitalist society.

degree of social integration would have facilitated the state's mobilization of public opinion in support of entrepreneurship.

Finally, we believe that entrepreneurial security also increased as attitudes toward industrialization became more favorable after 1848. Industrialists and bankers have been described as insecure during the 1840s (Hamerow, 1958). But the rapid growth of industry as a result of private initiative after 1850 suggests that there was much willingness to embark on entrepreneurial ventures, which we link partly to the greater degree of security.

Aristocratic opposition to entrepreneurship, even though a cause of insecurity before 1850, is believed to have had positive effects for German entrepreneurship very similar to those we have described for Britain and France, e.g., on the *desire for* status respect. Thus Visser (1969) argues that the opposition actually promoted the rise of capitalism and entrepreneurs because it represented an obstacle against which to struggle. Tilly (1967) makes a similar point regarding the effects of the state's restrictive monetary policies upon the banking system. As in Britain and France, the opposition was not severe enough to quash emerging entrepreneurs.

As for psychological characteristics supportive of entrepreneurship, we have no evidence that there was a psychological transformation around 1850 sufficiently extreme to account for the post-1850 industrial growth. The area in which we have the most evidence regarding the importance of psychological orientations is that of the relative importance of pecuniary motives. Veblen (1939) has been the most well-known representative of the view that German entrepreneurs were less driven by economic motives than entrepreneurs in other societies, arguing that they were more interested in technology and craftsmanship than the mercenary captains of business and finance in the United States. But Dawson (1911, p. 78) has said, "In Germany trade is a passion. . . . It is not an incident in a man's life . . . , but the chief, primary, absorbing concern," which leads us to question Veblen's characterization. We suspect that German entrepreneurs were motivated neither more nor less by the possibilities of economic gain than were entrepreneurs in other societies. They possibly were caught up by the nationalistic appeals surrounding formation of the German Empire in 1871, but we have no evidence to indicate that nationalism motivated their economic behavior to any appreciable degree.[42]

Therefore we believe that the sociocultural environment functioned in the German case in the manner we predicted. Before 1850 the limited legitimacy of entrepreneurship, the lack of social mobility of entrepreneurs, and the lack of entrepreneurial integration and security *prevented* German entrepreneurs from

---

[42]Visser (1969, p. 323) says, "Contemporary observers in the academic world . . . had their doubts about the businessmen's dedication to the common good." This causes us to have doubts about German entrepreneurs' nationalistic sentiments. Krupp was hardly a selfless patriot—he charged the German government twice as much as foreign governments for armor and often accrued profits of 100 percent (Manchester, 1968).

taking full advantage of the available economic opportunity conditions. The influx of foreign entrepreneurs in this period indicates that opportunity conditions were favorable. Their presence also gave German entrepreneurship the marginal quality that our model of "outsider" entrepreneurship predicts. However we regard the German case as a *quasi-outsider* type before 1850 because indigenous entrepreneurs do not appear to have been drawn from marginal groups. We attribute the greater representation of foreign entrepreneurs in Germany than in France primarily to the combination of *more favorable* economic conditions and *less favorable* noneconomic conditions that existed in the Germanic states at this time in comparison to France.

Public entrepreneurship took up part of the slack during this period but it was not sufficient to create rapid industrial growth. Hence the unfavorable quality of the sociocultural characteristics before 1850, the period in which we believe German entrepreneurship had negative causal significance, kept German entrepreneurship from emerging in proportion to the favorableness of opportunity conditions.

The Revolution of 1848 brought important changes in the sociocultural climate. The legitimacy of entrepreneurship increased, as did the possibility of social mobility, so that individuals were freer to enter the entrepreneurial role. The blockage of nonentrepreneurial roles, which distinguished the German case from the French, combined with the increased legitimacy of entrepreneurship to promote its emergence. Entrepreneurial security also increased, along with the integration of entrepreneurs within the system through their coalition with the Junkers. Foreign and public entrepreneurship both declined, and German entrepreneurship moved from a quasi-outsider type to the mainstream type. Its mainstream nature is also evident from the fact that entrepreneurs primarily came from mercantile and artisan backgrounds.[43] Thus the transformation of the sociocultural barriers to entrepreneurship around midcentury *liberated* entrepreneurship, allowing it to emerge in proportion to the favorableness of economic opportunity conditions.

Conceivably, the great changes which occurred after mid-century were partly due to a decisive increase in the willingness of German entrepreneurs to take risks. But we believe they are explained more cogently as the result of a significant decline in the *noneconomic* risks of entrepreneurship. Before 1850 the level of economic risk was less in Germany than in France, but the level of noneconomic risk was somewhat higher, and it was appreciably higher than in Britain. Consequently, the diminution of noneconomic risk after 1850 spurred entrepreneurial emergence.

---

[43]We link the rise of engineer-entrepreneurs to the opportunity conditions of the time which were more favorable in technologically more complex heavy industry. The importance of bankers as industrial entrepreneurs suggests that those with more capital were better able to respond to the existent opportunity conditions before 1850.

Another decrease in noneconomic risk came with the achievement of political unification in 1871. This was partly the result of the increased social integration that unification brought, and partly a consequence of the legitimizing effects of an ideology that advocated industrialization as the means of making the new nation strong militarily. It is almost certain that sociocultural factors were most favorable to entrepreneurship during this period. Entrepreneurship emerged disproportionately as a result, and it had positive causal significance.

How do we explain the improvement in these noneconomic characteristics after 1850? They may constitute another of the effects of backwardness. It has been suggested that the economic characteristics of "latecomer" societies are not the only important ones. "The effort of catching up calls forth entrepreneurial and institutional responses that, once established, constitute powerful stimuli to continued growth" (Landes, 1969, p. 336). This evidently is what happened in Germany.

But it is equally evident that this did not happen automatically. Our later discussion of the Russian case will show that backwardness by itself cannot promote sociocultural change. In the German case, the state played an important part in the transformation of noneconomic opportunity conditions in addition to its role in improving economic opportunity conditions. Its ending of guild restrictions made entry into the entrepreneurial role easier. The continual interest of many Prussian government officials in industrialization, and later actions, such as the protection given to cartels, helped increase entrepreneurial legitimacy and entrepreneurial security. Its support of heavy industry, which resulted from militaristic goals, helped to increase the prestige of entrepreneurs involved in that sector. The military goals coincided with the German economic opportunity conditions, with both favoring the development of heavy industry. But to make full use of the opportunity conditions it was necessary that the sociocultural environment also coincide.

We pointed out earlier (Chapter 2) that the government's role is not a truly exogenous factor because it may be influenced by the actions of entrepreneurs. The extent to which this was true in the German case is in question. The political influence of German entrepreneurs did increase after 1848 as a result of their alliance with the Junkers. Alfred Krupp, though possibly an extreme case, exemplifies the close relationships that were possible between entrepreneurs and government officials. And Visser (1969) claims that German entrepreneurs wielded political power, especially after 1848, comparable to that of entrepreneurs in Britain and the United States. But in Tilly's opinion (1966a) German entrepreneurs never attained the political influence that British and American entrepreneurs did. Our feeling is that they had some influence, but that it was not of major importance.

The juxtaposition of political, economic, and sociocultural changes after 1850 does make it difficult to determine which should be considered most important. If the major changes in economic opportunity conditions had not occurred, but the sociocultural changes had, it is likely that more entrepreneurship would have been forthcoming than in the past. Or if the opposite had happened, it is also likely that more entrepreneurship would have emerged. But the crucial point about the German case is that *both* the economic and noneconomic opportunity conditions improved at about the same time and they thereby substantially increased industrial growth and entrepreneurial emergence. Because the state helped promote changes in both of these areas, it represents a very important exogenous factor in the German case.

7

Japan

At about the same time as Germany began its period of most rapid industrialization, on the opposite side of the world Japan began to replicate in the Oriental world the pattern that Great Britain had displayed a century earlier in the West. Japan, after a revolutionary change of government in 1868, reversed centuries of history as a feudal rural society and, under the government of the Meiji Restoration, began to industrialize at a pace far more rapid than other Asian societies, just as Britain had pulled ahead of its Continental competitors after 1750. The similarities are even greater. Both societies were insular, both were relatively densely populated, and both were confronted by a more populous mainland society—Great Britain by France and Japan by China. Both also made the transition to industrialization on the strength of their consumer goods sectors. Thus one may regard Japan as the "Great Britain of the Orient."

But in many ways the Japanese case was more similar to the industrial transition described in the last chapter. Like Germany, Japan's transition was stimulated by the establishment of a new political order. The state played an important role as industrial entrepreneur in both societies, yielding in time to the increased participation of private entrepreneurs. Large-scale industrial organizations became prominent in both societies; at the same time a major sector of their economies remained tied to traditional small-scale modes of production. And industrial growth became intimately linked with militaristic expansion in both societies.[1] Eventually, after both societies had reached an advanced level of industrialization, they joined forces against much of the rest of the industrialized

[1]Bendix (1964) credits Japan with pursuing industrialization prior to militarization, the opposite of the German pattern.

160

world. Although this alliance is not the object of our concern, it may not have been coincidental. The combination of rapid industrial development and limited democratic development, the major role of the government in catalyzing the industrial transition, and the onerous position of being challengers to the established powers very likely provided conditions conducive to their becoming partners against the "haves" of the twentieth century.

Japan was the first Eastern society to industrialize; hence it is an important case to study. India and China, the two largest societies in the East, still are struggling to attain what Japan has achieved twice, the second time after World War II. So an analysis of Japanese entrepreneurship is of particular significance for assessing the importance of entrepreneurship for economic growth and development and the conditions under which it emerges.

The story of Japan's about-face actually began in 1853 with the appearance of Admiral Perry and his fleet of ships off Tokyo. Japan's contact with the West before that time had been on its own terms and under its control. But the incursion of the military strength of the industrialized West changed the rules, and Japan was forced to confront the possibility of becoming colonized. Fifteen years later the Tokugawa empire was overthrown and the government of the Meiji Restoration established. We begin our study of Japanese entrepreneurship at this point and extend it beyond the end of the Meiji period (in 1911) to 1927. Because the subsequent actions of the Meiji rulers were of critical importance for entrepreneurship, we begin our analysis with a consideration of them.

ROLE OF THE JAPANESE GOVERNMENT

The Meiji rulers followed their takeover of the reins of power with a rapid-fire succession of policies which broke the bonds of feudalism and improved the economic conditions for industrialization. Lockwood (1954) notes their greater reliance on economic than on political incentives, but many of their policies enabled them to solidify their political position and were formulated with that intent.

The following major actions were taken: As early as 1868 all guilds were abolished and trade barriers and checkpoints along highways were removed. The local clan governments (*hans*) were prohibited from participating in commercial activities in 1869. Two years later, in 1871, the *hans* were abolished and the prefectural system of administration was established, thus marking the end of feudalism. In that year and the following year permission was granted to all social classes to engage in any occupation, the right to private ownership of land was granted, commoners were allowed to take family names and to marry noncommoners, and peasants were allowed to sell their rice instead of using it to pay tribute to the samurai class. A pension system was established for the samurai at the same time (Hirschmeier, 1964; Horie, 1965; Takahashi, 1968). In addition, the bases of recruitment for the civil service were radically changed after 1868 so that family background declined in importance and the possession of nontraditional skills, such as Western education, increased (Silberman, 1966).

The Meiji government instituted a major land tax reform and began to construct model factories in 1873. Compulsory education was established in 1877, the same year as the Satsuma (or Saigo) Rebellion, the last gasp of feudalism (Horie, 1939, 1965). Extensive efforts were made to stimulate the cotton textile industry, through subsidies and the construction of cotton mills, after 1879. Many of these ultimately were sold to private entrepreneurs, along with other types of enterprises, in the 1880s. The Bank of Japan was established in 1880 and in 1882 it was made the central bank. Finally, an Industrial Bank was formed to directly provide capital for industrial development in 1902 (Maddison, 1969; Patrick, 1967).

Thus in about thirty years the Meiji rulers instituted a number of policies with far-reaching social and economic consequences.[2] There have been warnings against exaggerating the significance of the government's role after 1868 (Hartwell, 1971; Lockwood, 1954). Recently it has been argued that the government did not have a conscious industrial promotion policy and that it actually hindered the efforts of industrial entrepreneurs in many cases (Yamamura, 1974). But the general opinion has been that the efforts of the Meiji rulers were overwhelmingly positive for industrial development (Hirschmeier, 1964; Maddison, 1969; Patrick, 1967). We find it difficult not to be impressed by the changes that were wrought in Japanese society in a very short period. Whether the consequences were always the intended ones, the Meiji government appears to have made a decisive improvement in socioeconomic conditions, compared to the performances of the governments of France and Russia.

Why did the Meiji rulers take such drastic steps? First, they were very much concerned about maintaining their economic and political independence from potential Western invaders, and they saw industrialization as a means to that end (Hirschmeier, 1964; Marshall, 1967; Smith, 1965). Second, they perceived particularly the *military* potential of industrialization; in this respect they were similar to their Tokugawa predecessors (Smith, 1965). And third, several of the specific policies they instituted were intended to solve the problem of the samurai. Their concern about the samurai may have emanated from a genuine interest in samurai welfare or from a realistic appraisal of their potential to be a political nuisance (Horie, 1939; Smith, 1965).[3]

[2]Horie (1965) has suggested the government's actions had four major consequences—the attainment of political stability, economic liberalization, the promotion of social mobility, and industrial stimulation.

[3]The Meiji leaders' ability to implement their policies was enhanced by the high quality of the Japanese civil service (Silberman, 1966). But in some cases they did not rely upon the civil service solely. Ranis (1959) tells, for example, of entrepreneurs being summoned directly to the Imperial Palace and "encouraged" to volunteer their services.

OPPORTUNITY CONDITIONS FOR
JAPANESE ENTREPRENEURSHIP

The actions of the Meiji government had a major influence on the favorableness of economic opportunity conditions for Japanese entrepreneurship after 1868. At the time of the Meiji assumption of power, the Japanese level of economic development was far behind that of most of the other societies we are considering, comparable perhaps to that of sixteenth-century England (Orchard, 1930). As of 1870 Japanese real gross national product was about one-fourth that of England, and it was even lower than Russia's. Fully three-fourths of the Japanese employed population was in the agricultural sector in 1872 (Maddison, 1969, p. xvi).

Meiji Japan did, however, inherit some of the foundations of industrialization from the Tokugawa period. Product and factor markets were well enough developed by 1868 so that "the mechanism of relative price changes succeeded in allocating and mobilizing scarce resources" (Duffy & Yamamura, 1971, p. 422). Much of the agricultural system was operated on a commercial basis and the economy was almost completely monetized (Duffy & Yamamura, 1971; Takenaka, 1969). Industrial enterprises, including shipyards, mines, arms factories, cotton-spinning mills, iron smelteries and foundries, glassworks, and sake and soy processing plants were in existence (Allen, 1965; Takahashi, 1968; Takenaka, 1969), and there was also a sizeable number of businessmen (Takezawa, 1966). So Japan's level of economic development was probably quite high in 1868 relative to her Asian neighbors, even though it was far behind the industrializing Western countries.

Therefore the supply of investment capital for industry was probably quite low and further limited by the tendency of those with wealth to invest in land rather than in manufacturing (Orchard, 1930). This lack may not have been as serious as the low level of economic development and the investment propensities would suggest. The existent inequalities of wealth and the general disfavor toward material consumption may have promoted capital formation (Lockwood, 1954), and capital requirements in textiles, the dominant industry, were very small.

The Meiji government stepped into the breach with a number of measures which increased the supply of capital. The device used extensively at first was direct subsidization of industrial entrepreneurs (Hirschmeier, 1964; Lockwood, 1954). Subsidies were given to industrial activities ranging from the first private cotton spinning mill in 1875 to the chemical industry in 1915.[4] The subsidization policy was adopted primarily because the government was not allowed to use tariffs, a condition forced upon it in 1858 by the Western powers which remained

---

[4]Yamamura (1974) says that these were not always given eagerly. Iwasaki, founder of the Mitsubishi *zaibatsu*, had to force the government to subsidize his shipping firm.

in effect until 1899. The policy of direct subsidization declined after about 1885, and in Lockwood's (1954) opinion it was never as important as the government's tax and credit policies.

The development of the banking system after about 1876 was a second major contribution, and it served as the principal source of capital for industry throughout much of the rest of the Meiji period. The system included both private and quasi-public banks and eventually the Industrial Bank, which was modeled after the French *Crédit Mobilier* and was designed to provide loans directly to industrial entrepreneurs, to encourage foreign portfolio investment, and to create a market for corporate and government bonds (Patrick, 1967). A postal savings system, which had larger deposits than the private savings banks, was another capital-mobilizing facility (Lockwood, 1954).

The Japanese banking system was particularly praiseworthy, operating on a "supply-leading" basis in relationship to the textile industry until the 1890s at least and vis-à-vis heavy industry until World War I. The Meiji leaders wisely stimulated its growth by transferring tax revenues to it, rather than simply using it as an alternative to taxation (Patrick, 1967).

The government's tax policies were also of significance. One positive feature of the tax system was that it transferred resources from agriculture to industry as a result of the land tax reform of 1873.[5] The feasibility of drawing capital from this source increased after about 1880 as the result of improvements in agricultural productivity stemming from land reforms instituted by the government. Allowing farmers to own land and ending the system of feudal rights led to an extension of total land under cultivation, an extension of doublecropping, and increases in yields (Gould, 1972). The increased income resulting from these gains was siphoned off by the tax system and made available to industry.[6] As a result of the productivity increases, the direct tax burden on agriculture was less than half of what it had been under the Tokugawa regime, even though the Meiji tax rate was higher (Nakamura, 1966, p. 433).

The regressive nature of the tax structure benefited entrepreneurs directly. Both the taxes on agriculture and indirect taxes on consumer goods extracted proportionately more income from peasants and consumers than from landlords, merchants, and industrial entrepreneurs (Nakamura, 1966; Ranis, 1959).[7] Entrepreneurs also were allowed to amass large amounts of wealth, as inheritance taxes were not imposed until 1905.

Moreover, the government's monetary policies were beneficial for the

[5]Lockwood (1954, p. 521) estimates that agriculture provided more than 80 percent of revenue until 1882; Ranis (1959, p. 445) places the amount at over 70 percent.

[6]Gould (1972) suggests that this created a far more favorable situation than occurred in Russia, where similar tactics were attempted but agricultural productivity was not increased and the agricultural sector declined. The Japanese gains in productivity also were greater than they had been in Britain (Landes, 1969).

[7]Ranis (1959) asserts that the lower-income groups actually *increased* their rate of voluntary savings during this period in spite of the heavy tax burden placed on them.

supply of capital. For example, even though it engaged in deficit financing, so that the national debt was almost 30 percent of national income, it was able to avoid inflation (Ranis, 1959). The Meiji leaders also discouraged foreign equity investment, thus maintaining their economic independence, but encouraged foreign investment in government bonds. Consequently foreign equity investment was minimal except for the period 1896–1914.

The government did have some negative influences on capital supplies which also should be noted. First, the banking system tended to benefit large-scale industries and public utilities at the expense of small-scale entrepreneurs (Patrick, 1967), although the overall effect well may have been positive. Second, the government's easy money policies may have led to a waste of capital (Lockwood, 1954). Third, the high level of military expenditures was probably most serious. These amounted to between 40 and 50 percent of national revenue between 1895 and 1935 (Lockwood, 1954, p. 577). They accounted for half of government consumption even in the peacetime years 1903–13, and were much higher during the Sino-Japanese (1894–95) and Russo-Japanese (1904–05) wars (Maddison, 1969, p. 14). These expenditures undoubtedly reduced the supply of capital available for industrial entrepreneurs, but they also stimulated industries, such as shipbuilding, and they did have financial payoffs, such as the reparations from China after the Sino-Japanese War which amounted to about a third of Japanese gross national product (Maddison, 1969, p. 15).[8] They also enabled the Japanese to destroy the Russian fleet in 1905, a startling turnabout from the Western powers' bombardment of Shimonoseki in 1864, only forty-one years earlier.

We do not believe these negative features detracted sufficiently from the positive effects of other actions to conclude that the government's overall effect on capital supplies was negative. It is probable that the capital supply was increased to a favorable level. Furthermore, the predominance of light consumer industries meant that capital requirements were not that great.[9]

The Meiji government also helped to improve the supply of technology. We have shown in the preceding three chapters that a vast stock of technologies had been developed in Europe by 1868. Japan benefited from their existence and their easy accessibility (Lockwood, 1954). There also has been a greater appreciation in recent years of the extent of technological development during the Tokugawa period. Some Japanese nobles had studied Dutch industrial techniques before 1800, and there had been some experimentation with them after 1800.[10]

The Meiji rulers built upon these foundations. They incorporated

[8]These were used to finance the Yawata Steel Mill in the early 1900s.

[9]Gould (1972) points out that Japan was very similar to Great Britain in its relatively low rate of investment. It was markedly less than that of the United States where capital-intensive techniques were in greater use after 1850.

[10]For example, metallurgical laboratories had been established before 1850, several reverberatory furnaces were built between 1850 and 1853—on the basis of instructions in a Dutch book—and an iron gun was cast in 1853 (Hagen, 1968).

technological innovations in the model factories they constructed. They sent Japanese entrepreneurs abroad and imported foreign technicians with the understanding that they would provide training to indigenous personnel.[11] Like the German government, they promoted the use of capital-intensive techniques because of their greater potential productivity, even though the relatively large labor supply would have made labor-intensive techniques a more logical choice (Hirschmeier, 1964). In the cotton industry they generally promoted innovations in spinning because they thought they would provide greater returns there than in weaving (Orchard, 1930).[12] The government's action no doubt had a generally positive effect on the availability of technology and technological knowledge.

The market was a third area in which the Meiji government made major contributions. Although a reasonably integrated market system had been inherited from the Tokugawa era, it is probable that the domestic market for manufactured goods was rather small because of the low economic level and the extensiveness of domestic industry. The market problem was exacerbated by the negative orientation toward material consumption espoused by Confucianism (Lockwood, 1954). But the effect of Confucianism on the demand for goods is unclear. On the one hand, there was substantial importing of luxury goods as early as the first years of the Meiji period (Miyamoto, Sakodo, and Yasuba, 1965), which implies that the market potential was greater than it might seem and that Confucianism had limited influence on the upper classes. On the other hand, it appears the demand for luxury goods promoted the continued vitality of small-scale traditional modes of production because it could not be fulfilled by factory production (Allen, 1965). So it is difficult to know exactly what the domestic market potential was; we conclude that it was limited at first and then increased. Much of this increase was due to the rapid growth of the Japanese population which increased from 34 million in 1870 to 61 million in 1927 (Ranis, 1959, p. 444; Uyeda, 1938, p. 145).

The opening of Japan to trade with the West after 1853 increased the potential of the foreign market, but it also exposed Japanese entrepreneurs to the threat of competition from Western goods. We have noted that tariffs could not be used as a means of protection. But in this market the Japanese had the advantage of producing a good that was in great demand in the West—silk. They were further blessed by the increased demand for silk goods which followed the decline of the European silk industry in the 1860s.

The outbreak of World War I was another helpful fortuitous circumstance. It suddenly increased the domestic market for munitions and uniforms, removed

---

[11]In 1880 ten sets of 2,000-spindle units were imported from England and sold to private cotton entrepreneurs on a ten-year credit basis. Only one of the units proved successful, partly because they were too small and hence uneconomical (Yamamura, 1974).

[12]Yamamura (1974) argues that state technological promotion was not complete, citing the case of the public Tomioka silk filature where interested entrepreneurs were not allowed to observe the new machines. We believe that was an exception and not fully relevant because the major effects of technological innovation were felt in cotton spinning rather than in silk.

foreign competition, and opened up the large Asian market. This demand was reduced radically at the end of the war, and the result was a severe depression which was to have political repercussions in the 1930s.[13]

Various actions of the Meiji government improved the market situation. The early prohibition of commercial activities by the *hans* removed a source of competition for entrepreneurs, and the early removal of trade barriers promoted market integration. Government demand was also a substantial proportion of total demand, starting with railroad construction in the 1870s.[14] Military expenditures also were a stimulus to production from the 1880s on. In addition, the Meiji leaders worked to curtail imports and to expand exports. They discouraged the importation of luxuries by taxing consumer goods and they simultaneously promoted exports as a means of earning foreign exchange (Gould, 1972; Hagen, 1968; Islam, 1960; Nakamura, 1966).[15]

Therefore through a combination of internal changes, government actions, and unplanned external events—the destruction of the French silk industry by disease and World War I—the market potential for Japanese entrepreneurs improved after 1868.

The two areas in which the Meiji government had the least impact on opportunity conditions were labor and raw materials. The major favorable characteristic of the Japanese labor force was its low cost; the major unfavorable characteristic was its low level of skill. The abundant supply of low-cost labor resulted from the rapid growth of population in rural areas that were already overpopulated. In fact Takahashi (1968) claims that there was actually an *oversupply* of labor during the Meiji period, and Gould (1972) says that substantial amounts of *underemployed* agricultural labor were available for small-scale industry. The low cost was somewhat negated by high labor turnover. Many workers returned to the land, a pattern similar to France, and many worked only part-time. But wage costs were substantially lower than in most of the other societies we are considering.[16]

The low skill level was the result of the labor force's rural origin and its lack of technical training. The major contribution made by the government in this area was the establishment of a comprehensive system of general and technical education, begun in 1877. By 1900 much progress had been made in providing a basic four-year education (Hirschmeier, 1964; Lockwood, 1954). Whether this,

[13]Miyamoto, et al. (1965) credit foreign trade primarily with stimulating technological innovations, but it is apparent that it also provided favorable opportunities for expansion.

[14]The state was the chief customer for the electrical, cement, brick, paper, glass, and leather industries, and tended to buy from the most daring private entrepreneurs (Hirschmeier, 1964).

[15]In Gould's view (1972, pp. 267–68), the restraint on luxury consumption admirably distinguished Japan's experience from that of Russia, but he also notes that "Japan was extremely fortunate in finding good opportunities for export expansion."

[16]In 1914 they averaged one-sixth of German and one-twelfth of American wages (Ferguson & Bruun, 1958, p. 789). In 1926 wages in cotton-spinning mills in Georgia and the Carolinas averaged around five times the Japanese level in comparable mills (Orchard, 1930, p. 368).

however, had any significant effect on the quality of the labor force is questionable (Taira, 1971).[17]

The Japanese faced severe shortages of raw materials, except for silk and a few others. Water power was available and it provided the majority of electrical power after about 1900. Domestic cotton supplies were adequate until about the same time, but substantial imports were necessary after that. Copper was the only major mineral that was available (Orchard, 1930). The lack of coal and iron ore constituted the most grievous inadequacy. The available coal was not suitable for coke production and iron ore simply was not present. Thus it was necessary to rely upon the textile industry to finance imports of these materials (Orchard, 1930). The Japanese were favored in this regard by the timing of their industrial growth because there was relatively free access to these materials in the world market (Lockwood, 1954). The government promoted the importation of coal and iron ore and encouraged Japanese investment in Manchuria and China after 1900 to deal with this problem (Orchard, 1930). Later it moved to political control of these areas, a policy which contributed to the outbreak of World War II.

Thus Japan began the Meiji period with a lack of capital and raw materials and with relatively limited market potential; but it had an abundant supply of low-cost labor, and a large assortment of technological innovations was available from the industrializing nations of the West. The Meiji government improved capital supplies and promoted domestic and foreign trade through the policies we have described, thereby facilitating the import of necessary raw materials and machines. Therefore we believe that the economic opportunity conditions for entrepreneurship improved substantially after 1868. In Lockwood's (1954, p. 513) terms, "new incentives and opportunities to use wealth" became available.

The government also improved conditions for entrepreneurs *directly*, through its sale of most of its enterprises to them, often at extremely low cost, in the 1880s.[18] Of course, the purchasers had to operate them efficiently and profitably if they were to survive, but the technological groundwork had been laid for them, and the enterprises were often available at bargain prices; that in turn made assumption of the entrepreneurial role far easier than if it were necessary to start from scratch.

Opportunities were more favorable for entrepreneurs in agricultural pursuits, such as primary food production, than in industrial activities in the early part of the Meiji period because of the rise in food prices that had occurred (Hirschmeier, 1964). By World War I university graduates were beginning to

---

[17]The state intervened very little in the area of labor relations, a policy which may have had either negative or positive effects on productivity.

[18]These included shipbuilding yards, silk filatures, glass factories, chemical works, porcelain works, silk- and cotton-spinning mills, wool-spinning and weaving mills, linen mills, cement and brick plants, soap-making plants, typefounding plants, paint-making firms, iron and steel plants, agricultural machinery plants, sugar refineries, and paper-making plants (Lockwood, 1954; Maddison, 1969; Orchard, 1930; Takahashi, 1968).

choose business, rather than the civil service, for careers (Takezawa, 1966); that choice indicates the more favorable *relative* opportunity conditions available in business by that time. Thus we believe that relative opportunity conditions for entrepreneurship also improved during the Meiji period.

NONECONOMIC FACTORS INFLUENCING JAPANESE ENTREPRENEURSHIP

Because a number of the Meiji government's policies also had direct effects on the sociocultural environment, we shall now consider the nature of the noneconomic opportunity conditions for entrepreneurship.

The legitimacy of entrepreneurship was decidedly low at the beginning of the Meiji period, largely because of Confucianism's disapprobation of economic activities which brought individual profit to their participants. According to Marshall (1967) the Confucian emphasis on selfless devotion to duty and to the public interest was fundamentally opposed to profit and calculations of private interest. Commercial transactions which brought private profit were regarded as exploitative. In addition, the merchant class had been assigned the lowest rung on the social ladder, beneath even farmers, in the Tokugawa status hierarchy. Their position had improved by the end of the Tokugawa period, but they were still not respected, partly because many of them were believed to be dishonest (Hagen, 1962; Hirschmeier, 1964). Bankers, however, did have high prestige (Hirschmeier, 1964; Patrick, 1967).

Certain components of the Japanese normative-evaluative system did, perhaps, indirectly provide legitimacy for entrepreneurial activities. Confucianism promoted leadership by commoners (Horie, 1965), which might have promoted commoner entrepreneurship. It has been suggested that Japanese society also was characterized by positive evaluations of achievement, and that meritorious performances were rewarded (Pelzel, 1954; Vernon, 1971).[19] Individual competition, also presumably supportive of entrepreneurship, was sanctioned in the Tokugawa period, but it was individualism within a group context with one's contribution to the group of primary importance (Takezawa, 1966).

That Japanese entrepreneurs made vigorous attempts to increase the prestige of entrepreneurship early in the Meiji period implies that its legitimacy was really quite low in spite of these indirect supports. Such efforts constituted a veritable ideological assault in which entrepreneurs presented themselves as the embodiment of samurai ideals, devoted to the tenets of Confucianism. Their campaign had two main themes: that entrepreneurs were devoted to the welfare

---

[19]Frank (1969) suggests that role recruitment was based on achievement, whereas rewards within a role were allocated on an ascriptive basis.

of society and that they were uninterested in private profit.[20] The government supported the program, by granting presidents of enterprises special favors, such as the right to bear swords and to have family names. As a result of this combined effort of government and entrepreneurs, the image of the entrepreneur was improved at an earlier stage in the industrial transition than was the case in a society such as Russia (Hirschmeier, 1964). The Japanese application of traditional values to new structural conditions rather than their rejection (Lipset, 1967) is nowhere clearer than in the linking of Confucianism with the entrepreneurial role.

Social mobility had increased to some degree by the end of the Tokugawa period. Earlier there had been a sharp division between the samurai or warrior class, which constituted only 7 percent of the population and was in complete control, and the commoner classes; but these class lines had become less distinct (Yoshino, 1968). The lower samurai especially had fallen upon hard times, and many of them had been reduced to being merchants or putters-out. The samurai as a whole had become dependent upon merchants to convert the rice stipends they received from the peasantry into money for use in the increasingly monetized economy. They did maintain political superiority over merchants, though, and political power remained the major determinant of status (Pelzel, 1954; Takahashi, 1968; Takenaka, 1969).

One of the first steps the Meiji leaders took was to dissolve the prevailing class system and to destroy the samurai. They devised the ingenious solution of converting the samurai warriors into respectable businessmen in order to prevent their revival of feudal traditions and to encourage industrialization.[21] A major component of their solution was a system of compensation, consisting of government bonds that could be used only as collateral for the establishment of business enterprises, to replace the rice payments the samurai had received from the peasantry (Bronfenbrenner, 1969; Hirschmeier, 1964).

Ending the power of the samurai undoubtedly increased the possibility of social mobility. So did the series of measures adopted shortly after 1868 which abolished the guilds and *hans,* changed the basis of recruitment for the civil service, and allowed land ownership and intermarriage. Social mobility was allowed "an almost free rein" during this period (Vernon, 1971).

Even though social mobility increased appreciably, so that opportunities for upward mobility via entrepreneurship also increased, Japanese society certainly did not become anarchical. Hirschmeier (1964) emphasizes the general stability, cohesion, and discipline that prevailed. There appear to have been two reasons for the new regime's ability to achieve rapid integration. First, the Meiji

---

[20]Shibusawa, one of the prime movers of the program, coined the term *jitsugyoka* (someone who works with honesty for the establishment of industry) for the entrepreneurial role (Hirschmeier, 1964).

[21]But Redlich (1958) says that the promotion of industrialization was actually an unexpected consequence of their plan.

leaders were able to draw upon traditional integrative mechanisms, such as Confucianism and its emphasis on the lack of change inherent in life (Hirschmeier, 1964). There was also a pervasive emphasis upon cooperation and consensus within the society.[22]

More important was the second factor—the ability of the Meiji government to prevent the potentially explosive situation which existed in 1868 from getting out of control. The Satsuma Rebellion of the samurai in 1877 was the most serious incident of conflict and it was effectively crushed. Labor agitation around 1900 and in the 1920s never reached sufficient proportions to be seriously disturbing. Thus the Japanese case has been characterized as distinctive for the degree to which political and economic elites were able to combine their efforts for the common goal of industrialization (Lockwood, 1954; Vernon, 1971).

Entrepreneurs, therefore, were highly integrated in a system that promoted their activities. It also has been suggested that the Meiji leaders enjoyed freedom from outside interference during the critical early years of their rule. The Western powers were involved in conflicts of their own—the American Civil War had just ended and France was participating in its Mexican adventure under Napoleon III. This breathing space allowed the leaders to consolidate their control (Takahashi, 1968). It is probable that the earlier examples of Western interference in the 1850s and 1860s further facilitated integration of the new political system.

Nationalism was the Meiji leaders' ideological support, and it also became part of the ideology of many Japanese entrepreneurs who combined it with Confucianism and the samurai tradition (Hirschmeier, 1964: Horie, 1965).[23] There is a striking resemblance between the worldly asceticism of the Protestant Ethic and the Confucian emphasis upon one's devotion to duty. The main difference between the two is in the former's stress upon the *individual* and the latter's on the *collectivity*. Hence Confucianism may have provided an ideological support for entrepreneurship, like that which Protestantism allegedly provided in Europe, but entrepreneurship for the good of the group rather than the individual.

The difference of opinions regarding the influence of the Protestant Ethic on entrepreneurship has been duplicated by a controversy over the actual influence of the combination of Confucianism and nationalism on Japanese entrepreneurs. Some have concluded that entrepreneurs were motivated primarily by noneconomic incentives in a manner similar to the Calvinist entrepreneur laboring to fulfill his calling. The good of the nation, rather than individual salvation, was the goal according to this view. In other words, Japanese entrepreneurs really were motivated by the goals espoused in their entrepreneurial ideology.[24]

[22]Orchard (1930) offers the fact that Japan was an island nation as a factor promoting integration. Japan was like England in this respect, of course.

[23]Hirschmeier (1964) avers that nationalism may also have been an obstacle to entrepreneurship by encouraging individuals to enter political or military roles instead.

[24]Ranis (1955) has devised the term *community-centered* to refer to this characteristic of Japanese entrepreneurs and has suggested that it distinguishes them from entrepreneurs in other societies that industrialized early.

But recently this view has been disputed with the suggestion that actions are better indicators of motivation than statements (Yamamura, 1968). Yamamura (1974) describes Iwasaki and Yasuda, two of the most prominent entrepreneurs, as "extreme profit maximizers," unmotivated by nationalism.[25] Hirschmeier (1964, pp. 194, 198) has provided a slightly different analysis of Japanese entrepreneurs' profit orientation, describing them as showing "persistence and continued pioneering in spite of low returns over long periods." This implies that profits were not of major importance to them, but he also says that they calculated their future returns on the basis of a long time horizon and unusually optimistic discounting factors. That is, they were willing to defer gratification and anticipated great returns from so doing. So it is conceivable that their interest in profit maximization was similar to that of entrepreneurs in other countries but that they estimated their profits differently than other entrepreneurs did.[26]

We see that there has been much skepticism regarding the extent to which nonpecuniary motives influenced Japanese entrepreneurs. Our feeling is that they may have been influenced by the Confucianism-nationalism combination, but that economic motives were more weighty than has been suggested by some.

Hagen (1962) has used Japan as one of his examples of the manner in which the withdrawal of status respect produced entrepreneurship. According to him, wealthy merchants, the samurai, and wealthy peasants all suffered this affliction during the Tokugawa regime and this led to entrepreneurship on the part of at least the first two groups.

We shall show later that the extent of entrepreneurship by these two groups may not have been as great as Hagen thinks. Here we wish to suggest that an explanation in terms of *increasing status inconsistency* appears more satisfactory than one involving the withdrawal of status. Under the Tokugawa the samurai had seen their economic position decline at the same time as their prestige remained relatively stable. Their loss of power after the Meiji takeover was more an economic than a prestige loss, and they had little choice but to invest the bonds which the government had given them. Thus they definitely were in a status inconsistent position. Merchants, by comparison, experienced the opposite form of status inconsistency. Their economic position improved, but their political power and prestige did not. As a result they may have been highly motivated to achieve. The government's actions in regard to entrepreneurship after 1868 also may be construed as a *bestowal,* and not a withdrawal, of status respect. Therefore we find Hagen's argument unpersuasive.

Finally, it is possible that entrepreneurial security also increased as the legitimacy of the role increased and as entrepreneurs became more integrated into

[25]Iwasaki's requiring payments in Mexican dollars in order to increase his profits does not appear very nationalistic, for example (Yamamura, 1974).

[26]However, the political wisdom of appearing uninterested in personal profit, given the traditional negative attitudes toward it, has also been called to attention (Marshall, 1967).

the system during the Meiji period. The major concerns of entrepreneurs by 1900 were the loyalty of their labor force and the possibility of class conflict (Marshall, 1967; Yoshino, 1968), which suggests that their position still was not completely secure. But this type of insecurity should have been less damaging to entrepreneurship than the widespread opposition to it at the beginning of the Meiji period.

Therefore the sociocultural environment became more favorable for entrepreneurship during the course of the Meiji era, partly as a result of government actions and partly as a result of entrepreneurs' actions. We believe the greater legitimacy of entrepreneurship and the increased potential of social mobility were of primary importance. These were buttressed by the ideological support of nationalism, although there is some question as to how influential it actually was for entrepreneurs.

CHARACTERISTICS OF JAPANESE ENTREPRENEURSHIP

The improvement of economic and noneconomic opportunity conditions under the influence of the Meiji government led to a variety of entrepreneurial actions, that, on the basis of our descriptions of the British, French, and German cases, should by now be fairly predictable. However, there were unique aspects to the Japanese response.

Innovations

Japanese entrepreneurs, like the Germans, borrowed extensively from the technological innovations available in the West. Whereas the Germans borrowed from Britain and France, the Japanese borrowed from all three of these European countries and from others. Unlike German entrepreneurs, however, Japanese entrepreneurs added few significant technological innovations to those they borrowed.[27] Thus they stand as the prime example of technological *imitation* among the societies we are analyzing. In addition to the variety of machines they imported, they also made extensive use of foreign technical experts. These included Frenchmen and Italians in the silk industry; Swiss in hemp-braiding; Germans in brewing, zinc and steel smelting, and chemicals; Frenchmen and Germans in dyeing; and Austrians and Americans in paper manufacturing (Orchard, 1930). According to Hirschmeier (1964), they had an almost naive optimism about the potential of technological innovations and the ease with which they could be adopted which sometimes led them to dismiss too quickly the technical experts they had brought in.[28] This optimism very likely was benefi-

---

[27]Miyamoto, et al. (1965) credit them with occasional simple innovations but do not say what they were.

[28]Islam (1960) notes that there was a very high turnover of these personnel, which squares with Hirschmeier's observation that they were often released prematurely.

cial; if they had been more aware of the problems they faced, they probably would have been more cautious.

The silk-reeling industry, which was to become the major earner of foreign exchange to finance machine imports, was the first to be affected by the wave of technological innovations. European machines were adopted and first water and then steam power were applied. By 1928, 95 percent of the silk output was being reeled by machines (Orchard, 1930, p. 104). Cotton spinning was next to be transformed by machines and steam power, and this industry was almost completely mechanized by the 1920s. Cotton weaving long remained a household industry, however.[29]

Foreign technology also was indispensable in metallurgy. The Yawata steel works, erected in 1901, was modeled after the Krupp works in Germany and all the equipment for it was imported from there. But not all the available technological innovations were borrowed by Japanese entrepreneurs. Standardized production techniques were not adopted to any significant degree, partly because few industries constructed products with a number of components; the bicycle industry was one of the few in which it was used (Uyeda, 1938).

Japanese entrepreneurs generally adopted labor-intensive technologies (Miyamoto, et al., 1965), a reasonable choice given the low cost of labor. Since the trend in the West at this time was toward capital-intensive, labor-saving technologies, this meant that they often procured obsolete machinery (Orchard, 1930) that was probably less costly than more modern machinery would have been. The technologies that were borrowed quite often were simply transferred to Japan with no modifications.[30] The transfer was even more complete in metallurgy, with entire plants purchased from the United States and rebuilt in Japan (Orchard, 1930).

Not only were Western technological innovations imported and adopted, but so also were the products of Western industry. They were imported and copied and became the basis of new small-scale industries. These included rubber goods, bicycles, and electric lamps. The bicycle industry is an interesting case because entrepreneurs in it thought they could simply copy the product. They found, though, that they were unable to do so with their primitive technology, so they waited until the technology could be imported and then produced bicycles by that means (Uyeda, 1938). No Japanese machine industry of any note developed (Allen, 1965), which indicates the low level of technological knowledge in the society.

Product innovations were of little significance in the textile industry, which

[29]The number of power looms in operation finally equalled the number of hand looms by 1923 or 1924, and by 1928 only a fourth of the looms in operation were hand looms (Orchard, 1930, pp. 96, 117, 379).

[30]Orchard (1930) reports a case in which imported textile machines were too large for Japanese female workers and they were forced to stand on benches, but Miyamoto, et al. (1965) suggest that adaptations were made so as to better fit the imported technologies into the Japanese industrial structure.

remained the dominant industry until the end of the period we are studying, except for the introduction of wool in the 1890s. The silk-reeling industry did make some improvements in the quality of its goods. But the need for improved quality became less important because of the monopoly position which the Japanese attained as a result of the decimation of the French silk industry. The government actually found it necessary to institute quality controls on the industry in order to maintain this position (Orchard, 1930).

There appears to have been a sizeable amount of diversification into the production of new goods by Japanese entrepreneurs.[31] The *zaibatsus,* a form of entrepreneurship we shall discuss soon, were highly diversified, going either from manufacturing into nonmanufacturing areas or vice versa.[32]. This diversification reduced the economic risks they would have confronted if they had been involved in only one of the areas (Islam, 1960). Cotton entrepreneurs who moved to the production of woolen goods constitute another example of diversification (Uyeda, 1938).

The Japanese proclivity for borrowing did not extend to organizational innovations, and in this area they did make significant contributions themselves. There was a relatively limited transition from the domestic system to factory production. It was most extensive in cotton spinning, which had converted to factory production almost completely by the 1920s, and in metallurgy, but less extensive in silk-reeling. A number of silk-reeling enterprises did make the familiar progression from domestic production to a small factory to a larger enterprise with several branches, but the majority of enterprises did not (Orchard, 1930). The transition was least extensive in the weaving sectors of the silk and cotton industries, both of which still remained essentially household industries in the 1920s, and in the woolen industry (Allen, 1965; Orchard, 1930).

But the lack of factory production, which seemingly would limit increases in output and productivity, was compensated for in other ways. According to Gould (1972, p. 148), Japan "made exceptional use of rural industry, with an extensive network of putting-out industry linked to central factories, thus making use of cheap rural labor and minimizing the need for costly factory buildings." This sounds very much like the British practice of subcontracting a century earlier. There was less need for *intraorganizational* innovations in Japan than in societies which made a more complete transition to the factory system. And the Japanese were most hesitant to borrow Western innovations in this area. But they were perfectly willing to make use of technological innovations from the West, because that was the only place they were available.

This hesitance was not due to ignorance of the need for managers for

[31]Shinohara (1970) makes this characteristic a major point of contrast between samurai and nonsamurai entrepreneurs, indicating that the former were more likely to expand and the latter more likely to diversify.

[32]Mitsubishi displayed the former pattern, expanding from shipbuilding and shipping into banking and mining. Mitsui exemplified the latter, diversifying from banking into mining, foreign trade, and manufacturing (Shinohara, 1970).

example (Takezawa, 1966). Some entrepreneurs founded business schools and private universities to provide themselves with the necessary managerial corps (Hirschmeier, 1964). Instead it was a consequence of the feeling that "impersonal and contractual relationships between Western employers and employees and Western discrimination among employees were indecent and immoral" (Hagen, 1968, p. 234). The Japanese preferred to rely upon existing patterns of authority relationships, and so they developed a system of management based upon their merchant and samurai traditions that stressed the reciprocal obligations of employers and managers (Marshall, 1967; Takezawa, 1966). It basically involved a resident apprenticeship, starting in early adolescence and lasting about twenty years (Takezawa, 1966).

For most of the Meiji period nonmanagerial employees remained under the control of worker-bosses whose performance was not very satisfactory (Shinohara, 1970). With a restive labor force after 1900, however, Japanese entrepreneurs developed a system of labor management based on the *ie*, the traditional family unit, which has been termed *familial paternalism*. Under the new system the enterprise became a "family," a cooperative, harmonious partnership with the entrepreneur at its head. This system also involved a diffuse set of reciprocal obligations on the part of both employer and employee, with the former taking responsibility for the latter's needs and the latter responding with loyalty and obedience (Marshall, 1967; Takezawa, 1966; Yoshino, 1968).[33]

The system of familial paternalism constituted a combined organizational-labor innovation that exemplified "great creativity" according to Hagen (1968, p. 234). Entrepreneurs also found it necessary to provide dormitory facilities and other amenities in a manner similar to their British predecessors in order to retain and maintain their largely female labor force. But this increased labor costs, as did the practice of providing discharge allowances for dismissed workers which was an outgrowth of the system of familial paternalism (Takezawa, 1966; Uyeda, 1938). These extra costs made actual labor costs anywhere from a third to nine-tenths higher than the wages that were paid (Orchard, 1930, p. 361).

Japanese entrepreneurs also made market innovations under the influence of the Meiji government. The most important was their rapid utilization of the foreign market. The value of Japanese exports increased from $0.6 million to $331 million between 1859 and 1914, a rate of increase more rapid than any of the other industrializing countries (Maddison, 1969, pp. 27–28; Takahashi, 1968, p. 93).[34] They also moved rapidly into the Asian market during World War I; by 1918 the value of exports had skyrocketed to $1.2 billion. Throughout

---

[33]Two logical offshoots of this system were the lifetime commitment by a worker to the enterprise and a length-of-service wage system that developed in the twentieth century (Shinohara, 1970).

[34]Japanese foreign trade increased a hundredfold between 1864 and 1914 (Ferguson & Bruun, 1958, p. 789), an increase which is not quite as startling when one considers the almost complete lack of foreign trade before the Meiji era.

the period manufactured goods became an increasingly important part of the export trade. They comprised only 1.1 percent of exports in 1868; by 1924–27 they comprised about 40 percent (Orchard, 1930, p. 229; Takahashi, 1968, p. 80).[35]

Lastly, Japanese entrepreneurs' major material inovation, in addition to the limited use of coke, was the replacement of wood by other materials. This change shows the technological gap which the Japanese confronted. Iron, which had been used in Europe for several centuries, had not been used to any extent because of the lack of iron ore.

Therefore, the borrowing of Western technological and product innovations was the most noteworthy aspect of Japanese entrepreneurs' innovational actions. They added to these their own blend of organizational and labor innovations, rooted deeply in their social traditions. The adoption of these innovations enabled them to exploit the foreign, particularly the Oriental, market. (We will consider the development of the *zaibatsu*, which may be considered partly a financial-organizational innovation, in the context of entrepreneurial identity.)

Degree of innovation. Introduction of these innovations wrought major changes in Japanese society. For example, Orchard (1930) describes the great interest that was aroused when a modern silk filature was constructed in a brick building; the use of bricks was as unique as the mechanization of the production process. However, these changes were modified somewhat by the retention of a small-scale industrial sector and the concentration on light industry. Female workers, for example, had been an important component of the domestic textile industry, as in Britain, and hence the transition to factory production was probably less traumatic than it would have been without this prior experience. The Japanese solution to the problem of labor management undoubtedly lessened the shock, also. A rapid buildup of heavy industry—the German pattern—might well have had more shattering consequences.

The increases in productivity resulting from these innovations no doubt were comparable to those yielded by the British textile innovations after 1750. But Japanese productivity lagged in comparison with other industrializing societies after 1868. This was due to several factors—the quality of the labor force, the borrowing of machines that often were obsolete in the West, and further the lower efficiency of machines built in Japan as imitations of borrowed machines (Orchard, 1930). In 1926 Japanese spinning mills operated with only one-half to one-seventh as many spindles per worker as mills in Georgia and North and South Carolina. On the average three times as much labor was required in Japanese mills to get the same output as in mills in the United States

---

[35]But even with this great increase in exports Japan experienced a negative balance of trade in most of the years between 1895 and 1927 (Orchard, 1930). Islam (1960) has suggested that the extensive reliance on both imports and exports prevented monopolistic excesses by the *zaibatsus* and technological stagnation.

(Orchard, 1930, pp. 367, 370).[36] Improvements were made in both spinning and weaving, but as the indices in Table 15 show, they mainly involved increasing the number of spindles and looms per worker. Productivity on a per-spindle basis actually declined in cotton spinning.

Table 15
Indices of Productivity in the Japanese
Cotton Industry, 1927
(1913 = 100)

Cotton yarn per worker	105
Number of spindles per worker	140
Cotton yarn per spindle	75
Weaving productivity per worker	150
Number of looms per worker	145
Productivity per loom	107

Source: Uyeda (1938, p. 64, diagram 30; p. 71, diagram 32).

The failure to improve productivity also was partly organizational. Although cotton spinning has been described as well organized (Uyeda, 1938), Orchard (1930) describes the inefficiency of the Yawata steel works which did not store its raw materials next to its coke ovens and blast furnaces.

A major negative effect of the failure to improve productivity was neutralizing any advantages Japanese entrepreneurs might have enjoyed from the relatively low cost of labor. It is estimated that American wage costs per pound of yarn were only about 75 percent greater than Japanese, and that American wage costs in cotton weaving were actually about a third less than they were in Japan (Orchard, 1930, pp. 370, 374).

Expansions

Japan, like France and Germany, retained a dual industrial structure, with a large sector of small-scale traditional enterprises and a small sector of large-scale more modern enterprises. This dualism appears to have been more extreme in Japan than in either France or Germany. The Japanese small-scale sector, however, seemingly expanded its output, without extensive mechanization, rather than remaining stagnant and nonexpansive as the comparable sector in the French economy apparently did.

Industrial expansion was very slow until the government established cotton-spinning mills and provided entrepreneurs with subsidies around 1880. More entrepreneurs came forward after the state's incursion into the area. Later, during World War I, entrepreneurs did not show nearly the hesitance they had

[36]The gap was even greater in cotton weaving. Japanese mills used an average of seven times as many workers per loom as American mills and American output per worker averaged about 7.5 times Japanese output per worker (Orchard, 1930, p. 473).

thirty years earlier. A number of industries—cotton, wool, bicycles, chemicals, silk, and metallurgy—responded to the new opportunities. The number of factory workers increased by 70 percent and the production of manufactured goods almost quintupled during the war (Orchard, 1930, p. 232; Takahashi, 1968, p. 93). In fact, capacity was overextended, and many enterprises were forced to close in the depression following the war. The level of factory employment attained in 1921 was not reached again until 1926 (Orchard, 1930, p. 185).[37]

Degree of expansion. So Japanese entrepreneurs responded more readily as the Meiji period progressed. There was great variance in the scale of their operations and hence great variance in the capital costs associated with their expansions because of the dualistic industrial development. As elsewhere, it was possible to start on a small scale early in the industrial transition, but the scale increased with time. The first three cotton mills, established between 1863 and 1875, were equipped with 720, 2,000, and 3,600 spindles. The government helped found about a dozen factories of 2,000-spindle size after 1879. By 1882 a group of entrepreneurs constructed a mill with 10,000 spindles and a capitalization of 250,000 yen (Orchard, 1930, pp. 92–93; Uyeda, 1938, pp. 21–22). This mill was about one-fourth the size of mills being constructed in England after 1830 (Chapman, 1972, p. 26), and it was probably comparable in size to English cotton mills of the late eighteenth century.

The data available on the relative proportions of workers employed in enterprises of different sizes also reveal the great variance in the scale of operations. Table 16 shows that the overwhelming majority of factories had fewer than

Table 16
Japanese Factories, Proportions of Workers,
and Output, 1909

Size of Factory (number of workers)	Percentage of All Factories	Percentage of All Factory Workers	Percentage of Factory Output
5–29	85.6	34.8	20.5
30–99	10.6	21.7	18.8
100–500	3.4	22.6	29.4
Over 500	0.4	20.9	31.3
	100.0	100.0	100.0

Source: Takahashi (1968, p. 86, table 16).

[37]The amount of expansion is shown by the following data: the number of cotton spindles increased from 6,000 in 1863 to 6.1 million by 1927, the number of industrial firms had reached about 12,000 by 1918, the number of factories with ten or more workers was over 22,000 in the same year, and the number of factory workers in factories with five or more workers was almost two million by 1928, having been over two million as a result of the wartime boom (Takahashi, 1968, p. 93).

thirty workers, but that these factories accounted for only a little over a third of all factory workers and only about a fifth of total factory output. At the other extreme, factories with over 500 workers constituted only a very small percentage of total factories, but they employed about one-fifth of all factory workers and provided almost a third of total factory output. Thus in the smallest factories a third of all workers produced one-fifth of total output, and in the largest factories a fifth of all workers produced a third of total output, which indicates the greater productivity of the largest factories.[38]

The Japanese have been praised for their ability to obtain large increases in production with relatively low levels of investment, which has been attributed to their extensive reliance on the small-scale sector and its close ties with the large-scale sector by means of the *zaibatsu* (Gould, 1972). They also have been praised for reinvesting their profits to a large degree (Ranis, 1959). The combination of these factors led to the Japanese small-scale sector's not being the drag on growth that it was in France. The silk industry was dominant in this sector, however, and we have seen how it benefited from improvements in the market.

Entrepreneurial Identity

The government was the major entrepreneur in Meiji Japan until the 1880s, operating enterprises that had been started during the Tokugawa period as well as new enterprises. The government set up about a dozen cotton-spinning mills after 1879—there were only three mills in existence by 1879—and we have noted that these and other public enterprises were sold to the private sector in the 1880s. This action was taken partly because of opposition to state involvement as an entrepreneur, but the sorry financial condition of the public enterprises was a more important factor (Horie, 1939; Smith, 1965). Public entrepreneurship was generally more successful in nonmanufacturing areas, such as mining and railroad construction (Hirschmeier, 1964; Orchard, 1930).

Public entrepreneurship declined greatly after the 1880s, but there were occasional resorts to it in areas where the private sector lagged. The most prominent example was the Imperial Steel Works, constructed at Yawata in 1901. This plant, erected at a cost of $70 million, comprised virtually all Japanese iron and steel capacity until World War I. The war prompted construction of a number of new steel plants by private entrepreneurs but many of these failed in the depression after the war. As a result, the Yawata works produced two-thirds of the

---

[38]These data mask the very great differences between industries, however. In the wool industry, for example, 94 percent of factories employed fewer than fifty workers in 1929, and about two-thirds employed fewer than ten (Uyeda, 1938, p. 151, table 69). The average cotton-weaving enterprise contained only five looms as of 1928 (Orchard, 1930, p. 117). But in 1924, 95 percent of workers in cotton spinning were employed in factories with 500 or more workers, and in metallurgy 73 percent were so employed. The Yawata Steel Works employed 20,000 workers by 1930 (Orchard, 1930, p. 172).

country's pig iron and 57 percent of its steel by 1926 (Orchard, 1930, p. 239).[39] Like its predecessors, the Yawata works was hardly a financial success. It returned a profit during the war, but in other years suffered annual losses of between $500,000 and $875,000. Thus it is not too surprising that in 1927 a commission recommended that the government withdraw from the iron and steel industry (Orchard, 1930, pp. 107, 222).

Japanese manufacturing entrepreneurship can be considered as primarily private for the 1868–1927 period, despite the extensive government role, because the private sector was more active in manufacturing, whereas the government was more involved in areas such as mining and transport. The issue is clouded because the public and private sectors were closely linked. The *seisho*, or political merchants, a group of entrepreneurs who relied primarily upon government concessions and favors, were prominent in the early Meiji years (Hirschmeier, 1964; Horie, 1965). Later many of the *zaibatsus* had close links with the government, with many of their higher personnel being former civil servants. In some cases the presidents of firms were appointed by the government (Hirschmeier, 1964). So it is more accurate to characterize a portion of Japanese entrepreneurship as *mixed,* involving both public and private sectors.[40] Horie (1939) and Lockwood (1954) have stressed that the state's entrepreneurial activities did not compete with the private sector but supported it. In this respect the Japanese case is similar to the German.

The state did account for a substantial portion of industrial investment—approximately 40 percent (Maddison, 1969, p. 23)—mainly because of its role in the iron industry, mining, transport, and the armaments industry. But its proportion of the labor force was much smaller. In 1914, 12 percent of all factory workers were employed in state-run plants and this percentage declined after that date (Allen, 1965, p. 890). This was a higher percentage than in Germany, where one-tenth of the workers in industry, commerce and transport were in public enterprises in 1907 (Henderson, 1958, p. xiii).[41]

Collective forms of entrepreneurship superseded individual entrepreneurship, or individual entrepreneurs converted to collective entrepreneurship, during the Meiji period, as in the other societies we are considering. The first three cotton-spinning mills initiated after 1868 were the work of individuals, for example, and the *zaibatsus* were begun by individuals. By the 1920s the silk industry remained the province of individual entrepreneurs, whereas all enterprises in the cotton-spinning industry were at least partnerships by that time (Orchard, 1930).

[39]Public entrepreneurship accounted for fully four-fifths of Japanese pig iron output in 1926—from Yawata and the Toyo Manufacturing Company, a firm operated by the state after 1921 (Orchard, 1930, p. 239).

[40]Marshall (1967) claims that many private entrepreneurs were favorable to public entrepreneurship and felt that there should be more of it.

[41]The difference was actually greater than suggested by these data because the German percentage includes workers in commerce and transport.

Joint-stock companies began to appear in the 1880s and increased thereafter. Joint-stock organization was first used for a cotton mill in 1882; after 1887 all new cotton mills were organized on that basis. Hirschmeier (1964), studying fifty industrial leaders who were prominent before 1894–95, found the transition from individual to joint-stock forms quite apparent between the older and younger entrepreneurs.

We have mentioned the *zaibatsu* several times in this chapter. It constituted a distinctive form of *multi-organizational* entrepreneurship, similar in some ways to the German cartels and the American trusts and holding companies of the late nineteenth century. Four of these "money houses"—Mitsui, Mitsubishi, Sumitomo, and Yasuda—were dominant by World War I (Allen, 1965; Orchard, 1930). Some began as offshoots of established trading houses from the Tokugawa period, taking advantage of the new economic opportunities and government support of the Meiji period to expand into manufacturing. Others got their start at the time of the government's sale of its firms in the 1880s.

A *zaibatsu* typically consisted of a holding company that controlled a cluster of subsidiaries, with each cluster having one or more banks and insurance companies (Vernon, 1971). Personnel and capital flowed easily between the various firms within a *zaibatsu* and this provided great flexibility. They differed in such characteristics as industrial composition (although they were most prominent in heavy industry), their styles of management, and their relationships to the government, but they were all highly diversified (Hirschmeier, 1964). Lockwood (1954), p. 562) has described them as "huge agglomerations of miscellaneous enterprises in a wide variety of fields."

Finance, production, and trade were all under one control in many cases. As might be expected, those with their own banks or trust companies tended to be the largest and most successful (Islam, 1960; Patrick 1967). The *zaibatsus* also were intricately related to the small-scale sector of the economy, providing enterprises in that sector with capital, orders, and materials (Allen, 1965). These conglomerates, which reached the zenith of their power in the 1920s, therefore constituted virtual economies within the Japanese economy. They controlled more phases of the entrepreneurial role than did the German cartels which were primarily concerned with pricing. And they differed from the American trusts and holding companies in their diversification, their closer ties to the public sector, and their direct control of their own banks. They are a unique form of entrepreneurship among the societies we are studying.[42]

Family entrepreneurship was quite prominent in Japan. On the one hand, the *zaibatsus* were usually under the control of families. The Sumitomo family, for example, dated from 1591 (Orchard, 1930). On the other hand, the vast majority of small-scale enterprises at the opposite end of the economic spectrum, in the

---

[42]Japanese entrepreneurs have been commended for their willingness to cooperate (Hirschmeier, 1964; Takenaka, 1969) which would have been necessary for the development of such forms of multi-organizational enterprise.

silk industry, for example, also were organized on a family basis.[43] Japanese family entrepreneurship does not appear to have had the negative effects attributed to French family entrepreneurship. In the Tokugawa period, service to the lord was more important than the welfare of one's family, and fathers often adopted sons to inherit their property if they feared their first-born sons were incompetent (Hagen, 1968). This practice continued after 1868 among entrepreneurs who formerly had been samurai. Individuals also took potential entrepreneurs into their families through marriage (Kindleberger, 1958). These practices may have prevented the problems often associated with family entrepreneurship.

Foreign entrepreneurship was not significantly represented at any time after 1868.[44] It was proportionately greater in manufacturing than in other areas, generally being involved in import-substitution, and it often involved cooperation with indigenous entrepreneurs in joint enterprises. Joint enterprises increased in the 1920s, particularly in the electrical engineering industry. Direct foreign capital investment was therefore very limited, constituting only 5.5 percent of the total foreign capital investment between 1896 and 1913, for example. Eighty-five percent of the foreign investment of that period represented borrowing by the Japanese government (Islam, 1960, p. 66).

There were two major reasons for the lack of foreign entrepreneurship. First, the Meiji leaders restricted it out of a concern for maintaining economic independence; foreigners were not allowed to own land or mining rights as a result. Second, the *zaibatsus* had developed to the point where they constituted monopolistic competitors supported by the state by the time foreigners became seriously interested in entering the Japanese economy, hence opportunities for foreigners were limited (Islam, 1960).

Although Japanese entrepreneurship was not marginal in the sense of having a large contingent of foreign entrepreneurs, the issue of the extent to which indigenous entrepreneurs were marginal is unresolved and very complex. It also involves the related issue of the role of the former samurai class in industrial entrepreneurship. First, it is not clear which social origins should be considered marginal. The samurai were dominant and the *heimin* (commoner) class was subordinate, or marginal, under the Tokugawa regime. But these positions changed, and possibly reversed, with the destruction of samurai power after 1868. Or, perhaps, marginal individuals from both the samurai and commoner classes tended to become entrepreneurs.

We have described the program of compensation for the samurai—bonds which were to be invested in business enterprises. In the past, the great extent to

[43]Ranis (1959) says that the system of primogeniture encouraged family entrepreneurship by allowing one son to inherit an enterprise, but Takezawa (1966) claims many Meiji entrepreneurs did not inherit their enterprises.

[44]There were some cases of foreign entrepreneurship around 1900—the British Dunlop Company in the rubber industry and the American General Electric Company in the electric lamp industry (Allen, 1965; Orchard, 1930; Uyeda, 1938).

which the former samurai did in fact use the bonds for that purpose has been stressed, but recently that interpretation has been challenged. Redlich (1958) and Hagen (1962) represent the former viewpoint, while Takezawa (1966), Horie (1965), and Yamamura (1974) represent the challengers to that point of view. We will discuss the evidence for the former viewpoint first.

Hirschmeier (1964) and Yoshino (1968) have provided estimates of the proportions of entrepreneurs who had originally been samurai—46 percent and less than 25 percent, respectively. When compared with the samurai's earlier 7 percent share of the population, both estimates indicate that samurai were over-represented. The early role of samurai in industries such as cotton spinning has been noted also (Orchard, 1930; Uyeda, 1938).[45] There also is evidence of increased entrepreneurial participation by the samurai after the unsuccessful Satsuma Rebellion (Hirschmeier, 1964). Takahashi suggests that a number of the highest-level samurai were involved in the public enterprises that were sold to the private sector; Hagen (1968) credits lower-level samurai with the majority of samurai entrepreneurship.

By contrast, Takezawa (1966) claims that the samurai opted for political roles, whereas commoners were more inclined toward business, and Takahashi (1968) has asserted that lower samurai were the ones more likely to be involved in political affairs, in direct contradiction of Hagen's suggestion regarding their economic activities. And it also has been suggested that upper-level commoners were of primary importance in manufacturing (Yoshino, 1968).

Part of the confusion may occur because the samurai were more likely to go into banking than manufacturing (Hirschmeier, 1964; Shinohara, 1970). This apparently was not due to any profound distaste on their part for manufacturing, but to their greater success in banking (Hirschmeier, 1964). Hence those who have stressed the importance of samurai entrepreneurship perhaps have lumped banking and manufacturing together, whereas those who downplay its importance have concentrated on manufacturing.

The blurring of class lines by the end of Tokugawa probably is a more important reason for the lack of consensus. Hagen (1968) admits that it is impossible to determine whether entrepreneurs were samurai or not in some cases. Some of the lower samurai had become merchants by 1868 and some commoners had become samurai. Iwasaki and Yasuda, who ultimately became heads of two major *zaibatsus,* were born to peasant families but bought into the lower rural samurai class (Yamamura, 1974). Thus some entrepreneurs identified as former samurai may not have been. Hirschmeier (1964) suggests that the samurai contributed neither as much nor as little to the supply of industrial entrepreneurs as different scholars have claimed. We tend to agree with him because of the possibility of misidentification.[46]

[45]The first two cotton mills were established by the Lord of Satsuma, for example.

[46]But the fact that the samurai comprised only 7 percent of the population in the Tokugawa period suggests that the estimates of Hirschmeier and Yoshino probably would still show samurai overrepresentation, even if all samurai were correctly identified.

The problem of the extent of marginality among indigenous entrepreneurs extends beyond the samurai issue to the relative importance of entrepreneurs from different occupational backgrounds. According to Hirschmeier (1964), Meiji entrepreneurs were drawn from three groups—bankers, foreign traders, and political merchants. The first and third of these were mainstream occupations, but foreign trade was less so. That some of the *zaibatsus* began as established trading houses, and that many entrepreneurs came from business families, also suggests that nonmarginal origins were predominant. The puzzle concerns the role of the wealthy urban merchants who were undoubtedly mainstream. It has been pointed out that the most significant group of these, from the city of Osaka, were very hesitant to participate in manufacturing, preferring banking instead. Their conspicuous absence from entrepreneurship in manufacturing implies that Japanese entrepreneurship was not wholly mainstream.[47]

The representation of entrepreneurs from artisan backgrounds, whom we have seen were very prominent in Britain, France, and Germany, also appears to be limited. Most accounts of Japanese entrepreneurship have paid little attention to them, but we suspect this is due to their continuation of traditional modes of production during the Meiji period. A number of them continued to produce a variety of light consumer goods, such as matches, pottery, wooden and bamboo ware, mats, and lacquer ware (Orchard, 1930). There were instances of their conversion to quasi-factory modes of production, e. g., the sword makers of Sakai who diversified into bicycle production (Uyeda, 1938), but such conversions were exceptional.

So the evidence regarding the marginality of Japanese entrepreneurship is inconclusive and conclusions depend partly upon the determination of which social groups should be considered marginal.

In summary, Japanese entrepreneurship in manufacturing was primarily public in the early part of the Meiji period; but private entrepreneurship rapidly replaced it, although the government maintained close ties with the *zaibatsus*. The usual transition from individual to collective entrepreneurship was evident and carried to an extreme in the form of the multi-organizational *zaibatsus*. Family entrepreneurship crosscut the industrial structure, from the *zaibatsus* at the top to the small-scale traditional enterprises at the bottom. Japanese entrepreneurship was overwhelmingly indigenous, and thus not marginal in terms of being external to the society, but it is not clear whether or not indigenous entrepreneurs were marginal to any appreciable degree.

Our earlier discussion of the opposition to entrepreneurship in the early part of the Meiji period indicates that the marginality of Japanese entrepreneurship was cultural rather than social. If the Confucian strictures against entrepreneurship were as strong as has been suggested, then entrepreneurs definitely were deviants. However, the dominant role of the Meiji government in the promotion

---

[47]Relatively well-to-do *rural* merchants were involved in manufacturing, though (Hirschmeier, 1964; Horie, 1965; Orchard, 1930).

of industrialization transformed entrepreneurship into a mainstream role. The entrepreneurs' ingenious development of an ideology incorporating both Confucianism and nationalism may have been the key to that transformation.

THE RATE OF JAPANESE INDUSTRIAL GROWTH

The annual rate of industrial growth in Japan has been estimated at 4.6 percent between 1874 and 1900 by Shinohara (1970, p. 284), and at 5.5 percent between 1879 and 1913 by Maddison (1969, p. 31), although he suspects his estimate is somewhat high. This rate of growth did not differ from that of other countries industrializing at that time—notably Germany, the United States, and Russia—but it was higher than the rates for Great Britain and France, and much higher than the growth rate of any other Asian country. The rate increased to 7.5 percent between 1913 and 1925–29 which was much higher than the growth rates of any of the other societies we are considering. Their industrial growth rates for this period were as follows: Great Britain—0.3 percent; France—1.4 percent; Germany—0.3 percent; United States—3.7 percent (Patel, 1961, p. 319, table 2). This huge difference is partly due to Japan's smaller industrial base than the Western industrial nations at this time and partly to the Western nations' being enmeshed in World War I while the Japanese were benefiting from it. But it also indicates a very great willingness to respond to opportunity conditions on the part of Japanese entrepreneurs.

Thus Japan made amazing progress in a period of approximately sixty years. This was achieved in large part by means of its textile industries, which accounted for half of all factory workers, 45 percent of the total value of manufactured products, and 69 percent of the value of exports in 1928 (Orchard, 1930, p. 115; Takahashi, 1968, p. 73). Japan's significance on the world scene was still limited, however. As of 1927, for example, Japan had fewer total cotton spindles, although more per capita, than India (Orchard, 1930, p. 221).[48] Japanese pig iron production also was less than India's, and only about one-fourth Belgian output and one-third the output of Luxembourg by the end of our period of study (Orchard, 1930, p. 223).

Internally, changes also had not been as extensive in Japan as elsewhere. As late as 1925, 50 percent or more of the Japanese population still was dependent on agriculture, compared to Germany's 31 percent, France's 42 percent, Britain's 7 percent, and the United States' 26 percent (Orchard, 1930, pp. 182–83). Japan was ahead of only Russia on this indicator, but in comparison to the past and to its geographical neighbors it was far ahead.

[48]The total number of Japanese spindles was only slightly more than the total number in Bristol County, Massachusetts, and the increase in spindles between 1880 and 1927 was approximately equal to the increase in either North *or* South Carolina during the same period (Orchard, 1930, pp. 218–19).

THE CAUSAL SIGNIFICANCE OF
JAPANESE INDUSTRIAL ENTREPRENEURSHIP

Our conclusion on the basis of the foregoing evidence is that Japanese entrepreneurship must be accorded some degree of positive causal significance, particularly in the latter part of the period 1868–1927. This conclusion is based primarily on Japan's ability to attain a rate of industrial growth comparable to that of Germany and the United States before 1913, and a substantially higher growth rate than those two countries after that date. We feel that economic opportunity conditions in Japan were less favorable than those in Germany and the United States and only slightly more favorable than similar conditions in France and Britain. Hence we feel that Japanese entrepreneurs improved upon these conditions. That there was significant improvement in opportunity conditions during the Meiji period makes us hesitant to assign a *high* degree of positive causal significance to Japanese entrepreneurship, though. The Meiji government should be given much credit both for improving opportunity conditions and for inducing entrepreneurs to emerge.

As we have observed, Japan entered the Meiji period at an economic level lower than that of most, if not all, the societies we are discussing. In addition, the society was going through the throes of a dramatic political change. The outlook for Japanese industrialization could not have been very bright in 1868. Capital supplies were limited. There was an ample supply of low-cost labor, but its skill level was very low. The lack of raw materials for heavy industry made the German strategy of concentration on that sector an unrealistic option. Objectively, there was great potential for technological change because of the large quantity of available technologies from the Western world. But this was negated by the Japanese market situation which was probably the bleakest of all the economic opportunity conditions because of the country's low level of economic development and the impossibility of using tariffs to protect infant industries.

The Meiji government and Japanese entrepreneurs took steps to deal with each of these problems. Capital supplies were increased by government tax and banking policies. Concentrating on industries in which Japan had a comparative advantage and where capital requirements were small helped alleviate this problem, as did the development of the *zaibatsu*. Entrepreneurs responded to the large supply of low-skill labor by using labor-intensive techniques and by developing a system of labor management which likely increased productivity, although not to the level found in Western societies. Instead of concentrating on heavy industry, for which raw materials were lacking, the Japanese concentrated on industries for which materials, such as silk, were available. This strategy paid off in a vastly enlarged export trade.

We have described Japanese entrepreneurs' eager adoption of Western technologies, but also their limited adoption of the factory system of production. Instead they made use of a complex system of interrelationships between the small-scale and large-scale sectors of the economy and a combination of traditional and modern organizational arrangements. They also were quick to adopt new products from the West and to begin producing them on their own and to diversify their production. And the market situation improved as the government pushed for the curtailment of imports, as the world demand for silk products accelerated, and as foreign competition was diminished by World War I.

Therefore we do not feel that the rate of industrial growth achieved in Japan can be attributed solely to improved economic opportunity conditions. Japanese entrepreneurs themselves made important contributions, guided (or prodded) by the Meiji government. Their foremost contribution was the ability to combine the old and the new, the traditional and the modern, as exemplified by their system of management and the ties between the small-scale and large-scale sectors. The Japanese system of organization has been described as "an extraordinary blend of the feudal family structure, the government agency, and the modern corporation" (Vernon, 1971, p. 225), which expresses succinctly the combination of old and new that was involved.[49]

Because Japanese entrepreneurs did not respond immediately after 1868, Japanese entrepreneurship might be considered to have had no causal significance, or even to have had *negative* causal significance, in the early Meiji period. The Japanese pattern in this respect is very similar to the German experience before 1850. The increase in entrepreneurial responsiveness followed government stimulation—through the construction of model factories, the sale of its enterprises, subsidies to entrepreneurs, and the promotion of technological innovation. The government's actions substantially reduced the economic risks of industrial entrepreneurship. Entrepreneurs increasingly came forward as these risks were reduced and ultimately exceeded the potential of the available opportunity conditions. So the Japanese case is very similar to the German in this respect, too.

THE IMPORTANCE OF NONECONOMIC FACTORS FOR JAPANESE ENTREPRENEURSHIP

The sociocultural and political changes which took place in Japan after 1868 are quite similar to those that occurred in Germany about twenty years earlier. In both, government actions *freed* potential entrepreneurs by cutting down

[49]Japan, like Germany, confronted the possibility of exploiting the advantages of backwardness in 1868, chiefly because of the availability of technologies. But in order to do so it was necessary to change other economic opportunity conditions, such as capital and market supplies and the size of the market. It has been pointed out that Japan differs from Gerschenkron's model of the consequences of backwardness, both in terms of its development of light, rather than heavy, industry, and in its ability to recruit a labor force (Gould, 1972). Both of these deviations from the model are partly explainable in terms of opportunity conditions existing in Japan, but they also are partially the result of the entrepreneurial capacity to develop opportunity conditions more fully.

many of the noneconomic barriers to entrepreneurship. Government actions did not merely neutralize these barriers, but in both cases the government threw extensive *positive* support behind the cause of industrialization. Thus in both cases the *social* risks of entrepreneurship also were reduced.

We believe this decrease in social risks was more important for the emergence of entrepreneurship than any psychological changes which may have occurred. For example, we do not feel there was a substantial increase in the willingness to take risks because several entrepreneurial actions, such as the wholesale adoption of existing technologies and products and the creation of the *zaibatsus,* actually minimized risk. We have noted the possibility that Japanese entrepreneurs utilized a somewhat different economic calculus than did Western entrepreneurs, but we feel this characteristic, if present, also was less important than the sociocultural changes which occurred.

The identity of Japanese entrepreneurs also suggests that a great improvement in the sociocultural environment took place. In the Tokugawa period Japan undoubtedly fit our model of "outsider" entrepreneurship, given the prevailing opposition to the Western world and its ways and to economic activities. We have noted the despised position of merchants at that time, for example. This outsider quality was less pronounced after 1868. In contrast to Germany, marginal entrepreneurship was indigenous rather than foreign as the result of the state's opposition to foreign entrepreneurs and the emergence of indigenous entrepreneurs. Entrepreneurship became less and less marginal as the sociocultural and political support for it became stronger, and we would regard Japan as fitting our model of mainstream entrepreneurship well before 1900.

The confusion concerning the participation of the samurai and the wealthier merchants in industrial entrepreneurship indicates to us the quasimarginality characteristic of the period after 1868. In this respect Japan was similar to Germany and France. None of these societies corresponds fully with our model of outsider entrepreneurship. Some marginality was characteristic of both Japanese and German entrepreneurship in the context of a supportive socioeconomic and political environment. In France there was also some marginal entrepreneurship in a less supportive environment. We see a clearcut case of outsider entrepreneurship only when we come to Russia.

Japan shares two important characteristics with Germany. The first is a transition to entrepreneurship that had positive causal significance. The second is the importance of the government in promoting this transition through its effects on economic and noneconomic opportunity conditions. A more drastic break with the nonindustrial past was achieved through government action in these two countries than was the case in France. This did result in limited political development and the alliance of industrialization and militarism in Japan and Germany, but economically the more complete break with the past was more beneficial than the less complete break achieved in France. In Japan the power of the aristocracy was broken and they were manipulated into compliance with the goals of the state. In Germany the aristocracy allied itself with entrepreneurs. But in France the aristocracy remained influential enough to cause the government's role to be equivocal, but not strong enough to produce marginal entrepreneurship only.[50]

Therefore we believe that the factors promoting the emergence of entrepreneurship were very similar in Japan and Germany. Economic opportunity conditions improved, thereby promoting entrepreneurial emergence, but the improvement of noneconomic opportunity conditions under the state's influence also was necessary for the realization of the potential of the economic conditions.

---

[50]By contrast, in Russia we shall see the continuing strength of the aristocracy, and of a government allied with it, creating the conditions which promoted marginal entrepreneurship. The ultimate effects of this were revolutionary, and eventually the new Soviet leaders instituted a program of mainstream entrepreneurship under state control.

8

The United States

From Asia we turn to the New World, to the first example of industrialization in the Americas. The United States is the only New World society, as well as the only new *nation,* in this study. Germany achieved political unification during the course of its industrial transition through the amalgamation of a number of Germanic states. The Meiji Restoration in Japan was a major political transformation, but it involved a nation-state dating back many centuries. Only in the case of the United States do we find a totally new society and state being founded.

Despite the uniqueness of the American situation, we will find similarities between industrialization in the United States, Britain's former colony, and in the mother country. We will also find differences. And we shall see that by the end of the nineteenth century the United States had surpassed Britain to become the foremost industrial power in the world. In this chapter we are interested in determining the extent to which American entrepreneurship accounted for this feat. We shall consider its importance and characteristics during the period 1810 to 1880.

OPPORTUNITY CONDITIONS
FOR AMERICAN ENTREPRENEURSHIP

As of 1810, approximately twenty years after its establishment, the United States was an overwhelmingly agricultural society. The people's need for manufactured goods was met by domestic production and imports from Great Britain, with the latter predominant. There was little manufacturing, and "business . . . consisted mainly of shipping, brokerage, wholesaling, and retailing" (Cochran, 1967, p. 229). There had been only one factory in existence in 1790, and by 1808 there were just fifteen cotton mills (North, 1965). Capital supplies were no doubt relatively limited, though probably greater on a per capita basis than in Germany, France, Russia, and Japan.[1] The vast unexplored reaches of the new country promised an agricultural future for the new society, as a provider of raw materials for industrializing Europe and as a consumer of European goods. The potential of this course was limited only by the geographic separation of the new nation from the European continent.

The domestic market proved to be one of the most, if not the most, favorable of the opportunity conditions confronting American entrepreneurs (Chandler, 1963). It was characterized by rapid growth, a favorable composition, and specific improvements which combined to yield a very favorable situation. Demand increased faster than in Europe, and there was never the reluctance to buy mass-produced goods that there was in Britain, for example (Strassman, 1959).

The domestic market provided the initial impetus for American industrialization after 1810 as a result of the curtailment of imports from Britain occasioned by the Embargo Act of 1807 and the War of 1812. These developments removed the competition of superior British goods and increased awareness of the need for the new country to develop its own industrial system (Cochran & Miller, 1961; Holton, 1969). After 1812, therefore, many of the larger trading firms in New England began to switch to manufacturing, banking, transportation, and the purchase of land, with those firms that had the largest import trade and an existing distribution system leading the way (Cochran, 1967; North, 1963).

The rapid growth of the domestic market was the result of a combination of economic growth and rapid population increase. The population increased about seven times between 1810 and 1880 (from 7.2 million to 50.2 million), a vastly greater increase than that of any of the other societies included in our analysis. The growth resulted partly from a high rate of natural increase, due to a relatively high birth rate and a relatively low death rate, and partly from immigration. The other societies we are discussing were losing population to the new nation during this period.[2]

The improvements in the domestic market included changes that increased the demand for specific goods and that increased its integration. The 1820s and 1830s were characterized by an improvement of transportation and distribution systems, including port facilities, warehousing, and the spread of roads and turnpikes. The development of the canal system was the major focus of the 1830s

---

[1]As of 1840 American domestic per capita product was about $60, compared to $47 in France, $60 in Holland and Belgium, and $84 in England and Wales (Gallman, 1961, p. 401).

[2]Net in-migration constituted 5 percent of the average population and 16.5 percent of the net decennial change in population between 1821 and 1850. These increased between 1851 and 1880 to 5.9 percent of the average population and 23.5 percent of the net decennial change. After 1880 these percentages increased even more (Kutznets, 1966, p. 57).

and 1840s. These changes caused interregional trade to grow, which further stimulated demand, and especially expanded the market for the metallurgical industry (North, 1965; Temin, 1964). There also was a large and growing market for firearms in the frontier country (Saul, 1970), and the demand for agricultural tools and implements also increased as the population moved west. Urbanization further increased industrial demand. By 1840 11 percent of the population was urban; this had grown to 28 percent by 1880 (Carman, Syrett & Wishy, 1961, p. 23).

A major improvement in the domestic market occurred in the 1850s with the beginning of extensive railroad construction. The railroad boom served as the primary stimulus to the economy until 1870 or 1880, by increasing the demand for products of the metallurgical and machine industries. It was particularly significant in the United States because of the large distances that had to be traversed. It also promoted manufacturing in regions other than New England, which at the time accounted for three-fourths of the nation's employment in manufacturing (North, 1965).[3]

In the 1860s the Civil War produced a significant increase in demand that primarily benefited Northern entrepreneurs. They, especially those operating on a large scale, were able to avoid the destruction of the war and they received large government contracts for military goods. By the middle of the war some of them were paying dividends of between 40 and 50 percent. Consequently the war ended with Northern industry in a much more powerful position than it had enjoyed before the war (Cochran, 1961).

The demand for manufactured goods stayed ahead of production until the depression of 1873. After that critical period, the market was not sufficiently strong to absorb the continually increasing output of goods pouring out of American factories (Chandler, 1969). But throughout most of the period we are studying it constituted an extremely favorable condition for American entrepreneurs. The only major inadequacies were the absence of a suitable protective tariff before 1861 and the severity of American business cycles. Whether the lack of a very high tariff was a disadvantage is debatable; the consensus is that it was not a severe impediment. The business cycles, which were more extreme than in Europe, also had mixed effects (Cochran, 1955). They no doubt led to the ruin of some entrepreneurs, but they were used to advantage by innovative and perceptive entrepreneurs (Strassman, 1959).[4] Thus these problems did not detract greatly from the overall favorableness of the market.

The foreign market was far less favorable than the domestic because of the competition of Britain and the other European industrializers. We shall see that it was not a very significant outlet for American entrepreneurs.

Lack of capital was a hindrance to industrial entrepreneurs at least until

[3]Fogel (1964) has questioned the impact of railroad construction on the demand for iron, but his argument does not diminish the overall effects of the railroads, which were similar to their effects in Germany.

[4]Carnegie, for example, built up his reserves during boom periods and made major investments and bought out his competitors during depressions (Davis, Hughes & McDougall, 1965)

about 1850 (Carman, et al., 1961). Working capital was in shortest supply at the beginning of the industrial transition, as in other industrializing societies, and interest rates were high, higher than in Britain, for example (Livesay & Porter, 1971; North, 1965). According to Cochran and Miller (1961, p. 186), "Since the beginning of the industrial revolution in America, most enterprises in almost every *new* [emphasis in the original] industry . . . started with shoestring financing." And Strassman (1959) has shown the negative effects of the lack of capital on entrepreneurs' innovational actions.

A financial market had developed in the Northeast around the foreign and cotton trades, but there was much competition for capital from other sectors (Cochran & Miller, 1961; North, 1963). Transportation facilities, for example required large amounts of capital. Moreover, foreign investors avoided manufacturing at the time, and the banking system was slow to develop (Cochran, 1955).

Beginning in the 1820s, however, the need for capital for the construction of transportation facilities stimulated the development of capital-mobilizing mechanisms, such as banking and insurance companies (North, 1963). Investment bankers began to supply capital to industry also, or to serve as intermediaries between investors and entrepreneurs, and they provided the largest share of manufacturing capital until 1857 (Cochran & Miller, 1961). Insurance and real estate companies also got into the act occasionally, and increasing amounts of foreign capital were invested.

The capital supply increased more rapidly after 1850, doubling in that decade as the result of the discovery of gold in California and of increased foreign trade and foreign investment (Carman, et al., 1961). The Civil War also prompted some improvements in the capital market and helped put money in the hands of potential investors via inflation (Cochran, 1961). Large-scale financiers provided substantial amounts of capital by 1875, and American industry underwent what has been called the transition from industrial to finance capitalism.

Thus capital supplies increased dramatically from an initially low level. Although foreign capital was not important relatively, it was substantial in absolute terms. The United States was a net capital importer until almost 1900 and a far larger borrower than the other early industrializers (Gould, 1972). Yet foreign capital amounted to only about 4 percent of total capital invested between 1820 and 1860, and only slightly more after that (Kravis, 1972, p. 404). It was even less important for manufacturing than for other sectors, particularly transportation. Foreign investment in other sectors, however, did have the unintended consequence of freeing domestic capital for manufacturing (Cochran & Miller, 1961; Jenks, 1944).[5]

[5]The inadequacies of capital-mobilizing facilities not only led to capital imports but they offered "greater scope . . . for making money through financial manipulation and personal advantage in access to sources of capital" (Gould, 1972, p. 170). The financial wheeling-and-dealing of the period of railroad construction and of the later industrial financiers are evidence of the accuracy of this assertion.

The favorableness of American labor for entrepreneurship was limited at first, but improved as a result of immigration. The major handicap was the lack of skilled labor, especially in the producer goods sector. Consequently labor was a high-cost factor in comparison to Great Britain (North, 1965). The early development of a system of free education in the Northeast did improve the supply of skilled labor (Cochran & Miller, 1961). And the labor force was relatively mobile, rather passive, and more willing to accept technological innovations than was the British labor force (Strassman, 1959). This last characteristic undoubtedly was a latent consequence of the early scarcity of labor because there was little fear of unemployment at the time (Burn, 1931).

The rapid influx of immigrants overcame the obstacle created by the limited supply of labor. In fact, Cochran (1955) insists that it had created a labor *surplus* in the East by the 1840s, and the problem was to get this surplus to areas where scarcities existed. In addition, the immigrants were willing to work at low wages and were highly skilled, notably the earlier immigrants from northern and western Europe (North, 1963).[6]

The new nation was favored with a bountiful supply of natural resources in most instances. The textile industry, supplied by the Southern cotton plantations, certainly had had no supply problems after the invention of the cotton gin. The metallurgical industry faced somewhat greater handicaps. One problem it confronted was the geographic separation of ore and coal deposits. Adequate transportation facilities were available, however, by the time this problem became crucial. Second, American iron ore was too phosphoric for the Bessemer process, but it was about right for the Siemens-Martin process. In addition, the discovery of good Bessemer ores in the Lake Superior region in the 1870s occurred at just the right time for exploitation of the process. Third, American coal was not very suitable for coking, but the development of large anthracite deposits obviated that problem until the technological problems could be ironed out. Fourth, the lack of suitable raw materials similarly delayed the production of blister and cast steel before 1850 (Redlich, 1940). There were ample supplies of wood and water, though, and the abundant supply of water in the Northeast played an important part in the early localization of manufacturing in that area.

American entrepreneurs were able to draw upon a large supply of technologies as early as 1810. So, a lack of technology was not a problem, except for isolated instances, such as the lack of crucibles for making cast steel which handicapped the early steel industry for a time (Redlich, 1940).[7] In addition, as American entrepreneurs added their own innovations to this supply, complementarity, or *dovetailing* as Strassman (1959) calls it, between innovations was an unforeseen consequence. This was most apparent in the metallurgi-

[6]Diamond (1967) believes the immigrants offered entrepreneurs another advantage, the possibility of playing off workers of different nationalities against each other in order to keep costs low.

[7]Saul (1970) has suggested that many European inventions, especially in the steel industry, were particularly suitable for American industrial conditions.

cal, machine-tool, and power equipment industries, but much less common in the textile industry. It increased in the 1850s when railroad expansion, the development of iron turbines and the Corliss steam engine, and the application of interchangeable manufacture to new products supported each other (Strassman, 1959). The ongoing growth of technological and scientific knowledge also made technological innovations easier.

Strassman (1959) has concluded, on the basis of a detailed analysis of the metallurgical, textile, machine-tool, and electrical industries, that the risks of technological innovation really were not very great. He has divided these risks into four types: customer, interference (from labor and the government, for example), timing, and production. Of these four, only production risks were of significance in his opinion.[8] Customer and interference risks were lower than they were in Europe. Innovation was riskier in the textile industry than in other industries, at least after 1850, because of the slower expansion of demand and the lesser dovetailing between innovations from other industries and that industry. In the machine-tool industry, by contrast, new tools quite often were less expensive than existing ones.

Therefore we conclude that economic opportunity conditions became extremely favorable for industrial entrepreneurship in the United States in the years after 1810. Capital and labor supplies were least satisfactory at first, but they both improved rather quickly. Raw material supplies generally were favorable. The supply of technology also increased rapidly, building upon a base provided by Great Britain. We have singled out the rapid expansion of the domestic market as the most favorable of these opportunity conditions. Cochran (1955, p. 372) notes that "a very large part of the capital goods created . . . had ultimate economic value," indicating that very few entrepreneurial actions were unprofitable in the unindustrialized new nation. This depended on the continued growth of the market of course, and we have seen that that did take place throughout the period. Opportunity conditions were most favorable in the Northeast at first because the domestic market was concentrated there, extensive water power was available, and it had the best capital and labor markets because it was the center of the import trade and of immigration (North, 1965).

THE ROLE OF THE GOVERNMENT

We mentioned the lack of a sufficiently high tariff as a factor which possibly reduced the favorableness of the market situation for entrepreneurs. The general impression has been that *deficiencies* such as this characterized government policies during the period 1810–80, and that they followed a classical laissez-

---

[8]Production risks were greatest when an innovation involved a new process and/or the use of a new raw material. These risks were greatest before about 1830 and declined after that as scientific knowledge increased.

faire pattern in regard to industrial entrepreneurship. This impression is at least partly erroneous. The government did play a role and it did improve opportunity conditions in certain instances.[9]

Although at the outset the Jeffersonian Republicans were hesitant about industrialization, they did promote technological innovations.

> Beginning with George Washington and Alexander Hamilton,[10] officials of the Federal Government promoted mechanization by patronizing textile factories, issuing testimonials, and even arranging for imports of superior sheep as a patriotic necessity. The Federal Government also took the lead in developing or supporting interchangeable manufacture, battery-driven electric motors, the Bessemer process, hydraulic steel-mill equipment, the large scale use of alloys and aluminum, and many other innovations (Strassman, 1959, p. 190).

The government also promoted innovations by lending military technicians to the private sector and by establishing the land-grant colleges (Strassman, 1959).[11]

The support provided by state and local governments for the construction of transportation facilities was another major contribution of the pre-1850 period (Broude, 1959). In the 1850s the federal government's largesse fell upon the railroad builders who were granted approximately 200 million acres of land (Cochran & Miller, 1961). They also were given "the right to finance construction by the issuance of bank notes the only security for which was the *proposed* [emphasis in the original] railroad" (Cochran & Miller, 1961, p. 80). These actions improved the market, as did the government's demand for goods during the Civil War.

The government also promoted corporate formation by the establishment of limited liability in the years between 1800 and 1830 (Handlin & Handlin, 1945). Before the Civil War it remitted taxes on new enterprises and subscribed to corporate bond issues (Cochran, 1961). After the war the Supreme Court upheld the right of corporations to engage in interstate commerce which further strengthened their hand.

Policies regarding the banking system were probably the weakest part of the government's support for entrepreneurship.[12] The lack of government action in this area has been linked to the appearance of manipulative and speculative types of entrepreneurship which we shall describe later (Gould, 1972). Government demand for goods also did not constitute a sizable component of total demand. As of 1870 its expenditures as a proportion of gross national product

[9]Hartwell (1971) believes that its role has been underestimated, and Broude (1959, p. 25) describes it as "surely more than minimal."

[10]Hamilton helped establish the Pennsylvania Society for the Encouragement of Manufactures and Useful Arts in 1789.

[11]Murphy (1967), however, regards the governement as neutral toward the transfer of technologies from Europe.

[12]The fact that a central banking system was not established until 1913 illustrates the lack of government involvement in this area.

were less than those of the governments of Germany, Japan, and Great Britain (Maddison, 1969, p. 14).

Thus the government's role was generally supportive, with the exceptions just cited, and involved a greater variety of actions than often has been supposed. Its actions resulted partly from entrepreneurs themselves becoming an increasingly influential force promoting policies in accord with their interests. They began to mobilize politically in the period between 1816 and 1832 when they pushed for favorable tariff and banking laws. There was a lull between 1840 and 1860, but railroad men and metallurgical entrepreneurs played a major role in the adoption of the tariff in 1861.[13]

Entrepreneurs, led by the railroad builders, made ample use of monetary incentives, i.e., graft, to achieve their political goals. This strategy became more blatant after the Civil War and reached its highpoint in Grant's corruption-ridden administration when businessmen competed with each other in bribing legislators. But about 1875 a transition occurred, which Cochran and Miller (1961) describe as a change from ''political business'' to ''business politics.'' Businessmen began playing roles within the political system rather than being dependent upon politicians for favors, and their political influence became even greater.

CHARACTERISTICS OF AMERICAN ENTREPRENEURSHIP

How did American entrepreneurs respond to the favorable opportunity conditions they confronted and that they helped to create through their political actions? We will look first at what they did and then at who they were.

Innovations

American industrial growth between 1810 and 1880 was propelled by a plethora of innovations—technological, organizational, material, and product. Many of these innovations were borrowed from Europe, being brought over by immigrants in some cases. At the same time indigenous entrepreneurs added a significant number of innovations to this stream. Many of these innovations were organizational rather than technological, so the American case should not be seen solely as the triumph of technology. And not all technological innovations were adopted with equal rapidity. In several areas, as we shall note, diffusion was slow and entrepreneurs approached innovations with utmost caution. Perhaps the genius of American entrepreneurs was their ability to adopt or improve those

[13]In Fine's (1956) view, businessmen had become the dominant political figures by 1865 and they were very careful to distinguish between government interference and government aid, resisting the former but welcoming the latter.

innovations which were particularly relevant in the American context. In steel, for example, not a single fundamental contribution was made, but "incredible feats of refinement of existing procedures and machines . . . were accomplished . . . . the Americans concentrated, as soon as it was discovered that the process would work, on means to increase production" (Chamberlain, 1968, p. 173).[14]

The pattern of technological innovations was quite similar to Britain's—diffusion proceeding first in the textile industry and then in metallurgy. The introduction of the power loom in 1814 was followed in the 1820s and 1830s by additional mechanization on the basis of innovations borrowed from England. The only American contributions to textile technology were the ring-spinning machine, Lowell's power loom and Draper's automatic loom (North, 1965; Strassman, 1959). After about 1840, when machines were becoming increasingly complex, indigenous innovations in the textile industry dropped off sharply, although diffusion of English innovations continued (Saul, 1970). By that time "original changes were almost entirely limited to attachments and gradual increases in speed and scale" (Strassman, 1959, p. 114).[15]

Technological innovation in the iron industry was quite slow before about 1850. The industry was almost completely traditional in 1830, and British imports, such as puddling and rolling, were being adopted slowly.[16] The introduction of iron bottoms in puddling furnaces facilitated use of the puddling process, but rolling was used more extensively in the period before 1850 (Temin, 1964).

The American metallurgical industry only began to move forward rapidly at the time of the Civil War, aided by two more English imports—the Bessemer process in 1864 and the Siemens-Martin process in 1868.[17] Adoption of the Bessemer process was very slow at first, partly because American iron ores were too phosphoric. Adoption was more rapid, and steel output expanded rapidly in the 1870s, as a result of the opening of the Lake Superior ore fields and improvements in the process itself (Redlich, 1940; Temin, 1964).

The third major change, in addition to mechanization and the application of new processes, was the use of inanimate power sources for manufacturing. Steam power was not used very extensively yet in 1850, and its diffusion was relatively slow after that. By 1860 it accounted for only 52 percent of primary-power capacity in manufacturing (Rosenberg, 1972, p. 63); it was, however,

[14]Gould (1972) reports the British admiration of the American ability to devise minor improvements.

[15]North (1965) describes the period from 1840 to 1860 as involving the spread of mechanization to new industries; Cochran and Miller (1961) view the 1850s as a period of technological refinement.

[16]Unlike England and Germany, puddling and rolling were utilized in the United States before cast steel was produced (Redlich, 1940).

[17]Redlich (1940) reports that a Kentucky ironmaster claimed to have developed the Bessemer process before Bessemer, but he does not say whether there was any substance to this claim.

rapidly applied to the railroads.[18] A major reason for the slowness in adopting steam was the abundant supplies of wood and water.

The American forte in technological innovation was machine and machine-tool production, particularly in the *light,* metal-working industries, and the development of self-acting or automatic machine tools (Rosenberg, 1972; Saul, 1970). The British had made the initial innovations in this area, but American entrepreneurs made numerous additions to the supply of such tools. British observers of these innovations were particularly impressed by the American facility at "adapting special apparatus to a single operation in almost all branches of industry" (Rosenberg, 1972, pp. 96–97n).

Innovations in, and development of, the machine-tool industry had two major consequences for American industrialization. First, it made possible the use of standardized interchangeable parts, both for consumer and producer goods. The development of tools that could precisely shape unlimited numbers of parts made standardization, the production of identical parts, possible. Standardization in turn made interchangeability possible.[19] Interchangeability made both assembling and servicing a product immeasurably easier and it in turn led to the second consequence—*mass-produced* standardized *products*—which is regarded by some as the most distinctive feature of American industry (Schapiro, 1946; van der Haas, 1967).

The use of interchangeable parts was spreading rapidly by 1840 (Murphy, 1967). Makers of firearms, such as Eli Whitney, who were aided by the great demand for guns, were the first major users of this technology.[20] By the 1850s its use in the firearms industry was "the most famous of the early American technologies" (Saul, 1970, p. 6). The rest of the world was introduced to the technology by the American display of firearms at the Crystal Palace Exhibition in London in 1851 (Rosenberg, 1972). The technology spread to other countries, especially the manufacture of sewing machines, after the 1850s and ultimately to other consumer durables. Twenty-five years after the London exhibition the use of interchangeable parts in steam engine construction was a highlight of the Philadelphia Exposition celebrating the centennial of the United States.

The earmark of American industry therefore was the extent to which, and the rapidity with which, the use of interchangeable parts was adopted, compared to the European societies. Americans far exceeded the British in this respect, even though they had followed them chronologically in the development of some

---

[18]It is rather surprising that the milling industry was the major user of industrial power in 1870, using four times as much steam power as the cotton industry and more than even the iron industry (Rosenberg, 1972, p. 110).

[19]Before parts were standardized each and every part had to be manufactured individually. Because tools were not precise enough to make these parts identical, much time and energy (and cost) was required when assembling a product from parts in order to fit the parts together. And, if new parts were required, these too had to be shaped anew and the process of fitting the part repeated.

[20]Whitney usually has been credited with introducing the principle of interchangeable parts, but Landes (1969) claims that the technique goes all the way back to a Swede, Polhem, in the 1720s.

of the necessary tools.[21] The earlier British production of inexpensive textiles was limited in comparison.

It generally has been agreed that the relatively high cost of labor was a stimulus for technological innovation in the United States (North, 1965; Saul, 1970). "The typical 'bold' American innovation was the initial substitution of an ingenious mechanism for manual labor" (Strassman, 1959, p. 224). "The result was a more capital-intensive industry at a very early stage which was able to compete successfully with lower-wage, more labor-intensive industries abroad" (North, 1965, p. 676). Labor costs were influential in the choice between mule and ring spinning in the textile industry and in the steel industry in the mechanization of raw material handling, for example (Gould, 1972).[22]

Often it also is assumed that American entrepreneurs were extremely daring innovators. Men like Carnegie are popularly portrayed as reckless and willing to take extreme risks. But Strassman (1959) has painted a different picture of their willingness to take risks. According to him, the adoption of innovations was "not heroic gambling, but cautious exploitation of vast and multiplying opportunities" (p. 226). Entrepreneurs preferred to invest in innovations that had been successful in Europe rather than indigenous ones, and "the men who introduced the most radical technological changes of American origin preached extreme caution, and insisted that innovations should be no more than secondary and supplementary to the regular operations of a firm" (p. 64). Their caution increased disproportionately with the cost of an innovation.[23]

Their hesitance before 1850 may have been due to a lack of technological knowledge, but after that time it appears mainly due to fear or to the inability to foresee consequences. For example, "The fact that in certain producers' goods industries innovations time and again dovetailed with developments in complementary industries and resulted in windfall profits did not seem to penetrate into entrepreneurial consciousness" (Strassman, 1959, p. 210).[24]

Strassman (1959) has provided a number of other interesting observations about technological innovations among American entrepreneurs. He notes that only a small minority was involved in *absolute* innovations in accordance with

[21]Although a system of mass production can be traced back to the Middle Ages, it enjoyed its fullest development in the United States after 1850 (Klemm, 1964).

[22]The influence of labor costs on technological innovation may have been somewhat less than we are suggesting. Saul (1970), for example, claims that interchangeability was not necessarily adopted as a means of cutting labor costs.

[23]Others have concurred with this description of entrepreneurial caution. Redlich (1940) points out that Carnegie was far from a reckless gambler and that he adopted innovations only after he was convinced of their merits.

[24]Rosenberg and Landes have offered interesting explanations of why new technologies are slow to replace old ones. Landes (1965a) emphasizes the improvements that are made in the old technology in response to the new technology and the demand possibilities it creates and picturesquely describes this process as an "Indian summer of growth and achievement in obsolescence." Rosenberg (1972) stresses the long time it takes for a new technology to reach its optimum cost and efficiency levels.

our view of the rarity of absolute innovations. He also suggests that the boldest innovators were those who had superior information (which he interprets as access to superior opportunities), that intraindustrial diffusion was more rapid than interindustrial, and that innovation did not decrease with the rise of finance capitalism.[25] And he claims that depressions encouraged cost-cutting innovations and worked to the benefit of those who had adopted such innovations just prior to the economic downturn.

Overall it appears that American entrepreneurs did not take full advantage of their very favorable opportunity conditions. Cochran (1955) claims that it was possible for them to achieve good returns from mass production by means of simple machines because of the favorableness of opportunity conditions. So they very likely were able to obtain satisfactory returns without making the more costly innovations Strassman indicates they could have made.

Organizational innovations were an important supplement to the technological innovations of the period. Industrial entrepreneurs were preceded in this area by those who ran the burgeoning railroad system after midcentury, and who were the first to confront the problems connected with very large-scale operations, or, as Chandler (1967, p. 242) describes them, "the new ways of oligopolistic competition and large-scale, professionalized, bureaucratic management."

Textile entrepreneurs appear to have been oriented to factory production on an integrated basis from a very early time. In 1814, for example, the first cotton mill in the world to include all operations from the raw material stage to the finished product under one roof was erected in Massachusetts (van der Haas, 1967).[26] The transition to factory production in textiles was quite rapid, as it surpassed domestic production in 1837 (Cochran & Miller, 1961), a mere two years after the English passed that milestone. The factory system was dominant in New England by the Civil War, and enterprises there were significantly larger than elsewhere in the country (North, 1965). Yet as late as 1850, "The factory— . . .—was a rarity outside the textile and iron industries." A much more rapid transition to factory production took place after 1850, and by 1880, 80 percent of the workers in mechanized industry were employed in factories (Chandler, 1969, p. 27).

There is disagreement regarding the extent to which American entrepreneurs made innovations in the organization of production after the Civil War.[27] Carnegie has been credited with major managerial innovations during this period, such as the introduction of cost accounting and the selection of managers strictly on the basis of talent (Davis, et al., 1965; Redlich, 1940), but the

[25]But Cochran (1955) argues that it did decrease.

[26]North (1965) credits the Boston Manufacturing Company, which started at Lowell in 1813, with leadership in the specialization of functions.

[27]Cochran and Miller (1961) believe that entrepreneurs did not make advancements in organizing the production process after the Civil War so that by the 1890s they were behind Europeans in this area. But Strassman (1959) praises them for their ability at large-scale handling, and Sawyer (1954) also commends them in this respect.

evidence of continued American progress in this area is inconclusive. It is possible that there was less success in devising new systems to organize production within the factory than in organizing relationships between firms.

As of 1870 "nearly all American industrial enterprises were mere manufactures." By 1900, integrated firms, producing their own raw materials, manufacturing and transporting goods, and engaging in wholesaling and sometimes retailing, were dominant (van der Haas, 1967, pp. 30-31). Thus the trend after about 1875 was one of integration and combination of industrial enterprises, especially in the producer goods sector, in response to the vast growth of industrial output resulting from the introduction of technological innovations.[28] Overexpansion and competition resulted in attempts to control them by means of combination. And an innovation such as the Bessemer process created the need for stricter control of raw material supplies which led to the creation of backward linkages into raw material production (Strassman, 1959).

The metallurgical industry had moved toward an increasingly larger scale of production in individual enterprises after the Civil War under the leadership of the "classical" generation of entrepreneurs—men such as Ward (Redlich, 1940). But that generation was unable "to bring about well-integrated industrial combinations comprising more than two stages of production" (Redlich, 1940, p. 109). The following generation, the Carnegie generation, led by its namesake and men such as Frick and Oliver, *was* able to make the next integrative step, the creation of backward linkages to sources of raw materials and forward linkages to transportation and distribution systems (Redlich, 1940). Thus after 1880, Carnegie and Frick, "formed a great vertical combine of coal fields, coke ovens, limestone deposits, ore mines, ore ships, and railroads" (De Santis, 1963, p. 246).[29]

At the same time as these vertical integrative ties were being constructed, there also was a trend toward horizontal combinations, of manufacturers producing the same goods, as a means of reducing the perils of unbridled competition. Although tendencies to restrict competition may have been present from the beginning of the American industrial transition (Kirkland, 1961), efforts to develop cooperative arrangements in manufacturing increased after the Civil War, following the example set by the railroads. The Bessemer Steel Association was formed in 1875, for instance (Temin, 1964).

These organizational innovations were similar to changes occurring in Germany and Japan at about the same time—the rise of the cartels and the *zaibatsus*. So they do not constitute a unique American development. American

---

[28] "The machine, an instrument of competition, tended always to become mother to monopoly" (Cochran & Miller, 1961, p. 61).

[29] The next integrative step was taken in the 1890s as these mammoth industrial combines fell under the control of financiers such as Morgan, who established the U.S. Steel Company in 1901 through a merger of Carnegie and ten other companies. The formation of this company is regarded sometimes as marking the end of industrial capitalism and the beginning of finance capitalism.

entrepreneurs, however, were ahead of the British in the movement toward integration and combination.[30]

The corporation was the predominant means of amassing large amounts of capital before 1880, and its use constitutes one area in which American entrepreneurs did have temporal priority. It was in greater use in America than in England or on the Continent even before 1800 (Handlin & Handlin, 1945), and the adoption of the practice of limited liability between 1800 and 1830, although slow, preceded its development in England and France where rigid legal restrictions on corporations remained in force.[31]

The railroads provided leadership in the use of the corporation in the nineteenth century. Almost one-half of all the business corporations chartered between 1800 and 1860 were chartered in the 1850s, the period of the railroad boom, for example (Cochran & Miller, 1961, p. 70).[32] The corporate innovation also appears to have been used innovatively. A common practice after the Civil War was to capitalize corporations in excess of their physical assets, thereby increasing the profit potential for speculators (Cochran & Miller, 1961). Here, too, the railroads provided the example through financial manipulators such as Gould.

American entrepreneurs initially responded to the scarcity of labor both by introducing labor-saving innovations and by an extensive use of women and children. In 1816, for instance, 90 percent of the 100,000 people employed in cotton manufacturing were women and children, and women constituted two-thirds of the total factory labor force (Cochran, 1967, p. 234). Entrepreneurs also actively encouraged immigration. A group formed the American Emigration Company in the 1860s which sent agents to Europe in search of workers (Cochran & Miller, 1961), and Chinese workers were recruited for the iron industry (Redlich, 1940). And some Southern entrepreneurs made much more extensive use of slave labor than has been realized heretofore. About 5 percent of the slave population was employed in industry in the 1850s. By 1861 the Tredegar Iron Company of Richmond, the leading Southern iron mill and the iron mill with the third largest work force in the country, employed about 450 slaves—half of its labor force (Starobin, 1971, pp. 11, 15).[33]

[30]This trend was really in its infancy before 1880 and increased sharply after that. The years between 1898 and 1902, for example, have been described as involving "the greatest merger movement in American history" (Chandler, 1969, p. 31).

[31]Handlin and Handlin (1945) argue, however, that limited liability was not really very important at that time because corporations were used in areas where risk was minimal and the government was willing to come to their rescue.

[32]Jenks (1944) claims that financing corporate growth from within was an American innovation contributed by the railroads.

[33]In addition to the iron industry, slave workers were prominent in tobacco factories, rope factories, the machine industry, shoemaking, tanning, papermaking, brick works, sugar refining, rice and grist milling, cotton ginning and pressing, mining, lumbering, railroad construction, the turpentine industry, and shipbuilding. Approximately four-fifths of industrial slaves were owned; the others were hired. Slave labor was actually cheaper than free labor. Tredegar, for example, reduced its labor costs 12 percent by introducing slave workers (Starobin, 1971).

The immigrant labor was not always satisfactory because of its technological conservatism and thus sometimes had to be replaced by indigenous workers (Kindleberger, 1958). Some entrepreneurs, such as Whitney (and later Ford), preferred to train unskilled laborers to operate machines because they believed they were less likely to have negative working habits (Davis, et al., 1965). But Southern slave labor probably was more efficient than free labor because of its greater tractability (Starobin, 1971).

Apparently little ingenuity was shown in managing labor during the period we are studying. After 1865 there was little interest in increasing labor efficiency[34] and little sympathy to workers' demands (Cochran & Miller, 1961). "Like so many industrialists of his time . . . Carnegie found the aims of organized labor completely incomprehensible" (Davis, et al., 1965, p. 136). The employment of technically trained personnel, which began to occur after the Civil War, was a much more noteworthy accomplishment. These employees pushed entrepreneurs to adopt the Bessemer process, for instance, and Strassman (1959) reports that there was a direct relationship between the innovativeness of an enterprise and the influence of its technical personnel after 1870. Along with the establishment of the industrial research laboratories, the first of which was set up by the Bell Telephone Company in 1876, this labor innovation enabled American entrepreneurs to attain an alliance of science and industry similar to that which Germany achieved at this time.

The adoption of material innovations was relatively slow, both because of the large supplies of less expensive materials, such as wood, and because of problems connected with their introduction. Material innovations or process innovations incorporating new materials and new technologies comprise the very few cases in which innovations were not immediately successful (Strassman, 1959). The use of coke and the Bessemer process are prime examples. Coke was introduced around the 1830s but it was not used very extensively because anthracite coal made better-quality pig iron.[35] Charcoal was still widely used for smelting at the time of the Civil War and coke was not used in the Southern iron industry until after 1873 (Redlich, 1940). We have earlier noted the slowness of diffusion of the Bessemer process until after the discovery of nonphosphoric ores.

New materials were more significant for the machine and machine-tool industries. Many of the early American technological innovations had evolved from the woodworking industry (Saul, 1970), but from about 1835 on, machines were constructed from metal rather than wood, and this required new tools to make the machines (Strassman, 1959). In the 1870s the introduction of steel

---

[34]Entrepreneurs using slave labor devised a number of methods to discipline their labor force, including both rewards and punishments. They also trained some slaves to be managers and often linked slave workers with skilled technicians or had technicians train slaves in skilled jobs. Thus several slaves became puddlers at the Tredegar Iron Company (Starobin, 1971).

[35]Only 13 percent of pig iron was smelted by means of coke by 1860, whereas almost all of British pig iron was made in this manner already in 1800 (Rosenberg, 1972, p. 77).

alloys was a major material advancement for the machine-tool industry which allowed the production of more durable products (Klemm, 1964).

American entrepreneurs did not respond to the favorable domestic market situation that we have described by introducing very many new products, except for producer goods, such as machinery and machine tools. The early textile industry concentrated on using power looms to produce lower-cost grades of cloth rather than producing new goods, for example (North, 1965). There was a relatively rapid increase in the proportion of producer goods in the product mix after 1860, however, so that by 1880 consumer goods accounted for only 44 percent of total industrial output, which was less than the comparable German and British proportions in 1895 and 1871, respectively (North, 1965, p. 694; Patel, 1961, p. 322, table 3).

Entrepreneurs did display an interesting combination of diversification and specialization in response to the market though, especially in the machine industry. Textile and arms makers who had diversified into machine production were the major machine producers before about 1855. The textile manufacturers had become involved first, and they developed a variety of heavier machine tools, such as lathes, planers, and boring machines. The lighter machine tools—turret lathes, milling machines, and precision grinders—were spin-offs of the firearms industry. In addition, locomotives were produced by foundries, machine shops, and textile machine shops (Rosenberg, 1963, 1972).[36] After 1855 this pattern changed and highly specialized machine-tool firms began to appear (Rosenberg, 1972; Saul, 1970).

The metallurgical industry was much slower to diversify into both the production of cast steel and of rails for the emerging railroad system (Rosenberg, 1972). Carnegie did not begin producing steel until the 1870s for example. By 1880, however, metallurgical entrepreneurs were concentrating on rail production almost exclusively (Chamberlain, 1968), which resulted in some of the overproduction which prompted the movement toward integration.

The major market innovation of American entrepreneurs consisted of recognizing the potential of mass production for the domestic market and acting on that perception.[37] After an initial expansion and accumulation of resources and the rationalization of the use of those resources, the typical entrepreneur expanded into new markets and new lines to promote the full use of his resources (Chandler, 1962). As the economy grew many entrepreneurs realized the possibility of operating their firms on a nationwide basis (Evans, 1957). This pattern continued until the 1870s, when the depression of 1873 motivated industrial entrepreneurs to gain greater control of the market through the organizational innovations we have described.

---

[36]This pattern of diversification into machine production is identical to the pattern of the early British machine industry.

[37]Van der Haas (1967) commends American entrepreneurs for their orientation to the market, and Redlich (1940) credits Carnegie with being the first in metallurgy to visualize the potential of the mass market.

Compared to most of the other societies being considered, American entrepreneurs did not make substanial use of the foreign market. The United States accounted for only 8.8 percent of world foreign trade, compared to Great Britain's 24 percent, France's 10.8 percent, Germany's 9.7 percent, and Russia's 4.5 percent by the period 1870–80 (Kuznets, 1966, p. 306). The relatively greater significance of the American domestic market is apparent when we compare these percentages for the United States, Germany, and Great Britain with their shares of world industrial output in Table 17.

Table 17

Relationship Between Shares of World Industrial
Output and Foreign Trade

Country	Percentage Share of World Industrial Output, 1870	Percentage Share of World Foreign Trade, 1870–80
United Kingdom	32	24.0
Germany	13	9.7
United States	23	8.8

Source: Kuznets (1966, p. 306, table 6.3A); Patel (1961, p. 326, table 2).

Thus American entrepreneurs borrowed numerous technological innovations and added significant improvements to them. To these they also added organizational changes—integrative ties in the producer goods sector—and financial changes—the early use of the corporation. This combination of changes enabled them eventually to meet the demand of the rapidly growing domestic market. Labor and material innovations were a relatively less significant part of their actions.

Degree of innovation. American entrepreneurs attained significant gains in productivity as a result of their adoption of technological innovations, but these gains did not always come immediately. The iron industry has been criticized for its inefficiency (Cochran & Miller, 1961), and the Bessemer process required a long period of experimentation before it yielded high-quality steel. Furthermore, interchangeability has been criticized for leading to low-quality goods (Saul, 1970)[38]

But production costs generally had been lowered by 1860, and this trend continued. American Bessemer converters were from three to five times as efficient as British ones by 1876, for example (Chamberlain, 1968, pp. 172–73). The transition to vertical integration in heavy industry also appears to have had positive consequences, as it did in Germany. For instance, between 1880 and 1900 annual rates of growth in the producer goods sector in the United States and

---

[38]Saul (1970) also notes that contemporary observers often criticized the cheapness and flimsiness of American machinery, although he does acknowledge that British machinery could have been similarly criticized.

Germany were much higher—5.1 percent and 5.4 percent respectively—than they were in the much less integrated British producer goods sector which had an annual rate of growth of 2.0 percent between 1881 and 1907 (Patel, 1961, p. 324, table 4). This discrepancy cannot be attributed solely to this organizational innovation, but it was no doubt an important factor.[39]

Expansions

It appears to have been relatively easy to initiate both initial and subsequent expansions throughout the period 1810–80. Chandler (1962) notes the ease of subsequent expansions, and Redlich (1940) comments upon the relative ease of initial expansions in the steel industry in comparison to Britain and Germany. According to Cochran (1955), there was a great deal of movement into and out of industrial entrepeneurship, which also indicates that it was relatively simple to expand.

In fact, American entrepreneurship was characterized by a persistent tendency toward *overexpansion*, resulting from overly enthusiastic investing whenever the business cycle took an upswing (Cochran, 1955). Consequently, although the growth of manufacturing output followed a generally smooth course during the nineteenth century (Gould, 1972), there were numerous expansive spurts. In 1808, for example, there had been only 15 cotton mills, but in the following year 87 were established (North, 1965, p. 680). Just in the decade 1860–70 the number of manufacturing establishments increased by 80 percent (Carman, et al., 1961, p. 79). This recurrent tendency to overexpand played a major part in the movement toward integration and combination in the producer goods sector before 1880.

It is probable that increased capital requirements and the greater concentration of industrial control by 1880 made the entry of new entrepreneurs more difficult. The capital requirements of the Bessemer process were a restrictive factor, for example,[40] and established entrepreneurs attempted to restrict entry even more (Redlich, 1940). But forces were working in the opposite direction as well. According to Temin (1964, p. 185), "As the heavy products typical of the early years of steel gave way to more varied objects, the limits on entry due to heavy capital costs declined for finished products." And, according to Chandler (1969), the recruitment of new entrepreneurs continued for at least a generation after the onset of the trend toward concentration.

From an early period American entrepreneurs tended to finance their subsequent expansions by reinvesting their profits (Cochran, 1955). They became more dependent upon outside finance after midcentury, but an entrepreneur like

---

[39]The consequences of the transition to factory production were dramatic. "In 1800, only one free man in four was an employee; in 1900 a majority were" (Letwin, 1969, p. 11).

[40]Redlich (1940, p. 97) says, "The first outlay was so large, the details of the process so unknown, and the prejudices so powerful that manufacturers hestitated and preferred to wait." Strassman (1959) also mentions this innovation as one of the riskier ones that was confronted.

Carnegie continued to finance expansions from within even though outside capital was available. Ultimately though his company was no longer able to swim against the tide and it too fell under the control of outside financiers.

Degree of expansion. The size of expansions increased greatly over the course of the period we are studying, as it did in all of the other industrializing societies, with the biggest increases coming after 1850. Early in the period most factories were small, with $10,000 representing a substantial investment for buildings and equipment. The majority of businesses were still either small or medium-sized by 1850, except in the textile and shoe industries and in New England (North, 1965). And the iron industry remained predominantly small-scale until about 1850 (Redlich, 1940).

The Civil War and the subsequent adoption of technological innovations prompted a substantial increase in scale in metallurgy. The Bessemer process particularly increased capital requirements because it increased the minimum economic plant size (Temin, 1964). Thus American entrepreneurs, both new and old, initiated increasingly larger expansions in the years between 1810 and 1880. In fact they often expanded beyond the scope of their market and were forced to bring the situation under control with organizational innovations.

Entrepreneurial Identity

American industrialization often is portrayed as a history of outstanding individual entrepreneurs, such as Rockefeller, Carnegie, and Ford, and financiers, such as Gould and Morgan. Such a portrayal should not blind one to the fact that from 1810 to 1880 the identity of American entrepreneurs did not differ greatly from that of their contemporaries in the other societies we are studying. There was a transition from individual to collective entrepreneurship and increasing use of the corporation. Between 1810 and 1830 chartered corporations were more prominent than joint-stock companies in manufacturing because they were able to grant their investors limited liability. But the number of joint-stock companies increased after 1830 and especially after 1850 with the extension of this provision to them (Cochran, 1967; Cochran & Miller, 1961). The majority of corporations were involved in the construction of canals and railroads, though, and the corporation did not become dominant in manufacturing until after the depression of 1873 (Edwards, 1938).

The partnership was predominant in manufacturing, at least until the Civil War (Livesay & Porter, 1971). Individual entrepreneurs continued to be significant after the war, however, both "general" entrepreneurs (Cochran, 1955), who were involved in different but related lines of business, and men like Carnegie, who has been described as "almost the classic Schumpeterian entrepreneur" (Davis, et al., 1965, p. 134). But Carnegie cannot be considered a completely individualistic entrepreneur like British entrepreneurs of a century earlier. One of his assets was his willingness to surround himself with assistants who were more knowledgeable than he in areas such as technology and to rely upon their advice (Cochran & Miller, 1961; Strassman, 1959). So, although individuals were important entrepreneurs they acted somewhat less individualistically than earlier entrepreneurs in other countries.

Family entrepreneurship was particularly prominent in the beginning of the New England textile industry (Lamb, 1952).[41] It began to decline in industry in general before 1850 (Chandler, 1969), but we do not fully agree with Cole's (1959) claim that it was rare in the United States. As for the negative effects of family entrepreneurship, it has been suggested that nepotism possibly limited change (Cochran, 1949), but there is little evidence of any other bad effects.

American entrepreneurship, like British, was virtually completely private. The earliest corporations were "conceived as an agency of government, endowed with public attributes, exclusive privileges, and political power, and designed to serve a social function for the state" (Handlin & Handlin, 1945, p. 22). But this linkage to government had disappeared by the time they were significant in manufacturing.

During the period 1810–80 American entrepreneurship became increasingly mainstream, although it retained a slightly marginal quality through the period because of the large representation of immigrants who became entrepreneurs. We consider it only slightly marginal because, even though we have classified migrant entrepreneurs as marginal, many of the migrants came from Great Britain and from the societal mainstream there.[42] By 1880 mainstream entrepreneurship was the norm:

> . . . the typical industrial leader of the 1870's [was] American by birth, of a New England father, English in national origin, Congregational, Presbyterian, or Episcopalian in religion, . . . born and bred in an atmosphere in which business and a relatively high social standing [were] intimately associated with his family life (Gregory & Neu, 1952, p. 204).

We see that American entrepreneurship became increasingly mainstream in terms of religious origins, too. Many of the earliest entrepreneurs in New England were Nonconformists who had left England to avoid religious persecution (Smith, 1968). But the preceding quotation indicates that by 1880 entrepreneurs were drawn primarily from the higher-status, more established Protestant denominations.

---

[41]Merchant families provided substantial amounts of capital for the early entrepreneurs: In Boston, the Appletons, the Jacksons, and the Cabots financed the new textile mills of Lowell and Lawrence. In New York, the Phelps and the Dodges started the brass industry in the Connecticut Valley. . . . They not only raised the funds for plants and machinery, but also supplied a large amount of the cash and credit that the new manufacturers needed as working capital to pay for supplies and labor (Chandler, 1969, p. 26.)

On the basis of such financing, fifteen Boston families controlled 20 percent of the country's cotton spindleage, 30 percent of Massachusetts' insurance capital, and 40 percent of Boston's banking resources by 1850 (Cochran & Miller, 1961, p. 71).

[42]Redlich (1940) has described the "foreign-born adventurer," which would appear to be a more marginal type of entrepreneur, as unique to the United States. But he also observes that such entrepreneurs tended to be less innovative than indigenous entrepreneurs were, at least in metallurgy.

Socioeconomically there was a significant mainstream component by 1810 in the form of the established trading houses and shipping magnates that diversified into manufacturing (Cochran, 1967; North, 1965). Merchants continued to be a source of industrial entrepreneurship, and a primary source of industrial capital, until the Civil War (Livesay & Porter, 1971). Redlich (1940, p. 86) asserts that successful large-scale manufacturers who had received their training in retail trade were unique to America, but this assertion is questionable in light of the development of the British textile industry, and he is probably referring only to metallurgy.

Artisans and craftsmen were also important, particularly in the early years of the iron industry. Many manual workers moved into industrial entrepreneurship after 1810, often forming partnerships with wholesalers in order to obtain the capital they needed (Cochran, 1955). "Virtually every ante-bellum manufacturing firm which successfully produced for markets outside its local area developed as a partnership between merchants and manufacturers." And, as had occurred in Britain, "In almost all such cases merchants dominated the partnership" (Livesay & Porter, 1971, p. 64).

American entrepreneurs were drawn from occupations other than these. Redlich (1940, p. 68) has emphasized the low socioeconomic origins of many entrepreneurs: "Already in the eighteenth century people arose from relatively low strata who could hardly have become entrepreneurs in Europe at that time." By contrast, there were entrepreneurs from white-collar and professional backgrounds (Cochran, 1955).[43] So American entrepreneurship, although predominantly from artisan or merchant origins, came from an uncommonly broad range of socioeconomic origins, a pattern very similar to that which we have described for British entrepreneurship. This range of origins narrowed somewhat as industrialization proceeded, and a larger proportion of entrepreneurs were recruited from manufacturing or mercantile backgrounds (Stepanek, 1960). At the same time, opportunities opened for entrepreneurs with technological backgrounds in new industries, such as the electrical industry in which men such as Edison, Westinghouse, Brush, Thomson, Sprague, and Stanley began to appear around 1880 (Passer, 1953). This development was identical to the appearance of engineer-entrepreneurs in Germany at the same time, and kept the range of entrepreneurial origins from being seriously narrowed.

THE RATE OF AMERICAN INDUSTRIAL GROWTH

The American industrial transition did not proceed as rapidly as one might think. Industrial growth was more rapid after 1850 than before, and even more rapid after 1880, as in Germany; but the rate of growth after 1880 was not as great as in

---

[43]Geissenhainer, a clergyman, was involved in the promotion of anthracite as fuel in the iron industry, for example (Redlich, 1940).

Germany. Nevertheless the American accomplishment was striking. In 1810 the United States had been far behind its former mother country in industrial output, and as late as 1850 it still could be considered an underdeveloped area in comparison to Great Britain (Cochran, 1955). But by 1860 it was second to Britain in total industrial output (North, 1965, p. 682), and by 1870 American per capita gross national product was 69 percent of the comparable British figure and ahead of all the other early industrializers (Maddison, 1969, p. xvi).

The American annual industrial growth rate of 4.3 percent during the period 1860–80 was higher than that of Britain (2.4 percent), France (2.4 percent), and Germany (2.7 percent). But the growth rate of American industry was surpassed by Japan, Germany, and Russia between 1880 and 1900, and it appears to have been lower than the Japanese rate after 1900 (Maddison, 1969, p. 31; Patel, 1961, p. 319, table 2; Shinohara, 1970, p. 284). Thus the American rate was not as high as rates attained later by other industrializing societies, but it was relatively high for the period 1860–80.

THE CAUSAL SIGNIFICANCE OF AMERICAN ENTREPRENEURSHIP

We have described the economic opportunity conditions for entrepreneurship in the United States between 1810 and 1880 as very favorable and we have shown the responses American entrepreneurs made to these conditions. And we have seen that between 1860 and 1880 the American industrial growth rate was higher than that of Britain, France, and Germany. Therefore, we conclude that entrepreneurship was causally *insignificant* in the American industrial transition.

We will indicate our two main reasons for that conclusion because it is possibly a controversial one. First, our judgment is that the opportunity conditions were more favorable in the United States than in any of the other early developers during the period 1860–80. Hence, that the American industrial growth rate was also the highest of any of the early industrializers does not justify an inference of causal significance. It is exactly what we expect on the basis of the economic model of entrepreneurship.

Second, we do not feel that the opportunity conditions in the United States in the period 1860–80 were substantially *less* favorable than were the opportunity conditions in Germany in the period 1880–1900, or in Japan from 1913 to 1925–29; instead we feel they were approximately equal. So a comparison of annual industrial growth rates for these periods—4.3 percent for the United States in 1860–80; 5.3 percent for Germany in 1880–1900; and 7.5 percent for Japan in 1913 to 1925–29 (Patel, 1961, p. 319, table 2)—leads us to conclude that entrepreneurship had *positive* causal significance in Germany and Japan for those periods, but causal *insignificance* in the United States.[44]

Furthermore, in a number of areas, American entrepreneurs were not as innovative and expansive as the mythology surrounding them may lead one to believe. First, we noted the lack of innovation in the textile industry at even a relatively early time. Second, the metallurgical entrepreneurs were slow to respond to the demand for goods created by the railroad boom. It is particularly noteworthy that the German, Krupp, confronted by similar raw material problems, solved them and sold a large portion of his railroad wheels and rails to the American railroads. Third, we have also noted the slow diffusion of steam power, which was partly due to the bountiful supplies of timber and water. (This was one of several instances of large supplies of raw materials hindering innovation that we have noted throughout this study. Many times scarcities may be blessings in disguise for industrial entrepreneurship.) Fourth, the foreign market could have been exploited more, although American entrepreneurs may have suffered from greater cost disadvantages than we think.

The one area in which Americans made the greatest technological contribution, the mass production of standardized goods, can be explained largely in terms of a marriage of basically European technology with the favorable American domestic market. We have noted that good returns could be attained by using relatively simple machines for this type of production. Americans did make many improvements that increased productivity, but most of the basic ideas were of British or European origin.

NONECONOMIC FACTORS INFLUENCING AMERICAN ENTREPRENEURSHIP

Why, then, was the response of American industrial entrepreneurs not more dynamic than it was? We have argued that the economic risks of entrepreneurship were not that significant. Were there possibly noneconomic risks connected with entrepreneurial behavior that were not great enough to prevent entrepreneurship from emerging in proportion to the favorableness of the economic opportunity conditions but of sufficient magnitude to prevent a disproportionate emergence?

[44]Two considerations cause us to qualify this conclusion somewhat. First, we may have overestimated the capital supply for manufacturing. We noted that there was a sizable increase in this supply after 1850, but we may not have given adequate weight to the competition for capital from other sectors, such as transportation. Second, we may have overestimated the favorableness of raw material supplies as well, not giving enough attention to the phosphoric nature of the available iron ore. Germany and France, however, faced these problems, and did not have the benefit of as rapidly an expanding domestic market as the United States did.

Or were there psychological characteristics of the American people or American entrepreneurs that were inimical to entrepreneurship?

Given the importance of industry in twentieth-century America, it is a bit surprising to find very different opinions regarding the legitimacy of entrepreneurship during the nineteenth century. On the one hand, there is much evidence of values supportive of entrepreneurship. Cultural characteristics, such as the positive evaluation of material wealth, the emphasis on personal advancement, and the willingness to accept innovations, have been regarded as particularly conducive to entrepreneurial behavior (Cochran, 1949; Sawyer, 1954; Strassman, 1959; Williamson, 1955). This value constellation was supported by a legal system which "expressed a preference for property as an institution for growth rather than security" (Diamond, 1967, p. 573). In addition, it has been pointed out that many immigrants, especially from Great Britain, came with favorable attitudes toward entrepreneurship (Cochran, 1955).

Letwin (1969) is a prime representative of the viewpoint that entrepreneurship had high legitimacy, arguing that it was positively evaluated from the beginning because the colonies began as commercial ventures. The Northern aristocracy, such as it was, was not anti-business and the Southern aristocracy gradually lost power and was unable to make its negative attitudes influential. There was more opposition to commerce or trade than to manufacuring, and opposition after the Civil War was primarily directed at the railroads. Thus the businessman was at the top of American society, an unusual situation because "elsewhere businessmen have been despised or, if condoned, relegated to an inferior level of the social order" (Letwin, 1969, p. 1).

On the other hand, there *was* substantial opposition at times. In one view:

> American industrialists in the half century after 1812 were hated by southern planters, vilified by New England radicals, despised by landed gentry and Quaker merchants. . . . before the Civil War, unlike their English competitors after the struggle with Napoleon, [they] were only a subordinate group in a society dominated by farmers and merchants (Cochran & Miller, 1961, pp. 119–20).

There also was strong opposition to the use of corporations at the beginning of the industrial transition (Vernon, 1971).

Our conclusion is that there was some opposition to entrepreneurship, especially during the Jacksonian period, but that it was opposition to *industrial* entrepreneurship and not to entrepreneurship *per se*. The Southern slaveowners certainly were entrepreneurs! And this opposition pales in comparison to the degree of opposition in societies like France, Germany, Japan, and Russia. The economic success of the industrial entrepreneurs was the most powerful weapon disarming this opposition after the Civil War. By the Gilded Age, the entrepreneur was celebrated as a hero (Bendix, 1956), and he "embodied the common aspirations and symbolized the working life of most Americans" (Letwin, 1969, p. 8).

We believe the possibility of upward social mobility was greater in the

United States than in any of the other societies considered in this study; to a large extent it was the "land of opportunity" it was perceived to be by the millions of foreigners who descended upon its shores in the nineteenth century. This had not been the case in the eighteenth century, though, because the colonies, being outposts of English society, were characterized by the same restraints that existed there. But it was impossible to maintain these restrictions in the context of the new society. The need for a labor force especially "made it impossible to reproduce the rigidity of social structure characteristic of contemporary Europe. . . . Position in the new society became primarily a function of direct economic activity" (Diamond, 1967, pp. 565, 570).

Newcomers to the society therefore found virtually open-class communities without established leadership (Cochran, 1955). In Europe the nobility had provided such leadership, but this was absent in the United States. Europeans repeatedly marveled at "the absence of rigidities and restraints of class and craft; the freedom from hereditary definitions of . . . tasks or hardened ways of going about them; . . . the mobility . . . of Americans" (Sawyer, 1954, p. 376). As a result the possibility of using the entrepreneurial role as a means of ascending the status hierarchy was unequaled in the United States.[45]

Various sectional and local rivalries were the major factors inhibiting integration of the new society before the Civil War. Industrial entrepreneurs occasionally suffered the slings and arrows of the Southern planter aristocracy, but they shared many common interests, as entrepreneurs, with Northern farmers (Letwin, 1969). Merchants who shifted into manufacturing were also well integrated into the social system. The Civil War, of course, threatened to disintegrate the new society, but we have already seen some of the positive economic effects of that conflagration. Socially a major consequence of the South's defeat was the entrenchment of Northern industrialists' power which ultimately resulted in greater societal integration.

The war itself, although a potential cause of entrepreneurial insecurity, did not seriously endanger Northern entrepreneurs—many of whom evaded military service by buying substitutes (De Santis, 1963)—or their enterprises. Following the war, their increased political power increased entrepreneurial security still further. The right of private property was secure, and the government did little to interfere.

This may have been too much of a good thing. It has been hypothesized that the *absence* of government interference actually created *insecurity* for entrepreneurs, mainly in the area of capital investment. Thus the hands-off policy is

---

[45]Cochran (1955, pp. 342–43) says:
Trade and manufacturing necessarily became chosen avenues for social mobility. . . . As business success came increasingly to be the avenue to social prestige, a large supply of men was available for entrepreneurial pursuits. In addition, many occupations that in a foreign nation would not have been regarded as entrepreneurial or conducive to innovation or expansion in capital investment turned out to be such.

believed to have made the precipitous business cycles of the time even more severe (Carman, et al., 1961). The free license given to corporations also created insecurity (Cochran, 1955; Cochran & Miller, 1961). So the generally high degree of entrepreneurial security must be balanced against the unstabilizing effects of the very free economic environment.

Even so, the social risks of entrepreneurship do not appear to have been great in the United States. They may have been a slight barrier to entrepreneurship before the Civil War, but after the war the place of the entrepreneur in American society was assured. The generally supportive nature of the American sociocultural milieu corresponds with our earlier description of American entrepreneurship as being minimally marginal at first and then becoming overwhelmingly mainstream.

There also has been much speculation concerning the extent to which nineteenth-century American people and American entrepreneurs possessed a unique psyche especially conducive to entrepreneurship. A number of contemporary European observers of the American scene apparently felt that the Americans were a peculiar people (Burn, 1931).[46] These observers saw a variety of characteristics, including:

> the high focus on personal advancement and drives to higher material welfare; . . . adaptability . . . and . . . boundless belief in progress . . . initiative, originality, systematic effort, and boldness; . . . ; . . . ceaseless search and ready adoption of the new and more efficient; the intense responsiveness to shifting opportunities and expanding horizons; [and] the "go-aheadism" . . . at the root of the "immense drive" of American manufacturing (Sawyer, 1954, pp. 376–77).

This perception may, however, have resulted from the contrast between what they saw in the United States and what they had experienced at home because: "The American innovations that looked so bold to foreign visitors were mostly in fields where interference and customer risks were much lower in America than in Europe. . . . but there were also European innovations which looked bold to Americans" (Strassman, 1959, p. 224).

Cochran (1955) provides a slightly different perspective, suggesting that innovative personalities were normal in the United States because of the continued changes that were occurring. This implies that the entire population was psychologically affected by the nature of the economic opportunity conditions.[47]

McClelland (1961) has used the American case, along with the British, to support his need-achievement theory. In his view, achievement imagery in children's readers declined slightly between 1810 and 1830 and then ascended to a

---

[46]In the view of one observer in 1836, "There is, probably, no people on earth with whom business constitutes pleasure, and industry amusement, in an equal degree with the inhabitants of the United States" (Cochran, 1955, p. 344).

[47]He also observes that the optimistic business climate often induced professional men to become entrepreneurs.

peak in the period 1880–1900. This increase in achievement imagery preceded an increase in the rate at which patents were issued, and so he believes that need-achievement promoted industrial growth. We are skeptical of this interpretation for the pre-1880 period because of the smoothness of the growth of manufacturing throughout virtually the entire nineteenth century (Gould, 1972). The rate of industrial growth did increase somewhat after 1850, which would allow for a twenty-year lag from the 1830 date marking the upturn in achievement imagery. But the rate of growth had been increasing before 1850 also, and so a decline in industrial growth following the 1810–30 decline in achievement imagery is not apparent.[48]

Yet the theory of need-achievement and Hagen's (1962) theory of the withdrawal of status respect both can be linked to the great significance of foreign migrants in the American case. We agree with Williamson (1955) that a process of selective migration was operative. Those who migrated either may have had high levels of need-achievement, or they may have suffered from the withdrawal of status respect in their home societies and may have seen the new society as an optimal setting for achieving prestige. Thus the immigrants who made it to the new nation may have had psychological predispositions promoting entrepreneurial behavior.

The degree to which economic motives were uncommonly strong in the United States has been another focus of debate. Entrepreneurs have been described as interested in the price, volume, and quality of goods from the beginning (van der Hass, 1967), and they have been portrayed as wanting riches, but not being "high livers" (De Santis, 1963, p. 243). However, there also is evidence of nonmonetary incentives being important for some. Carnegie's goals were to become a philanthropist, retire when he had made a modest fortune and devote himself to public service, and mingle with the "great" in politics, learning, and the arts (Cochran, 1955, p. 365). Obviously it was necessary for him to pay attention to economic profits and losses in order to attain these goals.

Lastly, perception may also have been a significant psychological factor. The most successful innovators had the ability to perceive opportunities far in the future (Sawyer, 1954; Strassman, 1959). Their native ability to see ahead, or their greater awareness of the need for information on the future, probably gave them an advantage in calculating the costs and benefits of their actions. Even with this capability, though, most innovating entrepreneurs nevertheless underestimated the profitability of their innovations (Strassman, 1959).

So there is at least some evidence, mostly conjectural, for the presence of

[48]His argument appears more cogent for the early twentieth century. The degree of achievement imagery increased between 1880 and 1900 and then decreased, and the rate of industrial growth continued to increase until 1913 when World War I intervened. This extraneous event makes it impossible to judge whether the rate of industrial growth would have declined after 1914 in accord with the theory.

psychological traits which promoted entrepreneurship in the American situation.[49] Could these traits account for American entrepreneurship's not being more dynamic than it was? At first glance, it does not seem so; but upon further reflection, it is at least plausible. In reviewing the descriptions of American entrepreneurship one is stuck by their perplexing variety. We have noted the tendency of entrepreneurs to *overexpand* . We have seen that they were drawn from a very wide range of occupational backgrounds, including the professions and white-collar occupations in which financial rewards should have been relatively high. This aspect of American entrepreneurship suggests the intriguing possibility that entrepreneurs in the United States may have been *extreme* risk-takers, not the moderate risk-takers specified by the need-achievement model.

Or they may have been extremely oriented to profit opportunities. Or the opportunity conditions may have been so favorable that they became overoptimistic. In other words, the combination of conditions in the United States may have promoted *speculative* or *adventurer* entrepreneurship, rather than the sober ascetic style of entrepreneurship described by Weber. The main concern of *adventurer* entrepreneurship would have been financial gain and not production. In the heady atmosphere of the time this would have led to overexpansion and the pattern of movement into and out of entrepreneurship that we have described. It would also help to explain the passion for integration, combination, and financial manipulation characteristic of railroad men and industrialists after the Civil War.

But Strassman's (1959) persuasive description of entrepreneurs' caution regarding innovations and Chandler's (1969) suggestion that production did not catch up with demand until the 1870s are in sharp contrast. How could the lack of dynamism they describe occur simultaneously with overexpansion? The most satisfactory explanation we can conceive is that entrepreneurial insecurity was greater than we have imagined, not because of aristocratic opposition, but because of the cutthroat competitiveness and the severe fluctuations of the American economy. The actions of the speculative financially oriented entrepreneurs may have resulted in an insecure situation to which industrial entrepreneurs reacted with hesitance.

If this were the case, then we believe that it was the result of a unique combination of conditions. Broude (1959, p. 22) has described the American case as "a special set of circumstances plus a series of unique specific events." We agree with this succinct description. The United States was the only case, among those we are considering, of a totally new nation populated by migrants from a variety of lands. The broad reaches of the untamed new land surely must have inspired optimism about its potential which became mythologized in ideologies such as "manifest destiny." The migrants came, likely anticipating "streets paved with gold." Furthermore we strongly suspect that those who did

---

[49]As would be expected, given the predominance of Protestantism in the United States, the Protestant Ethic also has been cited as a motivational influence on American entrepreneurs (van der Haas, 1967).

choose to leave their home countries were either unusually optimistic or unusually willing to take risks.[50]

These sociopsychological characteristics were reinforced in turn by the favorable economic opportunity conditions in the new nation. We have mentioned that virtually all capital goods had value, for example. The favorable combination of economic, social, cultural and psychological conditions also likely led to the broad representation of classes and occupations in the entrepreneurial role. Migrants came with optimism or a willingness to take risks; they saw the potential for social mobility and the favorable opportunity conditions in the new nation; hence the entrepreneurial role was viewed as a viable option by probably a larger proportion of the people than in any of the other early industrializers. And this in turn strengthened the tendency toward adventurer entrepreneurship. This combination of conditions and the responses to it therefore could have led to a lower rate of industrial growth than a more sober, less speculative version of entrepreneurship would have.

We must also consider less positive aspects of the American situation. We believe two elements of the American experience—slavery and the Civil War—may have directly hindered industrial growth. Whether one attributes the existence of chattel slavery in ostensibly the most democratic of societies to economic advantage or to the desire to maintain an aristocratic lifestyle, the fact stands that the system of slavery kept the South locked into an agricultural vise which precluded extensive industrialization. Only after slavery had been driven from the scene did the industrial potential of the South begin to be realized. The effects of this anachronism on American industrial growth are probably unmeasurable.

In addition the war which slavery helped to spawn very likely had greater negative effects than we have described previously. Although it did strengthen Northern entrepreneurs and provide them with windfall profits (which would have reinforced the speculative tendencies we have noted), it and the political conflict following it left the South in ruins and had continued disintegrative influences during the period of Reconstruction. If we compare the effects of this event and its aftermath with political developments in Germany at about the same time—political unification and a smashing *victory* over an external enemy in the Franco-Prussian War—or the Meiji Restoration in Japan, the comparison makes clear that what happened in Germany and Japan was more propitious for industrial growth.

That the governments in these three societies played very different roles indicates the importance of government actions for entrepreneurship and industrial growth. In Germany and Japan the state was in the forefront of industrialization and helped to break the ties of the feudal past. In the United States it played a much less active role in stimulating industrialization and it proved unable to solve

[50]In fact one might regard "willingness to migrate" as an indicator of willingness to take risks.

the problem of slavery without resort to bloodshed. If the American government had done more in either area, it is quite likely that a higher rate of industrial growth would have been achieved. But the unique aspects of the American situation intrude here again. A larger government role was *impossible* in a nation founded on the basis of opposition to an established government and peopled by immigrants, many of whom had come to escape political repression. The political consequences of these differences in the respective governments' actions were ultimately more favorable in the United States, but it is probable that a more active government role would have promoted more rapid industrial growth.

9

Russia

Russia constitutes our negative case—the only one of the societies we are studying that did not achieve industrialization during the period in which we analyze it. By 1913 industry still accounted for only about 20 percent of Russian national income and employed only about 5 percent of the labor force (Goldsmith, 1961, p. 442). Because it is our only negative case, we are particularly interested in the extent to which the failure to achieve industrialization can be linked to the nonemergence of entrepreneurship. We shall explore that possibility for the years between 1800 and 1917, the beginning of the Bolshevik Revolution.[1]

OPPORTUNITY CONDITIONS FOR RUSSIAN ENTREPRENEURSHIP

At the beginning of the nineteenth century Russian industry was

> a somewhat bewildering patchwork. There were state enterprises, using the ascribed labor of state peasants; votchinal enterprises, using serf labor; merchant enterprises, using both hired labor and possessional peasants . . .; serf enterprises, using hired labor; and . . . myriad small rural and village handicraft manufactures (Falkus, 1972, p. 30).

[1]The failure of Russia to achieve industrialization makes it the most similar, of the six countries included in this review, to current societies which also remain unindustrialized. We will not draw any parallels between Russia and these societies, but the similarities should be obvious to anyone acquainted with the situations of these societies.

The limited extent of industrial development at this time is very apparent: the domestic sector made the largest contribution to total manufacturing output; fewer than 200,000 workers were employed in factories (Blackwell, 1968, p. 37).

The motley industrial structure had been inherited largely from the reign of Peter the Great (1682–1725) who had endeavored to Westernize Russia through a vigorous campaign of industrialization under state initiative. The practice of using unfree serf labor for industry, whereby entrepreneurs were allowed to purchase entire villages of serfs, had begun under his rule. State-owned serfs were used in state enterprises, and government subsidies given to entrepreneurs to stimulate industrial activities. As a result of these efforts it is estimated that Russia was the largest producer of pig iron in the world around 1750 (Maddison, 1969, p. 89). By 1800 it still produced a third of the world's pig iron, and its iron exports were larger than those of any other country (Blackwell, 1968, p. 56).

Nevertheless the level of economic development must have been extremely low. As late as 1870, for example, Russian per capita gross national product was approximately a third that of Great Britain, although slightly higher than that of Japan (Maddison, 1969, p. xvi). In the 1890s, "the level of living was so low that the average income was inadequate even for necessities" (Carson, 1959, p. 133). We can only guess at how low it must have been in 1800.

Therefore the potential supply of industrial investment capital undoubtedly was severely limited. The textile industry had suffered from a serious lack of capital in the 1700s, for example (Mavor, 1965). The scarcity of capital was aggravated further by the split within Russian society between a nobility oriented to the consumption of luxury goods and the peasant masses living at a subsistence level. There was also a strong tendency for available capital to flow into land rather than into industry (Carson, 1959; Portal, 1965). Unlike Japan, productivity of the agricultural sector did not increase, so there was little surplus from that sector to be siphoned off for industry. And from a relatively early period, capital requirements were large even in the textile industry (Miller, 1926). We have observed that in other societies the textile industry was one in which entrepreneurs invariably could begin on a small scale. But, as we shall discuss more fully later, cotton mills were very large scale in Russia by 1850.

A significant improvement in capital supplies did not occur until about 1880, when large amounts of foreign capital (and foreign entrepreneurs) began to pour into the country with the active encouragement of the Russian government. The degree to which Russia relied on foreign capital is illustrated in Tables 18, 19, and 20. These tables clearly show the increased role of foreign capital after about 1885 and its decline sometime after 1900, its predominant role in new capital investment during the 1890s, and its concentration in particular industries and areas, for example southern heavy industry, the mining industry in general, and Russian Poland. Thus Russia was far more dependent on foreign capital than any of the other societies we are analyzing, but this massive flow of outside

Table 18
Foreign Percentages of Total Russian
Industrial Capital

Year or Period	Foreign Percentage
1860	15
1889	25
1891–1903	50
1914	33

Source: Blackwell (1968, p. 246); Portal (1965, p. 825).

Table 19
Foreign Percentages of Russian New Capital
Investment, 1885–1914

Year or Period	Foreign Percentage
1885–1913	50
1893–1900	55
1898	67
1904–1914	25

Source: Maddison (1969, p. 91); McKay (1970, pp. 29, 380).

Table 20
Foreign Percentages of Russian Industrial
Capital, Selected Industries
(1900–1914)

Industry	Year	Foreign Percentage
Total metallurgical industry	1900	42
Total machine industry	1900	50
Southern steel industry	1900	78
Southern mining and metallurgy	1900	90
Total mining and manufacturing	1914	33
Total mining industry	1914	90
Total metallurgical industry	1914	40+
Total chemical industry	1914	50
Total textile industry	1914	28
Polish manufacturing	1913	62
Polish metallurgical industry	1913	86

Source: Falkus (1972, pp. 70–71); Maddison (1969, p. 91); McKay (1970, p. 297); Portal (1965, pp. 851, 859).

capital still was not sufficient to meet the needs of industrial entrepreneurs even when it was at its maximum in the 1890s (Spengler, 1959).[2]

A severe economic depression, which lasted until 1908 or 1909, partly accounted for the sharp decline in foreign capital after the turn of the century. The decline was also partly attributable to Russian banks' finally beginning to play a capital-mobilizing role at that time. Before the 1890s the private joint-stock banks had been content to provide mainly working capital to existing industrial enterprises; but in the 1890s they began to play a much more active part, backed by the financial resources of the Russian State Bank. Industrial entrepreneurs came increasingly under their control, for "The tendency . . . was to finance business by means of financial reorganization, or by enlarging the capital of existing companies, or by transforming individually owned firms into companies" (Crisp, 1967, p. 228).

The banks were even more active after the depressed period 1900–08 and were also more tightly linked with foreign banks. Thus foreign influence was still strong, although less direct, and one cannot describe the capital provided by the banks as purely private and domestic (Falkus, 1972). Crisp (1967) has criticized the joint-stock banks for ignoring the needs of smaller entrepreneurs and of light industry at this time, but the positive effects of the concentration on heavy industry were probably more significant. Although the Russian investment banks never played as large a role as the French and German investment banks (Henderson, 1968), adequate domestic financial institutions were finally present in Russia by the end of our period of study. But just as a reasonably adequate supply of industrial capital became possible, Russia fell into the whirlpool of World War I.

The situation in regard to labor was equally unfavorable. This was partially attributable to the tradition of using serf labor, which had declined somewhat by the nineteenth century but remained strong in metallurgy.[3] Greater reliance was placed upon free labor in the cotton industry in which *obrok* serfs constituted the majority of the labor force (Falkus, 1972).[4] Although the use of serf labor in factories was officially prohibited in 1840, the practice hung on after that time (Mavor, 1965).

The serf laborers, working under deplorable conditions for the most part, were virtually unskilled. Furthermore, the *immobility* of the peasantry had led to the system of unfree labor in the first place. Miller (1926, p. 224) describes the

[2]In 1914 France accounted for a third, England a fourth, and Germany a fifth of total foreign investment in Russia. Foreign investment in Russian banks was even greater than in manufacturing—comprising 42.6 percent of the capital in the 18 major banks in 1914 (Portal, 1965, p. 851).

[3]In the iron industry as of about 1800, 65 percent of the work force was unfree, and this percentage increased up to the time of the emancipation of the serfs in 1861 (Blackwell, 1968, p. 58).

[4]*Obrok* serfs fulfilled their obligations to their masters by payment of a yearly quit-rent rather than by personal labor (Rosovsky, 1954).

Russian peasantry as having an intense love for the land, which was exemplified by their response to emancipation. Many of them fled from the factories into which they had been coerced, and as a consequence, numerous metallurgical entrepreneurs were forced to suspend operations. Thus labor immobility remained a major problem even after emancipation.

Emancipation also did not increase the number of *obrok* serfs who had constituted the backbone of the textile industry's labor force (Portal, 1965). In addition, structural restrictions on labor mobility remained in effect in the post-emancipation period. The village commune, or *mir*, was strengthened by the reforms accompanying emancipation and it continued to restrict the movement of labor. It retained the ownership of land and placed barriers in the way of members who wished to sell their land and leave. Those who did leave remained members of the commune and liable to it for taxes (Gould, 1972; Harcave, 1959).

The situation improved to some degree only after about 1880, when an increasing number of former serfs migrated to urban areas in search of employment (Hayes, 1939). But they became restive and especially hostile to foreign employers after 1900 (McKay, 1970). The combination of severe economic depression at the time and the disastrous Russo-Japanese War culminated in the Revolution of 1905 in which they took an active part. The economic dislocations and scarcities precipitated by World War I produced worker revolts once again and the downfall of the czarist regime.

So the Russian labor problem was not resolved before World War I. Even changes, such as emancipation, which seemingly would have improved the supply and quality of available labor did so only very gradually.[5]

The potential of the domestic market was a third equally unfavorable condition in Russia. It was the extreme opposite of the favorable American market we have described in the previous chapter because of the low level of Russian economic development and the failure of the economy to grow. In addition, the peasant masses were deeply involved in domestic production, or *kustarny* industry, and opposed both to factory-produced goods and to industrialization. Hence *kustarny* industry was able to meet their needs for manufactured goods (Portal, 1965). Moreover, potential entrepreneurs faced serious competition from the influx of goods from other European countries. The tariff protection provided made the inferior products of Russian factories more expensive than foreign goods and increased costs for Russian entrepreneurs (Miller, 1926).

Population growth did occur—from 36 million in 1796 to 74 million in 1861 to 171 million by 1913 (Harcave, p. 161; Portal, 1965, pp. 811, 844)—an

---

[5]The seriousness of the problem is shown by the fact that foreign entrepreneurs in Russia at the time believed Russian labor was *more* costly and less productive than labor in their home societies (McKay, 1970).

increase of 375 percent in 117 years[6]—but the level of demand remained low. Mavor (1965) has succinctly described the Russian domestic market as compact, but with a very low level of effective demand. About the only positive feature was the general wearing of cotton clothing (Miller, 1926), and thus the cotton industry enjoyed the largest potential market.[7]

By the 1870s and 1880s, the demand for industrial goods primarily depended upon government orders, the size of harvests (which determined peasant demand), and foreign consumers (Portal, 1965), and none of these three factors was very reliable. Some improvement in the market for producer goods, as well as in the movement of raw materials and goods, occurred with the beginning of railroad construction in the 1880s.[8] But given Russia's immense land area, the development of its railroad system was pitifully inadequate. The United States, the only early industrializer with a land area comparable to Russia's, had 213,000 miles of railroad in 1904; Russia had only 39,000 miles. The Russian system lagged, even in comparison with the European countries, despite the fact that she led them in railroad construction between 1890 and 1913 (Miller, 1926). Her 39,000 miles of railroad in 1904 constituted 32 miles per 100,000 population—half that of France (Harcave, 1959, p. 328). The poor transport especially hampered development of the Urals region where large supplies of raw materials were located.

In spite of these obstacles, domestic demand did increase in the 1880s and enlarged even more in the 1890s. Much of this demand was for consumer goods and hence affected the textile industry (Portal, 1965). The depression after 1900 reduced demand but it recovered with the general economic upturn around 1909. Between 1909 and 1914 the demand for industrial goods was actually greater than the supply, and "the real problem [was] why Russian industrial production . . . could not meet the demand" (Portal, 1965, p. 46). Thus, from very poor beginnings, the potential of the Russian market finally began to improve in the late 1880s.

Opportunity conditions for Russian entrepreneurship were much more favorable in two other areas than they were in the three areas we have just discussed. One of these was technology and the other was raw material supplies. The technological innovations being developed in Great Britain were as available to Russian entrepreneurs as they were to entrepreneurs in France and Germany before 1850 and to Japanese entrepreneurs after 1850. All the major innovations of the First Industrial Revolution had been perfected for the textile and metallurgical industries by the time Russian industry finally began to move in the 1880s. During this decade the innovations which produced the Second Industrial Rev-

[6]The United States population increased by about 600 percent in the 70 years between 1810 and 1880.

[7]The potential of the foreign market was hardly any better. In that arena Russian entrepreneurs faced competition from Britain, France, and Germany. These countries provided many of the luxury goods purchased by the Russian nobility.

[8]As of 1855 Russia had only 650 miles of railroad to cover its area of over 6 million square miles (Harcave, 1959, p. 328).

olution also began to appear. So, all other things being equal, extensive borrowing of available technologies was a viable option for Russia, as Japan showed.

Moreover Russia's rich natural resources gave her an advantage over Japan in raw material supplies. Coal and iron ore were located close together in the Ukraine, and supplies of these were even greater in the Urals. Russia also had large oil deposits. Cotton was the only major raw material that was unavailable domestically, but it could be imported from the United States. After a setback in the 1860s as a result of the American Civil War, cotton imports were resumed and the textile industry was not affected seriously (Mavor, 1965). The major problem confronting Russian manufacturing entrepreneurs was the failure of the country to develop the resources it had. Coal and iron ore were not available in large quantities until foreign entrepreneurs rushed onto the scene in the late 1800s.

So the availability of foreign technologies constituted the most favorable opportunity condition for Russian industrial entrepreneurship. Raw materials were present, but were not developed to any extent until the 1880s. Capital supplies and the potential of the domestic market were severely limited until approximately the same time. And Russian labor did not undergo any noteworthy upgrading in the years before 1917.

THE ROLE OF THE RUSSIAN GOVERNMENT

The Russian czars did little to improve the economic opportunity conditions for entrepreneurship until the late nineteenth century, and even then often took some actions which were barely helpful. Their equivocation in regard to industrialization, which resulted from their dependence upon the aristocracy for support against the latent resentment of the peasants, was even more extreme than that of the French government. Perhaps *paranoia* better expresses their attitudes toward industrialization, as the following observation illustrates:

> In 1834, and 1845, the Minister of Finance pointed out that in Russia the development of factories was more advantageous, since the industrial workers were in reality peasants who returned to their land as soon as they left factory employment; hence, the employers couldn't have too great an influence upon them, and the workers themselves were not likely to congregate in a dangerous way (Bendix, 1956, p. 178).

Industrialization was to be encouraged, but as a means of throttling the dangerous entrepreneurs and the even more dangerous peasantry! The actual situation was more complex than that. Opposition to industrialization was greatest at local administrative levels, where the nobility was strongest, whereas officials of the central government were more favorable (Bendix, 1956). Nevertheless the pervasive fear of the social consequences of industrialization prevented the government from taking decisive steps to promote it.

Thus its role in the first half of the nineteenth century was primarily a controlling rather than a promotive one. A change in government attitudes began to appear as a result of the Crimean War debacle (1854–56) when the political leaders began to grasp the military potential of industrialization (Carson, 1959). The desirability of industrialization was further enhanced for them about 1870 when changes in the world grain market made an agricultural future appear less viable for Russia.

But no comprehensive industrial policy was developed until late in the century when several ministers of finance who were favorable to industrialization gained power. Foremost among these was Witte (1892-1903) who feared that Russia was becoming a colony of the western powers and who favored the development of heavy industry by the private sector (Crisp, 1967; Ellison, 1965). Under his influence therefore the government embarked upon a furious program of industrial promotion. "It was literally omnipresent, granting subsidies, providing concessions and privileges, adjusting tariffs, advancing credits, and encouraging private investment" (Harcave, 1959, p. 325). Another military defeat, this time in the Russo-Japanese War (1904–05), stimulated additional government support. And by this time the government, and Russia, benefited from the availability of capital, machinery, and expert advice on a much larger scale than had been the case a half-century earlier for France and Germany (Henderson, 1968).

The government's actions at this time left few areas untouched. First, it pushed railroad construction and eventually required that the railroads use only Russian-made products (Miller, 1926). Second, an especially high tariff was enacted in 1891 which stimulated the development of the iron industry by foreign entrepreneurs. Third, foreign capital was sought openly and foreign trade was pushed vigorously. Fourth, adoption of the gold standard in 1897 increased financial stability (Harcave, 1959). Fifth, development of the oil industry was encouraged (Hidy, 1950). Sixth, tax revenues were transferred to the banking system, and the State Bank was urged to promote industry. By 1900 the State Bank was the chief banker and moneylender in the economy. Seventh, industrial combinations were allowed, although not strongly encouraged (Miller, 1926). Thus the government's actions constituted the major cause of the economic growth of the 1890s (Falkus, 1972).

But, as had been the case in France, there were glaring inadequacies in the state's policies, and the positive effects of some were cancelled by the negative effects of others. Railroad construction was pushed, but if it had been pushed more enthusiastically, the demand for producer goods would have been greater and raw material supplies developed more rapidly. We have noted the inadequacy of the system of tariffs, which perhaps can be described as too little too early and too much too late. Capital supplies were improved, but the banking system was required to maintain an excessively high reserve (as in France) and entrepreneurs were taxed heavily (Kahan, 1967).[9]

---

[9]In 1900 taxes were 27.3 percent of the gross value of industrial output which represented an improvement over 1885 when they were 51.3 percent of gross value (Kahan, 1967, p. 463).

The tax system has received especially strong criticism—for being used primarily as a source of revenue rather than as a means of stimulating industry (Kahan, 1967; Portal, 1972), and for falling mainly on the peasantry and thereby smothering demand (Maddison, 1969).[10] As we noted in our discussion of the Japanese case, the reason this attempt to squeeze an economic surplus out of agriculture was less successful in Russia than in Japan was Russia's inability to improve agricultural productivity. The inability to solve the problems of agriculture may well have been the ultimate failure of the Russian government, or more precisely, the ultimate fault was *ignoring* the problem—Witte did not include it in his programs, for example. A tentative attempt to deal with this vexatious problem was finally made in 1906 by means of the Stolypin reforms, but they had little success and the problem still plagues the Soviet government today. Moreover the Russian government actually aggravated the problem through programs which encouraged the continuation of *kustarny* industry.

Thus it is quite clear that the policies of the Russian government were supportive of industrial entrepreneurship for only a very short period before 1917, and even then they had major weaknesses.

CHARACTERISTICS OF RUSSIAN ENTREPRENEURSHIP

On the basis of our discussion of the factors promoting entrepreneurship and economic growth at the beginning of this study, one would expect that Russian entrepreneurship was neither very expansive nor very innovative throughout much of the nineteenth century. The highly unfavorable economic opportunity conditions before about 1880 made entrepreneurship a risky proposition. After 1880, however, the improvement in opportunity conditions should have stimulated more extensive entrepreneurship and more rapid economic growth. We shall now see whether the facts of the Russian experience support our expectations.

Expansions

The expansion of Russian industry was relatively slow until after the emancipation of the serfs in 1861, and even then it did not increase very rapidly or uniformly.[11] Before 1861 new entrepreneurs were reluctant to enter the field, and existing entrepreneurs failed to reinvest their profits in their enterprises, preferring to invest in other sectors. The Demidovs, for example, who were among the more dynamic entrepreneurs in the iron industry, tended to invest their surplus in land, copper mines, and gold fields (Blackwell, 1968).

---

[10]Taxation was also the one function carried out most efficiently by the generally corrupt Russian civil service. This has led Crisp (1967, p. 233) to describe Russia as "a very rich state in a very poor country."

[11]However the number of industrial enterprises did increase from 14 or 15 thousand to 38 thousand between 1866 and 1887 (Portal, 1965, p. 815).

The failure to expand was both the result and the cause of the continued vitality of the *kustarny* sector in textiles and metallurgy. In fact this sector actually experienced a revitalization during the 1800–61 period because factory production stimulated rather than discouraged it. A weaver who worked in a factory for wages, for example, would buy his own yarn and go into business for himself, selling to merchants who bought from him and from competing factory producers. Sometimes this occurred after factories had failed, and sometimes factory entrepreneurs themselves encouraged it (Mavor, 1965).[12] The *kustarny* sector began a period of slow decline after 1861; but it remained unusually strong, and the significance of *kustarny* entrepreneurs who employed entire peasant villages increased at this time (Harcave, 1959). Only after 1900 did the decline of this sector become rapid when it fell under the control of wholesale traders (Portal, 1965).

A substantial amount of initial expansion occurred after about 1885 as a result of the step-up of foreign entrepreneurship. The typical pattern of expansion for these entrepreneurs involved a pioneer who was followed by a swarm of competitors (McKay, 1970). The number of factories in the Ukraine increased from four to seventeen between 1890 and 1900 (Portal, 1965, pp. 821, 828), and the number of industrial enterprises overall increased by 26 percent during this decade (Bendix, 1956, p. 175). Foreign entrepreneurs were forced into retrenchment and reorganization of their firms by the depression after 1900, however. And from about 1909 on, there was a significant burst of expansion by indigenous entrepreneurs.

Degree of expansion. One of the more unusual features of Russian entrepreneurship is the extremely large scale of production reached at a rather early stage of industrial development.[13] The mammoth scale of operations achieved by 1861 increased even more after that date.[14] The change in the proportions of different-sized factories between 1866 and 1890 is shown in Table 21.[15] By 1914, 90 percent of Russian factory workers were in establishments with more

[12]Miller (1926) reports cases of peasants imitating the production methods of nearby factories.
[13]According to Blackwell (1968, p. 393):
A mill with over 20,000 spindles was regarded as "gigantic" in the United States in 1830. During the same decade . . . several such large-scale factories were built in St. Petersburg, some exceeding 40,000 spindles. In 1860, the largest cotton spinning plant in Philadelphia, which at that time was considered the foremost textile manufacturing city in the United States, had 27,000 spindles, while the city and its suburbs claimed 400,000. In 1858, the four largest factories in St. Petersburg had a quantity of spindles equal to the total for all of the Philadelphia area and the Neva factory alone operated 160,000.
[14]In 1880 about half of cotton textile production came from enterprises employing over 100 workers; by 1894 three-fourths did (Falkus, 1972, p. 68).
[15]In 1900 14 percent of German factory workers were employed in factories with more than 500 workers, compared to the 34 percent of Russian workers shown in Table 21, and eight percent of German workers were employed in factories with more than 1000 workers versus Russia's 24 percent (Henderson, 1968), p. 238).

than fifty workers (Maddison, 1969, p. 92), a very high percentage in comparison with other societies. The large scale of production in heavy industry was especially evident in the Ukraine, where foreign entrepreneurship predominated; in the Urals, where indigenous entrepreneurship prevailed, the scale of production was substantially smaller.[16]

Table 21
Percentages of Russian Factories of Different Sizes, 1866 and 1900

Size of Factory (number of workers)	Percentage (1866)	Percentage (1900)
1000 and over	6.5	24.0
500–999	14.0	10.0
100–499	79.5	56.0
	100.0	100.0

Source: Henderson (1968, p. 238); Portal (1965, p. 823).

Thus Russian industry was characterized by extremes. As Henderson (1968, p. 203) says, "[There was] hardly any intermediate stage between small workshops and large factories." This difference in scale between the two industrial sectors sharply reveals the gulf that separated the old and the new in Russia. Furthermore, it means that new entrepreneurs could not begin on a small scale because it was not profitable (Miller, 1926). But the extremely large scale of production should not be taken solely as evidence of inordinate entrepreneurial expansiveness. It was due primarily to the low productivity of Russian labor (Falkus, 1972; Gould, 1972). Entrepreneurs found it necessary to employ unusually large numbers of workers in order to achieve even fairly respectable levels of production.

Innovations

Like other latecomers, Russia's move toward industrialization was based upon the technological innovations developed in the countries that were leading the march to industrialization, and we said earlier that the availability of these technologies was the most favorable opportunity condition for Russian entrepreneurship. Inventions did appear in Russia in the nineteenth century, but they

[16]In 1900, 65.2 percent of Urals factories, and only 18.2 percent of Ukraine factories employed fewer than 500 workers. None of the Urals factories, but 13.6 of the Ukrainian factories, employed more than 3000. In addition, the average Urals factory produced 45.1 tons of pig iron annually and the average Ukrainian factory 287.5 tons (Portal, 1965, p. 830).

were not followed by innovations, i.e., industrial applications of the discoveries.[17]

The adoption of borrowed innovations proceeded generally in the same order in Russia as elsewhere, except that the printing and finishing of cloth was modernized before spinning (Blackwell, 1968). Spinning machinery had been introduced in 1798 and this was followed by the introduction of steam power in 1805 (Ellison, 1965). The 1840s was a period of more rapid mechanization of cotton spinning and the application of steam power to it (Falkus, 1972). As of midcentury almost all the necessary machines had to be imported because of the limited development of Russian machine industry and the concentration of such machine shops as did exist on the production of other goods (Portal, 1965). Only about 39,000 workers were employed in mechanized industries in the cotton industry and almost 90,000 were still employed in enterprises using hand labor by 1860, and the annual output of the latter was twice that of the former (Blackwell, 1968, p. 390). The 1860s and 1870s were marked by more rapid mechanization, including the adoption of power looms (Falkus, 1972; Portal, 1965). Mechanization of the cotton industry was all but complete by the 1890s and in 1891 Russia had more cotton spindles than any other Continental country (Henderson, 1968), but that must be seen in light of its larger population.

Technological innovations were adopted very slowly in the metallurgical industry until the late 1800s. Puddling was not introduced until the 1830s, and by 1860 it accounted for only half of the industry's output (Falkus, 1972). The rate of innovations was still slow after 1860, and it required an infusion of foreign entrepreneurs after 1885 to stir the industry out of its lethargy. McKay (1970) has provided some valuable information regarding the foreign entrepreneurs' innovational practices. First, they generally introduced proven technologies from their home countries without modification, and experimented very little with new technologies in Russia. Second, they concentrated on capital-intensive technologies, the type operative in their home countries, although the quality of Russian labor was more amenable to labor-intensive methods.[18] Third, although they were not always the first to make use of a particular innovation, they adopted innovations universally once they had been introduced, and thus their impact was significant.

The rate of adoption of technological innovations after 1861 was not sufficiently rapid to enable Russia to keep pace with the other industrializing

---

[17]Blackwell (1968) mentions Savonov's water turbine in the 1830s and Schilling's invention of the telegraph a decade before Morse as examples of indigenous invention, but neither of these received any support and Russia actually ended up using Morse's system of telegraphy. He also notes that Russian technicians attempted to make improvements in the spinning jenny and the Jacquard loom. Harcave (1959) credits Jacob with inventing what probably was the first electric motor in 1838 and Popov with developing a system of radio-telegraphy before Marconi, but neither of these received any encouragement either.

[18]McKay (1970) observes that they apparently did not even consider the possibility of using less complex technologies.

societies. In 1861 she was not far behind either England or the United States in the application of steam power to key industries and only about twenty-five years behind England in the mechanization of cotton cloth production (Blackwell, 1968). But between 1860 and 1885 she was far outdistanced by her competitors (Goldsmith, 1961). We have seen that this was a period of extensive expansion and innovation in Germany and the United States particularly.

The slow rate of technological diffusion was accompanied by an equally leisurely transition to factory production. The *kustarny* sector remained strong as factory entrepreneurs found it impossible to lure sufficient amounts of labor from it, and the less successful they were, the more successful the *kustarny* sector was. Some *kustarny* producers, however, did shift to factory production. In metallurgy, for instance, many family workshops were converted into small factories (Portal, 1965), and some of the *kustarny* textile producers achieved large-scale specialization by allocating the responsibility for a single production operation to an entire village of peasants (Harcave, 1959).

The output of the *kustarny* sector exceeded factory output, and only 1 percent of the Russian population was employed in factories as of 1861 (Portal, 1965, pp. 808–09). *Kustarny* production had decreased to a third of total factory output by 1897 (Falkus, 1972, p. 79), but there were still eight million part-time and four million full-time workers employed in the domestic sector in 1904 (Harcave, 1959, p. 328). When we compare these figures with the *three* million factory workers in *1913*, the unusual staying power of domestic production is obvious.

Foreign entrepreneurs were primarily responsible for speeding up the transition to factory production. They made this transition in the same way in which they introduced technological innovations. Forms of organization that had been used at home were transferred with scarcely any modifications. This procedure was not completely satisfactory, as these firms had difficulty in dealing with their environments and with Russian workers, but even so, they were able to develop a highly integrated steel industry in southern Russia which comprised "the most important economic achievement of Russia's industrial surge" (McKay, 1970, p. 113.)

The most important organizational change after 1900 was the rise of cartels, or syndicates, similar in some respects to the German cartels, in response to the economic crisis of the time (Portal, 1965). They differed from German cartels in that they were "rather loose associations concerned almost solely with marketing," but they also had "extensive control of operations within individual industries," which implies that they partially fulfilled the entrepreneurial role. *Prodamet*, the metallurgical cartel, marketed the production of enterprises that accounted for 90 percent of that industry's output in 1913 (Falkus, 1972, pp. 77–78).

The development of the cartels and the simultaneous existence of a sizable domestic sector highlighted the extreme dualism of Russian industry, as did the contrast between very large factories and small workshops.[19] The dualism in Russia was even more extreme than in France, Germany, or Japan, which suggests that the conflict between the old and the new, the traditional and the modern, was most intense in Russia.

Material innovations also diffused very slowly until the invasion of foreign entrepreneurs in the 1880s. The use of coal was slowed by the large amounts of available timber (Henderson, 1968). Coke was introduced in 1869 but its use spread slowly, so that most iron, particularly in the Urals region, was still being produced by charcoal in the 1890s (Carson, 1959). Nevertheless the rapid diffusion of coke production under foreign initiative in the Ukraine at that time promoted its use elsewhere (McKay, 1970).

Product and market innovations were limited, too. A machine industry was slow to develop, and its output in 1860 was only slightly greater than the output of the American machine industry in 1810 (Blackwell, 1968). Consumer goods remained predominant, constituting 67 percent of industrial output in 1913 (Patel, 1961, p. 322, table 3), despite the large increase in the producer-goods sector after 1885. The cotton industry dominated the production of consumer goods, and woodworking was the major component of the *kustarny* sector (Miller, 1926). By 1912–13 metallurgy still accounted for only about 20 percent of total industrial output (Miller, 1926, p. 255). A significant increase in the export of manufactured goods was achieved under government stimulation in the 1890s, but as of 1913 agricultural products still accounted for a larger share of the export trade (Gould, 1972).

Corporations were used at a slightly earlier stage of industrialization in Russia than in the other societies we have considered because of her late start. Most enterprises in newer industries, such as metallurgy and machine construction, began as joint-stock companies. In the older industries, such as textiles and food processing, share associations were used more often. Shares could not be sold to third parties without the consent of the other partners in these organizations; thus they constituted a sort of cross between a partnership and a joint-stock company (Crisp, 1967). The most rapid increase in the formation of joint-stock companies occurred after 1861 (Falkus, 1972; Maddison, 1969). Later in the century many enterprises which had been under individual or family control converted to the corporate form. By 1900, 74 percent of the capital invested in industrial or commercial companies was corporate capital, and by 1914, 86 percent was (Crisp, 1967, p. 184).

Russian entrepreneurs made no real progress in solving the labor problem

[19]In Portal's (1965, p. 850) words:
The peculiarity of Russian economic development was that at a time when capitalism was in full advance, it was still far from permeating the entire economy, and allowed old forms of industrial organization to survive in the shape of a very active artisan industry; and yet at the same time, in the most important sectors of activity (mines, metallurgy, oil), it was already moving into its extreme forms . . . the subordination of industrial business to the banks, and the progressive formation of industrial and financial monopolies leading to trusts.

before 1917. This problem was severe for foreign entrepreneurs, too, but they were more ingenious in dealing with it than were indigenous entrepreneurs. For example, they attempted to solve the problem of a lack of skilled labor by using Polish workers in technical positions and Jews in financial positions. But the hostility of Russian workers forced them to replace non-Russian personnel with Russians after 1904 (McKay, 1970.)

Indigenous entrepreneurs generally continued to rely upon strict subordination of workers, which is not surprising considering the long history of unfree serf labor, as well as the response of many serfs to emancipation.[20] The system of labor management was paternalistic and absolute. Some entrepreneurs built barracks to house their workers, and they also attempted strict control over their lives. Bendix (1956) has emphasized the entrepreneurs' lack of success in developing an ideology and a work ethic before the establishment of large-scale industry. British entrepreneurs had done this, as we noted earlier, and thereby alleviated many of their labor problems.

The Russian government reinforced entrepreneurs' rigidity in dealing with workers because of its dread of worker revolts. It repeatedly stepped in to regulate labor relations (a very different pattern than we observed in Japan), for example in response to worker agitation in the 1870s and 1880s. Bendix (1956) suggests that the government took action reluctantly at that time for fear its intervention would indicate to workers that their grievances had merit! In addition, he points out that the Russian entrepreneurial ideology, such as it was, was a collaborative effort of the government and entrepreneurs, in contrast to Britain where it had been formulated by entrepreneurs themselves.

The government's intervention in labor relations was not exceptional because it maintained an extensive system of control over entrepreneurial actions through the nineteenth century.[21] This pattern of control extended to foreign entrepreneurs also. Nicholas I (1796–1855) required them to become Russian subjects, for instance (Blackwell, 1968). This stipulation was withdrawn in 1860, just before the serfs were emancipated; but later in the century foreign entrepreneurs were obligated to form joint enterprises with indigenous entrepreneurs (McKay, 1970). This policy, though, may well have enabled Russia to maintain a modicum of economic independence in the face of the flood of foreign entrepreneurs at that time.

The effects of the strict controls placed on indigenous entrepreneurs have generally been viewed negatively. Although the controls were substantially weakened after about 1840, it has been suggested that the tradition of state tutelage caused entrepreneurs to be overly dependent upon state initiatives

[20]Although the use of unfree labor had been prohibited officially in 1840, estimates of the proportion of workers who were still unfree at the time of emancipation range from 13 to 33 percent (Mavor, 1965, p. 368; Shimkin, 1949, p. 26).

[21]According to Miller (1926), only the textile and possibly the sugar-refining industries developed more or less independent of state control.

(Gerschenkron, 1963; Miller, 1926).[22] It is our feeling that this dependence on the government was less serious than the state's failure to promote more favorable opportunity conditions for entrepreneurship at an earlier date.

In sum, all types of innovation that were introduced diffused at a very slow rate, except possibly financial innovations, until the entry of large numbers of foreign entrepreneurs in the 1880s. These entrepreneurs brought numerous innovations with them and stimulated indigenous entrepreneurs to greater innovativeness shortly before World War I. The contrast between these two groups of entrepreneurs is shown vividly by the differential development of the Urals and Ukraine regions. The former, under indigenous control, did not begin to expand and innovate until just before World War I even though raw material supplies there were far more abundant than they were in the Ukraine (Portal, 1965).

Degree of innovation. The great difference between foreign and indigenous entrepreneurs carried over into differences in the productivity improvements which resulted from innovations. The southern foreign iron works were "considerably more productive" than the northern indigenous works (Falkus, 1972, p. 58). Productivity was even higher in Russian Poland where the foreign element was still more extensive (Portal, 1965).[23] And, even though improvements in productivity had been realized in the textile industry after about 1845 (Falkus, 1972), we have observed that extremely large-scale operations were required to attain a satisfactory level of production.

NONECONOMIC FACTORS INFLUENCING RUSSIAN ENTREPRENEURSHIP

As we predicted on the basis of the disadvantageous economic opportunity conditions characterizing most of the nineteenth century in Russia, entrepreneurial expansions and innovations were restricted until the late nineteenth century. Earlier we allocated a share of the blame for the unfavorable situation to the actions of the Russian government. We must now consider the nature of the noneconomic characteristics of nineteenth-century Russia and the part they played. Were sociocultural conditions equally unfavorable for entrepreneurship? Did major improvements in these conditions occur in the late nineteenth century correlative with the improvement of economic opportunity conditions?

Clearly, the legitimacy of entrepreneurship in Russia was very low throughout much of the nineteenth century.[24] From the time of Peter the Great

---

[22]The reader will remember a similar criticism of French entrepreneurship.

[23]But even so Russian iron plants generally used more labor per furnace or per ton of output than did German or British plants operating with comparable equipment (Landes, 1965a, p. 590).

[24]Smith (1968) argues that Russia was the only one of the European industrializers in which the political elite had sharply negative attitudes to private business, which appears an exaggeration in light of our discussion of the opposition to entrepreneurship in France and Germany.

until the emancipation of the serfs in 1861 there was a perpetual triangular conflict among the dominant aristocracy, the serfs, and the rising merchant class. This conflict, often focused upon obtaining favors from the government, was basically between the aristocracy and the merchants—the pattern we have seen in Britain, France, and Germany—with the serfs caught in the middle. The aristocracy were strongly opposed to industrial entrepreneurship by the merchants because it recognized the dangerous political potential of the increased economic power which would result. Because many nobles were in precarious financial positions, they supported serf entrepreneurship as a means of insuring payment of their annual tribute. As a consequence the merchants were hard pressed by serf competition and wanted greater economic benefits from the government (Bendix, 1956; Blackwell, 1968).

The economic and political power of the merchants increased incrementally and the position of the nobility became more tenuous during the first half of the nineteenth century. Emancipation of the serfs effectively slashed the power of the nobility, since many had been dependent on serfs for labor, but their negative attitudes toward industrialization lingered. They were joined in this sentiment by the intelligentsia and the developing populist movement. But the Marxist movement developing at the same time advocated industrialization and the growth of capitalism in order to foster the creation of a revolutionary working class. The clash between the opposing groups became concentrated in the 1880s upon the incursions of foreign entrepreneurs into Russia (McKay, 1970).

The degree of legitimacy of entrepreneurship during this period was a direct corollary of the struggles for political power that were occurring. The nobility was not opposed to entrepreneurship in and of itself, as many of them were involved in entrepreneurial activities and they supported such activities by the serfs, but they were opposed to *merchant* entrepreneurship.[25] Therefore it appears likely that the legitimacy of entrepreneurship was generally lower in Russia than it was in the other European societies we have considered, although possibly no lower than it was in Japan at the beginning of the Meiji period.

Russia also inherited an extremely rigid social system at the beginning of the nineteenth century. The continuation of the system of serfdom speaks for itself, and it actually had become increasingly widespread and unbending in the last half of the eighteenth century.[26] There were 18 million serfs and 13 million state peasants in a total Russian population of 36 million in 1800, and only 6 percent of the peasant population were freeholders. The typical estate comprised between 100 and 500 peasants and the largest number of serfs belonging to any

[25]The tradition of petty commerce in Russia might be regarded as evidence of the legitimacy of entrepreneurship but Mavor (1965) points out that it tended to strengthen *kustarny* industry.

[26]Under Elizabeth (1741–1762) the right of nobles to ascribe free peasants as serfs had been established. Under Catherine (1762–1796) large numbers of free peasants were transformed into state peasants after the secularization of lands formerly owned by the Russian Orthodox Church. She herself enserfed approximately 800,000 peasants and also revoked the rights of serfs to appeal the treatment (Harcave, 1959).

single individual was 200,000 (Harcave, 1959, pp. 162, 166, 239). The rights of the nobility had also been formalized in the late eighteenth century.[27]

Thus at the beginning of its industrial transition Russian social structure was more static, and there was less potential for social mobility, than in any of the other societies we have considered. The oppressive system did begin to unravel between 1800 and 1861. Nicholas I's reduction of some of the powers of the nobility resulted in the lower nobility's becoming impoverished (Harcave, 1959), a process of downward mobility identical to that suffered by the lower samurai in the last years of the Tokugawa period. Peasant unrest also increased precipitously, and non-Russian nobles from the Baltic regions began to move into positions in the vast Russian bureaucracy, thereby further threatening the position of the Russian nobility.

By 1861 there were 21 million serfs working the land, 1.4 million household serfs, and 24.7 million state peasants in a population of 74 million (Harcave, 1959, p. 277). Emancipation did not give the two groups of serfs absolute freedom but replaced the power of the landlord with the power of the *mir*, as we noted previously. The state peasants received larger grants of land, but they too were subservient to the commune. Thus social mobility and social flexibility remained more restricted after emancipation than one might assume.

The extreme lack of social mobility before 1861 is also shown by the weakness of the Russian urban middle class. As Harcave (1959, p. 72) says, "One of the peculiarities of Russian development has always been the absence of a strong middle class," a feature he attributes to the consolidation of czarist rule before such a class had a chance to emerge. It is probable, however, that emancipation of the serfs increased the potential for its emergence via the entrepreneurial role.

The combination of limited entrepreneurial legitimacy and suppressed social mobility corresponds perfectly with the model of outsider entrepreneurship that we presented at the beginning of this study. Other aspects of Russian society also correspond to that model. For example, a tightly integrated society, with the czar at the apex, was one of the derivatives of the harsh system of feudalism. Harcave (1959, p. 51) describes the system as originally established:

> . . . a nearly complete ring of obligations had been forged: the peasant was obliged to help maintain the landlord and the state—by payment of dues to the first and taxes to the latter; the landlord was obliged to support the state as a soldier or as an administrator; and the state was obliged to guarantee the landlord economic security.

---

[27]In 1785 the Charter of Nobility granted the nobility absolute rights over their lands and the products thereof and made the noble status hereditary. According to Harcave (1959, p. 133):
  The Charter of the Nobility established the nobles in a very secure position. Their rights, privileges, and property were no longer dependent upon service, and yet they retained first choice of important administrative and military stations. In local government they had a position of primacy, and in central government they retained a position of influence.

The system became less integrated with increased peasant unrest and the decline of the nobility after 1800. Status divisions *within* the nobility became accentuated and they became a source of grievances (Harcave, 1959). Earlier, the czars had been able to maintain integration by playing contending groups against each other—granting favors first to the nobility and then to the merchants (Bendix, 1956). But after 1800 this strategy became less effective. Nicholas I was forced to institute the secret police known as the *Third Section* and he also persecuted dissident religious groups vigorously (Harcave, 1959). The emancipation of the serfs continued the trend of an increasing "loosening" of Russian society, as did the uprisings after 1900. Yet it is conceivable that the trend eventually would have stopped short of revolution if World War I had not broken out.

Consequently it also is doubtful that entrepreneurial security was ever very great before 1917, except perhaps for the springtime years of 1909–14. The opposition of the aristocracy continued after 1861 and the conflict between capitalist and proletariat was superimposed upon it. Workers became increasingly hostile and threatened even foreign entrepreneurs in Russia. It seems that a measure of entrepreneurial security existed only after about 1910 and it was destroyed by the outbreak of World War I, four years later.

Finally, Russia also lacked a powerful ideological force to promote either entrepreneurship or industrialization. Peter the Great's attempts to Westernize the country had been far from successful. The issue of whether Russia's future lay with the industrializing Western societies or with a continued reliance upon agrarianism remained alive in the 1800s, with first the Slavophiles and then the populist *Narodniki* advocating a continuation of the rural past (Harcave, 1959). The Russian Orthodox Church, probably more otherworldly than Roman Catholicism, was hardly an ideological support for industrialization, rather, it buttressed the rigidity of the social system.

Thus we believe that the sociocultural supports for entrepreneurship were weaker in Russia than in any of the other societies we have viewed. Japan came closest to Russia in this respect, with Germany probably next closest. But in those two societies the government stepped in and deliberately instituted changes which reduced the noneconomic risks of entrepreneurship. The Meiji rulers' actions after 1868 are a stellar example of positive government actions in this regard. The Russian government, by contrast, did not act decisively. It vacillated, tossed to and fro by contending forces, and was often oblivious to the severity of the situation. When forced to, the czarist government finally did emancipate the serfs, thereby "freeing up" the monolithic social structure somewhat. But it was a rather half-hearted step and new restrictions were imposed through the *mir*. Its attempts to improve the educational system, a step which probably would have improved the quality of the Russian labor force, were similarly unenthusiastic (Carson, 1959; Mavor, 1965).

Therefore, before 1917, and particularly before about 1880, the Russian government, like the French government before about 1850, failed to achieve the crisp break with the feudal past that was needed to promote industrial entrepreneurship. Because the feudal system was more entrenched in Russia than it had been in France, a *more* resolute break was required in Russia. It took forces from the outside to achieve this break in the late nineteenth century.

ENTREPRENEURIAL IDENTITY

The portrait we have just sketched of a sociocultural system inhospitable to industrial entrepreneurship presages a distinct type of entrepreneurial identity in nineteenth-century Russia. Our earlier presentation of the attributes of what we have labeled *outsider* entrepreneurship and the factors promoting its emergence, coupled with this most recent description, suggests that Russian entrepreneurship should come closest, of the six societies under consideration, to fitting the parameters of this model.

And the most noteworthy characteristic of Russian entrepreneurship *is* the degree to which it emerged from *marginal* groups, both indigenous and foreign. Blackwell (1968, pp. 193–94) says, "In contrast to the European pattern, the Russian capitalist class was recruited as much from outcasts, outsiders, and disadvantaged elements of society . . . as from the indigenous commercial classes." Domestically, serfs and religious minorities were the most noteworthy outsider entrepreneurs, but, as we have repeatedly indicated, the influence of foreign outsiders was more significant for Russian industrialization. We shall discuss these marginal groups in that order.

Serf entrepreneurs first appeared in northern Russia in the eighteenth century. Agricultural land was less productive there than in the south, and hence the practice of *obrok* had developed with industrial activities offering a means of paying that form of tribute. There also were greater opportunities for urban work, a greater demand for the goods serfs could produce, and less competition from free peasant producers than in the south. Thus serfs began to produce the calico, cotton, and silk goods with which they were familiar. As we noted, the nobility encouraged them in their endeavors (Bendix, 1956; Gutmann, 1954: Rosovsky, 1954).

Some serf entrepreneurs became leaders in the textile industry around 1800.[28] Grachev, for example, began in 1751 with one small plant in Ivanovo in which he printed cotton cloth. He bought his freedom in 1795, and by 1798 he employed 121 people in his factory; by 1807 he employed 722. The Garelins, another serf family, ran a factory employing 1,407 workers by 1817. Serf entrepreneurs such as these changed Ivanovo from "a small village . . . to the textile

---

[28]Henderson (1968, p. 208) observes, "There were serfs whose industrial careers would have rejoiced the heart of Samuel Smiles." Samuel Smiles was a leader in the formulation of the English entrepreneurial ideology (Bendix, 1956).

city which came to be known as the 'Russian Manchester' '' (Blackwell, 1968, p. 207). Many of them used their profits to buy their freedom, as Grachev had done, but many were swindled by their noble masters in the process. Yet "In the end in many cases, he [the serf] regained his properties, rebuilt his fortune, expanded his enterprise, and aspired to new empires" (Blackwell, 1968, pp. 207–08). Serf entrepreneurship gradually declined after 1800, with the rise of entrepreneurs from merchant backgrounds, and thus was most significant early in the 1800–1917 period, but it constituted a unique chapter in entrepreneurial history.[29]

The Old Believers, a sect which originated in the seventeenth century in opposition to reforms instituted by the Russian Orthodox Church, was the most prominent religious minority to become entrepreneurs. Members of the sect were persecuted until the early 1800s, but as persecution decreased many went to Moscow where a number of the wealthier became textile entrepreneurs. Their major asset was capital, some of which was derived from the monopoly they enjoyed in the sale of religious articles, and some from bequests of individual property required of their adherents. One branch of the Old Believers, the Theodosians, held all property in common and allowed no family inheritance, thus amassing large amounts of capital.

With their austere, puritanical ways, they displayed the worldly asceticism of Weber's Calvinists, but according to Blackwell (1965), their industrial ventures were not strongly influenced by any Calvinistic "calling." Instead the elders of the group invested the group's capital in their own industrial enterprises, or aspiring entrepreneurs converted into the group to obtain loans. The Old Believers began to decline in the 1830s, both as textile entrepreneurs and as a religious community, as secularization seized the newer generations. Increased persecution by the state rapidly destroyed their religious uniqueness in the 1840s and they quickly passed from the scene (Blackwell, 1965, 1968).[30]

As these two groups of domestic outsiders declined in importance during the nineteenth century, the representation of foreign outsiders increased, starting slowly after 1800.[31] The foreign contingent increased more rapidly during the 1840s, particularly in the cotton textile industry. The most important foreign entrepreneur in that period was Ludwig Knoop, a German or German-Englishman, who founded most of the large cotton mills at the time (Falkus, 1972; Miller, 1926). Knoop apparently came from a merchant or banking background and was a bit of an exception because most foreign entrepreneurs were involved in commerce rather than in industry before 1860 (Blackwell, 1968).

---

[29]Many serfs remained entrepreneurs in the *kustarny* sector after 1861 (Redlich, 1958).

[30]Jews are now believed to have played a more important role in manufacturing than was originally thought. They were involved primarily in the woolen and sugar-beet refining industries (Blackwell, 1968).

[31]The first factory to produce steam engines had been founded in 1792 by a foreigner, Baird, for example (Blackwell, 1968).

Foreign entrepreneurs began to enter the potential growth industries—metallurgy, mining, and oil—in large numbers in the 1870s,[32] and after 1885 the stream of foreigners became a deluge. The depression which hit Russia after 1900 stifled further foreign expansions, however, and after 1909 foreigners declined in importance as indigenous entrepreneurs came forth. So the period of intensive foreign entrepreneurship actually was quite short—only about twenty years. The outbreak of World War I and the Bolshevik Revolution prevent us from determining whether the decline after 1909 marked the beginning of the end of foreign entrepreneurship and the start of self-sustained economic growth based upon indigenous private entrepreneurs, or whether it constituted a temporary pause. According to McKay (1970), Russia was very close to entrepreneurial self-sufficiency by 1914, but World War I revealed manifold weaknesses in the industrial capabilities of indigenous entrepreneurs.

Foreign entrepreneurs came mostly from England, France, Germany and Belgium—the four most highly industrialized European countries—although Swedes largely carried out development of the Russian oil industry which led the world in oil production from 1870 to 1900 (Harcave, 1959; Henderson, 1968). They specialized among industries on the basis of the countries from which they came. The British were the most important foreign representatives prior to 1875 and were concentrated in cotton, iron, and machine-building. The earliest efforts of the French were directed to development of the Russian railroad system, but in the 1890s they and the Belgians became the most significant entrepreneurs in the southern (Ukrainian) steel industry. By 1914 the French were the most prominent foreign entrepreneurs, with controlling interests in the coal and iron industries and substantial investments in the textile, gas, electric, engineering, construction, and chemical industries, as well as insurance and banking (Cameron, 1961).

German entrepreneurs were involved in sawmills, rope factories, iron foundries, and sugar refineries in the early 1800s. After 1830 they became involved in cotton textiles (Blackwell, 1968), and later they became involved in railroad construction and the woolen industry (Henderson, 1968). And the German electrical industry founded a number of firms in the 1890s (Holzer, 1970).

McKay (1970) has described three main types of foreign entrepreneurship in Russia. The first involved a foreign firm establishing an affiliate in Russia and retaining a strong minority position in order to control its operations. The parent firm's main contributions were capital and technological and organizational skills. The second type resulted from the efforts of individual promoters, living in Russia and either Russian citizens or foreign businessmen, to encourage foreign firms to initiate activities in Russia. A group of foreign firms which joined together to establish an enterprise in Russia constituted the third type.

Most cases of foreign entrepreneurship therefore were joint enterprises,

---

[32]In 1869, for instance, John Hughes, a Welshman, began iron production in the Donetz region of the Ukraine (Harcave, 1959).

involving partnerships with Russians, and were not completely foreign operations, as we noted earlier. This system also proved to be the most satisfactory. Foreigners were much more proficient at dealing with internal technical and organizational problems than with the environment, and dealings with the government bureaucracy and with Russian workers were handled most effectively by Russian personnel. Thus enterprises were most successful when this type of division of labor was worked out (McKay, 1970).

The foreign entrepreneurs entered Russia primarily because they saw an opportunity for large profits. The high Russian tariff also made it more profitable to produce goods in Russia than to import them. But profit considerations were not the sole determinant. McKay (1970) indicates that they perceived their greatest opportunities in industries for which they possessed the necessary technology because they did not always enter the industries with the highest profits. And generally their profit expectations were not met—McKay estimates that the average rate of return on foreign investments during this period was between four and seven percent—which also played a part in their diminished participation after 1900.

It is impossible to calculate precisely the actual proportion of foreign entrepreneurship in Russia during the 1885–1900 period.[33] Falkus (1972, p. 70) reports that the number of foreign companies increased from 12 to 269 between 1888 and 1900. By 1914 there were "two thousand or so" companies in existence and about one-third of their capital was foreign, which is a very rough indicator of the extent of foreign entrepreneurship (Portal, 1965, p. 851). We do know, though, that it was more extensive in Russia than in any of the other countries under consideration.[34]

Despite their relatively short tenure foreign entrepreneurs did manage to put several sectors of Russian heavy industry on their feet. Their greatest accomplishment was the development of the oil, coal, and metallurgical industries of southern Russia. McKay (1970) perhaps has given an overly optimistic account of their achievements, but he does rightly credit them with utilizing underused resources, making steel available at lower prices, replacing foreign personnel with indigenous workers, supplying capital and technology to the Russian economy, infusing the economy with dynamism and an outlook favoring growth, and stimulating a larger supply of indigenous entrepreneurs. So overall we feel that foreign entrepreneurs made a very positive contribution in Russia.[35]

[33]We presented data earlier on foreign capital investment, but that does not correspond precisely with the extent of foreign entrepreneurship.

[34]Foreign participation was not spread evenly among regions, being more extensive in the Ukraine than in the Urals: "In Russian eyes . . . the Urals were a bulwark of Russia's industrial independence." It was even more extensive in Russian Poland, where industry was "almost entirely in the hands of foreigners." It was also more extensive in mining than in manufacturing (Portal, 1965, p. 859).

[35]The Russian experience with foreign entrepreneurship clearly was the harbinger of similar experiences for currently developing societies. Many of the arguments about foreign entrepreneurship raised today repeat the points made for and against foreign entrepreneurship in Russia.

Thus, of the six countries we have considered, Russia is the best illustration of "outsider" entrepreneurship and the conditions promoting it. The combination of low entrepreneurial legitimacy and a virtual absence of social mobility discouraged the emergence of "mainstream" entrepreneurship. Serf entrepreneurs' access to other mobility channels was blocked obviously, and they also benefitted from the relative security provided by the ongoing conflict between the aristocracy and merchants. If the aristocracy had joined with the merchants in opposition to serf entrepreneurship, it is doubtful that it would have emerged to the extent that it did.

Serf entrepreneurs very likely possessed a degree of integration as an outcast group, but the Old Believers better exemplify the importance of this noneconomic factor. Their integration as a group having a distinct religious identity in opposition to the established church compensated for their lack of integration with the larger society. When they became less integrated as a result of secularization and persecution, they diminished both religiously and economically (Blackwell, 1965).

Foreign entrepreneurs in Russia bring to light another factor which we noted in our previous discussion of traits conducive to entrepreneurship, namely the importance of possessing necessary *resources*. They were more immune to the hostile Russian socioeconomic environment (although not completely immune as they found out) because they had the technology and capital needed to convert the *potential* Russian opportunity conditions into *actual* ones. Serf and Old Believer entrepreneurs possessed resources also, the former technological knowledge and the latter substantial amounts of capital. In all three cases, having these resources decreased the economic risks of entrepreneurship, and the marginal position of each group decreased the noneconomic risks.

Russian entrepreneurship also was distinguished by the somewhat greater involvement of the aristocracy in industrial activities, compared to our other five societies. In the eighteenth century they had been one of the three major groups of entrepreneurs, along with merchants and serfs (Rosovsky, 1954), and Bendix (1956) credits them with being the prime force promoting economic growth in that century. Emancipation of the serfs dealt them a fatal blow and after 1861 many of them were forced to sell their enterprises (Blackwell, 1968). However, the government did issue bonds to some of them like the Meiji government did for the samurai, as compensation for their freed serfs, and these bonds were often used for financing industrial enterprises as they were in Japan (Maddison, 1969).

In other respects the identity of Russian entrepreneurs was more similar to that of other industrializing societies. Although entrepreneurs from merchant backgrounds were relatively less important than in the other societies under consideration, they were the most important group in the textile industry. Wealthier merchants who moved to urban areas generally were the ones who became involved as industrial entrepreneurs (Blackwell, 1968; Redlich, 1958).

Russia had a tradition of public entrepreneurship dating from Peter the Great, but it diminished after 1800, although the state remained "a significant owner of manufacturing and mining properties'' (Carson, 1959, p. 116). In manufacturing it was most active in machine-building, operating enterprises such as the Alexandrovsk machine works in St. Petersburg in which the first Russian steam engines and railway equipment were produced. Public entrepreneurship did increase again after about 1870 or 1880, but its role in manufacturing was very limited.[36] So throughout the 1800–1917 period Russian manufacturing entrepreneurship was predominantly private (McKay, 1970).[37]

There was also a transition from individual to collective entrepreneurship, in the form of corporations and share associations as we saw earlier. There also were other instances of collective entrepreneurship. Among the peasantry, for example, cooperatives, or *artels,* were important sources of entrepreneurship in the *kustarny* sector, and they remained prominent after 1861 (Harcave, 1959). Foreign entrepreneurship involved both single organizations and combinations of organizations as did the entrepreneurship provided by the Russian banks around 1900.

Individual entrepreneurship was most significant before emancipation, and many individuals, especially in textiles, had become very wealthy by 1861. Blackwell (1968, p. 190) says, "If New York had twenty millionaires by 1855, Moscow at the same time had at least a dozen, St. Petersburg an equal number (although many of these were of foreign birth), and Ivanovo, three." We also have observed that individuals sometimes played major roles in the entry of foreign entrepreneurs in the late 1800s.

Family entrepreneurship was prominent in Russia, too, in both the *kustarny* and factory sectors, before emancipation. Serf entrepreneurs, for instance, typically passed their enterprises on to their sons. Many family dynasties, such as the Grachevs and Garelins in the textile industry, were formed in this way during the 1820s and 1830s (Blackwell, 1968). According to Crisp (1967) the majority of the firms, especially in Moscow, were family partnerships after emancipation as well. But family entrepreneurship declined in significance as corporate forms of organization increased rapidly in the last half of the century, except in the Urals where the pressure of joint-stock organization was not felt until after 1900 (Portal, 1965). The decline, when it came, was so complete that by 1917 many of the family names that had been prominent in industry were no longer in existence (Blackwell, 1968).

So there were some similarities between Russia and our other case studies in regard to entrepreneurial identity. But the differences are more important. Throughout the nineteenth century and until just shortly before World War I,

[36]The state's entrepreneurial role was most pronounced in the railroad system, which was purchased from the private sector in the 1890s (Carson, 1959), and in the alcohol monopoly initiated in 1894 (Miller, 1926). It was also more prominent in the Urals than in the Ukraine (Portal, 1965).

[37]About one-third of the state's annual budget, a substantial portion of which may have gone to the state arsenals, was devoted to industries maintained by the government in 1900 (Harcave, 1959, p. 325). In 1913, 27 percent of government expenditures was devoted to state undertakings (Miller, 1926, p. 131).

Russian entrepreneurship was largely "outsider" entrepreneurship, involving domestic "outsiders" first and their replacement by foreign "outsiders." The influx of foreign entrepreneurs was accompanied by a rapid switch to collective forms of entrepreneurship and a swift decline of family entrepreneurship. After we have considered the rate of Russian industrial growth we will be in a position to determine the causal significance of Russia's "outsider" entrepreneurship.

THE RATE OF RUSSIAN INDUSTRIAL GROWTH

A number of estimates of the rate of growth of Russian industry are available for the 1860–1913 period, or for portions of that period, which are included in Table 22. We lack quantitative evidence of the rate of industrial growth between 1800 and 1860, except for Blackwell's (1968, p. 42) estimate that Russian factory industry more than doubled during that time. That can be converted roughly into an annual growth rate of about two percent, but it does not include the output of the *kustarny* sector.[38] The number of manufacturing plants did increase a little more than six times between 1804 and 1860 and the number of factory workers by about the same amount, but it is not possible to convert these data into increases in production.

Table 22
Estimates of Annual Rates of Growth of Russian
Industrial Production, 1860–1913

Period	Rate (%)
1860–1913	5.0
per capita	3.5
1880–1900	6.4
1890–1899	7–8
textiles	7.8
metallurgy	8.4
1900–1913	4.8
1907–1913	6.0–6.25

Source: Carson (1959, p. 130); Falkus (1972, pp. 46, 66); Goldsmith (1961, pp. 443, 469, 470, 475); Patel (1961, p. 319, table 2).

Table 22 reveals several things. First, it clearly shows the high rate of growth achieved in the 1890s as a result of the activities of foreign entrepreneurs. Second, it also shows the dropoff in industrial production immediately after 1900 and its rise again after 1907. Third, the annual industrial growth rate of 6.4 percent for the 1880–1900 period was higher for that period than that of any of

---

[38] According to Falkus (1972), the earlier view that Russian industry stagnated until emancipation is incorrect.

the other societies we have analyzed; Germany was next highest with a rate of 5.3 percent. Fourth, the Russian rate of 4.8 percent between 1900 and 1913 was less than that of the United States (5.2 percent), but greater than Germany's (4.4 percent) for that period (Patel, 1961, p. 319, Table 2). And the Russian rate of growth for the period from 1885 to 1914 was higher than that of any other industrial country (Falkus, 1972, p. 82; McKay, 1970, p. 4). Fifth, the growth rate in *per capita* industrial output from 1860 to 1913—3.5 percent—was also *higher* than that of any of the other countries included in this study (Goldsmith, 1961, p. 475). But, because of the extremely slow rate of growth of the Russian agricultural sector, the Russian per capita *economic* growth rate—only .9 percent between 1870 and 1913—was *lower* than the comparable rates for France, Germany, Japan, and the United States (Gould, 1972, p. 22), and undoubtedly also Great Britain.[39]

Thus Russia's economic position, relative to other industrializing societies, did not improve appreciably between 1860 and 1913. Russian real per capita income in 1913 was approximately the level of Italy's and only one-third the level of the United States' and Great Britain's and one-half of German's real per capita income. It was approximately 50 percent greater than Japan's though. So, in Goldsmith's (1961) view, Russia was relatively worse off in comparison to the United States and Japan in 1913 than she had been in 1860.[40] The differential effects of World War I on Russia and Japan were to be tremendously important. Japan prospered from the industrial demand created by the war; Russia underwent a revolution which, together with the war, threw its industrial production into chaos.

Russia has been cited as the best exemplification of the "advantages of backwardness" because of the rapid growth of its heavy industry (Gould, 1972). The above data support this and our discussion has shown the crucial part foreign entrepreneurship played in achieving this rate of growth. If foreigners had not entered and widened the cracks that were appearing in the Russian social fabric, it is improbable that the advantages of backwardness would have been realized.

[39]There also were serious inconsistencies in the growth of Russian industry after 1860 which gave it a "two steps forward and one step backward" quality. The cotton industry experienced a severe decline between 1887 and 1890 with raw cotton consumption dropping by almost a third. It did not expand at all between 1900 and 1906 because of the depression at that time (Falkus, 1972; Portal, 1965), but by 1914 it was fourth in world output (Miller, 1926, p. 249). Pig iron production also declined after 1860, concomitant with emancipation, and again after 1900. By 1906 it had surpassed the 1900 level of annual output, but by 1908 it had once again dropped below even the relatively low 1901 level. Annual iron and steel production also fluctuated widely. Between 1897 and 1900 it increased by about 60 percent, between 1900 and 1906 it decreased by about 18 percent, and between 1908 and 1913 it once again increased rapidly—by 67 percent (Falkus, 1972, pp. 52, 79; Portal, 1965, pp. 827, 844). During that period of expansion annual pig iron production increased by 63 percent.

[40]This judgment appears correct for the United States; in 1870 the Russian level of per capita real gross national product was about half the American level. It appears less correct vis-à-vis Japan because the Russian level was about 37 percent greater than the Japanese in 1870 (Maddison, 1969, p. xvi).

But foreign entrepreneurship could not solve all of Russia's problems—the periphery of the society remained undeveloped (Portal, 1965)—and the latent tension between class and mass went unresolved.

THE CAUSAL SIGNIFICANCE OF ENTREPRENEURSHIP IN RUSSIA

Should foreign entrepreneurship in Russia in the late nineteenth century be credited with *positive* causal significance? We think it should. It achieved an industrial growth rate between 1880 and 1900 which was higher than that of any of the other countries we have studied.[41] Economic opportunity conditions had improved to some degree by this time, but the quality and supply of labor were still quite poor and so was the domestic market. So we believe that during these years the foreign invaders dramatically improved upon the potential of the Russian opportunity conditions. It should be realized that they had advantages over many indigenous entrepreneurs; they had greater capital resources and they could bring their technologies and their organizations with them. Yet they also showed greater adroitness in dealing with the Russian environment than most indigenous entrepreneurs did which no doubt enabled them to achieve the results they did.

Although the half century before 1860 would appear to constitute a classic case of the *negative* causal significance of a *lack* of entrepreneurship, we do not draw that conclusion. We regard Russian entrepreneurship as causally *insignificant* during this period because we believe that the economic opportunity conditions for entrepreneurship at the time were the least favorable of any of our six societies, and the rate of industrial growth probably the lowest also. Opportunity conditions obviously could have been improved greatly by appropriate government actions, but the important point is that they were not. The only really favorable condition confronting Russian industrial entrepreneurs was the availability of foreign technology, but the lack of investment capital made that largely a mirage. We think that Russia probably absorbed as much technology during that period as she was able to. Raw materials for heavy industry were also available—in the ground—but the failure of the government and mining entrepreneurs to develop them more rapidly cannot be laid upon manufacturing entrepreneurs.

Therefore we view the Russian situation during this period as a more extreme case of what we saw earlier in France—unfavorable opportunity conditions and an aristocratically controlled government failing to improve those conditions. The performance of the Russian government in this period was much less helpful than even the French government's, and the Russian opportunity condi-

[41] Sweden's rate during this period has been estimated at 8.1 percent, however (Patel, 1961, p. 319, Table 2).

tions were worse than the French.[42] The very slow growth before 1860 we believe was commensurate with an equally slow improvement in opportunity conditions. If Russian opportunity conditions had been equal to those in France or Germany at the time and Russian industrial growth had been as slow as it was, then we would have concluded that the lack of entrepreneurship did in fact have negative causal significance.

We believe Russian entrepreneurship was causally *insignificant* in two other periods: 1860–1880 and 1909–1914. The slight improvement of the rate of growth in the former period corresponded with continued improvement of the opportunity conditions. Emancipation of the serfs, although necessary for long-run development, did have short-run negative effects on the labor supply but these very likely were balanced by the greater supply of available technology at that time. It was at this time especially that the Russian government did not move deliberately to improve opportunity conditions, but remained captive to a frightened aristocracy and hence emancipation had only partially positive effects.

We appraise entrepreneurship as causally insignificant in the 1909–1914 period also because the injection of foreign entrepreneurship in the 1880–1909 interim substantially improved opportunity conditions in the areas of raw materials, technology, and capital. The government also finally moved with some resolution to improve opportunity conditions and indigenous entrepreneurs responded accordingly to the improved conditions.

This discussion places the contribution of foreign entrepreneurship in Russia in perspective. Its rapid penetration of the system constituted a shock which yielded a "great leap forward." The government's actions supplemented and complemented this sudden transfusion of entrepreneurial energy and thus opportunity conditions were markedly improved by about 1910. Or, to phrase it in terms of risk, foreign entrepreneurs radically decreased the risks of entrepreneurship, both by action and by example, and the government's actions helped keep the level of risk lower than it had been.

THE RELEVANCE OF NONECONOMIC FACTORS
FOR ENTREPRENEURSHIP

Where, then, does this leave the noneconomic factors we have discussed? Have we rendered them inconsequential? By no means. In fact, we have learned a great deal about the relevance of noneconomic factors for the emergence of entrepreneurship from our "negative" case. If these factors had been more supportive of entrepreneurship throughout the nineteenth century, then we think that Russian entrepreneurs would have "beat the odds" and Russian entrepreneurship would

---

[42]We feel the Russian situation before about 1860 was roughly comparable to the later years of the Tokugawa period in Japan.

have had positive causal significance. But as we have seen, the noneconomic opportunity conditions duplicated the economic opportunity conditions. As one improved the other also improved, although both improved very slowly indeed.

Instead the major impact of these noneconomic factors was upon the identity of the entrepreneurs who did emerge, and the fact that they were drawn from marginal sources to a greater extent in Russia than in the other five societies. The massive noneconomic risks of entrepreneurship created by the sociocultural environment led to entrepreneurship on the part of those marginal actors who were either more willing to take risks or who were not as affected by the level of risk because they were marginal. Serf entrepreneurs had no other possibilities for upward mobility. Old Believers had their own avenue to social status. And foreign entrepreneurs undoubtedly were less concerned about whether or not their actions brought disapprobation from the Russian "mainstream" than native Russians were.

The influence of the Russian government was of great significance here, too, as it was for the economic opportunity conditions. Greater support of merchants against the aristocracy, for example, would have increased the legitimacy of entrepreneurship and spurred social mobility, and more merchants would have become industrial entrepreneurs in all probability. This did take place slowly before 1860 as the system unraveled, and serf and Old Believer entrepreneurs began to decline in importance. Thus the improvement in the sociocultural environment correlated very highly with the gradual transition from "outsider" to "mainstream" entrepreneurship. But the fact that the government did not make dramatic moves after 1861 to improve the sociocultural environment for entrepreneurship meant that another group of "outsiders" was the only group capable of getting the industrialization process rolling more rapidly. If decisive steps had been taken during this crucial period, then it is likely that Russian industrialization would have been carried forward by indigenous "mainstream" entrepreneurs rather than by foreign "outsiders."[43]

Therefore the industrial experiences of Russia and Japan in the last half of the nineteenth century offer striking contrasts even though there were great similarities between them before that time. The Russian government in 1861 and the Japanese government in 1868 confronted similar crises and both responded with measures ending feudalism. The actions taken by the Meiji government were swift and determined—the disaffected samurai were defeated and manipulated into supporting the government's industrialization policies. The actions of the czarist government were partial and halting. Control by the *mir* replaced control by the landowner and the power of the aristocracy was *not* completely broken.

[43]Gerschenkron's (1962) argument that negative attitudes toward entrepreneurship can only delay its appearance unless they are fortified by specific government policies is particularly cogent for the Russian case, as is his claim that opposition to entrepreneurship tends to produce periods of rapid growth once entrepreneurs break through it.

Moreover the Meiji leaders also moved quickly to improve opportunity conditions and to put traditional norms and values at the service of industrialization. The Russian leaders did little to improve opportunity conditions and retained a desire for the simplicity of the past. In order for changes to have been achieved in Russia comparable to those that occurred in Japan another Peter the Great would have been necessary or Russian Orthodoxy would have had to be transformed into a this worldly nationalistic ideology.[44]

So in Japan government actions reduced the economic and social risks of entrepreneurship very rapidly and the country began its industrial transition. In Russia these risks were scarcely diminished until the appearance of foreign entrepreneurs after 1880 reduced primarily the economic risks of entrepreneurship. Complementary actions of the Russian government helped to diminish both the economic and social risks of entrepreneurship at the same time. And as a result indigenous entrepreneurs appeared after 1909 to a degree not seen before (or to be seen again) in Russia.[45]

---

[44]We have noted several times the differential success of the two governments in dealing with the agricultural sector. In Japan agricultural productivity was improved and the surplus used for industrial purposes. In Russia agriculture was ignored and attempts to tax it produced stagnation.

[45]Russia and Germany could be compared also, but we find a comparison with Japan more meaningful because of the greater similarity of opportunity conditions and feudal traditions at the mid-nineteenth century in it and Russia.

10

Entrepreneurship: Cause or Effect?

We set out to answer two closely linked questions about the phenomenon of entrepreneurship in this study. First, what is its significance for economic growth and development? Is it a crucial factor in the development process, or is it an extraneous factor, outwardly significant but actually a surrogate for more basic ''causes'' of economic growth and development? Second, what factors induce entrepreneurship to appear in a society? Does it emerge primarily in response to the economic conditions present in a situation, as economists have generally argued, or are noneconomic aspects the major inducement mechanisms? At the outset of this study, we claimed that these two questions are really inseparable. If entrepreneurship is found to have causal significance, then that is attributable to the influence of noneconomic characteristics promoting its inordinate emergence or preventing it from appearing.

Our strategy for answering the first question involved comparisons of the rate of industrial growth achieved by a society and the favorableness of the economic opportunity conditions for entrepreneurship within that society. Entrepreneurship was judged to have causal significance in either of two situations. If the rate of industrial growth achieved by a society was significantly *greater* than the favorableness of the opportunity conditions present in that society, then we inferred that entrepreneurship had an independent *positive* ''causal'' effect on economic growth and development. And if the rate of industrial growth was substantially *lower* than the favorableness of the economic opportunity conditions, then our judgment was that entrepreneurship had a *negative* ''causal'' impact. Entrepreneurship was judged to have no independent effect on economic growth and development in cases in which the rate of industrial growth was *proportionate* to the favorableness of economic opportunity conditions.

This strategy required a comparative study so that judgments could be made regarding the relative favorableness of the opportunity conditions promoting entrepreneurship and the relative rates of industrial growth that were achieved. By looking at six different societies, five of which achieved industrialization and one which did not, it has been possible for us to determine whether a specific society's opportunity conditions and rate of industrial growth should be regarded as favorable or high respectively (or unfavorable or low).

To answer the second question we supplemented our analysis of the economic opportunity conditions for entrepreneurship with a consideration of several noneconomic factors which we believed would influence entrepreneurial emergence—the legitimacy of entrepreneurship, the extent of social mobility, social integration, entrepreneurial security, ideology, and psychological motivational influences. We anticipated that these factors would have promoted a disproportionate emergence of entrepreneurship in cases in which it had positive causal significance, and would have prevented its emergence in cases in which negative causal significance was inferred.

In addition to the economic and noneconomic opportunity conditions influencing entrepreneurship, we analyzed three characteristics of entrepreneurship itself: the *type* of entrepreneurial actions initiated, the *size* of the changes these actions involved, and the *identity* of the actors playing the entrepreneurial role. We assumed that these characteristics would constitute important links between the economic and noneconomic opportunity conditions, on the one hand, and the extent to which entrepreneurship emerged, on the other hand. To state it more succinctly, we hypothesized that the characteristics of entrepreneurship would vary with the opportunity conditions present in a situation and would in turn influence the causal significance of entrepreneurship.

There obviously has been a sizable judgmental component in this study, involving questions such as: Were opportunity conditions for entrepreneurship in society A at time X more, or less, favorable than opportunity conditions for entrepreneurship in society B at time Y? We feel that the qualitative evidence we have presented provides sufficient justification for the conclusions we have reached even though we have not always been able to marshall hard quantitative evidence to support them. The most noteworthy aspect of the study is that it simultaneously compares entrepreneurship in six different societies and hence enables us to put the phenomenon into a perspective that a study of one society could not provide.

MAJOR CONCLUSIONS

The analysis of entrepreneurship in these six societies which we have presented in the preceding chapters leads us to three major conclusions. First, entrepreneurship was of little causal significance in the industrial transition in these societies. It did have definitional significance, in the sense in which we used that term earlier, and it may well have causal significance in other societies experiencing industrialization. But in these societies any independent causal effect that it had on industrial growth was really quite limited.

Second, the two sets of factors with which we have been concerned—the economic and the noneconomic—both constitute *necessary* conditions for the emergence of entrepreneurship.[1] In other words, both types of factors must be favorable for entrepreneurship to appear. We were impelled to this conclusion by the striking similarity in the favorableness of the two sets of factors in each of our six societies. Statistically speaking, we discovered a high degree of *multicollinearity* between them. If one was favorable, then the other also tended to be favorable, and entrepreneurship emerged in proportion to the degree of favorableness. By contrast, if one was unfavorable then the other was unfavorable, too, and entrepreneurship was slow to appear. Consequently it is impossible on the basis of this study to conclude that either set of factors is a sufficient condition for entrepreneurial emergence; both apparently are required.

Third, the actions, or inactions, of governments are very influential for entrepreneurship through their effects on both economic and noneconomic opportunity conditions. We had not expected the government's role to be very significant in our six societies because we were focusing upon entrepreneurship in the eighteenth and nineteenth centuries, well before the current extensive involvement of governments in economic and social affairs. Yet we could not help but conclude that in almost all of the societies we considered it was truly consequential. Hence models of entrepreneurship cannot exclude government actions.

We will discuss these conclusions more fully in the remainder of this chapter and will also summarize our conclusions regarding the relevance of the characteristics of entrepreneurship found in different situations for economic growth and development.

THE CAUSAL SIGNIFICANCE OF INDUSTRIAL ENTREPRENEURSHIP

A brief recapitulation of our six case studies will help to clarify our general conclusion regarding the limited causal significance of industrial entrepreneurship. We first determined that it had little if any causal significance in Great Britain, the leader of the First Industrial Revolution. Opportunity conditions were quite favorable there and a relatively high rate of industrial growth was achieved. We also determined that it had limited causal significance in France, Britain's major economic and political rival of the century between 1750 and 1850. The rate of French industrial growth was approximately as much lower than the British rate as the opportunity conditions in France were less favorable

---

[1] We will show later that each appears to influence different characteristics of entrepreneurship, however.

than those in Britain. We feel that many past criticisms of French entrepreneurship have not given sufficient weight to the less favorable opportunity conditions there. Our interpretation is more in accord with recent discussions of French entrepreneurship.

We first found an example of causally significant entrepreneurship in Prussia-Germany, the third European society we considered. We concluded that the lack of entrepreneurship before about 1850 had negative causal significance, but that German entrepreneurship ultimately had positive causal significance after 1880, beyond the point at which industrialization had been achieved. The relative significance of entrepreneurship for Germany's rapid industrial growth after 1850 was minimized somewhat by the fact that the Prussian, and then German, governments improved both economic and noneconomic conditions that had been retarding the appearance of entrepreneurship.

Our conclusions regarding industrial entrepreneurship in Japan, the only non-Western society we considered, were very similar to those for Prussia-Germany. The actions of a government committed to industrialization improved opportunity conditions and entrepreneurs responded in increasing numbers. These actions paid off in the form of an extremely high rate of industrial growth in the twentieth century. Although this was partly the result of market improvements, we judged that the entrepreneurial response was disproportionate to the improvement and hence that Japanese entrepreneurship had positive causal significance at that time.

The United States, our fifth case, was also distinctive as the only new nation among those we analyzed. We concluded that the rapid influx of migrants from European countries plus the possibility of extensive technological borrowing from those countries were primarily responsible for the very favorable opportunity conditions for entrepreneurship that existed during much of the nineteenth century. The rate of industrial growth was quite high, though not as high as it was to be in Germany, Russia, and Japan later, and so we concluded that industrial entrepreneurship was causally insignificant.

It is fitting that our negative case, Russia, was juxtaposed with the United States so as to highlight the stark contrast in opportunity conditions for entrepreneurship in the two geographically largest societies in our study. We judged that opportunity conditions in Russia were extremely unfavorable before about 1860, that they made some improvement between 1860 and 1880, but that they were not greatly upgraded until the massive ingress of foreign entrepreneurs after 1880. We accorded positive causal significance to foreign entrepreneurship during that period because the rate of Russian industrial growth was higher than that of the other societies we considered for that period. The improvement in opportunity conditions resulting from the period of foreign intervention resulted in a burst of indigenous entrepreneurship in the five years or so before World War I, which we regarded as proportionate to the favorableness of opportunity conditions and thus causally insignificant.

We believe a *lack* of entrepreneurship should be judged as having *negative* causal significance in only one instance (Germany before 1850), and it is possible that on further reflection we would assign that case to the category of causally insignificant entrepreneurship. The cases in which we judged industrial entrepreneurship to be causally insignificant have included both favorable opportunity conditions correlated with relatively high industrial growth rates (Great Britain, the United States, Prussia-Germany from 1850 to 1880, Japan from about 1880 to 1914, and Russia from 1909 to 1914) and cases of less favorable or unfavorable opportunity conditions corresponding with relatively low rates of industrial growth (France, Japan from 1870 to 1880, Russia from 1800 to 1860).

In the few cases in which entrepreneurship did have positive causal significance, its impact was momentous. This is nowhere more true than in Russia, where foreign entrepreneurs achieved changes within two decades that Russia by itself had been unable to achieve for almost two centuries (if we date the beginning of Russian industrialization attempts from Peter the Great). Of course opportunity conditions for entrepreneurship were more favorable in 1880 than they had been in 1680, and foreign entrepreneurs had sizable technological and capital assets, but this should not detract from the contribution they made.

FACTORS INFLUENCING THE
EMERGENCE OF ENTREPRENEURSHIP

As we have said, our determination that economic and noneconomic factors both constituted *necessary* conditions for entrepreneurship in these six societies resulted from the great similitude of these two sets of factors in each of our societies. Both sets of factors were most favorable for industrial entrepreneurship in Great Britain and the United States and least favorable in Russia. In France both were noticeably less favorable than in Britain. Japan and Germany exemplify how government actions promoted a gradual improvement in both sets of factors, although Germany (before 1850) is the one case in which we believe the noneconomic opportunity conditions impeded entrepreneurship. After 1850, however, the two sets of conditions were in phase, and we believe that the combination of increased social mobility and the relative blockage of nonentrepreneurial roles were major contributing factors to the increased emergence of entrepreneurship at that time.

Even though we have concluded that the two sets of conditions constituted necessary conditions for entrepreneurship, we still believe that its emergence should be explained first in terms of the favorableness of economic opportunity conditions because it is primarily economic behavior, as we argued earlier. Noneconomic factors therefore are necessary conditions in the sense that they promote, or allow, the emergence of entrepreneurship *in proportion to* the favorableness of economic opportunity conditions. Thus neither set of factors can produce entrepreneurship by itself. If any of the societies we studied had combined the economic conditions of the United States, for example, with the noneconomic conditions of Russia, it is likely that entrepreneurship would have appeared to an extent intermediate to its appearance in these two societies. But we simply found little evidence of the two sets of conditions being sufficiently diverse to promote a *disproportionate* emergence or absence of entrepreneurship.[2]

Economic Factors

In our initial discussion of economic opportunity conditions we analyzed several determinants of the favorableness of these conditions for entrepreneurship. These can be grouped into two sets—those influencing the costs, and those affecting the rewards, of entrepreneurial behavior. We utilized these determinants in our examinations of the individual societies to ascertain the favorableness of economic opportunity conditions. Now that we have analyzed all six societies, it is possible to reach some conclusions about the impact of each of these determinants.

Capital. Landes (1969) claims that after about 1750 the Continental countries had less capital available for industrial investment and less-developed capital markets, that their capital was more likely to be invested in agriculture than in industry, and that they faced larger capital requirements than was the case in Great Britain. We agree with these assessments. All the societies which began to industrialize after Great Britain may be considered as having less favorable opportunity conditions in terms of capital supplies.

Sooner or later this inadequacy was dealt with in various ways—the development of mobilizing facilities (investment banks in France, Germany, and Russia), discoveries of new sources of gold (the United States), the reliance upon large amounts of foreign capital (Russia). Only in Japan was it possible to initiate production on a scale comparable to that in Great Britain. Generally it appears that as capital supplies increased entrepreneurship also increased, and the more rapidly the supplies increased the more rapidly entrepreneurs appeared. France and Russia are prime examples of the lack of capital for industrial pursuits impeding entrepreneurship and an adequate supply promoting it. Thus we conclude that capital supplies were very influential for entrepreneurship.

Labor. It has been suggested that labor was an extremely important factor for eighteenth- and nineteenth-century entrepreneurs because they made decisions largely on the basis of labor costs, because these costs constituted a rela-

---

[2]We suspect that such discrepancies are not likely to be found in many other societies either, and we further suspect that the multicollinearity of economic and noneconomic conditions is the result of either some unknown prior factor or factors or the reciprocal influence of the conditions on each other.

tively high proportion of total costs, and because labor was very immobile and mobility was more crucial than supply (Gould, 1972; Habakkuk, 1955, 1968). It is almost impossible to sort out the relative effects of labor supplies and labor mobility on entrepreneurship, though, because they tended to be correlated in the societies we studied. Labor on the Continent was generally cheaper, but also less mobile, than it was in Great Britain, for example (Landes, 1969). The American labor force was relatively high-cost but also highly mobile; the Russian labor force was at the opposite extreme on both counts.

In general, it appears that the potential advantages of low-cost labor were negated by the deleterious effects of labor immobility, with the Russian *kustarny* sector constituting the most extreme case of the tenacity of domestic modes of production which resulted from labor immobility. The German and Japanese cases offer sharp contrasts in methods of dealing with the problem of low-cost immobile labor. Germany circumvented the problem by plunging ahead with capital-intensive technologies, while Japan utilized labor-intensive methods. By contrast, the disadvantages of high-cost labor could be modified by the introduction of labor-saving innovations as was done in the United States.

In all cases, however, we believe that the tactics used in dealing with the labor problem depended upon the favorableness of other opportunity conditions. If they were favorable, then they predisposed a society to use some tactics rather than others. For example, the capital-intensive route was far more feasible for Germany than for Japan, whereas the world demand for silk products made an intensive use of labor a more viable option for Japan. Therefore we do not feel that labor supplies were as important as capital supplies in influencing the emergence of entrepreneurship. Labor problems could be solved more easily than capital could be created.

Raw materials. There was great variation in raw material supplies in the six societies we have examined. Great Britain had access to suitable quantities of cotton and ample supplies of coal and iron ore. France was handicapped by its limited supplies of all three of these. Germany lacked cotton but its supplies of coal and iron ore more than made up for that inadequacy. Japan, however, confronted the opposite situation—adequate silk supplies but an absence of coal and iron ore. The United States fared exceptionally well in raw materials, although coal and iron ore supplies were not developed as rapidly as they might have been. And Russia had access to cotton supplies but its large coal and iron ore deposits remained undeveloped throughout most of the nineteenth century. So what conclusions can we draw about the significance of this factor?

It has been argued (Gould, 1972) that technological innovations can compensate for raw material inadequacies, but it also has been argued that that is not the case in metallurgy (Landes, 1969).[3] Raw material problems do appear to have

---

[3] "Cheap ore and coal could cover a multitude of sins, and all the ingenuity in the world couldn't compensate for their absence" (Landes, 1969, p. 174).

slowed the metallurgical industry more than the textile industry. The cases of Germany, Russia, and the United States all reveal that growth of the metallurgical industry was hindered, to varying degrees of course, by tardiness in the development of domestic coal and iron ore supplies. Furthermore, it appears that the slowness with which these supplies were developed was partially the result of large quantities of other materials, e.g., timber.

A lack of raw materials clearly did not prevent entrepreneurship from emerging—witness the Japanese case. However, it did influence the direction which entrepreneurship took, as indicated by a comparison of the German and Japanese cases. In general, we believe that raw material supplies were not influential by themselves, but were highly correlated with other opportunity conditions. The more favorable these were, the more likely it was that raw materials were developed and made available to industrial entrepreneurs.

Technology. All of Great Britain's successors enjoyed the advantage of an existent supply of technologies, with later "latecomers" benefitting the most. But the differential experiences of Japan and Russia illustrate vividly that the objective availability of technology is not sufficient to yield entrepreneurial emergence by itself. As it turns out, a supply of technologies constitutes the most favorable opportunity condition for entrepreneurship if two other conditions are met—there is an inadequacy of some sort which the innovation can help resolve and other opportunity conditions are favorable. If existing technologies are adequate to yield satisfactory returns, and if other opportunity conditions are unfavorable, then technology is likely to have less of an effect on entrepreneurship than if the opposite conditions hold.

Market. The four factors we have just discussed all determine the probable costs of entrepreneurial behavior—the greater the supply of each, the less costly such behavior will be. The potential of the market constitutes the major determinant of the probable rewards from entrepreneurship. In our previous discussion we suggested that the size and the composition of the market would both be of significance.

Great Britain's leadership in foreign trade as well as in technological innovation, and her extensive colonial system, meant that her successors all had less favorable foreign markets than she did. Furthermore, each succeeding "latecomer" had a slightly less favorable foreign market situation than its predecessors because of increased competition for that market. This "disadvantage of backwardness" possibly cancelled the advantages resulting from the increased supply of technologies. However, Japan was probably in the second most advantageous position among our six societies on this factor because of its monopoly of the world silk trade following the demise of the French silk industry.

Domestically only the United States had a sufficiently large and expanding market to compensate for this foreign market disadvantage. France was hampered by a very slow rate of population growth and by a dichotomous class structure which precluded mass production of cheap goods. Germany was similarly handicapped by the latter plus economic fragmentation. Japan's population was growing but she was unable to use tariffs to protect her market, and Russia had the least favorable domestic market potential of all.

The changes in the market, both domestic and foreign, which occurred during the nineteenth century, make it difficult to determine the influence of market potential on entrepreneurial emergence, though. The development of transportation systems facilitated the movement of raw materials and finished products and increased the demand for producer goods.[4] As industrialization progressed consumption undoubtedly increased, thereby improving market potential as well.

Therefore instances of sudden, rather than gradual, improvements in market potential provide the clearest evidence of the importance of this factor. Two such instances stand out in the countries we studied—the change in the German market resulting from political unification in 1871 and the sudden enlargement of Japan's foreign market during World War I. In both of these cases rapid improvement in the market was followed by rapid entrepreneurial expansion. Furthermore, we also noted a rapid increase in population size and a tendency toward overexpansion in the United States that we do not feel was coincidental. Thus it appears that whether or not the market is expanding and the rate at which it is expanding are the most significant characteristics of the market for entrepreneurship's emergence.

Economic opportunity conditions and economic risks. The implication of the above discussion is that the effects of *combinations* of the determinants of economic opportunity conditions must be considered in analyzing entrepreneurial emergence. When this is done, we find that the societies we examined generally had either mostly favorable or mostly unfavorable opportunity conditions. For example, technology was the one factor on which Great Britain had a disadvantage relative to France, whereas for France, this one advantage could not compensate for its capital, labor, raw material, and market disadvantages. In Britain advantages on those factors encouraged innovations that filled the technological gap. Russia of course constituted a more drastic case. With insufficient capital and labor supplies, an inadequate market potential, and undeveloped raw materials, a simple injection of technological innovations was hardly sufficient to produce a transformation. The foreign entrepreneurs in Russia showed that technology could have a great impact, but they also possessed substantial capital and had a place in the foreign market.

The effects of combinations of economic opportunity conditions may of course be summarized in terms of the economic risks of entrepreneurship. The more conditions that are unfavorable, the greater will be the economic risks of

---

[4]Landes (1969) claims that improvements in transportation were more beneficial to heavy industry than to light industry because of their effects on the movement of raw materials.

entrepreneurship. If these are reinforced by unfavorable noneconomic conditions, and hence by a high level of noneconomic risks as well, then the emergence of entrepreneurship is very improbable.

Noneconomic Factors

We are also able to provide some generalizations concerning the effects of a variety of noneconomic factors on the emergence of entrepreneurship, having looked at all six societies. These constitute the determinants of the noneconomic risks of entrepreneurial behavior.

Legitimacy of entrepreneurship. The relationship between the degree of legitimacy of entrepreneurship and the extent to which entrepreneurship emerged was one of the most consistent patterns we found in this study. Great Britain and the United States stood at one extreme on this characteristic, while Russia occupied the opposite extreme. The degree of legitimacy in France was lower than in Britain and the United States, it was even lower in the Germanic states prior to 1850, and lower yet in Japan at the beginning of the Meiji period. Looking at another sociocultural characteristic which may be regarded as an indicator of the degree of legitimacy—the amount of aristocratic opposition to entrepreneurship—yields a similar ordering of societies (from least to most): the United States, Great Britain, France, Germany (before 1850), Japan, and Russia.

In virtually all cases in which the legitimacy of entrepreneurship increased, this increase was followed by an upsurge in entrepreneurial emergence. Increases in legitimacy occurred in France and Germany after about 1850, in Japan after about 1880, in the United States after the Jacksonian period, and in Russia after the invasion of foreign entrepreneurs. So the legitimacy of entrepreneurship was an important noneconomic influence on the emergence of entrepreneurship in these societies.

Social mobility. An identical argument can be made for the effects of the degree of social mobility in a society. These effects followed one of two patterns in the societies we analyzed. In those cases, notably the United States and Great Britain, in which there was relatively extensive social mobility, and in which entrepreneurship was a means of upward mobility, entrepreneurship was relatively more emergent. In other cases, entrepreneurship emerged to a greater degree following sociocultural changes which increased the possibility of social mobility. These changes were more evident in Germany and Japan than in Russia, for example, because of the varying degrees to which these societies broke with their feudalistic pasts, and consequently entrepreneurship was quicker to appear in Germany and Japan than in Russia. Moreover, the blockage of nonentrepreneurial mobility channels as in Germany increased the influence of this factor on entrepreneurial emergence.

Security. Entrepreneurial security did not seem to add much to our analysis, possibly because it is a surrogate for other factors, such as the legitimacy of entrepreneurship and the degree of government support for entrepreneurship. Normally improvements in these two factors increased entrepreneurial security. A distinction should be made, however, between economic and noneconomic security. The former, which is a function of the economic opportunity conditions influencing entrepreneurship, will be relevant to our upcoming discussion of innovations. The latter, a function of noneconomic opportunity conditions, is important for the identity of entrepreneurs in different situations, as we shall show.

Ideology. Germany and Japan provide the clearest examples of the positive effects of ideology on the emergence of entrepreneurship. In both societies nationalistic ideologies joined forces with the other noneconomic factors we have described to promote a disproportionate emergence of entrepreneurship. Russia, by comparison, offers the clearest example of the negative effects of an anti-industrial ideology, although clearly the ideology was simply one more barrier to entrepreneurship and not the sole factor preventing its emergence.

We do not feel that there is sufficient evidence from this study to regard the Protestant Ethic as a major influence on entrepreneurial emergence. Protestants were predominant among entrepreneurs in both Britain and the United States, and undoubtedly also in Germany, but these were predominantly Protestant societies. Dissenting Protestants appear to have been important as entrepreneurs only during very early stages of the industrial transition in Britain and the United States. We have further suggested that education was possibly a more important influence in Britain, and we have observed that mainstream Protestant denominations soon provided the bulk of American entrepreneurs.

Psychological factors. Neither have we uncovered much evidence to convince us that the various psychological traits that some have regarded as influential for entrepreneurship were in fact important in the six societies we surveyed. We have proposed that a desire for *status recognition* or situations of *status inconsistency* constitute more plausible explanations of entrepreneurial motivation than do the need-achievement or withdrawal of status respect theories. For instance, the desire for status recognition was likely strongest in Russia, followed by Japan, Germany, France, Great Britain, and the United States, if we can assume that it was in inverse proportion to the degree of aristocratic opposition to entrepreneurship. This ranking does not correspond with the degrees of entrepreneurial emergence in these societies, however, so this factor does not offer that satisfactory an explanation for entrepreneurial emergence either.

We speculated on the possibility that status inconsistency was a motivating force for the samurai in Japan and that the withdrawal of status respect or high need-achievement might have influenced Europeans to migrate to the United States and to become entrepreneurs after their arrival. But it has been impossible to separate the influence of these psychological characteristics from other noneconomic factors.

Some kind of motivational force is undoubtedly an additional necessary condition for the emergence of entrepreneurship, but we doubt whether a specific psychological trait can account for entrepreneurship in all situations. Instead we suspect that different traits will be operative in different situations and that they will be influenced by the economic and noneconomic conditions found in different situations. The very favorable conditions for entrepreneurship in the United States very likely produced a different psychological bent than the unfavorable conditions which prevailed in Russia.

It is conceivable that particular combinations of economic and noneconomic factors will produce especially powerful entrepreneurial motivations. Just a moment ago we questioned whether the motivation for status recognition could explain entrepreneurial emergence. But if we combine the influence of this factor with the favorableness of opportunity conditions, both economic and noneconomic, for all of our societies except Japan and the United States, we derive an interesting finding. A ranking of these two factors, from greatest to least as in Table 23, may provide a partial explanation for the dynamism of German entrepreneurship after 1850. Germany was characterized by the highest *combination* of motivation for status recognition and favorable opportunity conditions of these four societies.[5] In addition, after 1850 the opportunity conditions in Germany perhaps surpassed those in Great Britain a century earlier, because of the larger supplies of capital and technology, the increased legitimacy of entrepreneurship, and the greater potential for social mobility. Hence it is possible that pent-up motivations from the pre-1850 period were manifested in vigorous entrepreneurship because of the presence of favorable opportunity conditions after 1850.

Nevertheless, we remain skeptical of explanations of entrepreneurial

Table 23
Relationship Between Motivation for Status Recognition and Favorableness of Opportunity Conditions

Motivation for Status Recognition	Favorableness of Opportunity Conditions
Russia	Great Britain
Germany	Germany
France	France
Great Britain	Russia

[5]This becomes clearer if we assign values (from 4 to 1) to each column and assume the relationship between these two variables is multiplicative.

emergence that rely too heavily upon psychological causes. One can explain the emergence of entrepreneurship either in terms of degrees of *risk* or degrees of *willingness* to take risks, in our opinion. In every case in this study in which we have found either an extensive emergence of entrepreneurship or tentative attempts at emergence we believe that an explanation in terms of degrees of risk is far more persuasive than one couched in terms of willingness to take risks. The critical test of the two explanations comes in situations in which entrepreneurship has emerged suddenly, after a period of hesitation, as in Germany after 1850. In such situations we believe it is more likely that the degree of willingness to take risks has remained relatively constant and the degree of risk has diminished than that the degree of risk has held steady and individuals are suddenly more willing to take risks.

THE IMPACT OF GOVERNMENT ACTIONS ON ENTREPRENEURSHIP

Our third major conclusion was that governments, by their actions or their failure to act, greatly influence both the economic and noneconomic opportunity conditions for entrepreneurship.

Economic Opportunity Conditions

A comparison of the German and Japanese cases with the Russian reveals the most about the importance of government actions. In Germany and Japan the government moved to improve the opportunity conditions which were least favorable. In Germany these included capital and raw material supplies and the nature of the market. Supplies of the first two were substantially improved after 1850, and the market was improved through gradual expansion of the *Zollverein* and then greatly improved by political unification. Likewise programs undertaken on a broad front by the Meiji government in Japan improved capital supplies, and exploitation of the foreign market under government influence enabled Japan to compensate for its lack of raw materials for heavy industry.

The czarist governments in Russia, however, made only tentative attempts to improve economic conditions until the foreign invasion of the late nineteenth century. As in France, where government failures were less serious, there was equivocation regarding the desirability of industrialization and some policies were adopted that counteracted the potential positive influence of other policies.

Noneconomic Opportunity Conditions

The effects of government actions on noneconomic factors affecting entrepreneurship were possibly even greater than their influences on economic conditions. Again, Japan, Germany, and Russia provide the most informative comparison. The Meiji government achieved the most complete break with the past by decisively ending the system of feudalism and the power of the samurai. The Prussian and German governments' actions were somewhat less dramatic, but the legitimacy of entrepreneurship was increased greatly after 1850, and particularly after Bismarck's accession in 1861, when the government threw its weight behind the goal of rapid industrialization. But in Russia the government did not achieve a clearcut break with the past. Emancipation of the serfs was accomplished, a step outwardly similar to the Meiji leaders' cessation of feudalism, but it was only partial and noneconomic opportunity conditions were not improved greatly.

The governments in the other two societies, Great Britain and the United States, acted very similarly, no doubt because of the cultural linkage between the two, and very differently from the governments in Japan and Germany. In both cases overt government actions were relatively limited, but the governments created a climate supportive of entrepreneurship.[6] They interfered very little with entrepreneurs' activities, but intervened sufficiently to keep the industrialization process moving forward.

However, it should be noted that in both of these societies opportunity conditions for entrepreneurship were generally favorable and entrepreneurs were coming forth to take advantage of them. Either one or both of these conditions did not hold in Germany and Japan, and neither held in Russia. If entrepreneurs had been less emergent in Great Britain and the United States, or more emergent in Germany, Japan, Russia, and France, then it is plausible that the roles of the governments of these two groups of societies would have been at least partially reversed.

Although we have discussed the effects of governments' actions *upon* the noneconomic opportunity conditions for entrepreneurship, it is more likely that the actions operated in conjunction with these conditions. In Table 24, for example, we summarize the combined effects of government support for entrepreneurship and the degree of social integration prevailing in our six societies. Russia stands at one extreme, with a high degree of social integration under the czarist governments and the least government support for industrialization. The United States stands farthest toward the opposite extreme. We have included Germany (before 1850) and France in the neutral category of state support because we feel that the positive and negative policies in those instances cancelled each other out.

This table reveals several things. First, the combination characterizing Russia was particularly inhibitive of mainstream entrepreneurship and conducive to "outsider" entrepreneurship. Second, the combination in Great Britain and the United States yielded substantial economic growth by means of mainstream entrepreneurship. Third, the combination in Germany after 1850 (and even more

---

[6]We have noted the possibility that the lack of government involvement in the United States may have had negative effects in the form of entrepreneurial insecurity, though.

Table 24
Relationship Between Degree of Societal Integration
and Degree of Government Support for
Industrialization

| | | Degree of Societal Integration | |
		Low	High
	Negative		Russia
Degree of Government Support	Neutral	Germany (before 1850) Great Britain United States	France
	Positive		Germany (after 1850) Japan

after 1871) and in Japan—positive government support and high societal integration—produced two of our three cases of positively causally significant entrepreneurship.

Thus the combination of the degree of societal integration and the degree of government support for entrepreneurship was very significant in these six societies. Positive government support combined with high societal integration prompted an extensive emergence of entrepreneurship. The German case is again informative, because both factors increased substantially after 1850. Government opposition and high societal integration, however, inhibited it and stimulated "outsider" entrepreneurship in Russia. And entrepreneurship conceivably would have been more emergent in both Great Britain and the United States if those societies had been either more highly integrated or if government support had been more positive, rather than leaning toward neutrality.

Characteristics of Entrepreneurship

The governments in our six societies also influenced the characteristics of entrepreneurship directly, in addition to their indirect influence on entrepreneurship via opportunity conditions. For example, they played an important role in some cases in encouraging the adoption of innovations. Thus in both Germany and Japan the state forcefully promoted technological innovations. The Meiji government embarked upon an extensive program of model-factory construction which it then turned over to the private sector. Even the French government encouraged French entrepreneurs to utilize British innovations. In Russia, by contrast, and to a lesser degree in France, inventions were not transformed into innovations partly because of the lack of government support. Government support extended to organizational innovations as well. The government's ties to the *zaibatsus* in Japan, and its encouragement of the cartels in Germany constitute two prime examples.

The role of governments in influencing who played the entrepreneurial role also should not be overlooked. Obviously governments determined the extent to which entrepreneurship was relegated to the private sector. Less obvious is the fact that in the cases in which "outsider" entrepreneurship was present, government policies largely determined whether it was of domestic or foreign origin. The marginal German entrepreneurs were foreigners while in Japan marginal entrepreneurship was domestic because of the government's restrictions on foreign participation. In Russia also government restrictions on foreign entrepreneurs prior to 1860 promoted domestic marginal entrepreneurship, and the loosening of these restrictions after 1860 promoted the eventual preponderance of foreign entrepreneurship after 1880.

THE RELEVANCE OF CHARACTERISTICS
OF ENTREPRENEURSHIP

We paid special heed to three of the major sources of variation in the entrepreneurial role—who played the role, what they did in the role, and the extensiveness of the changes they initiated. These are of course the most tangible manifestations of entrepreneurship, more concrete than either opportunity conditions or rates of industrial growth. But the fact that they are more visible does not mean they are more important. The variation one finds in these characteristics may be interesting, but it may be largely inconsequential for economic growth and development. We did not expect that to be the case, however. Instead we felt that these characteristics would be important intervening variables between the opportunity conditions for entrepreneurship and the outcome of entrepreneurship, i.e., economic growth and development. So we will next see what we have learned from our study about their relevance in this respect by summarizing the relationships we have found between each characteristic and opportunity conditions and the causal significance of entrepreneurship.

Type of Entrepreneurship

Throughout this study we have concentrated upon two basic entrepreneurial actions, innovations and expansions, involving qualitative and quantitative changes respectively. Were these two types of entrepreneurship more likely under some conditions than under others? And was the occurrence of these two types associated with whether or not entrepreneurship was causally significant?

Relationship to opportunity conditions. The likelihood of entrepreneurs initiating innovations in the societies we have surveyed appears to have been a function of two factors: an inadequacy in regard to one opportunity condition and the favorableness of *other* opportunity conditions. Inadequacies, whether they involved supplies of capital, raw materials, or labor, the productivity of existing technologies, or the size of the market, created the *need* for innovations. But whether or not this need was met depended largely on the favorableness of the other opportunity conditions in the situation. If these were unfavorable, then in most instances the need went unmet.

The favorableness of the other opportunity conditions present in a situation appears to be the more significant of these two factors. Thus the lack of innovativeness in France and Russia can be explained more reasonably in terms of the unfavorableness of other opportunity conditions than in terms of the lack of a *need* for innovations in those settings. French entrepreneurs, for example, initiated innovations for which opportunity conditions were more favorable and failed to make innovations in areas where they were less favorable. In Russia, however, the unfavorableness of all opportunity conditions discouraged innovation. But there also were cases in which the need for innovation appears to have been relatively more important. We have noted several instances in which the adequacy of traditional fuels, for example, hindered entrepreneurs from adopting coal and converting to steam power. In Britain, by contrast, the inadequacy of water for power promoted adoption of this innovation.

Second, the *kinds* of innovations that were adopted were a function of the nature of a specific inadequacy, the favorableness of specific opportunity conditions, and the availability of innovations. The availability of innovations did become less important in the late nineteenth century when the Second Industrial Revolution was launched by a number of absolute innovations, but it was extremely important before that time, even in Great Britain. We have seen that many of the early British textile innovations built upon existing primitive technologies.

The different experiences of our six countries reveal the importance of these factors. British technological innovations were basically gap-filling, economizing on labor and resolving the problems of a lack of raw materials in specific areas—thread for the textile industry and water for power. France, however, concentrated on improving the efficiency of both water and steam power because the British innovations offered less cost advantages due to France's less expensive labor and more expensive coal. Germany's rapid adoption of innovations in heavy industry after 1850 was largely influenced by the availability of necessary technologies and the increased demand for producer goods. Available technology, the relative supplies of labor and raw materials, and the nature of the market encouraged Japan to concentrate on the production of consumer goods. In the United States a combination of a large market and relatively high-cost labor promoted the adoption of labor-saving mass production techniques. And in Russia opportunity conditions were too unfavorable to promote innovations of any significance, despite the great availability of technologies, until foreigners provided the impetus; even indigenous innovations were ignored there.[7]

Generally we also found that capital-intensive techniques were adopted where capital was abundant relative to labor and that labor-intensive techniques were utilized where labor was relatively ample. Germany constitutes the primary exception to this pattern, although its selection of the capital-intensive route was facilitated by the growth of capital-mobilizing mechanisms that had occurred by 1850 and the abundance of necessary raw materials. Japan was forced to go the more normal route, using labor-intensive technologies which meshed with its labor supply.

Organizational innovations in the countries we studied also exemplified the influence of these three factors. The domestic or putting-out system of production became inadequate as technological innovations were developed.[8] Thus the rapidity of the conversion to factory production depended largely upon the rate at which these innovations, especially steam power, were adopted. The British entrepreneurs who began the transition also had models of large-scale organizations from which to choose (Pollard, 1965). And the availability of capital, as well as the supply and mobility of labor, also influenced the rapidity of this transition. In general, societies in which the other opportunity conditions were most favorable made this transition most rapidly, and societies with the least favorable opportunity conditions, such as Russia, retained the strongest domestic sectors.

Financial innovations similarly arose from the inadequacy of capital supplies. The need for such innovations was greater in France than in Britain, for example, and we have noted the greater French progress in this area through the use of the *commenda*. Belgium provided the model for the *Crédit Mobilier*, and Germany in turn adopted and expanded upon that model. We attribute its greater development of this innovation in comparison to France to the more favorable opportunity conditions in Germany, as well as to the greater support of the German government.

The impact of these three factors is somewhat more difficult to discern in the case of market innovations. Specifically, these innovations may be interpreted as a consequence of either an inadequacy of one opportunity condition or the adequacy of another. Thus the British and American concentration on mass-production, as well as Britain's exploitation of the foreign market and the United

---

[7]Gould (1972, p. 241) says that the period between 1850 and World War I, "Thanks to a fortunate conjuncture of favorable circumstances . . . offered a quite remarkable, probably unique, opportunity for countries not only to exploit comparative advantage to the full . . . but, thanks to the rapid expansion of world trade, to achieve ongoing growth through such specialization."

[8]Landes (1969) points out that the conversion to factory production increased risk for entrepreneurs because more of their investment was tied up in fixed equipment, but that the increased productivity of the new mode of production counterbalanced this increased risk.

States' utilization of the domestic market can be explained in either way. The two countries' concentration on mass-production appears better explained by the adequacy of their markets than by some sort of inadequacy, unless one concludes that their markets for luxury goods were inadequate. Britain's expansion into the foreign market may be explained either in terms of the adequacy of that market or the inadequacy of the domestic market, whereas the American exploitation of the domestic market may be attributed to either domestic adequacy or foreign inadequacy. Likewise, France's continued production of luxury goods may be accounted for by the adequacy of the market for such goods or by the inadequacy of the market for mass-produced goods.

A third generalization we can make regarding the relationship between opportunity conditions and innovations is that some kinds of innovations are primarily the result of the favorableness of economic opportunity conditions whereas others appear to be influenced by the combination of economic and noneconomic conditions. Innovations which were less influenced by interpersonal relationships—particularly technological, material, product, financial and market innovations—were influenced mainly by economic conditions. Noneconomic factors were more influential in the adoption of innovations which involved interpersonal relationships, particularly organizational and labor innovations.

We have shown that the transition to factory production was a consequence of economic conditions and technological innovations. However, noneconomic factors influenced the type of intra-organizational innovations that were adopted, particularly the type of management. The fact that economies of internal scale were relatively limited compared to external economies during this period alleviated the need for major innovations in this area to some degree (Gould, 1972). But noneconomic factors were partially responsible for the British hesitance to use managers. Similarly the relatively small scale of many Japanese enterprises reduced the need for extensive intrafirm innovations, but the refusal of Japanese entrepreneurs to adopt Western management practices cannot be explained solely in terms of economic factors. Values and attitudes were a more important influence.

A combination of economic and noneconomic factors also seems responsible for the developments in interfirm organization that were achieved, such as integration and combination. The requirements of heavy industry for stable sources of supply created a need for integration, but we believe noneconomic factors were important in determining whether that need was met. The need undoubtedly was just as great in Britain as in Germany, but it was not met in Britain and it was carried to an extreme in Germany. Likewise the creation of combinations to provide entrepreneurs with stable markets was partly dependent upon their willingness to cooperate which was influenced by noneconomic factors.

The experience of foreign entrepreneurs in Russia is informative for the light it sheds on the relationships between organizations and their economic and sociocultural environments. Their discovery that organizational forms suitable to their home environments were less satisfactory in Russia than technological innovations, which could be transferred with few modifications, indicates the greater influence of the environment on organization than on technology.

The area in which entrepreneurs were least innovative during the eighteenth and nineteenth centuries was that of labor. There were exceptions to this generalization, such as Germany's and the United States' use of technically trained personnel and Japan's development of a unique system of labor management. But in general entrepreneurs were slow to develop incentives to improve labor productivity or to create more humane systems of labor management. Why was progress so slow in this area?

In part, there was no great need for labor innovations until the late 1800s. The gains in productivity resulting from technology often compensated for unproductive labor. But noneconomic factors were probably even more important. Marshall (1950) has described the sequential gaining of civil, political, and social rights by the working classes as a process that occurred simultaneously with industrialization. Although there were exceptions, such as the German system of social legislation adopted under Bismarck after 1880, in most cases the proletariat had not yet attained its social rights, the right to welfare and to life as an equal partner in society. Hence the sociocultural environments of the nineteenth-century industrializers were not conducive to the development of more humane methods of dealing with workers. Japan did develop a relatively humane system based on traditional feudal patterns, but its paternalistic qualities meant that workers were not viewed as social equals. Development of systems of labor management were probably least far along in Russia, and extensive conflict between workers and entrepreneurs was the result. Even in the United States, supposedly the most enlightened of nations, the work force was viewed as subordinate during this period.

The extent to which entrepreneurs in "latecomer" societies made significant additions to the stock of technologies they inherited was not a function solely of economic factors either. Some "latecomers" (Germany and the United States) made numerous additions to the existent supply. One, France, made fewer additions, and Russia and Japan made hardly any. We believe the American case partly exemplifies the impact of the market. Gould (1972) suggests that technological *improvements* are largely market-induced, and we have noted the American facility in that area. But the development of science and its linkage to industry in both the United States and Germany played a major role in their contributing innovations in the latter part of the nineteenth century. We attribute their leadership in this area primarily to the development of a system of technical education, especially in Germany, and to immigration of individuals with technological knowledge in the United States. Thus noneconomic factors were of importance in both countries.

Although French science was highly developed it did not develop the linkage between science and industry that Germany did. This we believe was due both to less favorable economic conditions and a lesser cultural appreciation of the industrial possibilities of scientific knowledge. We attribute the lack of independent technological innovation in Japan to its very limited development of scientific knowledge, and this, along with unfavorable opportunity conditions, accounts for the similar lack in Russia.

Entrepreneurial expansions appear to be somewhat easier to explain than innovations, in that they were primarily a response to the favorableness of opportunity conditions in the societies we analyzed. Both initial expansions and subsequent expansions were most evident in situations in which economic opportunity conditions were most favorable. However, we were unable to determine the relative proportions of these two types of expansion within a society with any specificity. Apparently both were either relatively present or absent in a society.

There was a decline in initial expansions in the late nineteenth century in some countries, particularly Germany and the United States, because of increased capital requirements and the concentration of heavy industry. But there were extensive initial expansions at about the same time in other societies—in France, involving products of the Second Industrial Revolution; in Japan, involving products borrowed from the West; and in Russia in the form of foreign entrepreneurship. These were largely in response to changes in opportunity conditions in our opinion.

There appears to have been a difference in the extent to which entrepreneurs initiated subsequent expansions on the basis of reinvested profits, which was closely linked to opportunity conditions, too. This practice was most apparent in Britain, Germany, the United States, and Japan, less apparent in France, and least apparent among indigenous Russian entrepreneurs. But the dualism in the French and German industrial structures indicates that not all German entrepreneurs reinvested profits and expanded and that the failure to reinvest was not universal among French entrepreneurs.

Those societies confronted by the least favorable opportunity conditions also retained the largest sectors of nonexpansive domestic production. This sector constituted a drag on industrial growth in Russia and France particularly. The Japanese and German small-scale traditional sectors were less of a hindrance to industrial growth, but these societies had more favorable opportunity conditions after 1850 than France had before that date and than Russia had throughout most of the 1800s. The Japanese small-scale sector benefitted from the demand for silk products and its close ties to the large-scale sector through the *zaibatsus*, for example. In France the two sectors served different markets, with the small-scale sector meeting the demand for luxury goods which did not increase that much.

The importance of competition. At various points in this study we have commented upon the relevance of competition for entrepreneurship. In our discussion of economic opportunity conditions, for example, we regarded extensive competition—for capital and for markets—as making these conditions less favorable. Thus, the more entrepreneurs competing for a fixed supply of capital, the less favorable the opportunity conditions for any one entrepreneur. We also noted that the apparent lethargy of French entrepreneurship has been linked to the absence of competition in the French economy, which implies that *too little* competition is more debilitating than too much. But we also raised the possibility that the high level of competition in the American case diminished entrepreneurial dynamism by engendering insecurity.

Upon further reflection it appears that competition is a double-edged sword for entrepreneurship. Too little competition makes the initiation of innovations and expansions easier, but it also makes them less necessary for entrepreneurs to survive. Conversely, a high degree of competition creates a greater need for innovations and expansions—if entrepreneurs do not they are likely to be eliminated by entrepreneurs who do so—but it simultaneously makes the initiation of innovations or expansions riskier because of the greater struggle for factor supplies and a share of the market.

Hence it is impossible to come up with a quick and easy answer to the question of the optimum level of competition for innovative and expansive entrepreneurship. Entrepreneurs in societies in which competition was high, such as the United States, faced risks if they innovated or expanded, but they also faced risks if they did not innovate or expand. Very likely the overall favorableness of opportunity conditions in a society like the United States tipped the balance in favor of action rather than inaction, but we have also noted Strassman's (1959) discussion of the caution of American entrepreneurs in the face of apparently optimal circumstances. For Russian entrepreneurs, however, the unfavorableness of opportunity conditions probably meant that innovating or expanding was riskier than not doing so. They did confront competition from the *kustarny* sector, but because that sector was not innovating or expanding either, the perils of their not innovating likely were not that great.

Relation to the causal significance of entrepreneurship. Clearly the more expansions and innovations that entrepreneurs initiate, the more likely it is that entrepreneurship will have positive causal significance, and the less expansive and innovative they are, the more likely it will have negative causal significance. But are there consistent relationships between the relative importance of innovations and expansions in the array of entrepreneurial actions and the causal significance of entrepreneurship? Or are specific types of innovations and expansions consistently related to causal significance?

A look at the cases in which entrepreneurship was causally significant in our six societies reveals that causal significance is more likely when innovations are predominant among entrepreneurial actions. All three instances in which we regarded entrepreneurship as having positive causal significance involved extensive innovation, although the nature of the innovations varied. Japan exemplified one pattern in this regard, with a number of innovations promoting rapid expansion of the production of consumer goods. Technologies were borrowed wholesale from the West. Distinctive organizational innovations, such as the development of the *zaibatsus* and a system of management, played a major role in the utilization of these technologies, as did the creation of a unique system of managing the labor force. The rapid movement into the foreign market during World War I constituted a market innovation, and some of the goods sold in that market were products that had been borrowed from the West, too. Only material innovations were relatively unrepresented.

German entrepreneurs and foreign entrepreneurs in Russia after 1880 reveal a different pattern, based on heavy industry and producer goods. Technological innovations and improvements were especially important, as were material innovations and the development of organizations and financial mechanisms. In both cases the foreign market was exploited, and labor innovations, although relatively less significant, were introduced. German entrepreneurs can be regarded as more innovative than the foreign entrepreneurs operating in Russia, because the latter group primarily transferred proven technologies and organizational forms whereas Germans developed many of them themselves. However, foreign entrepreneurs had to exhibit some ingenuity in dealing with the Russian socioeconomic environment.

So in these three societies innovative entrepreneurship was the key to the causal significance of entrepreneurship.[9] It made possible the expansions which had a more direct bearing on industrial growth but which by themselves very likely would not have yielded causal significance. A comparison of the highly innovative large-scale sectors and the less innovative small-scale sectors in those societies with dualistic industrial structures reaffirms the relatively greater significance of innovations. The domestic sectors in those societies tended either to remain stagnant, as in Russia, or to expand only very slowly, as in Germany or France, unless they were pulled along by the large-scale sector, as was the case in Japan.

Degrees of Innovation and Expansion

We referred to the second characteristic of entrepreneurial actions that we explored as the degree of innovation and expansion. These terms represent our attempts to grapple with the *sizes* of the innovations and expansions initiated by entrepreneurs. We assumed that different-sized changes would be more likely under some conditions than others, and that they would have relevance for the causal significance of entrepreneurship. It seemed logical that entrepreneurship would be more likely to have positive causal significance, the larger the innovations and expansions that were introduced.

[9]The negative causal significance of Prussian-German entrepreneurship before 1850 also can be attributed partially to the failure to adopt available technological innovations in the textile and metallurgical industries in the face of relatively favorable opportunity conditions.

Relationship to opportunity conditions. A fairly strong relationship between the favorableness of opportunity conditions and the degree of innovation is evident in the six societies we have examined. Those societies with more favorable opportunity conditions achieved greater increases in productivity as the result of technological innovations, for example. We found evidence of this in both the metallurgical and textile industries. In the former, the United States and Germany attained especially large productivity increases. Foreign entrepreneurs in Russia radically surpassed indigenous entrepreneurs in this regard, but they were less successful in comparison to American and German entrepreneurs, no doubt mainly because of the quality of the Russian labor force and the difficulty of operating in an alien environment. We have also seen that Japan was less successful in improving productivity in the textile industry than American entrepreneurs were, which can be explained by two factors. First, we have noted that the Japanese often borrowed technologies that were obsolete in the United States. Second, the Japanese labor force was less skilled than the American, and hence on that factor Japanese opportunity conditions were less favorable than they were in the United States.

The size of the expansions initiated by entrepreneurs was largely a consequence of the number and size of innovations that were initiated in a particular society. Thus the greater the productivity increases resulting from technological innovations, the larger the scale of operations that was possible. Organizational innovations were required to coordinate the larger scale of operations, and these, too, tended to appear more often where opportunity conditions for entrepreneurship were favorable. Japan constitutes an exception from the secular trend toward an increased scale of operations which occurred after 1750. It was largely able to replicate the earlier British pattern in textiles, but we have just noted that its innovations yielded smaller productivity increases, and hence it supports the greater importance of innovation also.

However, the movement toward a larger scale of operations was not wholly due to innovation. We have observed that the Russian textile industry attained an extremely large scale of operations already by 1850. In that case the increase in scale was a means of compensating for the low productivity of the Russian labor force.

Implications for the causal significance of entrepreneurship. In two of the cases in which entrepreneurship had positive causal significance, relatively ''large'' innovations were a prominent characteristic. In both Germany and Russia after 1880 substantial gains in productivity were achieved as a result of technological innovations and these were supported by the other types of innovations we have already mentioned. In Japan, however, the changes wrought by technological innovations was cushioned by the Japanese adeptness at ''pouring new wine into old bottles.'' So the degree of innovation appears more relevant in cases in which the causal significance of entrepreneurship derives from innovations in heavy industry than in cases, such as Japan, in which consumer goods are predominant.

Two interesting contrasts in the degree of expansion in different situations make clear that this characteristic of entrepreneurial actions is not consistently associated with the causal significance of entrepreneurship. The Russian textile industry displayed a very large scale of operations at a time when Russian entrepreneurship certainly was not causally significant, and Japanese entrepreneurship had positive causal significance at a time when its scale of operations was not especially large. Relatively large-scale operations were characteristic of the two other cases in which entrepreneurship was causally significant—Germany and Russia after 1880. So the degree of expansion is less consistently related to the causal significance of entrepreneurship than is the degree of innovation, which is what one would expect because of the partial dependence of expansions on innovations.

Entrepreneurial Identity

We used a number of categories to sort out the wide variety of individuals and groups who may play the entrepreneurial role. As indicated earlier, a basic assumption was that we would uncover consistent variations between the identity of entrepreneurial actors and either the opportunity conditions for entrepreneurship or the causal significance of entrepreneurship. Thus entrepreneurial identity would constitute an important intervening variable between the two. Some of our expectations were realized, others were not.

Relationship to opportunity conditions. The most interesting influence of opportunity conditions on entrepreneurial identity that we found involves whether "mainstream" or "outsider" entrepreneurship is characteristic of a society. We have seen that there was a high degree of multicollinearity between the economic and noneconomic opportunity conditions in a society. The predominance of "mainstream" or "outsider" entrepreneurship in a society was equally highly associated with the favorableness of opportunity conditions. The more favorable the opportunity conditions for entrepreneurship, the larger the "mainstream" component among a society's entrepreneurs; the less favorable these conditions the larger the representation of "outsider" entrepreneurs.

Great Britain and the United States enjoyed the most favorable opportunity conditions and their entrepreneurs were most uniformly "mainstream." France, with somewhat less favorable opportunity conditions, had a larger proportion of "outsider" entrepreneurs. Germany, having slightly more favorable economic opportunity conditions but less favorable noneconomic conditions than France before 1850, had a slightly larger contingent of "outsider" entrepreneurs than France during that period. These entrepreneurs were replaced by "mainstream" entrepreneurs after 1850 as both sets of opportunity conditions improved. Japanese entrepreneurship was also marginal at the beginning of the Meiji period, when opportunity conditions were least favorable, but it too became increasingly "mainstream" when both sets of factors improved. And Russia, with the least favorable opportunity conditions, revealed the largest proportion of "outsider" entrepreneurs. Domestic "outsiders" were of course predominant after 1880. Russian entrepreneurship became primarily "mainstream" only after 1909, when opportunity conditions had been greatly improved.

Although we cannot be certain because of the virtually perfect associations, we believe that noneconomic opportunity conditions had greater influence on entrepreneurial identity than did economic opportunity conditions. Germany before 1850 provides the most telling evidence because noneconomic factors were less favorable than economic factors during that period, and that is also the period when "outsider" entrepreneurship was most significant. Economic factors, however, appear more important than noneconomic factors for the relative proportions of innovations and expansions initiated by entrepreneurs in a society.

The favorableness of opportunity conditions also appears to be a partial determinant of the specific social origins from which "mainstream" entrepreneurs come within a society. The more favorable these conditions are, the *wider* the range of occupations and statuses from which they are drawn. The United States, with the most favorable opportunity conditions, was characterized by the widest range of backgrounds among its entrepreneurs; Britain, with the next most favorable opportunity conditions, had a very similar range.

The resources possessed by individuals in different social locations constitute an additional influence, however. We have seen that merchants or artisans were prominent among industrial entrepreneurs in all six societies, which no doubt was largely due to their possessing two important assets—capital and technical knowledge respectively. Furthermore, we have seen a sequence of social origins of entrepreneurs in several societies, which can be accounted for by means of the same factors. Artisans were most prominent in the initial stages of the First Industrial Revolution, when opportunity conditions were greatest for those with technical knowledge. As capital requirements increased, merchants came to the fore armed with that resource. We have seen that they quite often formed working relationships with artisans in industrial undertakings. The commencement of the Second Industrial Revolution in the late nineteenth century was accompanied by the need for even greater capital and a much higher level of technological knowledge. And in that period financiers and engineer-entrepreneurs became important.[10]

The same two factors—specific opportunity conditions and the possession of resources—seem to determine whether "outsider" entrepreneurs come mainly from domestic marginal groups or from foreign origins. The Russian case strongly suggests that indigenous marginal groups will come forward if they have at least some resources to take advantage of specific opportunities. We noted that serf and Old Believer entrepreneurs had technical knowledge and capital suffi-

---

[10]These factors also explain the relatively extensive participation of the Russian aristocracy and French and German private bankers in industrial entrepreneurship.

cient to take advantage of the limited opportunities in Russia. The later experience of Russia suggests that entrepreneurship will be truly "outsider," i.e., carried out by actors from outside the society, if those actors have sufficient resources to convert potential opportunities into actual ones and if they are strong enough to withstand the hostility of their hosts. We also have seen that foreign entrepreneurs mistakenly perceived Russian opportunity conditions to be greater than they were; their dreams of huge profits were thwarted for the most part. Hence *perception* of opportunities plays a vital part, too.

The other types of entrepreneurial identity revealed much greater uniformity across the six societies, and hence were less consistently related to the favorableness of opportunity conditions. Thus in all six societies there was a trend toward collective forms of entrepreneurship, due mainly to the increase in capital requirements in the course of each society's industrial transition. The six societies varied in the speed of this transition, with later "latecomers" making the transition more swiftly, but in all the trend was inexorable. Yet specific individual entrepreneurs remained significant in most societies, often as the heads of vast industrial empires. The crucial difference from an earlier period was that individuals were no longer able to fulfill all phases of the entrepreneurial role.

Second, there was also a decline in family entrepreneurship in each of the societies correlative with the transition to collective entrepreneurship. There were exceptions—the Japanese *zaibatsus* were family-run organizations, for example—and families were to delay their demise longer in some societies than in others, but this trend was relentless, too. It resulted from the inability to meet both the capital and technological requirements of later stages of industrialization. It does appear to have survived longer in societies, such as Japan, in which the family was a more important source of social identity, although inheritance patterns probably were of equal importance.

A third consistency among the six societies was the predominance of private entrepreneurship in manufacturing. Even societies which began their industrial transitions with a sizable public sector, such as Japan, Russia, Germany, and France, sooner or later converted to private forms of entrepreneurship. In some instances public entrepreneurship remained prominent in nonmanufacturing areas, for example Russia; in others it remained in a few specific industries, such as the Japanese metallurgical industry. But in all six societies entrepreneurship in manufacturing was predominantly private, and this constitutes one of the major differences between these societies and currently industrializing societies. The extensive reliance on private entrepreneurship does not appear to have had any strong economic basis, except possibly in the case of the miserable performance of the Japanese public sector. Rather it can be attributed to the ethos of the nineteenth century. Economic liberalism held sway, and no Soviet Union or People's Republic of China existed to serve as a model of socialist entrepreneurship.

Lastly, there was also a trend from new to old entrepreneurship in the six societies. As the industrial transition proceeded, as capital requirements increased, and as the control of industrial enterprises became more concentrated, it became increasingly difficult for individuals who had not acted entrepreneurially before to take on the role. There was enough leeway, however, that there were bursts of new entrepreneurship, particularly during the Second Industrial Revolution, but these were exceptions rather than the rule.

Relevance for the causal significance of entrepreneurship. Did who played the entrepreneurial role in these societies make any difference in whether entrepreneurship was causally significant or not? We see little evidence that it did in the three cases that were positively causally significant. Two of the cases, Germany and Japan, involved "mainstream" entrepreneurship at the time they were significant, while the third case, Russia, involved "outsider" entrepreneurship. Hence either of these types of entrepreneurship may be causally significant in particular situations.

Second, these three cases all involved primarily collective entrepreneurship, but so did cases which were causally insignificant. The same can be said for the private-public difference, because the majority of manufacturing entrepreneurship was private in all six societies. However, we have repeatedly noted the important role played by the governments of Germany and Japan in stimulating private entrepreneurship, and the Russian government also attempted to stimulate the private sector at the time when foreign entrepreneurship was most extensive.

Family entrepreneurship may be considered as significant in the Japanese case because of the importance of the *zaibatsus*, but it is likely that the collective nature of *zaibatsu* entrepreneurship was a more important factor. The Japanese case does indicate, though, that family entrepreneurship is not necessarily inimical to expansiveness and innovativeness as does the fact that cases of both dynamic and unaggressive family entrepreneurship occurred within the same society. We have earlier indicated that the timidity of French entrepreneurship was not so much due to the French family as to the unfavorableness of French opportunity conditions.[11]

Thus it appears that who plays the entrepreneurial role is not as important as what is done within that role. And what is done within the role largely depends upon the nature of opportunity conditions. If they are unfavorable, then marginal entrepreneurship may appear in sufficient quantity to promote extensive industrial growth and development, as it did in Russia after 1880. But the likelihood of this happening does not appear to be very great. The part played by foreign entrepreneurship in Russia looks very much like an exceptional case.

---

[11]However, family entrepreneurship may have been partially responsible for the lack of entrepreneurship in pre-1850 Germany, which constituted our only case of negative causal significance.

A COMBINED MODEL OF ENTREPRENEURSHIP

We present a model of entrepreneurship in Figure 3 which incorporates the three major conclusions of this study. First, the fact that entrepreneurship revealed little independent causal significance is exemplified by the absence of an arrow connecting E (entrepreneurship) and Y (industrial growth and development). Second, our conclusion that economic (O) and noneconomic (X) factors each constituted necessary conditions for the emergence of entrepreneurship is shown by the single arrow combining their effects upon E. Third, the influence of the state (S) as an exogenous factor is shown by arrows drawn from it to O, X, and E. This model therefore combines the two models of entrepreneurship which we presented in Chapter 2 and adds the influence of the state to them. Thus in cases in which entrepreneurship is found to have causal significance, either positive or negative, it will be attributable to actions of the state and/or noneconomic factors and not solely due to the latter.

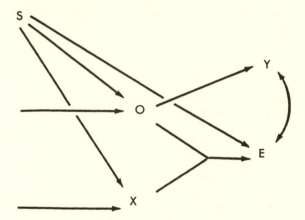

Figure 3   A Combined Model of Entrepreneurship

Was entrepreneurship a cause of industrial growth and development, or was it largely an effect of other factors, in the six societies we have considered in this study? It was a cause, but it was a cause in proportion to the favorableness of the economic, social, cultural, and political conditions characterizing these societies in most cases. We hope that this study induces others to study the combinations of these conditions which promote the emergence of entrepreneurship and economic growth and development. We also hope that this study has provided convincing evidence for the desirablility of considering economic and noneconomic factors in conjunction as equally important influences on entrepreneurship and the course of socioeconomic change.

Bibliography

Alexander, A. P. The supply of industrial entrepreneurship. *Explorations in Entrepreneurial History,* 1967, Series 2, *4*, 136–149.

Allen, G. C. The industrialization of the Far East. In H. J. Habakkuk & M. Postan (Eds.), *The Cambridge economic history of Europe* (2nd ed.) (Vol. 6, II). Cambridge: University Press, 1965.

Anderson, J. N. Buy-and-sell and economic personalism: foundations for Philippine entrepreneurship. *Asian Survey,* 1969, *9*, 641–668.

Apter, D. E. *The politics of modernization.* Chicago: University of Chicago, 1965.

Ashton, T. S. *The industrial revolution, 1760–1830.* London: Oxford, 1948.

Aubrey, H. G. Industrial investment decisions: a comparative analysis. In B. Okun & R. W. Richardson (Eds.), *Studies in economic development.* New York: Holt, Rinehart, Winston, 1961.

Awad, M. H. The supply of risk bearers in the underdeveloped countries. *Economic Development and Cultural Change,* 1971, *19*, 461–468.

Barber, E. G. The bourgeois way of life in eighteenth-century France. In B. Barber & E. G. Barber (Eds.), *European social class: stability and change.* New York: Macmillan, 1965.

Becker, H. S. *Outsiders: studies in the sociology of deviance.* New York: Free Press, 1966.

Bendix, R. *Work and authority in industry: ideologies of management in the course of change.* New York: Wiley, 1956.

Bendix, R. *Nation-building and citizenship.* New York: Wiley, 1964.

Blackwell, W. L. Old Believers and the rise of private industrial enterprise in early nineteenth-century Moscow. *Slavic Review,* 1965, *24*, 407–424.

Blackwell, W. L. *The beginnings of Russian industrialization: 1800–1860.* Princeton, Princeton University, 1968.

Bowen, R. H. The roles of government and private enterprise in German industrial growth, 1870–1914. *The Journal of Economic History,* Supplement, 1950, *10*, 68–81.

Brandenburg, F. Contribution to the theory of entrepreneurship and economic development: the case of Mexico. *Inter-American Economic Affairs,* 1962, *16*, 3–23.

Bronfenbrenner, M. The Japanese "howdunit." *Transaction,* 1969, *6*, 32–36.

Broude, H. The role of the state in American economic development, 1820–1890. In H. G. J. Aitken (Ed.), *The state and economic growth*. New York: Social Science Research Council, 1959.

Brozen, Y. Determinants of entrepreneurial ability. *Social Research*, 1954, *21*, 339–364.

Bruton, H. J. Contemporary theorizing on economic growth. In B. F. Hoselitz, J. J. Spengler, J. M. Letiche, E. McKinley, J. Buttrick, & H. J. Bruton (Eds.), *Theories of economic growth*. Glencoe, Ill.: Free Press, 1960.

Burn, D. L. The genesis of American engineering competition, 1850–1870. *Economic History*, Supplement to *The Economic Journal*, 1931, *2*, 292–311.

Bustamante, J. A. The "wetback" as deviant: an application of labeling theory. *American Journal of Sociology*, 1972, *77*, 706–718.

Cameron, R. *France and the economic development of Europe, 1800–1914*. Princeton: Princeton University, 1961.

Cameron, R. England, 1750–1844. In R. Cameron (Ed.), *Banking in the early stages of industrialization*. New York: Oxford, 1967a.

Cameron, R. France, 1800–1870. In R. Cameron (Ed.), *Banking in the early stages of industrialization*. New York: Oxford, 1967b.

Carman, H. J., Syrett, H. C., & Wishy, B. W. *A history of the American people* (Vol. 2). New York: Knopf, 1961.

Carr, J. C., & Taplin, W. *History of the British steel industry*. Cambridge: Harvard University, 1962.

Carson, G. B., Jr. The state and economic development: Russia, 1890–1939. In H. G. J. Aitken (Ed.), *The state and economic growth*. New York: Social Science Research Council, 1959.

Chamberlain, N. W. *Enterprise and environment: the firm in time and place*. New York: McGraw-Hill, 1968.

Chandler, A. D., Jr. *Strategy and structure: chapters in the history of the industrial enterprise*. Cambridge: M.I.T., 1962.

Chandler, A. D., Jr. "Entrepreneurial opportunity" in nineteenth-century America. *Explorations in Entrepreneurial History*, 1963, Series 2, *1*, 106–124.

Chandler, A. D., Jr. The railroads: pioneers in modern corporate management. *Business History Review*, 1965, *39*, 16–40.

Chandler, A. D., Jr. In C. Walton & R. Eels (Eds.), *The business system: readings in ideas and concepts* (Vol. 1). New York: Macmillan, 1967.

Chandler, A. D., Jr. The role of business in the United States: a historical survey. *Daedalus*, 1969, *98*, 23–40.

Chapman, S. D. Fixed capital formation in the British cotton industry, 1770–1815. *The Economic History Review*, 1970, 2nd Series, *23*, 235–266.

Chapman, S. D. Fixed capital formation in the British cotton manufacturing industry. In J. P. P. Higgins & S. Pollard (Eds.), *Aspects of capital investment in Great Britain, 1750–1850*. London: Methuen, 1971.

Chapman, S. D. *The cotton industry in the industrial revolution*. London: Macmillan, 1972.

Clapham, J. H. *The economic development of France and Germany: 1815–1914* (4th ed.). Cambridge: University Press, 1951.

Clemence, R. V., & Doody, F. S. *The Schumpeterian system*. Cambridge: Addison-Wesley, 1950.

Cochran, T. C. Role and sanction in American entrepreneurial history. In Harvard University Research Center in Entrepreneurial History, *Change and the entrepreneur*. Cambridge: Harvard University, 1949.

Cochran, T. C. Entrepreneurial behavior and motivation. *Explorations in Entrepreneurial History*, 1950, *2*, 304–307.

Cochran, T. C. The entrepreneur in American capital formation. In National Bureau of Economic Research, *Capital formation and economic growth*. Princeton: Princeton University, 1955.

Cochran, T. C. *The Puerto Rican businessman*. Philadelphia: University of Pennsylvania, 1959.

Cochran, T. C. Did the Civil War retard industrialization? *Mississippi Valley Historical Review*, 1961, *48*, 197–210.

Cochran, T. C. In C. Walton & R. Eels (Eds.), *The business system: readings in ideas and concepts* (Vol. 1). New York: Macmillan, 1967.

Cochran, T. C., & Miller, W. *The age of enterprise: a social history of industrial America* (Rev. ed.). New York: Harper, 1961.

Cole, A. H. *Business enterprise in its social setting.* Cambridge: Harvard University, 1959.

Collins, O., & Moore, D. G. *The organization makers: a behavioral study of independent entrepreneurs.* New York: Appleton-Century-Crofts, 1970.

Crisp, O. Russia, 1860–1914. In R. Cameron (Ed.), *Banking in the early stages of industrialization.* New York: Oxford, 1967.

Crouzet, F. Editor's introduction. In F. Crouzet (Ed.), *Capital formation in the industrial revolution.* London: Methuen, 1972.

Dahrendorf, R. *Society and democracy in Germany.* Garden City: Doubleday, 1967.

Dales, J. H. Approaches to entrepreneurial history. *Explorations in Entrepreneurial History,* 1949, *1,* 10–14.

Davis, L., Hughes, J. R. T., & McDougall, D. M. *American economic history: the development of a national economy* (Rev. ed.). Homewood, Ill.: Irwin, 1965.

Davis, S. Entrepreneurial succession. *Administrative Science Quarterly,* 1968, *13,* 402–416.

Dawson, W. H. *The evolution of modern Germany.* London: Unwin, 1911.

Deane, P. The industrial revolution and economic growth: the evidence of early British national income estimates. *Economic Development and Cultural Change,* 1957, *5,* 159–174.

Deane, P. & Cole, W. A. *British economic growth, 1688–1959: trends and structure* (2nd ed.). Cambridge: University, 1967.

De Santis, V. Industrialization and urbanization, 1865–1900. In L. Wright, *et al., The democratic experience: a short American history.* Chicago: Scott-Foresman, 1963.

Diamond, S. Values as an obstacle to economic growth: the American colonies. *The Journal of Economic History,* 1967, *27,* 561–575.

Duffy, W. J., & Yamamura, K. Monetization and integration of markets in Tokugawa Japan: a spectral analysis. *Explorations in Economic History,* 1971, *8,* 395–423.

Dunham, A. L. *The industrial revolution in France, 1815–1848.* New York: Exposition, 1955.

Easterbrook, W. T. The climate of enterprise. *American Economic Review,* 1949, *39,* 322–335.

Easterbrook, W. T. The entrepreneurial function in relation to technological and economic change. In B. F. Hoselitz & W. E. Moore (Eds.), *Industrialization and society.* Paris: UNESCO, 1963.

Edwards, G. W. *The evolution of finance capitalism.* New York: Longmans, Green, 1938.

Ellison, H. J. Economic modernization in imperial Russia: purposes and achievements. *The Journal of Economic History,* 1965, *25,* 523–540.

Evans, G. H., Jr. The entrepreneur and economic theory: a historical and analytical approach. *American Economic Review,* Supplement, 1949, *39,* 336–348.

Evans, G. H., Jr. A century of entrepreneurship in the United States, 1850–1957. *Explorations in Entrepreneurial History,* 1957, *10,* 90–103.

Evans, G. H., Jr. Business entrepreneurs, their major functions and related tenets. *The Journal of Economic History,* 1959, *19,* 250–270.

Falkus, M. E. *The industrialization of Russia: 1700–1914.* London: Macmillan, 1972.

Feller, I. Approaches to the diffusion of innovations. *Explorations in Entrepreneurial History,* 1967, Series 2, *4,* 232–244.

Ferguson, W. K., & Bruun, G. *A survey of European civilization* (3rd ed.). Boston: Houghton Mifflin, 1958.

Fine, S. *Laissez faire and the general welfare state: a study of conflict in American thought, 1865–1901.* Ann Arbor: University of Michigan, 1956.

Fischer, W. Government activity and industrialization in Germany (1815–1870). In W. W. Rostow (Ed.), *The economics of take-off into sustained growth.* New York: St. Martin's, 1963.

Flinn, M. W. Social theory and the industrial revolution. In T. Burns & S. B. Saul (Eds.), *Social theory and economic change.* London: Tavistock, 1967.

Fogel, R. W. *Railroads and American economic growth: essays in econometric history*. Baltimore: Johns Hopkins University, 1964.

Frank, A. G. *Latin America: underdevelopment or revolution*. New York: Monthly Review, 1969.

Gallman, R. E. Estimates of American national product made before the Civil War. *Economic Development and Cultural Change*, 1961, *9*, 397–412.

Gerschenkron, A. Comment. In National Bureau of Economic Research, *Capital formation and economic growth*. Princeton: Princeton University, 1955.

Gerschenkron, A. *Economic backwardness in historical perspective*. Cambridge: Harvard University, 1962.

Gerschenkron, A. The early phases of industrialization in Russia: afterthoughts and counterthoughts. In W. W. Rostow (Ed.), *The economics of take-off into sustained growth*. New York: St. Martin's, 1963.

Gerschenkron, A. The modernization of entrepreneurship. In M. Weiner (Ed.), *Modernization: the dynamics of growth*. New York: Basic, 1966.

Glade, W. P. Approaches to a theory of entrepreneurial formation. *Explorations in Entrepreneurial History*, 1967, Series 2, *4*, 245–259.

Goldsmith, R. W. The economic growth of tsarist Russia, 1860–1913. *Economic Development and Cultural Change*, 1961, *9*, 441–475.

Gough, J. W. *The rise of the entrepreneur*. London: Batsford, 1969.

Gould, J. D. *Economic growth in history: survey and analysis*. London: Methuen, 1972.

Gregory, F. W., & Neu, I. D. The American industrial elite in the 1870's. In W. Miller (Ed.), *Men in business: essays in the history of entrepreneurship*. Cambridge: Harvard University, 1952.

Gutmann, P. The serf entrepreneur in Russia: a comment. *Explorations in Entrepreneurial History*, 1954, *7*, 48–50.

Habakkuk, H. J. Family structure and economic change in nineteenth-century Europe. *The Journal of Economic History*, 1955, *15*, 1–12.

Habakkuk, H. J. The historical experience on the basic conditions of economic progress. In S. N. Eisenstadt (Ed.), *Comparative perspectives on social change*. Boston: Little, Brown, 1968.

Hagen, E. E. *On the theory of social change: how economic growth begins*. Homewood, Ill.: Dorsey, 1962.

Hagen, E. E. How economic growth begins: a theory of social change. *Journal of Social Issues*, 1963, *19*, 20–34.

Hagen, E. E. British personality and the industrial revolution: the historical evidence. In T. Burns & S. B. Saul (Eds.), *Social theory and economic change*. London: Tavistock, 1967.

Hagen, E. E. *The economics of development*. Homewood, Ill.: Dorsey, 1968.

Hamerow, T. S. *Restoration, revolution, reaction: economics and politics in Germany, 1815–1871*. Princeton: Princeton University, 1958.

Handlin, O., & Handlin, M. F. Origins of the American business corporation. *The Journal of Economic History*, 1945, *5*, 1–23.

Harbison, F. Prime movers of innovation. In C. A. Anderson & M. J. Bowman (Eds.), *Education and economic development*. Chicago: Aldine, 1965.

Harbison, F., & Myers, C. A. (Eds.), *Management in the industrial world: an international analysis*. New York: McGraw-Hill, 1959.

Harcave, S. *Russia, a history* (4th ed.). Chicago: Lippincott, 1959.

Harris, J. Some problems in identifying the role of entrepreneurship in economic development: the Nigerian case. *Explorations in Economic History*, 1970, *7*, 347–369.

Hartwell, R. M. *The industrial revolution and economic growth*. London: Methuen, 1971.

Hayes, C. J. H. *A political and cultural history of modern Europe* (Shortened rev. ed.) (Vol. 2). New York: Macmillan, 1939.

Henderson, W. O. *The state and the industrial revolution in Prussia, 1740–1870*. Liverpool: University, 1958.

Henderson, W. O. *Britian and industrial Europe, 1750–1870* (2nd ed.). Leicester: Leicester University, 1965.

Henderson, W. O. *The industrial revolution in Europe: Germany, France, Russia, 1815–1914.* Chicago: Quadrangle, 1968.

Hidy, R. W. Government and the petroleum industry of the United States to 1911. *The Journal of Economic History,* Supplement, 1950, *10,* 82–91.

Higgins, B. Economic development: principles, problems, and policies. New York: Norton, 1951.

Hirschman, A. Obstacles to development: a classification and a quasi-vanishing act. *Economic Development and Cultural Change,* 1965, *13,* 385–393.

Hirschmeier, J. *The origins of entrepreneurship in Meiji Japan.* Cambridge: Harvard University, 1964.

Hoffman, W. G. *British industry, 1700–1950* (W. O. Henderson & W. H. Chaloner, Trans.). Oxford: Basil Blackwell, 1955.

Hoffman, W. G. The take-off in Germany. In W. W. Rostow (Ed.), *The economics of take-off into sustained growth.* New York: St. Martin's, 1963.

Holmes, G. M. The study of entrepreneurship in nineteenth-century France. In G. Palmade, *French capitalism in the ninteenth century* (G. M. Holmes, Trans.). New York: Barnes and Noble, 1972. (Originally published, 1961.)

Holton, R. H. Business and government. *Daedalus,* 1969, *98,* 41–59.

Holzer, G. S. The German electrical industry in Russia: from economic entrepreneurship to political activism, 1890–1918 (Doctoral dissertation, University of Nebraska, 1970). *Dissertation Abstracts International,* 1971, *31,* 5320A. (University Microfilms No. 71–9564)

Horie, Y. Government industries in the early years of the Meiji era. *Kyoto University Economic Review,* 1939, *14,* 67–87.

Horie, Y. Modern entrepreneurship in Meiji Japan. In W. W. Lockwood (Ed.), *The state and economic enterprise in Japan.* Princeton: Princeton University, 1965.

Hoselitz, B. F. Entrepreneurship and capital formation in France and Britain since 1700. In National Bureau of Economic Research, *Capital formation and economic growth.* Princeton: Princeton University, 1955a.

Hoselitz, B. F. Reply. In National Bureau of Economic Research, *Capital formation and economic growth.* Princeton: Princeton University, 1955b.

Hoselitz, B. F. Economic growth and development—noneconomic factors in economic development. *American Economic Review,* 1957, *47,* 28–41.

Hoselitz, B. F. *Sociological aspects of economic growth.* Glencoe, Ill.: Free Press, 1960.

Hoselitz, B. F. Entrepreneurship and traditional elites. *Explorations in Entrepreneurial History,* 1963, Series 2, *1,* 36–49.

Ilchman, W. F., & Uphoff, N. T. *The political economy of change.* Berkeley: University of California, 1971.

Islam, N. *Foreign capital and economic development: Japan, India, and Canada.* Rutland, Vt.: Tuttle, 1960.

Jenks, L. H. Railroads as an economic force in American development. *The Journal of Economic History,* 1944, *4,* 1–20.

Kahan, A. Government policies and the industrialization of Russia. *The Journal of Economic History,* 1967, *27,* 460–477.

Katzin, M. F. The role of the small entrepreneur. in M. J. Herskovits & M. Horwitz (Eds.), *Economic transition in Africa.* Evanston, Ill.: Northwestern University, 1964.

Kemp, T. *Economic forces in French history.* London: Dennis Dobson, 1971.

Kerr, C., Dunlop, J. T., Harbison, F. H., & Myers, C. A. *Industrialism and industrial man.* Cambridge: Harvard University, 1960.

Kilby, P. Hunting the heffalump. In P. Kilby (Ed.), *Entrepreneurship and economic development.* New York: Free Press, 1971.

Kindleberger, C. P. *Economic development.* New York: McGraw-Hill, 1958.

Kindleberger, C. P. *Economic growth in France and Britain: 1851–1950.* Cambridge: Harvard University, 1964.

Kirkland, E. C. *Industry comes of age: 1860–1907.* New York: Holt, Rinehart, Winston, 1961.

Kirzner, I. M. *Competition and entrepreneurship.* Chicago: University of Chicago, 1973.

Klemm, F. *A history of western technology* (D. W. Singer, Trans.). Cambridge: M.I.T., 1964. (Originally published, 1954.)

Knight, F. H. *Risk, uncertainty, and profit.* New York: Harper and Row, 1965. (Originally published, 1921.)

Kravis, I. B. The role of exports in nineteenth-century United States growth. *Economic Development and Cultural Change,* 1972, *20,* 387–405.

Kriesberg, L. Entrepreneurs in Latin America and the role of cultural and situational processes. *International Social Science Journal,* 1963, *15,* 581–594.

Kunkel, J. H. *Society and economic growth: a behavioral perspective of social change.* New York: Oxford, 1970.

Kuznets, S. Quantitative aspects of the economic growth of nations. II. industrial distributions of national product and labor force. *Economic Development and Cultural Change,* Supplement, 1957, *5,* 1–111.

Kuznets, S. *Modern economic growth: rate, structure, and spread.* New Haven: Yale University, 1966.

Kuznets, S. *Toward a theory of economic growth.* New York: Norton, 1968.

Lamb, R. K. The entrepreneur and the community. In W. Miller (Ed.), *Men in business: essays in the history of entrepreneurship.* Cambridge: Harvard University, 1952.

Landes, D. S. French entrepreneurship and industrial growth in the nineteenth century. *The Journal of Economic History,* 1949, *9,* 45–61.

Landes, D. S. New-model entrepreneurship in France and problems of historical explanation. *Explorations in Entrepreneurial History,* 1963, Series 2, *1,* 56–75.

Landes, D. S. French business and the businessman: a social and cultural analysis. In H. G. J. Aitken (Ed.), *Explorations in enterprise.* Cambridge: Harvard University, 1965a.

Landes, D. S. Technological change and development in western Europe, 1750–1914. In H. J. Habakkuk & M. Postan (Eds.), *The Cambridge economic history of Europe* (2nd ed.) (Vol. 6, I). Cambridge: University Press, 1965b.

Landes, D. S. *The unbound Prometheus: technological change and industrial development in western Europe from 1750 to the present.* Cambridge: Cambridge University, 1969.

Letwin, W. The past and future of the American businessman. *Daedalus,* 1969, *98,* 1–22.

Lipset, S. M. Values, education, and entrepreneurship. In S. M. Lipset & A. Solari (Eds.), *Elites in Latin America.* New York: Oxford, 1967.

Livesay, H. C., & Porter, G. The financial role of merchants in the development of United States manufacturing, 1815–1860. *Explorations in Economic History,* 1971, *9,* 63–87.

Lockwood, W. W. *The economic development of Japan: growth and structural change, 1868–1938.* Princeton: Princeton University, 1954.

Maddison, A. *Economic growth in Japan and the USSR.* New York: Norton, 1969.

Manchester, W. *The arms of Krupp: 1587–1968.* Boston: Little, Brown, 1968.

Marczewski, J. Some aspects of the economic growth of France, 1660–1958. *Economic Development and Cultural Change,* 1961, *9,* 369–386.

Marczewski, J. The take-off hypothesis and French experience. In W. W. Rostow (Ed.), *The economics of take-off into sustained growth.* New York: St. Martin's, 1963.

Marris, P. *The social barriers to African entrepreneurship.* Institute of Development Studies, University of Sussex, England. Mimeo Series No. 22, January, 1969.

Marris, P., & Somerset, A. *The African entrepreneur: a study of entrepreneurship and development in Kenya.* New York: Africana, 1971.

Marshall, A. *Principles of economics* (8th ed.). London: Macmillan, 1936. (Originally published, 1890.)

Marshall, B. K. *Capitalism and nationalism in prewar Japan: the ideology of the business elite, 1868–1941.* Stanford: Stanford University, 1967.

Marshall, T. H. *Citizenship and social class, and other essays.* Cambridge: Cambridge University, 1950.

Marx, K. *Capital: a critique of political economy* (E. and C. Paul, Trans.). New York: International, 1929. (Originally published, 1867.)

Marx, K., & Engels, F. *The communist manifesto* (S. Moore, Trans.). Chicago: Regnery, 1954.

Mavor, J. *An economic history of Russia* (2nd ed.) (2 vols.). New York: Russell & Russell, 1965.

McClelland, D. C. *The achieving society.* New York: Free Press, 1961.

McClelland, D. C. The achievement motive in economic growth. In B. F. Hoselitz & W. E. Moore (Eds.), *Industrialization and society.* Paris: UNESCO, 1963.

McClelland, D. C. N achievement and entrepreneurship: a longitudinal study. *Journal of Personality and Social Psychology,* 1965, *1,* 389–392.

McClelland, D. C. Does education accelerate economic growth? *Economic Development and Cultural Change,* 1966, *14,* 257–278.

McClelland, D. C., & Winter, D. G. *Motivating economic achievement.* New York: Free Press, 1971.

McCloskey, D. N., & Sandberg, L. G. From damnation to redemption: judgments on the late Victorian entrepreneur. *Explorations in Economic History,* 1971, *9,* 89–108.

McKay, J. P. *Pioneers for profit: foreign entrepreneurship and Russian industrialization: 1885–1913.* Chicago: University of Chicago, 1970.

Miller, M. S. *The economic development of Russia, 1905–1914.* London: King, 1926.

Miyamoto, M., Sakodo, Y., & Yasuba, Y. Economic development in preindustrial Japan: 1859–1894. *The Journal of Economic History,* 1965, *25,* 541–564.

Moore, B., Jr. *Social origins of dictatorship and democracy.* Boston: Beacon, 1966.

Murphy, J. J. Retrospect and prospect. In D. L. Spencer & A. Woroniak (Eds.), *The transfer of technology to developing countries.* New York: Praeger, 1967.

Musson, A. E. Editor's introduction. In A. E. Musson (Ed.), *Science, technology, and economic growth in the eighteenth century.* London: Methuen, 1972.

Musson, A. E., & Robinson, E. *Science and technology in the industrial revolution.* Toronto: University of Toronto, 1969.

Nafziger, E. W. Indian entrepreneurship: a survey. In P. Kilby (Ed.), *Entrepreneurship and economic development.* New York: Free Press, 1971.

Nakamura, J. I. Meiji land reform, redistribution of income, and saving from agriculture. *Economic Development and Cultural Change,* 1966, *14,* 428–439.

Negandhi, A. R., & Prasad, S. B. *Comparative management.* New York: Appleton-Century-Crofts, 1971.

North, D. C. Industrialization in the United States (1815–1860). In W. W. Rostow (Ed.), *The economics of take-off into sustained growth.* New York: St. Martin's, 1963.

North, D. C. Industrialization in the United States. In H. J. Habakkuk & M. Postan (Eds.), *The Cambridge economic history of Europe* (2nd ed.) (Vol. 6, II). Cambridge: University Press, 1965.

Orchard, J. E. *Japan's economic position: the progress of industrialization.* New York: McGraw-Hill, 1930.

Palmade, G. *French capitalism in the nineteenth century* (G. M. Holmes, Trans.). New York: Barnes & Noble, 1972. (Originally published, 1961.)

Papanek, G. F. The development of entrepreneurship. *American Economic Review,* 1962, *52,* 46–66.

Parker, W. N. Entrepreneurial opportunities and response in the German economy. *Explorations in Entrepreneurial History,* 1954, *7,* 26–36.

Parsons, T. *Structure and process in modern society*. New York: Free Press, 1960.

Parsons, T., & Smelser, N. J. *Economy and society*. New York: Free Press, 1956.

Passer, H. *The electrical manufacturers, 1875–1900: a study in competition, entrepreneurship, technical change, and economic growth*. Cambridge: Harvard University, 1953.

Patel, S. J. Rates of industrial growth in the last century, 1860–1958. *Economic Development and Cultural Change*, 1961, *9*, 316–330.

Patrick, H. T. Japan. In R. Cameron (Ed.), *Banking in the early stages of industrialization*. New York: Oxford, 1967.

Pelzel, J. The small industrialist in Japan. *Explorations in Entrepreneurial History*, 1954, *7*, 79–93.

Peterson, R. A., & Berger, D. G. Entrepreneurship in organizations: evidence from the popular music industry. *Administrative Science Quarterly*, 1971, *16*, 97–106.

Pollard, S. *The genesis of modern management: a study of the industrial revolution in Great Britain*. Cambridge: Harvard University, 1965.

Portal, R. The industrialization of Russia. In H. J. Habakkuk & M. Postan (Eds.), *The Cambridge economic history of Europe* (2nd ed.) (Vol. 6, II). Cambridge: University Press, 1965.

Pounds, N. J. G. Economic growth in Germany. In H. G. J. Aitken (Ed.), *The state and economic growth*, New York: Social Science Research Council, 1959.

Ranis, G. The community-centered entrepreneur in Japanese development. *Explorations in Entrepreneurial History*, 1955, *8*, 80–97.

Ranis, G. The financing of Japanese economic development. *The Economic History Review*, 1959, 2nd Series, *11*, 440–454.

Redlich, F. *History of American business leaders* (Vol. 1). Ann Arbor: Edwards, 1940.

Redlich, F. The leaders of the German steam-engine industry during the first hundred years. *The Journal of Economic History*, 1944, *4*, 121–148.

Redlich, F. Business leadership: diverse origins and variant forms. *Economic Development and Cultural Change*, 1958, *6*, 177–190.

Riggs, F. W. *Administration in developing countries: the theory of prismatic society*. Boston: Houghton Mifflin, 1964.

Rosenberg, N. Technological change in the machine tool industry, 1840–1910. *The Journal of Economic History*, 1963, *23*, 414–443.

Rosenberg, N. *Technology and American economic growth*. New York: Harper & Row, 1972.

Rosovsky, H. The serf entrepreneur in Russia. *Explorations in Entrepreneurial History*, 1954, *6*, 207–233.

Rosovsky, H. Japanese capital formation: the role of the public sector. *The Journal of Economic History*, 1959, *19*, 350–373.

Rostow, W. W. The take-off into self-sustained growth. *The Economic Journal*, 1956, *66*, 25–48.

Rothman, S. Entrepreneurial behavior and political consensus in England and France. *Explorations in Entrepreneurial History*, 1956, *8*, 167–171.

Saul, S. B. Editor's introduction. In S. B. Saul (Ed.), *Technological change: the United States and Britain in the nineteenth century*. London: Methuen, 1970.

Sawyer, J. E. The entrepreneur and the social order. In W. Miller (Ed.), *Men in business: essays in the history of entrepreneurship*. Cambridge: Harvard University, 1952.

Sawyer, J. E. The social basis of the American system of manufacturing. *The Journal of Economic History*, 1954, *14*, 361–379.

Sayigh, Y. A. *Entrepreneurs of Lebanon: the role of the business leader in a developing economy*. Cambridge: Harvard University, 1962.

Schapiro, S. *Modern and contemporary European history (1815–1845)* (New ed.). Boston: Houghton Mifflin, 1946.

Schaw, L. C. *The bonds of work*. San Francisco: Jossey-Bass, 1968.

Schumpeter, J. A. *The theory of economic development*. New York: Oxford, 1961. (Originally published, 1934.)

Shapiro, S. *Capital and the cotton industry in the industrial revolution*. Ithaca, N.Y.: Cornell University, 1967.

Shimkin, D. B. The entrepreneur in tsarist and soviet Russia. *Explorations in Entrepreneurial History,* 1949, *2,* 24–34.

Shinohara, M. *Structural changes in Japan's economic development.* Tokyo: Kinohuniya, 1970.

Silberman, B. S. Criteria for recruitment and success in the Japanese bureaucracy, 1868–1900: "traditional" and "modern" criteria in bureaucratic development. *Economic Development and Cultural Change,* 1966, *14,* 158–173.

Smelser, N. J. *Social change in the industrial revolution.* Chicago: University of Chicago, 1959.

Smith, H. R. A model of entrepreneurial evolution. *Explorations in Entrepreneurial History,* 1968, Series 2, *5,* 145–157.

Smith, T. *Political change and industrial development in Japan: government enterprise, 1868–1880* (2nd ed.). Stanford: Stanford University, 1965.

Solo, R. A. *Economic organizations and social systems.* Indianapolis: Bobbs-Merrill, 1967.

Spengler, J. J. The state and economic growth: summary and interpretation. In H. G. J. Aitken (Ed.), *The state and economic growth.* New York: Social Science Research Council, 1959.

Starobin, R. S. *Industrial slavery in the old south.* New York: Oxford, 1971.

Stepanek, J. E. *Managers for small industry: an international study.* Glencoe, Ill.: Free Press, 1960.

Stolper, G., Hauser, K., & Borchardt, K. *The German economy 1870 to the present.* New York: Harcourt, Brace, World, 1967.

Strassman, W. P. *Risk and technological innovation: American maufacturing methods during the nineteenth century.* Ithaca, N.Y.: Cornell University, 1959.

Strassman, W. P. The industrialist. In J. J. Johnson (Ed.), *Continuity and change in Latin America.* Stanford: Stanford University, 1964.

Swerdlow, I. Economics as part of development administration. In I. Swerdlow (Ed.), *Development administration: concepts and problems.* Syracuse, N.Y.: Syracuse University, 1963.

Taira, K. Education and literacy in Meiji Japan: an interpretation. *Explorations in Economic History,* 1971, *8,* 371–394.

Takahashi, M. *Modern Japanese economy since 1868.* Tokyo: Kokusai Bunka Shinkokai, 1968.

Takenaka, Y. Endogenous formation and development of capitalism in Japan. *The Journal of Economic History,* 1969, *29,* 141–162.

Takezawa, S. Socio-cultural aspects of management in Japan: historical development and new challenges. *International Labor Review,* 1966, *94,* 148–174.

Taylor, N. W. Entrepreneurship and traditional elites: the case of a dualistic society. *Explorations in Entrepreneurial History,* 1965, Series 2, *2,* 232–234.

Temin, P. *Iron and steel in nineteenth-century America: an economic inquiry.* Cambridge: M.I.T., 1964.

Thiagarajan, K. M., & Whittaker, W. S. *Realistic goal setting as a key indicator of entrepreneurship: a cross-cultural comparison.* Rochester, N.Y.: Management Research Center, University of Rochester, Technical Report 30, September, 1969. (NTIS No. AD 700 284)

Tilly, R. *Financial institutions and industrialization in the Rhineland, 1815–1870.* Madison: University of Wisconsin, 1966a.

Tilly, R. The political economy of public finance and the industralization of Prussia, 1815–1866. *The Jouranl of Economic History,* 1966b, *26,* 484–497.

Tilly, R. Germany, 1815–1870. In R. Cameron (Ed.), *Banking in the early stages of industrialization.* New York: Oxford, 1967.

Trebilock, C. "Spin-off" in British economic history: armaments and industry, 1760–1914. *The Economic History Review,* 1969, 2nd Series, *22,* 474–490.

Uyeda, T. *The small industries of Japan: their growth and development.* New York: Institute of Pacific Relations, 1938.

van der Haas, H. *The enterprise in transition: an analysis of European and American practice.* London: Tavistock, 1967.

Veblen, T. *Imperial Germany and the industrial revolution.* New York: Viking, 1939.

Veblen, T. *The engineers and the price system.* New York: Harcourt, Brace, World, 1963. (Originally published, 1921.)

Veblen, T. *The theory of business enterprise*. New York: Kelley, 1965. (Originally published, 1904.)

Vernon, R. *Sovereignty at bay: the multinational spread of United States enterprises*. New York: Basic, 1971.

Visser, D. The German captain of enterprise: Veblen's *imperial Germany* revisited. *Explorations in Entrepreneurial History,* 1969, Series 2, *6*, 309–328.

Wallerstein, I. *The modern world-system: capitalist agriculture and the origins of the European world-economy in the sixteenth century*. New York: Academic, 1974.

Weber, M. *The Protestant ethic and the spirit of capitalism* (T. Parsons, Trans.). New York: Scribner's, 1958. (Originally published, 1930.)

Wilken, P. H. Catalysts of change? A comparative analysis of the significance of entrepreneurship in the eighteenth and nineteenth centuries (Doctoral dissertation, University of North Carolina, 1976). *Dissertation Abstracts International,* 1977, *38*, 1062A. (University Microfilms No. 77–17, 382)

Williamson, H. F. Comment. In National Bureau of Economic Research, *Capital formation and economic growth*. Princeton: Princeton University, 1955.

Wilson, C. The entrepreneur in the industrial revolution in Britain. *Explorations in Entrepreneurial History,* 1955, *7*, 129–145.

Wutzmer, H. Die herkunft der industriellen bourgeoisie Preussens in der vierziger jahren des 19. Jahrhunderts. In H. Mottek (Ed.), *Studien zur geschichte der industriellen revolution in Deutschland*. Berlin: Akademie-Verlag, 1960.

Yamamura, K. A re-examination of entrepreneurship in Meiji Japan (1868–1912). *Economic History Review,* 1968, Series 2, *21*, 144–158.

Yamamura, K. *A study of samurai income and entrepreneurship*. Cambridge: Harvard University, 1974.

Yoshino, M. Y. *Japan's managerial system: tradition and innovation*. Cambridge: M.I.T., 1968.

Young, F. V. A macrosociological interpretation of entrepreneurship. In P. Kilby (Ed.), *Entrepreneurship and economic development*. New York: Free Press, 1971.

Youngson, A. J. Marshall on economic growth. In B. Okun & R. W. Richardson (Eds.), *Studies in economic development*. New York: Holt, Rinehart, Winston, 1961.

Author Index

Page numbers in *italics* indicate where complete references are listed.

Alexander, A. P., 9, 43, *281*
Allen, G. C., 163, 166, 174, 175, 181, 182, 183, *281*
Anderson, J. N., 20, *281*
Apter, D. E., *281*
Ashton, T. S., 77, 79, 85, 93, 99, *281*
Aubrey, H. G., 15, *281*
Awad, M. H., 15, *281*

Barber, E. G., 128, *281*
Becker, H. S., *281*
Bendix, R., 10, 14, 53, 83, 86, 89, 91, 92, 95, 99, 160, 214, 227, 230, 235, 237, 239, 240, 244, *281*
Berger, D. G., 13, *288*
Blackwell, W. L., 222, 224, 229, 230, 232, 233, 234, 235, 237, 240, 241, 242, 244, 245, 246, *281*
Borchardt, K., 134, *289*
Bowen, R. H., 137, 144, 147, 155, *281*
Brandenburg, F., 13, 20, *281*
Bronfenbrenner, M., 170, *281*
Broude, H., 197, 218, *282*
Brozen, Y., 9, 10, 11, 13, 15, *282*
Bruun, G., 136, 141, 176, *283*
Bruton, H. J., 10, 15, *282*
Burn, D. L., 216, *282*

Bustamante, J. A., *281*

Cameron, R., 10, 78, 89, 100, 104, 105, 108, 110, 112, 114, 117, 118, 133, 149, 154, 242, *282*
Carman, J. H., 193, 194, 208, 216, *282*
Carr, J. C., 83, 88, *282*
Carson, G. B., Jr., 222, 234, 239, 245, *282*
Chamberlain, N. W., 199, 206, 207, *282*
Chandler, A. D., Jr., 192, 193, 202, 204, 206, 208, 210, 218, *282*
Chapman, S. D., 77, 81, 82, 83, 84, 88, 89, 90, 91, 105, 179, *282*
Clapham, J. H., 139, 140, 141, 142, 143, 146, 154, *282*
Clemence, R. V., 14, *282*
Cochran, T. C., 8, 9, 15, 20, 67, 192, 193, 194, 195, 196, 197, 198, 199, 202, 203, 204, 205, 207, 208, 209, 210, 211, 212, 214, 215, 216, *282*, *283*
Cole, A. H., 10, 13, 20, 24, 67, 91, 210, *283*
Cole, W. A., 86, *283*
Collins, O., 20, *283*
Crisp, O., 224, 228, 229, 234, 245, *283*
Crouzet, F., 78, 81, 88, 89, 92, 105, *283*

· Dahrendorf, R., 137, 154, 155, *283*

291

Index

Date Due